SPOLIATION OF EVIDENCE

Sanctions and Remedies for Destruction of Evidence in Civil Litigation

Second Edition

Margaret M. Koesel
Tracey L. Turnbull

Daniel F. Gourash
Editor

TORT TRIAL & INSURANCE PRACTICE

Cover design by ABA Publishing

10 09 08 07 06 5 4 3 2

Library of Congress Cataloging-in-Publication Data

Spoliation of evidence: a practitioner's guide to sanctions and remedies for destruction of evidence in civil litigation / written by Margaret M. Koesel and Tracey L. Turnbull; edited by Daniel F. Gourash.— 2nd ed.
    p. cm.
    Includes bibliographical references and index.
    ISBN 1-59031-622-3
    1. Evidence tampering—United States. 2. Civil procedure—United States.
I. Turnbull, Tracey L., 1969- . II. Gourash, Daniel F., 1957- . III. Title.

KF9421.K64 2005
347.73'6—dc22   2005034220

Contents

Chapter 8

Dedications

For Nancy, Mary Jo, Lori, and Joan.

M.M.K.

For Mom and Dad.

T.L.T.

Introduction

"Contra spoliatorem omnia praesumuntur."

More than 275 years ago, in *Armory v. Delamirie*, an English court confronted one of the first recorded instances of spoliation of evidence.[1] In that case, a chimney sweep found a jeweled ring and took it to a jeweler for appraisal. When the jeweler returned the ring without the stone, the chimney sweep brought an action to recover the gem. Since the jeweler had retained the stone, the judge instructed the jury to "presume the strongest against the [jeweler] and make the value of the best jewels the measure of . . . damages." The court announced the now familiar axiom that a party should be held accountable for improperly destroying evidence: "Contra spoliatorem omnia praesumuntur," that is, "All things are presumed against a spoliator."[2]

In the nearly three centuries since *Armory*, courts and practitioners have wrestled with spoliation of evidence in the context of civil litigation.[3] Since publication of the first edition of this text, evidence tam-

---

1. 93 Eng. Rep. 664 (K.B. 1722).

2. *Id.*; *see also* Sullivan v. General Motors Corp., 772 F. Supp. 358, 360 (N.D. Ohio 1991) (noting that at common law "it was proper to presume that evidence which had been destroyed, or 'spoliated,' could be construed against the party responsible for the destruction of that evidence"); Welsh v. United States, 844 F.2d 1239, 1246 (6th Cir. 1988) (discussing the modern application of *Armory v. Delamirie*); Warner Barnes & Co. v. Kokosai Kisen Kabushiki Kaisha, 102 F.2d 450, 453 (2d Cir. 1939), *modified*, 103 F.2d 430 (2d Cir. 1939) ("When a party is once found to be fabricating, or suppressing, documents, the natural — ndeed, the inevitable—conclusion is that he has something to conceal, and is conscious of guilt.").

3. *See* Rex v. Arundel, 1 Hob. 109, 80 Eng. Rep. 258 (K.B. 1617). Early decisions by American courts in which the spoliation inference was considered include *Pizarro*, 15 U.S. 227 (1817) and *Hanson v. Lessee of Eustace*, 43 U.S. 653 (1844). 2 JOHN H. WIGMORE, EVIDENCE IN TRIALS AT COMMON LAW 278, at 133 (Chadbourne rev. ed. 1979) ("It has always been understood . . . that a party's *falsehood or other fraud* in the preparation and presentation of his cause, his fabrication or suppression of evidence by bribery or spoliation . . . is receivable against him as an indication of his consciousness that his case is a weak or unfounded one.").

pering[4] has again created headlines suggesting the production of evidence "is a game whose rules can be broken."[5] One study from the early 1990s concluded that 50 percent of all litigators found spoliation to be either a frequent or regular problem.[6] A more recent study has concluded that "[i]t appears to be as difficult to find a commentator who thinks evidence tampering is under control as it is to find systematic empirical evidence confirming its ubiquity."[7]

As with the first edition, the authors intend this book to be a guide for practitioners as they confront spoliation issues in their civil practice. Although spoliation most often arises in litigation, it can touch on other practice areas—for example, in corporate document retention policies, which must be drafted with spoliation issues in mind. Spoliation can affect plaintiffs, defendants, and even third parties,

---

4. The term "evidence tampering" refers to a range of activities "by which parties alter the natural evidentiary 'emissions' of the transactions and occurrences that may give rise to suit." Chris William Sanchirico, *Evidence Tampering*, 53 Duke L. J. 1215, 1218 n. 4 (2004).

5. Sanchirico, *supra* note 4, at 1217. *See also* Bethany McLean and Peter Elkind, The Smartest Guys in the Room: The Amazing Rise and Scandalous Fall of Enron 381-83 (Portfolio 2003) (discussing Arthur Andersen's document shredding, which reportedly ended only after it received a subpoena from the Securities and Exchange Commission even though the SEC had announced its planned inquiry earlier). *See* United States v. Arthur Andersen, LLP, 374 F.3d 281 (5th Cir. 2004), *rev'd*, 125 S. Ct. 2129, 161 L. Ed. 2d 1008 (2005) (upholding conviction of an accounting firm for obstructing an official investigation by the SEC based on its directives to firm personnel to destroy or conceal documents). *See also* Mary Flood, *Some Judges Are Skeptical,* The Houston Chronicle (Apr. 28, 2005) (noting certain Supreme Court justices expressed skepticism about the accounting firm's conviction and concern about a chilling effect on businesses).

6. *See* Charles R. Nesson, *Incentives to Spoliate Evidence in Civil Litigation: The Need for Vigorous Judicial Action*, 13 Cardozo L. Rev. 793 (1991). Professor Nesson acknowledges an overwhelming incentive for spoliation, because typically an opponent is unlikely to discover either the spoliated evidence or the act of spoliation itself. *See also* Wayne D. Brazil, *Civil Discovery: Lawyers' Views of Its Effectiveness, Its Principal Problems and Abuses*, 1980 Am. B. Found. Res. J. 787, 829 (noting that it is "difficult to exaggerate the pervasiveness of evasive practices"); Edward J. Imwinkelried, *A New Antidote for an Opponent's Pretrial Discovery Misconduct: Treating the Misconduct at Trial as an Admission by Conduct of the Weakness of the Opponent's Case,* 1993 B.Y.U. L. Rev. 793, 794 (1993) (noting "deliberate obstructionism is commonplace").

7. Sanchirico, *supra* note 4, at 1239. For a detailed analysis of the empirical basis for the concerns voiced by commentators regarding evidentiary foul play, *see* Sanchirico, *supra* note 4, at 1230.

who may be required to retain evidence if they are on notice of possible litigation.[8]

This book is not a treatise; rather, it is a guide for the litigation practitioner faced with the loss of evidence in a civil suit in a state or federal court. Among other key topics, the authors discuss record-keeping obligations, the duty to preserve evidence, sanctions and other remedies for spoliation. In addition, the authors provide a brief analysis of the current state law and the law of each federal circuit to facilitate the practitioner's ability to locate key cases in his or her jurisdiction.

At the end of each substantive chapter, the authors include practical tips to assist the practitioner. Finally, the authors provide an annotated bibliography of treatises, law review articles, and practical publications on spoliation for those seeking more detailed information on specific issues.

---

8. *See* W. Russell Welsh & Andrew C. Marquardt, *Spoliation of Evidence*, 23 WINTER BRIEF 9, *36 (1994) (noting "all corporations . . . must consider their potential exposure to legal liability resulting from the destruction of records"). *See, e.g., In re* Prudential Ins. Co. of Am. Sales Practices Litig., 169 F.R.D. 598 (D.N.J. 1997), *rev'd on other grounds*, 133 F.3d 225 (3d Cir. 1998) (insurer sanctioned where company's top management recognized the company's obligation to preserve documents in connection with certain lawsuits, yet no one actively formulated, implemented, or communicated document retention policy).

Acknowledgments to the 2006 Edition

As we acknowledged in the first edition, spoliation of evidence is an unfortunate reality of modern-day civil litigation. Since the 2000 edition, there has been a virtual explosion of lawsuits involving electronic data in litigation. These cases have shown that spoliation can not only subject parties to tort liability or sanctions that may be outcome-determinative, but also that such cases involve significant negative publicity.

Most attorneys, whether they represent parties to litigation or are counseling clients who may be seeking to avoid litigation, at some point will face issues involving destruction of evidence. We have attempted to provide a resource for practitioners to turn to in those situations. We readily acknowledge that this book cannot answer all of the readers' questions; we will be satisfied if it serves as a useful starting point for attorneys in resolving these issues.

As with the first edition, our debts are numerous. First and foremost, we wish to acknowledge the support provided by our friends and colleagues at Porter Wright Morris & Arthur LLP. Without their support, this book would have not been possible,

We gratefully acknowledge the assistance, suggestions, and support provided by our editor and colleague, Daniel F. Gourash. Without Dan's help and gentle reminders, this book would not have been possible.

We are also grateful for the suggestions and insight provided by our colleague, Mason Evans, particularly in the area of electronic record retention and discovery.

We cannot say enough to thank Darlene M. Hudeck, Lynn Raby, and Lynna Wasyluk for their helpful assistance in preparing the manuscript. The dedication, energy, and enthusiasm of these talented professionals made it possible for us to produce a coherent document.

Although our former colleague and co-author David Bell could not assist us in preparation of this edition, we are grateful to him for his insight and encouragement.

We are grateful for the contributions of all of these people and are proud to call them friends and colleagues. For these special people and for everyone who helped us in any way, our thanks. We, of course, accept sole responsibility for any errors or omissions in the book.

Margaret M. Koesel
Tracey L. Turnbull
November 2005

About the Editor

Daniel F. Gourash

Mr. Gourash is a partner practicing in the Cleveland, Ohio, office of Porter Wright Morris & Arthur, LLP. He has a national practice in the area of complex civil litigation involving a wide variety of legal issues. He has broad experience at all levels of trial and appeal representing insurance carriers in coverage disputes. Mr. Gourash also has substantial trial and appeal experience defending manufacturers, distributors, and service providers in both land-based and maritime products liability actions involving claims for personal injury, wrongful death, and property damage. He has represented manufacturers and trade associations in a variety of mass tort matters. His experience further includes substantial involvement in the litigation of construction defect, ERISA, environmental, commercial, and securities fraud actions.

Mr. Gourash is admitted to practice in Ohio, the U.S. District Courts for the Northern District of Ohio and the Eastern District of Michigan, the U.S. Court of Appeals for the Fourth and Sixth Circuits, and the U.S. Supreme Court. He also has appeared pro hac vice in numerous state and federal courts across the country. He further has broad experience in a variety of alternative dispute resolution contexts, including arbitration under the rules of the American Arbitration Association and the National Association of Securities Dealers, and mediation and arbitration under private and court-annexed procedures.

Mr. Gourash graduated from the University of New Haven (B.A., summa cum laude, 1980) and received his law degree from Duke University School of Law (J.D. 1983). He has substantial involvement in the organized bar, having held numerous positions of responsibility in the American Bar Association, including serving as the chair of the Young Lawyers Division, serving several terms in the House of Delegates, and serving on a variety of special and standing committees within the Judicial Division Lawyers Conference and the Torts and Insurance Practice Section. He currently is serving as chair of the Lawyers Conference, is immediate past chair of the TIPS Publications Editorial Board and is a member of TIPS Council. Mr. Gourash is a fellow of the American Bar Foundation and served on its Board of Governors for a five-year term.

About the Authors

Margaret M. Koesel

Margaret Koesel is a partner with Porter Wright Morris & Arthur LLP in Cleveland, Ohio. She devotes the majority of her practice to assisting employers in avoiding and defending wrongful discharge and employment discrimination claims in state and federal courts throughout Ohio and has an active trial court and appellate court practice. She also has significant experience litigating commercial disputes, including claims involving ERISA, trade secrets, and unfair competition. She is admitted to practice in Ohio, the United States District Court for the Northern District of Ohio, and the Sixth Circuit.

Ms. Koesel graduated from Baldwin-Wallace College with a degree in business administration. She received her law degree from Cleveland Marshall College of Law (magna cum laude), where she served as an editor on the law review. Before she entered private practice, Ms. Koesel served as a law clerk for Judge Ann McManamon of the Eighth Appellate District of the Ohio Court of Appeals in Cuyahoga County.

Ms. Koesel is a member of the American Bar Association, Sections of Litigation and Labor and Employment, and the Ohio Bar Association. She has published numerous articles on employment- and spoliation-related topics and is a frequent speaker on employment law and destruction of evidence issues.

Tracey L. Turnbull

Tracey Turnbull is a partner in the Cleveland, Ohio, office of Porter Wright Morris & Arthur LLP. She has significant experience representing manufacturers of recreational vehicles, pharmaceutical products, and medical devices in products liability matters, as well as employers in harassment and discrimination claims in both state and federal courts. She is admitted to practice in the state of Ohio, the United States District Court for the Northern District of Ohio, and the Sixth Circuit Court of Appeals.

Ms. Turnbull received her undergraduate degree from Hamilton College with honors and received her law degree cum laude from Case Western Reserve University School of Law, where she served as an editor on the *Case Western Reserve Law Review.*

Ms. Turnbull is a member of the American Bar Association, the Defense Research Institute, and the Cleveland Bar Association. She has co-authored a number of publications on spoliation of evidence and wrongful discharge and is a frequent lecturer on destruction of evidence and electronic evidence issues.

The Duty to Preserve Evidence

1

The precedential implications of this ruling . . . are truly enormous. Future plaintiffs may likewise find themselves tossed out of court because they tossed out their junk. It could be a wrecked car, a severed body part, an item of clothing, a bandage, a dead cat. Who knows?[1]

Several issues arise in the context of analyzing the duty to preserve evidence. For instance, when does the duty arise to preserve evidence or items that potentially could become evidence? To whom does this duty extend? And, what items must be preserved? Answers to these three questions are of critical importance for attorneys who counsel their clients. There is potential exposure to sanctions or tort claims when documents or physical evidence is lost or destroyed and a lawsuit is filed, threatened, or should reasonably be anticipated.

The duty to preserve documents or tangible evidence in a given instance can arise from the existence of pending, threatened, or reasonably foreseeable litigation. This duty also can arise from a number of other sources, in-

---

1. Graves v. Daley, 526 N.E.2d 679, 682 (Ill. App. Ct. 1988) (Heiple, J., dissenting).

cluding a contract, a voluntarily assumed duty, a statute or regulation, or an ethical code.[2]

CHOICE OF LAW

As a threshold matter, a practitioner must determine what law applies to spoliation issues that arise during pending litigation or in the context of an independent tort claim for spoliation. Whether a duty to preserve evidence exists is a question of law for the court.[3] The forum in which spoliation occurs can have a substantial impact on the resulting remedies available to the non-spoliating party, because courts disagree, not only regarding the substantive law of spoliation, but in some instances, about what law applies.

Although state courts apply the forum law to spoliation claims, federal courts sitting in diversity disagree about whether spoliation that occurs during pending litigation is a substantive matter, to be governed by state law, or a procedural matter, subject to federal law.[4] A

---

2. Trevino v. Ortega, 969 S.W.2d 950, 955 (Tex. 1998) (Baker, J., concurring); Boyd v. Travelers, Ins. Co., 652 N.E.2d 267 (Ill. 1995); Callahan v. Stanley Works, 703 A.2d 1014, 1018 (N.J. Super. 1997).

3. Manorcare Health Servs. v. Osmose Wood Preserving, Inc., 764 A.2d 475, 479 (N.J. Super. 2001) (holding the duty to preserve evidence is a question of law for the court); Aetna Life & Cas. Co. v. Imet Mason Contrs., 707 A.2d 180, 184 (N.J. Super. 1998).

4. *See, e.g.*, Rowe v. Albertson's, Inc., No. 02-4186, 2004 U.S. App. LEXIS 20959 (10th Cir. Oct. 7, 2004) (affirming Utah district court's decision to apply Texas substantive law to spoliation questions in a diversity case); Hodge v. Wal-Mart Stores, Inc., 360 F.3d 446, 449-50 (4th Cir. 2004) (holding imposition of sanctions for spoliation is an inherent power of federal courts and the decision to impose them is governed by federal law); King v. Ill. Cent. R.R., 337 F.3d 550, 556 (5th Cir. 2003) (stating federal courts generally apply their own evidentiary rules in diversity matters; therefore, federal law governs whether a district court abused its discretion in declining to apply spoliation sanctions); American Family Ins. v. Black & Decker (U.S.), Inc., No. 3:00CV50281, 2003 U.S. Dist. LEXIS 16245 (N.D. Ill. Sept. 16, 2003) (holding a party's pre-suit duty to preserve evidence is a substantive rule of law requiring application of state law in a diversity case); Keller v. United States, 58 F.3d 1194, 1197-98 (7th Cir. 1995) (applying New Mexico law and noting that courts are split regarding whether state or federal law applies, in diversity actions, to the spoliation of evidence); Moyers v. Ford Motor Co., 941 F. Supp. 884, 885 (E.D. Mo. 1996) (applying federal law because sanctions are within court's inherent powers); Allstate Ins. Co. v. Sunbeam Corp., 865 F. Supp. 1267, 1278 (N.D. Ill. 1994) (holding that whether a plaintiff has a duty to preserve a defective product is a substantive issue to be decided by state law); State Farm

court analyzing the issue must first determine whether the result would differ under federal or state law.[5] If the result would be the same, then because there is only a "false conflict," the choice of law analysis is at an end. If the result would differ under the two jurisdictions' respective laws, then, of course, the court must determine which law applies.[6]

It appears no federal court has recognized a tort claim for spoliation under federal law.[7] Instead, tort claims for spoliation are analyzed under applicable state law.[8]

At least two federal courts have rejected an attempt to assert an independent tort claim of spoliation based on 29 C.F.R. § 1602.14, a provision that requires an employer to retain records relevant to a charge of employment discrimination against an employer.[9] For example, in *Lombard v. MCI Telecommunications Corporation*,[10] an Ohio district court held that such a violation was not "actionable *per se*" because the regulation does not provide the employee with the right to sue for damages. Rather, the court followed other decisions which establish

---

Fire & Cas. Co. v. Frigidaire, 146 F.R.D. 160, 162 (N.D. Ill. 1992) (finding "presuit duty to preserve material evidence is substantive and is controlled by state law rather than federal law"); Headley v. Chrysler Motor Corp., 141 F.R.D. 362, 364 (D. Mass. 1991) (explaining federal law controls regarding whether dismissal is proper for spoliation), *approved and adopted*, No. 881642MA, 1992 U.S. Dist. LEXIS 3758 (D. Mass. Jan. 23, 1992).

5. Toste v. Lewis Controls, Inc., No. C-95-01366-MHP, 1996 U.S. Dist. LEXIS 2359, at *18 n.2 (N.D. Cal. Feb. 28, 1996); Baliotis v. McNeil, 870 F. Supp. 1285, 1289 (M.D. Pa. 1994).

6. When a federal court has federal question jurisdiction, the "federal law of spoliation will be applied." Communities for Equity v. Mich. High School Athletic Ass'n, No. 1:98-CV-479, 2001 U.S. Dist. LEXIS 16019 (W.D. Mich. Sept. 21, 2001).

7. Lombard v. MCI Telecomm. Corp., 13 F. Supp. 2d 621, 627 (N.D. Ohio 1998). *See also* Catoire v. Caprock Telecomm. Corp., No. 01-3577, 2003 U.S. Dist. LEXIS 8812 (E.D. La. May 22, 2003) (rejecting claim for spoliation of evidence noting the absence of a private cause of action for relief under 29 C.F.R. § 1602.14).

8. Johnson v. Washington Metro. Area Transit Auth., 764 F. Supp. 1568, 1579 (D.D.C. 1991); Lewis v. J.C. Penney, Inc., 12 F. Supp. 2d 1083, 1086 (E.D. Cal. 1998) (addressing the applicable law for a spoliation claim and holding that in a diversity action the legal issues are governed by the substantive law of the forum state).

9. *See* note 6, *supra*.

10. 13 F. Supp. 2d 621 (N.D. Ohio 1998).

that the proper remedy for such a violation is a rebuttable presumption "that the destroyed document would have bolstered [the plaintiff's] case."[11] Although a number of states have recognized independent tort claims for spoliation of evidence, depending on the law of the forum state and whether it is brought in federal or state court, a party may have different duties regarding preservation of evidence and may face widely varying sanctions for violation of such a duty.[12]

Ohio, West Virginia, and Montana are among a handful of states that recognize an independent tort claim for spoliation of evidence, which allows a plaintiff who can establish the requisite elements of this tort to recover money damages.[13] Most states, however, do not recognize the tort of either intentional or negligent spoliation. Therefore, if spoliation occurs in these states, the non-spoliating party may seek only non-tort remedies, such as civil or evidentiary sanctions, against the destroyer.

Even then, disagreement can exist about the proper analysis for spoliation claims. In Illinois courts are split over whether to focus solely on the prejudice suffered by the non-spoliating party in determining the proper sanction or, instead, whether to consider the level of culpability of the party responsible for the destruction of evidence.[14] One lesson for the practitioner facing a spoliation issue is the importance of familiarizing herself with the law of the governing jurisdiction.

The choice of law analysis also could be important in determining whether there is insurance coverage for spoliated evidence. Typically, general liability insurance policies provide coverage for amounts a

---

11. *Lombard*, 13 F. Supp. 2d at 628.

12. *See* Hank Grzlak, *Federal, State Courts at Odds on Spoliation*, PENNSYLVANIA L. WKLY., July 22, 1996 at 1 (explaining that in Pennsylvania, "if a key piece of evidence is missing in state court, the case has a good chance of being dismissed, even if the allegedly defective part is preserved," whereas "[i]n federal court, the judge will impose some type of sanction, but the case is likely to survive").

13. *See* Smith v. Howard Johnson, 615 N.E.2d 1037 (Ohio 1993); Hannah v. Heeter, 584 S.E.2d 560 (W. Va. 2003); Oliver v. Stimson Lumber Co., 993 P.2d 11 (Mont. 1999).

14. *Compare* H & H Sand & Gravel Co. v. Coyne Cylinder Co., 632 N.E.2d 697 (Ill. App. Ct. 1994) (state of mind of spoliating party a factor to be analyzed) *with* Farley Metals, Inc. v. Barber Colman Co., 645 N.E.2d 964 (Ill. App. Ct. 1994) (upholding dismissal of complaint based on prejudice and stating that "when crucial evidence is destroyed, the offending party's intent becomes significantly less germane in determining a proper sanction"); *see also* David A. Bell, et al., *An Update on Spoliation of Evidence*, 85 ILL. B. J. 530 (1997).

tortfeasor is legally obligated to pay as damages for bodily injury or property damage caused by the tortfeasor's negligent conduct.[15] Currently, only a handful of states recognize a cause of action for negligent spoliation of evidence.[16] Some other states recognize a cause of action for spoliation of evidence, which requires a degree of recklessness or intent. Since most general liability policies exclude coverage for intentional conduct, typically there would be no coverage for the spoliation in states that require some degree of intentional conduct as an element of the tort.

WHEN THE DUTY TO PRESERVE EVIDENCE ARISES

Generally, no duty to preserve evidence arises before litigation is filed, threatened, or reasonably foreseeable unless the duty is voluntarily assumed or imposed by a statute, regulation, contract, or another special circumstance.[17] Absent notice of litigation, or another source of a duty to preserve evidence, a company or individual generally has the right to dispose of his own property, including documents and tangible objects, without liability.[18]

On the other hand, the duty to preserve potentially relevant evidence can arise prior to the commencement of a lawsuit if it is reasonably foreseeable that a lawsuit will be filed.[19] This situation can arise,

---

15. The typical general liability policy defines an "occurrence" to mean "an accident, including continuous or repeated exposure to conditions which result in injury or property damage neither expected nor intended from the standpoint of the insured." Also, most general liability policies contain an exclusion for intentional conduct.

16. *See* Smith v. Atkinson, 771 So. 2d 429 (Ala. 2000).

17. *Hannah*, 584 S.E.2d at 569; Wal-Mart Stores, Inc. v. Johnson, 106 S.W.3d 718 (Tex. 2003); Gilleski v. Community Med. Ctr., 765 A.2d 1103 (N.J. App. 2001); Kelly v. Sears Roebuck & Co., 720 N.E.2d 683 (Ill. App. Ct. 1999).

18. *See, e.g.*, Zubulake v. UBS Warburg, LLC, 220 F.R.D. 212 (S.D.N.Y. 2003) ("It goes without saying that a party can only be sanctioned for destroying evidence if it had a duty to preserve it."); Coleman v. Eddy Potash, Inc., 905 P.2d 185, 191 (N.M. 1995) ("We hold that in the absence of such a circumstance [requiring a duty to preserve evidence], a property owner has no duty to preserve or safeguard his or her property for the benefit of other individuals in a potential lawsuit.").

19. Fujitsu Ltd. v. Federal Express Corp., 247 F.3d 423, 436 (2d Cir. 2001); Kalumetals, Inc. v. Hitachi Magnetics Corp., 21 F. Supp. 2d 510, 520 (W.D. Pa. 1998); Howell v. Maytag, 168 F.R.D. 502, 505 (M.D. Pa. 1996); Shaffer v. RWP Group, Inc., 169 F.R.D. 19, 24 (E.D.N.Y. 1996); Moyers v. Ford Motor Co., 941 F. Supp. 883, 884 (E.D. Mo. 1996); Baliotis v. McNeil, 870 F. Supp. 1285 (M.D. Pa. 1994).

for example, if a potential defendant receives a demand letter or learns that a former employee is seriously contemplating a lawsuit, or if events or circumstances would reasonably put the company, or individual, on notice that a lawsuit likely will be filed.[20]

For example, in *Ferrel v. Connetti Trailer Sales, Inc.*,[21] the court criticized the plaintiffs for failing to bring a motor home to a service center for inspection and necessary repairs, as requested by the dealer. The dealer had offered to pick up the motor home, transport it to another state for inspection, and return it to the plaintiffs at no charge, but the plaintiffs refused. The trial court noted that on at least four or five occasions the manufacturer had requested an opportunity to inspect and repair the vehicle while the plaintiffs still owned it, but they denied those requests.

The *Ferrel* court criticized the plaintiffs for surrendering the vehicle to creditors when they were planning a lawsuit regarding the defective repairs and had threatened several times to do so. Moreover, as the manufacturer and dealer pointed out, under Rhode Island law, they had the right to inspect or test goods, a right that plaintiffs violated when they rebuffed the defendants' request to inspect the vehicle. The court noted that the plaintiffs were aware of the potential relevance of the motor home, yet refused to allow the manufacturer or the dealer to inspect it. The court, therefore, precluded all evidence of defective repairs.

On appeal, the Rhode Island Supreme Court reversed, finding that the trial court had gone too far in precluding all evidence of the defective repairs. Instead, the court remanded the case for a new trial, allowing the plaintiffs to introduce evidence of defective repairs and permitting the defendants to rebut this evidence "as best they can." However, the supreme court also instructed the trial court that, because the plaintiffs' conduct caused the motor home to be unavailable for inspection, the jury could infer that if the manufacturer and dealer had been allowed to conduct such an inspection, they would have discovered evidence indicating the repairs were not defective. This case illustrates the importance of not only taking steps to locate miss-

20. *See, e.g.*, Stevenson v. Union Pac. R.R. Co., 364 F.3d 739 (8th Cir. 2004) (sanctioning railroad because it destroyed evidence similar to what it had previously used to its advantage in another case, after an accident but before litigation commenced).
21. 727 A.2d 183 (R.I. 1999).

ing evidence and tracing it to third parties to the extent necessary, but also of cooperating in any requested inspection by a potentially adverse party.

These types of pre-litigation discussions or a history of previous litigation resulting from similar circumstances can trigger a duty to preserve relevant evidence. As one court explained:

> When a party may be deemed to be on notice [that evidence may be relevant to future litigation] is a function of the variable chronologies along which issues develop in a lawsuit. Thus, in one case it may be a discovery request, in another the complaint, in still another correspondence prior to the filing of a complaint, that puts a party on notice that material in its custody is, or reasonably should be considered, admissible evidence which the party has a legal duty to preserve.[22]

There is a straightforward rationale for requiring parties to preserve relevant evidence before a lawsuit is filed: Absent such a pre-litigation duty, a party might be able to "subvert the discovery process and the fair administration of justice" by destroying evidence before a potential litigant actually files a claim.[23]

There appears to be a "growing trend" for courts to attach a duty to preserve evidence even before a lawsuit is filed.[24] Several courts have held that once a party knows that information may be relevant to a reasonably foreseeable claim, a duty to preserve such evidence arises.[25]

---

22. Abramowitz v. Inta-Bores Acres, Inc., No. 98-CV-4139 (ILG), 1999 U.S. Dist. LEXIS 20005, *7-8 (E.D.N.Y. Nov. 16, 1999) (citing Kronisch v. United States, 150 F.3d 112, 126 (2d Cir. 1998)); *compare* Kanyi v. United States, No. 99-CV-5851(ILG), 2001 U.S. Dist. LEXIS 19814 (E.D.N.Y. 2001) (refusing to sanction a party where documents were destroyed after the lawsuit had been filed but before service of the first requests for production of documents) *with* Stevenson v. Union Pac. R.R. Co., 354 F.3d 739 (8th Cir. 2004) (sanctioning railroad that destroyed voice tapes immediately after an accident where railroad knew such tapes were relevant in earlier lawsuits).

23. *Trevino*, 969 S.W.2d at 955 (Baker, J., concurring).

24. Mary Kay Brown & Paul D. Weiner, *Digital Dangers: A Primer on Electronic Evidence in the Wake of Enron*, 74 Pa. Bar Assn. Q. 1, 3 (January 2003).

25. *See, e.g.,* Silvestri v. General Motors Corp., 271 F.3d 583, 590 (4th Cir. 2001) ("Spoliation refers to the destruction or material alteration of evidence or failure to preserve property for another's use as evidence in . . . reasonably foreseeable litigation."); Mathias v. Jacobs, 197 F.R.D. 29, 37 (S.D.N.Y. 2000) ("duty to preserve arises when a party . . . anticipates litigation").

For instance, one court found that an employer had a duty to preserve certain electronic records destroyed before an employee ever filed a charge of discrimination,[26] which would have triggered a statutory duty to preserve evidence. Acknowledging that a duty to preserve evidence does not arise "[m]erely because one or two employees contemplated the possibility that a fellow employee might sue," the *Zubulake IV* court explained that "it appears that almost everyone associated with [the employee] recognized the possibility that she might sue. . . . Thus, the relevant people at [the employer] anticipated litigation [before the employee filed her charge]. The duty to preserve attached at the time that litigation was reasonably anticipated,"[27] which the court held occurred months before the employee filed her discrimination charges.[28]

A recent district court case adopted a two-prong test for determining whether a duty to preserve evidence exists for potential litigation. The court held that "wherever such a duty exists, a defendant owes a duty of due care to preserve evidence if a reasonable person in the defendant's position should have foreseen that the evidence was material to a potential civil action."[29]

---

26. *Zubulake*, 220 F.R.D. 212 ("Zubulake IV").

27. *Id.* at 217.

28. *See also* Barsom v. NYC Housing Auth., 202 F.R.D. 396, 400 (S.D.N.Y. 2001) (holding plaintiff had a duty to preserve recording of a key conversation with her boss because she "knew or should have known that it was reasonably foreseeable that the tape would be relevant in future litigation," and she had already consulted an attorney).

29. Denton v. Northeast Ill. Reg'l Commuter R.R. Corp., No. 02C2220, 2004 U.S. Dist. LEXIS 7234, *5-6 (N.D. Ill. 2004). As the court explained, "One Illinois court has described this as a two-prong test for the existence of a duty to preserve evidence: (1) the relationship prong; and (2) the foreseeability prong. Unless both prongs are satisfied, there is no duty to preserve evidence." *Id.* (internal citations omitted). *See also* Urban v. United States of America, No. 03C6630, 2005 U.S. Dist. LEXIS 428 (N.D. Ill. 2005) (same); Albertson's, Inc. v. Arriaga, No. 04-03-00697-CV, No. 2004 Tex. App. LEXIS 8307 (Tex. App. 2004) ("a duty arises only when a party knows, or reasonably should know, that there is a substantial chance that a complaining party will file a claim and that the party possesses or controls material evidence relevant to that claim"). *But see* Royal & SunAlliance v. Lauderdale Marine Ctr., 877 So. 2d 843, 846 (Fla. Dist. Ct. App. 2004) (noting that Florida courts have held that there is no duty to preserve evidence when litigation is merely anticipated).

Once a party has notice that litigation has been filed, courts uniformly impose a duty to preserve potentially relevant evidence on parties to the lawsuit.[30] Perhaps the leading case delineating the scope of a party's duty to preserve evidence is *William T. Thompson Company v. General Nutrition Corporation.*[31] There, the plaintiff served the defendant with requests for production of documents shortly after filing suit. The court found the defendant had destroyed records, including electronic records, despite having pre-suit notice of their relevance in subsequent potential litigation. The court explained a litigant's duty to retain relevant documents:

> While a litigant is under no duty to keep or retain every document in its possession once a complaint is filed, it is under a duty to preserve what it knows, or reasonably should know, is relevant in the action, is reasonably calculated to lead to discovery of admissible evidence, is reasonably likely to be requested during discovery, and/or is the subject of a pending discovery request.[32]

William Thompson demonstrates the general rule in preserving evidence, that "[a] 'potential spoliator' need do only what is reasonable under the circumstances"[33] and does not have a duty to "take

---

30. *Trevino*, 969 S.W.2d at 954-55.
31. 593 F. Supp. 1443 (C.D. Cal. 1984), *aff'd*, 104 F.R.D. 119 (C.D. Cal. 1985).
32. *Id.* at 1455. *See also Howell*, 168 F.R.D. at 505 ("A party which reasonably anticipates litigation has an affirmative duty to preserve relevant evidence."); *Toste*, 1996 U.S. Dist. LEXIS 2359, at *8 ("As soon as a potential claim is identified, a litigant is under a duty to preserve evidence which it knows or reasonably should know is relevant to the action.") (citation omitted); Colfer v. Southwest Builders & Dev. Co., 832 P.2d 383, 385 (Nev. 1992) ("[E]ven where an action has not been commenced and there is only a potential for litigation, the litigant is under a duty to preserve evidence which it knows or reasonably should know is relevant to the action.") (citation omitted).
33. Hirsch v. General Motors Corp., 628 A.2d 1108, 1122 (N.J. Super. Ct. Law Div. 1993) (quoting County of Solano v. Delancy, 264 Cal. Rptr. 721, 731 (Cal. Ct. App. 1989), *opinion withdrawn*, No. S013565, 1990 Cal. LEXIS 488 (Feb. 1, 1990)). *See also Baliotis*, 870 F. Supp. at 1290 (quoting Fire Ins. Exch. v. Zenith Radio Corp., 747 P.2d 911, 914 (Nev. 1987) ("litigant is under a duty to preserve evidence which it knows or reasonably should know is relevant to the action"); Willard v. Caterpillar, Inc., 48 Cal. Rptr. 2d 607, 625-26 (Cal. Ct. App. 1995) (noting that some courts impose discovery sanctions only if party is on notice that documents are potentially relevant).

extraordinary measures to preserve evidence. . . ."[34] Thus, as two commentators have observed, "[t]he critical legal question, . . . is whether the litigation was reasonably foreseeable at the time the discoverable documents were destroyed. The existence of a legal duty depends on the answer to this . . . question."[35]

Often, a party will receive notice that certain documents or items are relevant when it receives the complaint or document requests from the opposing party.[36] To be effective as notice, however, the complaint must allege facts describing the conduct that affords notice to the party in possession of evidence.[37]

Discussing when a defendant's duty to preserve evidence arose in a claim for copyright violation, one court explained:

> All reasonable inferences lead inexorably to the conclusion that [the defendant] must have been aware that [plaintiff's] source code would be the subject of a discovery request long before it stopped destroying older versions, and I so find. It is inconceivable that after the [prelitigation] meeting, [defendant] did not realize that the software in its possession would be sought during discovery. Certainly, commencement of the action settled any doubts. Thereafter the request for production, followed by the motion to compel, provided repeated, insistent reminders of the duty to preserve this irreplaceable evidence. Yet the destruction proceeded. . . . Even assuming that maintenance of only a single, updated version of the source code was, in other circumstances, a bona fide business practice, any destruction of versions of the code [20 days after service of the complaint] could not be excused as a bona fide business practice.

Computer Assocs. Int'l, Inc. v. American Fundware, Inc., 133 F.R.D. 166, 169 (D. Colo. 1990).

34. *Id.*

35. J. Kinsler and A. MacIver, *Demystifying Spoliation of Evidence*, 34 Tort & Ins. L.J., 761, 768 (1999).

36. Turner v. Hudson Transit Lines, Inc., 142 F.R.D. 68, 73 (S.D.N.Y. 1991).

37. *Kelly*, 720 N.E.2d at 693; *see also* Valentine v. Mercedes-Benz Credit Corp., No. 98 Civ. 1815, 1999 U.S. Dist. LEXIS 15378 (S.D.N.Y. Sept. 30, 1999). Of course, parties to litigation should promptly request relevant records and documents from the opposing party lest unexplained laxness undercuts a claim of harm from a later failure to produce. In cases where "a party has had an opportunity to pursue discovery but has not aggressively done so, the courts have gone so far as to hold that the subsequent improper destruction of relevant evidence by the other side should not trigger any spoliation sanctions." Saul v. Tivoli Systems, Inc., No. 97CV2386 (DC) (MHD), 2001 U.S. Dist. LEXIS 9873, at *50 (S.D.N.Y. July 17, 2001); *Fujitsu Ltd.*, 247 F.3d at 435-36.

Notice can occur through other means as well. For instance, in *Sanchez v. Stanley-Bostitch, Inc.*,[38] counsel directed that the plaintiff take photographs of an allegedly defective pneumatic staple gun in anticipation of a lawsuit. Neither plaintiff nor counsel notified the manufacturer about the potential claim, nor did they identify the allegedly defective product for the manufacturer before it was lost. The court found that even though the plaintiff did not have possession of or exercise control over the gun, he could have informed the manufacturer of the potential lawsuit and asked his employer to preserve it for future inspection. The court held that because the plaintiff knew that litigation was possible and had retained counsel, he had an obligation to preserve the evidence.[39] Because the plaintiff did not take these steps, the court imposed an adverse inference instruction at trial.[40]

Courts have increasingly indicated that counsel must take affirmative steps to ensure that their litigation clients comply with the duty to preserve evidence. Emphasizing counsel's key role, one court explained, "Once on notice, the obligation to preserve evidence runs first to counsel, who then had a duty to advise and explain to the client its obligations to retain pertinent documents that may be relevant to the litigation."[41]

In a series of cases analyzing the obligation to preserve evidence, district court Judge Shira A. Scheindlin identified certain duties of counsel to parties to litigation "designed to promote continued preservation of potentially relevant evidence in the typical case," including:

- Issuing "litigation hold" letters to the company officials at the outset of litigation or whenever it is reasonably anticipated;
- Communicating directly with "key players," that is, the individuals identified in a party's initial disclosures, about the need to preserve evidence in their possession;
- Periodically reissuing litigation hold letters to employees and remindi ng key employees that the preservation duty still exists; and

---

38. No. 98 Civ. 0494, 1999 U.S. Dist. LEXIS 12975 (S.D.N.Y. Aug. 23, 1999).

39. *Sanchez*, 1999 U.S. Dist. LEXIS 12975.

40. *Id.* at *12.

41. Mary Kay Brown & Paul D. Weiner, *supra* note 24, at 5 (quoting Telecom. Int'l Am., Ltd. v. AT&T Corp., 189 F.R.D. 76, 81 (S.D.N.Y. 1999)).

- Instructing all employees to produce electronic copies of their relevant active files and make sure all backup media is identified and stored in a safe place.[42]

The limits of a litigant's duty of reasonableness are not, of course, always clear. As the quotation at the beginning of this chapter indicates, the danger exists that a party may innocently discard what appears to be not evidence but junk, and, subsequently, a court may determine that it was reasonably foreseeable that the spoliated materials were relevant evidence.

WHEN THE DUTY TO PRESERVE EVIDENCE ARISES INDEPENDENTLY OF LITIGATION

A duty to preserve evidence also can arise independent of litigation from (a) a contract, (b) a statute or regulation, (c) a document retention policy, or (d) in the case of attorneys, ethical duties. In these cases, the duty to preserve evidence may exist before litigation is contemplated, or may arise out of a pre-suit agreement to preserve evidentiary material.

Numerous federal and state statutes and regulations impose record-keeping obligations on individuals and organizations.[43] These laws require companies to retain certain types of documents for a specified

---

42. Zubulake v. UBS Warburg, LLC, No. 02 Civ. 1243 (SAS), 2004 U.S. Dist. LEXIS 13574 (S.D.N.Y. July 20, 2004) ("Zubulake V").

43. Discussing whether directing an expert to destroy drafts and notes is sanctionable, one commentator observed that Fed. R. Civ. P. 26(a)(2)(B) mandates disclosure of both a statement of all opinions and the data or information considered by the expert, which includes "documents provided by counsel to the expert and the expert's draft reports and notes." Gregory P. Joseph, *Expert Spoliation,* 15 THE PRACTICAL LITIGATOR 7 (Nov. 2004) (citing Corrigan v. Methodist Hosp., 158 F.R.D. 54, 58 (E.D. Pa. 1994)); Ladd Furniture v. Ernst & Young, 1998 U.S. Dist. LEXIS 17345, at *34 (M.D.N.C. Aug. 27, 1998); Hewlett-Packard v. Bausch & Lomb, 116 F.R.D. 533, 537 (N.D. Cal. 1987). *See also* Trigon Ins. Co. v. United States, 204 F.R.D. 277 (E.D. Va. 2001) (noting drafts of expert opinions may be useful for cross-examination and sanctioning party for destroying drafts of an expert's report). This same commentator also suggests that attorneys "[b]e slow to request any of this discovery from your adversary. You, too, have an expert. It is effectively impossible to insure that no potentially responsive documents are lost, however hard you try. Mutual assured destruction worked for decades. It still has legs." *Id.* at 11.

period of time. Some of these statutes and regulations also specify the required sanction for destruction of documents in violation of laws when it results in documents being unavailable in civil litigation. These statutes and regulations typically permit the opposing party to obtain an adverse inference instruction. Although a comprehensive list of these laws is beyond the scope of this book, Chapter 6 discusses selective statutory record-keeping requirements.

For example, regulations governing the Office of Federal Compliance Programs contain a record-keeping requirement, section 60-741.80 of Title 41 of the Code of Federal Regulations. This requirement governs record-keeping requirements for the Office of Federal Compliance Programs and requires that personnel and employment records made by a covered contractor be preserved for at least two years from the day of the record or the personnel action involved, whichever occurs later. This regulation provides that failure to preserve such records may result in the presumption that the information destroyed or not preserved would have been unfavorable to the party that failed to retain the records. This presumption does not apply if the contractor is able to establish that the destruction or failure to preserve resulted from circumstances outside of his control.[44]

Likewise, the Sarbanes-Oxley Act of 2002 imposes certain record-keeping requirements on corporate entities and creates penalties for failure to comply with these requirements. Among other things, the Act requires that "[a]ny accountant who conducts an audit of an issuer of securities to which section 10A(a) of the Securities Exchange Act of 1934 applies, shall maintain all audit and review work papers for a period of 5 years from the end of the fiscal period in which the audit or review was concluded."[45]

As discussed *infra*, in Chapter 2, a company also may have a duty, under its document retention policy, to preserve certain types of documents for a specified time period. A company's failure to retain documents as provided for in the policy, or to suspend the policy in light of pending litigation, can result in substantial sanctions.[46]

In addition, involvement in spoliation may subject attorneys to sanctions for violation of ethical codes. For example, the ABA's Model Rule

---

44. 41 C.F.R. § 60-741.80.
45. 18 U.S.C. § 1520(a)(1) (2002).
46. *See infra* at ch. 2.

of Professional Conduct prohibits a lawyer from unlawfully altering, destroying, or concealing documents or other material having potential evidentiary value. Likewise, Disciplinary Rule 7-102(A)(3) prohibits a lawyer from knowingly creating or preserving false evidence.[47]

WHAT EVIDENCE MUST BE PRESERVED?

In addition to determining whether a duty exists to preserve evidence, a party also must decide what evidence should be preserved. Essentially, the test is one of reasonableness, as seen from the perspective of the party charged with that duty. If a party on notice of a lawsuit, or threatened lawsuit, would reasonably believe that evidence in its possession is relevant, then it must take steps to preserve this evidence.

"Relevance" is given an exceedingly broad scope under the Federal Rules of Civil Procedure and analogous state rules.[48] As one court explained:

> The broad contours of the duty to preserve are relatively clear. That duty should certainly extend to any documents or tangible things (as defined by Rule 34(a)) made by individuals "likely to have discoverable information that the disclosing party may use to support its claims or defenses." The duty also includes documents prepared for those individuals, to the extent those documents can be readily identified (*e.g.,* from the "to" field in e-mails).[49]

Given the potential breadth of this duty, a party deciding whether to preserve particular items of evidence would be well advised to err on the side of caution.

Still, although parties must take reasonable steps to preserve relevant evidence, they are not required to make extraordinary efforts to retain evidence. In determining whether non-retention of a particular item of evidence is reasonable, courts will weigh such factors as safety, expense, and the cumbersomeness of retaining the evidence in question.

For example, in *Conderman v. Rochester Gas & Electric Corpo-*

---

47. *See* MODEL RULE 3.4(a); DR 7-102(A)(3).
48. *See, e.g.*, Corrigan v. Methodist Hosp., 158 F.R.D. 54, 57 (E.D. Pa. 1994) ("Relevance for discovery purposes is defined broadly.").
49. *Zubulake IV*, 220 F.R.D. at 218-19.

ration,[50] utility poles fell onto the plaintiffs' pick-up truck and power lines from the downed poles injured them as they were driving. The defendant utility company sent emergency crews to the scene. In the process of clearing the road, the crews cut the poles into four-foot lengths and removed them to a landfill. After filing a lawsuit, plaintiffs moved for summary judgment based on alleged spoliation of evidence by the utility company. The trial court granted the motion, essentially precluding the utility company from offering evidence to rebut a presumption of negligence.[51]

The appellate court reversed the grant of summary judgment on spoliation. It reasoned that the utility company was "responding to an emergency situation that affected public safety, and it would be unreasonable to have imposed upon [it] at the time the duty to preserve evidence, anticipating the possibility of future litigation."[52]

To ensure that "relevant evidence" is not destroyed or discarded during the pendency of a lawsuit, a party, of course, must determine what evidence is relevant. The potential relevance of evidence can be ascertained from the complaint, discovery requests, or a court order. If no lawsuit has been filed, a potential defendant may be put on notice by a demand letter from counsel for plaintiff, or it may have notice through a pattern of complaints received in the past regarding the particular product.[53]

Sometimes it is impossible or impractical for a party to retain all of the relevant evidence. For example, it may be unreasonably expensive, unsafe, or unduly disruptive of the company's business to preserve certain items of evidence. Courts will consider all of the surrounding circumstances to determine whether it was reasonable for the party not to retain the evidence in question.[54]

---

50. 262 A.2d 1068 (N.Y. 1999).
51. *Id.* at 1068-69.
52. *Id.* at 1069.
53. Lewy v. Remington Arms Co., 836 F.2d 1104 (8th Cir. 1988).
54. *See, e.g., Zubulake IV,* 220 F.R.D. 217 ("Must a corporation, upon recognizing the threat of litigation, preserve every shred of paper, every e-mail or electronic document, and every back-up tape? The answer is clearly, 'no.' Such a rule would cripple large corporations . . . ."); *Conderman,* 262 A.2d at 1069 (finding public safety justified failure to preserve evidence); *Sanchez,* 1999 U.S. Dist. LEXIS 12975 (finding plaintiff's retention of counsel who directed that certain evidence be photographed suggested plaintiff had a duty to preserve evidence); Concord Boat Corp. v. Brunswick Corp., No. LR-C-95-791, 1997 U.S. LEXIS 24068 (E.D. Ark.

Convolve, Inc. v. Compaq Computer Corporation[55] is illustrative. There, a technology company shared certain proprietary information with the manufacturers of a disk drive and a computer producer and distributor. The technology company claimed these computer makers misappropriated its trade secrets and infringed on its patents. The technology company sought sanctions against the computer makers for alleged spoliation of certain electronic data or wave forms used to evaluate the performance of disk drives. Rejecting the technology's company's request, the court explained:

> [T]he preservation of the wave forms in a tangible state would have required heroic efforts far beyond those consistent with [the computer maker's] regular course of business. To be sure, as part of a litigation hold, a company may be required to cease deleting e-mails, as to disrupt its normal document destruction protocol. But e-mails, at least, have some semi-permanent existence. . . . By contrast, the data at issue here are ephemeral. They exist only until the tuning engineer makes the next adjustment, and then the document changes. No business purpose ever dictated that they be retained, even briefly.[56]

On occasion a party may opt to retain photographs, videotapes, test results, or other "secondary evidence" rather than the actual physical evidence. In these situations, the non-spoliating party may argue that the preserved evidence is an inadequate substitute for the original evidence. Courts sometimes will accept this argument and exclude testimony based on the missing evidence.

For example, in *Cincinnati Insurance Company v. General Motors Corporation*,[57] an insurer filed suit against an automobile manufacturer, alleging that a defective motor vehicle caused a fire that damaged its insured's home. After the insurance company's expert

---

Aug. 29, 1997) (explaining "to hold that a corporation is under a duty to preserve all e-mail correspondence potentially relevant to any future litigation would be tantamount to holding that the corporation must preserve all e-mail. . . . Such a proposition is not justified.").

55. 223 F.R.D. 162 (S.D.N.Y. 2004).

56. *Id.* at 177. Among other authorities, the court referenced Proposed Fed. R. Civ. P. 37(f), which, if adopted, will impose some limits on the authority of district courts to sanction the destruction of electronically stored information.

57. No. 940T017, 1994 Ohio App. LEXIS 4960 (Ohio Ct. App. Oct. 28, 1994).

had examined the vehicle, someone destroyed the car but not the blower motor. Before it was destroyed, the insurer's expert took photographs of the vehicle and the surrounding area. Although the insurer gave the manufacturer's expert the photographs, that expert opined that he could not determine the origin and cause of the fire without examining the entire vehicle and possibly the area where the vehicle had been parked.

The trial court granted the manufacturer's motion and excluded the insurer's expert testimony. Thereafter, it granted summary judgment because without this expert testimony, the insurer could not prove its case. Affirming the trial court's decision, the court of appeals rejected the insurer's contention that its photographs provided the manufacturer with an adequate substitute for the destroyed evidence, explaining that the physical evidence itself is far more probative under these circumstances:

> The physical object itself in the precise condition immediately after an accident may be far more instructive and persuasive to a jury than oral or photograph descriptions.[58]

As another example, in *Dillon v. Nissan Motor Company, Ltd.,*[59] the district court barred testimony by the expert who inspected the allegedly defective vehicle and excluded any evidence derived from his inspection, including photographs of the vehicle he inspected, as a sanction for destruction of evidence. Rejecting photographic evidence offered to minimize prejudice to the manufacturer, the district court stated that the photographs were not comprehensive, were blurred, and failed to document the condition of crucial areas of the allegedly defectively designed vehicle.[60]

Before deciding to discard evidence and substitute photographs, a practitioner would be well advised to consider one court's remarks when an expert discarded evidence and then tried to substitute photographs and oral testimony for missing evidence:

---

58. *Id.* at *13-14 (quoting American Family Ins. Co. v. Village Pontiac-GMC, Inc., 585 N.E.2d 1115, 1118 (Ill. App. Ct. 1992)); *see also* State Farm Fire & Cas. Co. v. Frigidaire, 146 F.R.D. 160, 163 (N.D. Ill. 1992).

59. 986 F.2d 263 (8th Cir. 1993).

60. *Id.* at 268.

Plaintiffs were the only individuals with first-hand knowledge of the physical evidence which is far more probative under these circumstances in determining whether the [product] caused the fire than photographs and two wires taken from [the product]. . . . As a matter of sound public policy, an expert should not be permitted intentionally or negligently to destroy such evidence and then substitute his or her own description of it.[61]

These cases teach that a party that decides to discard relevant evidence because it is impractical or impossible to retain will bear the burden of showing that it did all that it could to provide a prospective adverse party with an opportunity to inspect the evidence before it elected to "preserve" that evidentiary material by photographs or other secondary means. As one court explained, "[a]t a minimum . . . an opportunity for inspection should be afforded a potentially responsible party before relevant evidence is destroyed."[62]

WHERE EVIDENCE IS IN THE POSSESSION OF THIRD PARTIES

As a general rule, there is no duty to retain evidence to aid in future legal action against a third party[63] "[a]bsent some special relationship or duty arising by reason of an agreement, contract, statute, or other special circumstance.]"[64] However, a duty to preserve evidence may extend beyond the parties themselves and include evidence entrusted to their agents, experts, insurers, attorneys, and the like. In such instances, a party may be held liable for spoliation committed by a third party to whom it entrusted the destroyed evidence.

For example, in *Jordan F. Miller Corporation v. Mid-Continent Aircraft Service, Incorporated*,[65] a buyer filed suit against the sellers

---

61. *State Farm Fire & Cas. Co.*, 146 F.R.D. at 163.

62. *Baliotis*, 870 F. Supp. at 1290-91; *see also Zubulake IV*, 220 F.R.D. 217 (observing that a party to a lawsuit must not destroy "unique, relevant evidence that might be useful to an adversary").

63. Wilson v. Beloit Corp., 921 F.2d 765 (8th Cir. 1990) (explaining that absent special relationship or duty, no duty exists to preserve possible evidence to aid in future legal action against third party).

64. Koplin v. Rosel Well Perforators, Inc., 734 P.2d 1177, 1179 (Kan. 1987).

65. No. 97-5089, 1998 U.S. App. LEXIS 2739 (10th Cir. Feb. 20, 1998).

of a jet aircraft. Shortly after purchase, the aircraft landing gear collapsed and severely damaged the aircraft. The buyer hired a company to repair the aircraft. Thereafter, the buyer filed suit against the sellers, and the buyer's insurer intervened.

The sellers served discovery requests, including a request that all of the aircraft component parts be made available for inspection or testing. Ultimately, during the deposition of the president of the aircraft repair company, the sellers learned for the first time that all but one of the aircraft's component parts had been destroyed.

The sellers filed a motion to dismiss based on spoliation of evidence. The buyers argued that only the insurer had a duty to preserve the landing gear, and that he had no such duty once it was in the possession of the repair company. The court rejected this argument, explaining that the buyer remained responsible for preserving the aircraft parts:

> [The buyer] knew that the damaged landing gear was relevant to his claims against [the sellers] and he, therefore, had a duty to preserve the evidence. His argument that only [the repair company] had a duty to preserve the landing gear is misguided. [The repair company] did not enter the suit as a party until almost a year after [the buyer] filed his complaint. Moreover, that [the repair company] may also have had a duty to preserve the evidence did not absolve [the buyer] of his duty to preserve evidence that was relevant to his own claims against [the seller].[66]

The court held that the buyer's conduct provided a basis for sanctions and, because the seller's experts testified they could not render an opinion without the missing evidence, the trial court appropriately dismissed the complaint.[67]

The third-party destruction of evidence issue also arises when relevant evidence has been turned over by a party to its insurer or expert retained to examine the evidence and to render an opinion. If the insurer or expert loses the evidence or subjects it to destructive testing, then the party that relinquished the evidence may be held liable for its loss.

---

66. *Id.* at *18-19.
67. *Id.* at *23.

Where evidence is in the possession of a party's insurer when it is lost or destroyed, courts typically hold that the party entrusting the evidence to the insurer retains the duty to preserve it. For example, in *Thompson v. Owensby*,[68] the court held that the relationship between the party and an insurance company in possession of evidence favors a finding that the party had a duty to preserve evidence. Courts also will find that when the party sought to be held liable for spoliation could have informed the party in possession that a lawsuit existed and requested the evidence be preserved, that party may be held liable for spoliation.[69]

A somewhat related situation occurs when a party claims it has been prejudiced by the loss or destruction of evidence and seeks to hold a third-party liable for its loss. In *Elias v. Lancaster General Hospital*,[70] the court considered whether Pennsylvania should recognize a cause of action in tort against a third party that had discarded relevant evidence. Although the court declined to rule on whether a separate tort claim was needed where spoliation was caused by a party to litigation, it did express the view that additional remedies adequate under those circumstances were needed.[71] Where the spoliator was not a party to the underlying action, the court reasoned that traditional negligence principles, rather than a separate tort of negligent spoliation, would suffice to remedy third-party spoliation.[72]

Moreover, noted the *Elias* court, "the law does not impose affirmative duties absent the existence of some special relationship, be it contractual or otherwise."[73] Applying traditional negligence principles to the facts before it, the court concluded that the hospital could not be held liable for failing to preserve pacemaker wires to aid an individual in his product liability action against the manufacturer of the wires. The court noted that the hospital had no contractual duty to do so, nor did the hospital agree to preserve these wires. The court rejected the plaintiff's argument that the hospital had "a general duty to preserve for inspection any foreign objects removed from its patients' bodies

---

68. 704 N.E.2d 134 (Ind. Ct. App. 1998).
69. *Sanchez*, 1999 U.S. Dist. LEXIS 12975.
70. 710 A.2d 65 (Pa. Super. Ct. 1998).
71. *Id.* at 67.
72. *Id.* at 67-68.
73. *Id.* at 68.

due to its relationship with its patients."[74] The court also held "that hospitals do not owe a general duty to their patients to preserve foreign objects extracted from their bodies."[75] Accordingly, the court affirmed the dismissal of plaintiff's spoliation claim.

Courts have taken conflicting positions on the issue of third-party liability for spoliation. For example, in *Holmes v. Amerex Rent-a-Car,*[76] the District of Columbia Court of Appeals considered whether, under District of Columbia law, a plaintiff may recover against a defendant who has negligently or recklessly destroyed, or allowed to be destroyed, evidence that would have assisted the plaintiff in pursuing a claim against a third party. The court held that such a claim is cognizable, provided, however, that the party seeking to assert that claim can establish the existence of a special relationship that would create a duty to preserve the evidence for use in future litigation.[77]

The California Supreme Court considered a similar issue in *Temple Community Hospital v. Superior Court of Los Angeles County,*[78] in which it determined whether a party may bring a tort claim against a person who intentionally destroys evidence that would be relevant in an underlying lawsuit to which the spoliator is not a party. The court held that no cause of action exists against a third party for spoliation that affects the existing lawsuit because of concerns over "endless litigation."[79]

Practice Tips

When advising clients on the obligation to preserve evidence, consider these principles:

- When deciding whether to preserve evidence, err on the side of caution, particularly where it is not inordinately expensive, cumbersome, or disruptive of one's business to preserve evidentiary material.

---

74. *Id.*
75. *Id.* at 69.
76. 710 A.2d 846 (D.C. App. 1998).
77. *Id.* at 849.
78. 976 P.2d 223 (Cal. 1999); *compare Stimson*, 993 P.2d at 16-17 (recognizing a cause of action for third-party spoliation).
79. *Temple Community*, 976 P.2d at 229.

- If evidence cannot reasonably be retained, provide all litigants, or prospective litigants, with a reasonable opportunity to inspect and test the evidence before it is destroyed. Be sure to keep a written record of any notice and opportunity to inspect given to a potential adverse party.

- Before destroying any physical evidence, to the extent feasible, make a photographic or videotape record of the evidence that must be discarded.

- Before discarding potential evidence, be sure that there have been no court orders or discovery requests covering this evidence.

- If evidence is to be turned over to third parties, including experts and insurers, instruct them not to dispose of or destroy the evidence without the express consent of the company and confirm that instruction in writing.

- When considering whether a particular piece of documentary physical evidence should be retained as relevant to potential litigation, bear in mind that your decision may be reviewed by a court that has the benefit of hindsight.

- Attorneys counseling clients regarding spoliation issues should be mindful of their ethical obligations under the applicable code of ethics.

- Once litigation is reasonably anticipated, corporate counsel should determine whether and to what extent its routine document retention programs should be suspended.

- Once litigation has commenced, outside counsel should take an active role in document preservation efforts, including issuing "litigation hold" letters and following up with company officials and in-house counsel throughout the litigation to ensure that relevant records continue to be preserved.

- Make discovery requests for documents, records and things promptly. Courts consider failure to timely pursue such materials pertinent to arguments regarding prejudice caused by loss of evidence.

- Once a party retains an expert, make sure that the expert is aware that every document he or she writes or receives should be retained and include that instruction in correspondence retaining the expert.

The Impact of Document Retention Policies | 2

. . . No more shredding. . . .[1]

Even in an era of computerized records, no company possibly can, or should, indefinitely retain all the documents that it receives or generates. The expense alone would be prohibitive. Some documents, such as a company's historical documents, may be appropriate for permanent retention. However, most documents should be kept for a specific period of time and then, absent special circumstances, they should be destroyed.

There are many reasons for a company to implement a document retention program. These include: (1) the expense of document storage, (2) the need to locate records efficiently, (3) the desire to avoid sanctions for improper destruction of documents, and (4) conversely, the potentially devastating consequences that can result from documents that should not have been subject to retention.[2]

---

1. Arthur Andersen, LLP v. United States, 125 S. Ct. 2129, 2133, 161 L. Ed. 2d 1008, 2005 U.S. LEXIS 4348 (2005) (reversing accounting firm's conviction for obstruction of justice under 18 U.S.C. § 1512(b)(2)(A) and (B) because the jury instructions did not properly convey the elements of a corrupt persuasion conviction under 15 U.S.C. § 1512(b)).

2. S. Ratliff, *Innovative Ideas in Records Retention Policies and Management—"What Do I Do With This Stuff?"*, ch. 3 in RECORDS RETENTION (Business Law, Inc. Aug. 1993); Comment: *A Wreck on the*

Despite these practical concerns and the existence of "countless long-standing document retention policies," many "businesses may be surprised to find that, because of the spoliation doctrine, they may be sued for spoliation of evidence or otherwise penalized as a consequence of their actions."[3] One commentator explained the tension between document retention policies and obstruction of justice laws as follows:

> Document retention policies request that a business enterprise destroy documents. Conversely, obstruction of justice laws seek the inherently opposite position, since they are designed to protect documents from being destroyed. Truth-seeking, impartiality, and the honor of the judicial and governmental system seem to necessitate more legal control over document retention policies because such policies are designed to destroy documents relevant to potential litigation.[4]

But a well-designed document retention policy can strike an appropriate balance between these seemingly contradictory views.[5] Achieving this balance requires that the policy calling for document destruction be suspended upon commencement of litigation or an official investigation into the company or when a company has reason to know litigation or an investigation is imminent.[6] But what provides a company with "reason to know?"

Info-Bahn: Electronic Mail and the Destruction of Evidence, 6 COMMLAW CONSPECTUS 75, 84 (Winter 1998); Note: *Document Retention Programs for Electronic Records: Applying a Reasonableness Standard to the Electronic Era*, 24 IOWA J. CORP. L. 417, 418 (Winter 1999).

3. Robert L. Tucker, *The Flexible Doctrine of Spoliation: Cause of Action, Defense, Evidentiary Presumption and Discovery Sanction*, 27 U. TOL L. REV. 67, 79 (Fall 1995) (citations omitted).

4. Christopher R. Chase, *To Shred or Not to Shred: Document Retention Policies and Federal Obstruction of Justice Statutes*, 8 FORDHAM J. CORP. & FIN. L. 721, 754 (2003) (citing Jamie Gorelick, et al., DESTRUCTION OF EVIDENCE 278 (1989)) (hereinafter *To Shred or Not to Shred*).

5. *Id. See also* Mary Kay Brown & Paul D. Weiner, *Digital Dangers: A Primer on Electronic Evidence in the Wake of Enron*, 74 PA. BAR. ASSN. Q. 1 (January 2003).

6. *Id.*; Gary G. Grindler & Jason A. Jones, *Please Step Away From the Shredder and the "Delete" Key: §§ 802 and 1102 of the Sarbanes-Oxley Act*, 41 AM. CRIM. L. REV. 67 (Winter 2004) (hereinafter *Please Step Away*). *See, e.g.,* Rambus, Inc. v.

Discussing the required nexus between the "persua[sion] to destroy documents and any particular proceeding" in the criminal case against the accounting firm in Arthur Andersen, the Supreme Court observed: "It is . . . one thing to say a proceeding 'need not be pending or about to be instituted at the time of the offense,' and quite another to say a proceeding need not even be foreseen."[7] The Court continued, a "knowingly . . . corrupt[t] persuade[r] cannot be someone who persuades others to destroy documents under a document retention policy when he does not have in contemplation any particular official proceeding in which those documents might be material."[8]

Document retention policies exist "in part to keep certain information from getting into the hands of others, including the government."[9] Under ordinary circumstances, "[i]t is . . . not wrongful for a [company] to instruct [its] employees to comply with a valid document retention policy."[10]

ISSUES TO CONSIDER WHEN DESIGNING A DOCUMENT RETENTION PROGRAM

A well-designed document retention policy "must be tailored to fit the specific needs of the business involved and should have a legitimate business purpose at its core."[11] When determining whether a document should be retained or destroyed as a matter of policy, the central inquiry must be the legal or business purpose for keeping or discarding the document, as opposed to the content of the document.[12] Docu-

---

Infineon Tech. AG, 222 F.R.D. 280 (E.D. Va. 2004) (noting "[e]ven valid purging programs need to be put on hold when litigation is reasonably foreseeable").

7. *Arthur Andersen*, 125 S. Ct. 2129, 2136-37.

8. *Id.*

9. *Arthur Andersen*, 125 S. Ct. at 2133 (citing *To Shred or Not to Shred, supra* note 4).

10. *Id.* at 2134.

11. Joseph P. Messina & Daniel B. Trinkle, *Document Retention Policies After Andersen*, 46 Boston Bar J. 18 (Sept./Oct. 2002).

12. *Id. See Rambus*, 222 F.R.D. at 296 (finding company "adopted its document retention program because it anticipated litigation" and that its document retention program was part of its litigation strategy); Carlucci v. Piper Aircraft Corp., 102 F.R.D. 472, 482 (S.D. Fla. 1984) (sanctioning aircraft maker where the purpose of its records retention policy was to eliminate document that could harm it in a lawsuit).

ment retention policies designed to eliminate potential "smoking guns" or other damaging documents will not withstand judicial scrutiny.[13]

In developing a policy, an organization must "consider the externally mandated laws and regulations that govern it . . . , as well as its duty to preserve data relevant to actual or reasonable anticipated litigation."[14] But records management programs and policies also serve "legitimate information, storage, access and retention needs of the organization,"[15] which courts have long recognized.[16]

To avoid questions about the motives for developing, changing and/or implementing a document retention policy, the policy should be created or revised and implemented at a time when "litigation or an investigation is not pending or foreseeable."[17] Companies should also regularly review their policies to insure that they are in compliance with new or current regulations. For example, by now accounting firms should have reviewed their policies to reflect retention requirements established by the Sarbanes-Oxley Act of 2002.[18]

Not only should a company insist upon strict compliance with its document retention policies, it should routinely remind employees about the need to follow its policies.[19] But "[r]eminders about document retention policies should be sent . . . in accordance with a regular sched-

---

13. *See* Reingold v. Wet 'N Wild Nevada, Inc., 944 P.2d 800 (Nev. 1997); Lewy v. Remington Arms, 836 F.2d 1104, 1112 (8th Cir. 1988); *Rambus*, 220 F.R.D. at 286; Kozlowski v. Sears, Roebuck & Co., 73 F.R.D. 73 (D. Mass. 1976).

14. THE SEDONA CONFERENCE, THE SEDONA GUIDELINES: BEST PRACTICE GUIDELINES & COMMENTARY FOR MANAGING INFORMATION & RECORDS IN THE ELECTRONIC Age 18 (Sept. 2004), *available* at www.thesedonaconference.org (hereinafter THE SEDONA GUIDELINES) (citing *Rambus*, 222 F.R.D. at 281); Zubulake v. UBS Warburg LLC, 220 F.R.D. 212, 216 (S.D.N.Y. 2003).

15. *Id.*

16. *Carlucci*, 102 F.R.D. 472; *Lewy*, 836 F.2d 1104.

17. *To Shred or Not To Shred, supra* note 4, at 754 (citing Lisa Shaheen, *Required Recordkeeping Sets the Record Straight,* PEST CONTROL 27 (Apr. 1, 2001)).

18. *Please Step Away, supra* note 6, at 89.

19. *See* THE SEDONA GUIDELINES at 37 (suggesting that, depending on a particular company's culture, in some companies it may be appropriate to require employees to sign written acknowledgment confirming that they understand the records retention policy just as like employees are asked to acknowledge their receipt of and understanding of other company policies); *see also* THE SEDONA PRINCIPLES: BEST PRACTICE RECOMMENDATIONS & PRINCIPLES FOR ADDRESSING ELECTRONIC DOCUMENT PRODUCTION (March 2003), *available at* www.thesedonaconference.org.

ule to avoid allegations that document destruction took place in connection with a particular matter."[20]

A document retention program should also consider procedures
for educating the workforce regarding the policy itself and the need
for everyone in the organization to follow it.[21] As the Arthur Andersen
"prosecution demonstrated, a comprehensive document retention
policy is useless unless properly administered."[22] Employees should
be educated about the perils of unwise document creation, warned
about the consequences of improper destruction of documents, and
encouraged to consult with in-house counsel or specified compliance
officers regarding questions or concerns about "the substance of certain documents and whether they should be destroyed."[23]

For example, absent an effectively enforced document retention
policy, employees may use company e-mail to poke fun at other employees or otherwise make comments that are unrelated to the
company's business.[24] These kinds of personal e-mails, even if not
demonstrative of company policy, can be subject to discovery in civil
litigation and may be highly damaging to the company.

As part of its records retention program, a company also should
consider an e-mail policy that restricts the dissemination of offensive
or disruptive e-mails. Implementation of such a policy can eliminate
the need to justify failure to retain these documents at some later time.

It sometimes can be as problematic for a company to improperly
retain non-business documents as it is to destroy documents that should
have been retained. For example, if a company is sued based on age
discrimination, it may be required to produce an employee's file that
contains such improperly preserved items as "over the hill" birthday
cards given to the employee. This type of record is discoverable, even

---

20. *Id.*

21. *Please Step Away, supra* note 6, at 89.

22. *Id.*

23. *Id.*

24. *See, e.g.,* Strauss v. Microsoft Corp., 814 F. Supp. 1186 (S.D.N.Y. 1993)
(sex discrimination suit based on e-mails). *See also* Martin Redish, *Electronic
Discovery and the Litigation Matrix*, 51 Duke L. J. 561, 588 (2001) ("E-mail is
often used with a lack of appropriate caution, given its near permanence—a fact
seldom realized by e-mail users, who think that when they trash a message it is
destroyed. Moreover, the distribution of e-mail messages is largely impossible to
control because they are so easily copied and forwarded.").

when there is no legitimate business purpose for having retained such a document, simply because it found its way into an employee's file.

Having a document retention policy is problematic unless it is followed regularly, because it leaves a company open to charges that its program is followed only when the company wants to destroy evidence of wrongdoing.[25] Therefore, depending on its size, a company should appoint a records retention officer or assign a high-level employee responsibility for overseeing its record retention program.[26] That person's responsibilities should include ensuring that the retention policy is being followed consistently and updated when necessary. The designated company record retention officer also should have authority to suspend the policy when the company anticipates or receives notice of pending or potential litigation to avoid destruction of relevant and discoverable documents.[27] A company also should conduct periodic audits to ensure that its employees comply with its document retention policy.

Courts examine a company's compliance with its own document retention policy when assessing the appropriateness of imposing sanctions for spoliation of evidence. Failure to comply with an existing document retention policy may support a finding that the company did not take its policy seriously or, worse, that it was a sham designed to permit the company to engage in deliberate document destruction.[28]

---

25. *See, e.g.,* United States v. Arthur Andersen, LLP, 374 F.3d 281, 287 (5th Cir. 2004), *rev'd,* 125 S. Ct. 2129, 2131 (May 31, 2005).

26. *See* THE SEDONA GUIDELINES, *supra* note 14, at 31.

27. *Please Step Away, supra* note 6, at 89.

28. *See Rambus,* 222 F.R.D. at 296 (finding company "adopted its document retention program because it anticipated litigation" and that its document retention program was part of its litigation strategy); *Carlucci,* 102 F.R.D. at 482 (sanctioning aircraft maker where the purpose of its records retention policy was to eliminate document that could harm it in a lawsuit); United States v. Taber Extrusions, L.P., No. 4:00CV0025, 2001 U.S. Dist. LEXIS 24600, at *8-9 (E.D. Ark. Dec. 27, 2001) 30 n.28 (analyzing reasonableness of destroying documents pursuant to retention policy and finding policy destroying documents after six years and three months appeared reasonable on its face and no evidence indicated government should have known the documents would become material). *See also* Bruce E. Jameson, *Document Retention and Electronic Discovery,* 15 THE PRACTICAL LITIGATOR 45 (Sept. 2004) (observing that "[o]nce a company develops a policy it must enforce it regularly. Having a policy but not enforcing it may be worse than having a policy at all.").

For example, records retention programs focusing on elimination of "bad documents" can lead to the imposition of severe sanctions.[29]

Not only is it advisable to have a document retention policy, once a company adopts a such a policy, it should "consider documenting its record retention efforts."[30] Among other things, a company should keep its training information, document any changes to its policies, and keep records of its implementation procedures.[31]

DOCUMENT RETENTION REQUIREMENTS

The time period for retaining documents depends on a number of factors, including the type of business in which the company is engaged, the legal requirements governing the documents at issue, and whether the company has knowledge of claims or a litigation history that might render the documents at issue subject to discovery in litigation. The appropriate time period for retaining non-permanent records can vary from as little as a month or two to as much as 40 years or longer. But "[u]nless there is an applicable retention obligation imposed by statute or regulation, or there is a legal hold imposed by virtue of litigation, audit or investigation, . . . organizations can legitimately prescribe retention (or deletion) periods for . . ." documents and records, including, "recorded communications, such as electronic mail, instant messaging, voice over IP, text-messaging, and voice-mails."[32]

Numerous federal statutes, including the Employee Retirement Income and Security Act of 1974 (ERISA), the Sarbanes-Oxley Act of 2002, the Health Insurance Portability and Accountability Act, the Internal Revenue Service codes, the Securities and Exchange Act, the Occupational Safety and Health Act (OSHA), and employment laws such as the Fair Labor Standards Act (FLSA), the Americans with Disabilities Act, and the Family and Medical Leave Act impose record-keeping obligations on companies. These requirements often include specific time periods for keeping such records.

In addition, state statutes may impose varying record-keeping requirements on companies. A comprehensive listing of these record-

---

29. *See, e.g., Rambus*, 222 F.R.D. at 286.
30. The Sedona Guidelines, *supra* note 14, at 30.
31. *Id.*
32. The Sedona Guidelines, *supra* note 14, at 27.

keeping obligations is beyond the scope of this book. However, as part of any record retention program, a company should thoroughly familiarize itself with applicable state and federal record-keeping requirements.[33]

A duty to retain records can arise not only from pending, threatened, or reasonably anticipated litigation or applicable statutory laws, but from other sources as well. For example, a contract provision in a collective bargaining agreement may obligate a company to retain certain records, such as union grievances, for a defined time period. Therefore, when preparing a document retention schedule, a company should look beyond federal and state statutory obligations and anticipated or pending litigation to obligations it may have undertaken in contracts with employees, unions, and third parties.

SUSPENSION OF DOCUMENT RETENTION POLICY— LITIGATION OR LEGAL "HOLD"

Among the key elements of a record retention policy is a provision for suspending and resuming the policy. Once a company has notice of a lawsuit or reason to know of a particular potential lawsuit, it must take all necessary steps to ensure that it preserves, and does not destroy or discard, potentially relevant documents and other evidence.[34] This includes an obligation to immediately suspend the document retention policy regarding documents relevant to that litigation.[35] A company may reinstate its document retention policy regarding unrelated or irrelevant materials after determining which

---

33. *See* RICHARD L. CLAYPOOLE & GLADYS QUEEN RAMEY, GUIDE TO RECORDS RETENTION IN THE CODE OF FEDERAL REGULATIONS (Diane Pub. Co. 2004).

34. *Arthur Andersen*, 125 S. Ct. 2131 (observing that someone who persuades another to shred documents under a company's document retention policy cannot have "knowingly" engaged in corrupt persuasion within the meaning of 18 U.S.C. § 1512(b) unless he has a particular official proceeding in mind in which those document might be relevant).

35. *See, e.g.,* Stevenson v. Union Pac. R.R., 354 F.3d 739, 747-48 (8th Cir. 2004) (finding railroad that destroyed audio tapes before lawsuit commenced that were the sole source of relevant evidence of that accident acted in bad faith because it was aware that accidents that caused serious injuries or death would result in litigation). *See also* THE SEDONA GUIDELINES, *supra* note 14, at 41 (citing cases).

documents are relevant to the litigation or investigation[36] and may fully reinstate its policy at the conclusion of the investigation or litigation at issue.[37]

If a company fails to suspend its policy when it is or should be aware of threatened or pending litigation and, as a result, documents subject to discovery are destroyed, sanctions may be imposed. For example, in *Reingold v. Wet 'N Wild Nevada, Inc.*,[38] the plaintiff filed a lawsuit against a waterpark for injuries suffered while walking toward a pool. During discovery, the plaintiff requested first-aid logs. The general manager of the waterpark testified that the logs for the relevant year were destroyed pursuant to a routine document destruction policy before the plaintiff filed the lawsuit.[39] The plaintiff requested an adverse inference instruction, which the trial court denied because it found no intent to willfully suppress the logs within the meaning of the applicable Nevada statute. On appeal, the supreme court reversed and reasoned as follows:

> There is no dispute that the records were "willfully" or intentionally destroyed. [The waterpark] claimed that all records are destroyed at the end of each season. This means that the accident records are destroyed even before the statute of limitations has run on any potential litigation for that season. It appears that this records destruction policy was deliberately designed to prevent production of records in any subsequent litigation.[40]

---

36. *See* Computek Computer & Office Supplies, Inc. v. Walton, 156 S.W.3d 217 (Tex. App. 2005) (finding an injunction overbroad because it prohibited a company from engaging in lawful, routine destruction of documents unrelated to the plainitff's claims). *See also* THE SEDONA GUIDELINES at 26 (noting that "[w]here an organization in good faith adopts a reasonable document retention policy, and its operation and procedures are rational, it should be permitted to continue those procedures after commencement of litigation, assuming reasoanble steps have been taken to preserve data relevant to actual or reasonably anticipated litigation, governmental investigation or audit.") (citing Redish, *Electronic Discovery and the Litigation Matrix*, 51 DUKE L. J. AT 621).

37. *To Shred or Not To Shred, supra* note 4, at 754. *See, e.g.,* Silvestri v. General Motors Corp., 271 F.3d 583, 590 (4th Cir. 2001) (noting that valid document purging progams must be put on hold when litigation is "reasonably foreseeable"); Thompson v. United States Dep't of Hous. & Urban Dev., 219 F.R.D. 93, 100 (D. Md. 2003) (same).

38. 944 P.2d 800 (Nev. 1997).

39. *Id.* at 970.

40. *Id.*

The *Wet 'N Wild* court concluded that the waterpark's deliberate destruction of the first-aid logs, before the statute of limitations had run, amounted to suppression of evidence. The court further held that if the waterpark chose to adopt such a records destruction policy, it must accept the adverse implications of that policy.[41]

As *Wet 'N Wild* demonstrates, blind adherence to a document retention policy will not shield a company from liability for destruction of documents, particularly where it is on notice that certain documents should be retained. As one court succinctly noted, a company cannot "blindly destroy documents and expect to be shielded by a seemingly innocuous document retention policy."[42]

Records retention programs represent a helpful way to avoid charges of spoliation of evidence, including those involving electronic data. But a records retention program may not be enough. The increasing significance and prevalence of electronic data mandates that any litigation hold address both paper and eletronic records. A "litigation hold" allows a party to maintain the status quo and prevent the destruction of potentially relevant information. Formulating and implementing an effective litigation hold that encompasses paper and electronic records requires planning and coordination with counsel and company executives, as well as the members of a company's information technology group.[43] An effective litigation hold requires clear boundaries and instructions to ensure proper compliance.

Sending "preservation letters" to all parties and clients represents an additional safeguard. These letters should explicitly identify the data and documents to be preserved. To the extent possible, counsel should segregate this data into easily identifiable categories. The duty to preserve is not satisfied by sending a single communication; counsel must actively monitor the potential sources of evidence.

On the other hand, there is no general duty to retain all documents on the theory that a lawsuit might possibly be filed at some unspecified future time. Consequently, where a company is not reasonably on notice that specific documents need to be preserved because of litiga-

---

41. *Id.*

42. *Lewy,* 836 F.2d at 1112.

43. Virginia Llewellyn, *Planning with Clients for Effective Electronic Discovery,* THE PRACTICAL LITIGATOR 7 (July 2003) ("The best electronic discovery response requires work well in advance of litigation.").

tion or potential litigation, the destruction of these documents pursuant to a regularly followed document retention program generally will not usually result in sanctions.[44]

Willard v. Caterpillar, Inc.[45] illustrates this general rule. In that case, a manufacturer had routinely destroyed documents relating to a 35-year-old product that had never been the subject of a lawsuit. The court based its analysis on factors that it developed from an examination of the *Restatement Second of Torts*, § 870. The *Willard* court examined four factors in determining whether to impose tort liability:

1. The nature and seriousness of the harm to the injured party;
2. The nature and significance of the interest promoted by the actor's conduct;
3. The character of the means used by the actor; and
4. The actor's motive.[46]

Applying those factors, the court held that the manufacturer was not obligated to preserve documents merely because a lawsuit might be filed at some undetermined point in the future.

There is one important caveat to this general rule: Where a company has been involved in similar lawsuits regarding a specific product in the past, some courts have found an obligation to preserve certain categories of records relating to that product. In those cases, courts have held companies responsible to retain records, even though a specific lawsuit may not have been foreseeable, because of a previous pattern of litigation related to that product or products. Therefore, if it is foreseeable that lawsuits about a specific product or product category are likely, then documents related to that product should be preserved to avoid sanctions or potential tort liability.

This was the case in *Lewy v. Remington Arms Co., Inc.*[47] There, a lawsuit arising from an accidental rifle discharge resulted in a substantial verdict and punitive damage award. On appeal, the gun manufacturer argued the trial court should not have given the jury an adverse

---

44. *A Wreck on the Info-Bahn: Electronic Mail and the Destruction of Evidence*, 6 COMMLAW CONSPECTUS at 84.

45. *Willard v. Caterpillar, Inc.*, 40 Cal. App. 4th 892 (1995).　　35 nn.45, 46

46. *Id.* at 915.

47. 836 F.2d 1104 (8th Cir. 1988). *See also Stevenson*, 354 F.3d at 747-48.

inference instruction based on its inability to produce documents destroyed under its record retention policy. Under this policy, the gun manufacturer destroyed complaints and gun examination reports in three years if no action regarding a particular record had been taken in that period. The gun manufacturer argued that destroying records pursuant to routine procedures did not support an adverse inference.

The court of appeals remanded and instructed the trial court to consider three factors in determining whether to give such an instruction: (1) whether the gun manufacturer's document retention policy was reasonable considering the facts and circumstances surrounding the particular documents; (2) whether lawsuits concerning the complaint or related complaints had been filed, the frequency of the complaints, and the magnitude of the complaints; and (3) whether the gun manufacturer had implemented its document retention policy in bad faith.[48]

Adherence to a routine policy of destroying documents, where a company has notice of a potential claim, can result in severe sanctions if the destruction causes prejudice to the non-spoliating party. For example, in *Blinzler v. Marriott International, Inc.*,[49] the decedent became ill while staying in one of the defendant's hotel rooms. The plaintiff called the hotel operator and requested an ambulance; however, the hotel's records showed that the operator waited 14 minutes before calling the ambulance. By the time that paramedics arrived, the decedent had suffered severe brain damage. He died three days later.[50] Approximately 30 days after the incident, the hotel destroyed the telephone log identifying the exact time the operator had called the ambulance.

The decedent's wife filed a lawsuit, alleging that the hotel's failure to call an ambulance promptly was a proximate cause of her husband's death. The court permitted the plaintiff to introduce evidence at trial of the missing log, and the jury returned a verdict for the widow on all claims. However, notwithstanding that verdict, the court entered judgment for the hotel on the emotional distress claim.[51]

On appeal, the court reinstated the verdict in its entirety, rejecting the hotel's argument that the trial court had erred by admitting the de-

---

48. 836 F.2d at 1112.
49. *Blinzler v. Marriott International, Inc.*, 81 F.3d 1148 (1st Cir. 1996)
50. *Id.* at 1150.
51. *Id.* at 1158.

struction of the telephone logs into evidence. The hotel maintained that this evidence should have been excluded because it destroyed the telephone log pursuant to an established document retention policy. The appellate court ruled that although a lawsuit had not been filed at the time the log was destroyed, the hotel knew of the decedent's death and was aware that his widow had attempted to discover the exact time that the hotel had called an ambulance.[52] Accordingly, the court held that the trial court was within its discretion in admitting the evidence.

Negligent destruction of documents in violation of company policy also can render a company liable for other sanctions. For example, in *In re: The Prudential Insurance Company of America Sales Practices Litigation*,[53] policy holders had filed a class action against an insurer based on allegedly deceptive sales practices. The court overseeing the litigation entered a preservation order requiring parties to "preserve all documents and other records containing information potentially relevant to the subject matter of this litigation."[54] After entry of this order, thousands of the insurer's relevant files were destroyed, allegedly pursuant to the insurer's document destruction policy.[55] The court found that the insurer had failed to disseminate the court's order regarding preservation of documents to its employees. It also found that the insurer otherwise had failed to provide its employees with relevant information, resulting in document destruction in violation of its order. The court concluded:

> While there is no proof that [the insurer], through its employees, engaged in conduct intended to thwart discovery through the purposeful destruction of documents, its haphazard and uncoordinated approach to document retention indisputably denies its party opponents potential evidence to establish facts in dispute. Because the destroyed records . . . are permanently lost, the court will draw the inference that the destroyed materials are relevant and, if available, would lead to the proof of the claim.[56]

After evaluating all relevant factors, the court imposed sanctions ordering the insurer (1) to give every employee a copy of its docu-

---

52. *Id.* at 1158-59.
53. 169 F.R.D. 598 (D.N.J. 1997).
54. *Id.* at 600 (quoting Sept. 15, 1995 Order).
55. *Id.* at 601.
56. *Id.* at 615.

ment preservation order, with an explanation of potential sanctions for failure to follow that order; (2) to submit a written copy of its document preservation policy to the court; (3) to establish a hotline to allow employees to report any improper document destruction; (4) to establish a certification process to ensure compliance with document retention policies; (5) to pay a $1 million fine; and (6) to reimburse the plaintiffs' counsel for the fees and costs associated with its improper conduct.[57]

CONSEQUENCES OF NOT HAVING A DOCUMENT RETENTION POLICY

The absence of a coherent document retention policy also can lead to severe sanctions. For example, in *Telectron v. Overhead Door Corporation*,[58] the defendant had destroyed numerous documents that were the subject of a document request. Although the defendant ostensibly had a document retention policy in place, the defendant company's president admitted he did not know any details about the policy. The court concluded that the defendant company's secrecy about the lawsuit and the type of documents requested constituted a "pervasive state of ignorance."[59]

After considering the source of its authority to issue sanctions, the willfulness of the destruction, prejudice to the plaintiff, and the inadequacy of lesser sanctions, the *Telectron* court concluded that the entry of default judgment against the defendant company "is the only sanction truly capable of punishing [it] for its willful subversion of the discovery process, and deterring others from embarking on a similar course of destroying potentially unfavorable evidence."[60]

ELECTRONIC RECORDS AND DOCUMENTS: SPECIAL PROBLEMS

No discussion of records retention can be complete without addressing electronic records. While electronic discovery is presently a "hot" or "emerging" topic, courts have been addressing this issue in various

---

57. *Id.* at 616-17.
58. 116 F.R.D. 107 (S.D. Fla. 1987).
59. *Id.* at 123.
60. *Id.* at 137.

forms for more than 30 years.[61] Likewise, the Federal Rules of Civil Procedure have acknowledged the significance of electronic records for purposes of litigation for 35 years.[62] As one court explained:

> A discovery request aimed at the production of records retained in some electronic form is no different, in principle, from a request for documents contained in an office filing cabinet. . . . [T]here is nothing about the technological aspects involved which renders documents stored in an electronic media "undiscoverable."[63]

Technology advancements have increased the scope of available electronic data. For example, in 2000 fewer than 10 billion e-mail messages were sent per day worldwide.[64] Today it is estimated that this number surpasses 35 billion messages. Nothing suggests that this trend will abate in the near future. Accordingly, records retention programs must address the unique issues associated with electronic data.

The significance of electronic data in litigation cannot be underestimated. Not only may failure to preserve electronic data subject a party to negative publicity (e.g., Arthur Andersen and Merrill Lynch), but in certain circumstances destruction of electronic data can be outcome-determinative in litigation. In several recent high-profile lawsuits, electronic data has provided "smoking guns." The potential rewards afforded by electronic data ensure that electronic discovery and related preservation issues will not disappear from the litigation arena.

---

61. *See, e.g.,* National Union Elec. Corp. v. Matsushita Elec. Indus. Co., 494 F. Supp. 1257 (E.D. Pa. 1980) (granting request to produce electronic data); Adams v. Dan River Mills, Inc., 54 F.R.D. 220 (W.D. Va. 1972) 39 n.61(granting motion to compel discovery of certain electronic payroll records to support discrimination claim).

62. The 1970 amendments to Rule 34 of the Federal Rules of Civil Procedure expanded the definition of "documents" to include: "data compilations from which information can be obtained, translated, if necessary, by the respondent through detection devices into reasonably usable form." *See* Fed. R. Civ. P. 34(a). In 1993, Fed. R. Civ. P. 26(a)(1)(B) was amended to include "data compilations" as a source of initial disclosure information.

63.   Linnen v. A.H. Robins Co., Inc., 1999 Mass. Super. LEXIS 240, *16
                (Mass. Super. Ct. June 15, 1999) 39 n.63

64. Gordon M. Shapiro & Brian A. Kilpatrick, *E-Mail Discovery and Privilege*, 23 Corp. Couns. Rev. 201, 201 (2004). *See also* Ken Withers, *Digital Discovery Starts to Work*, Nat'l L. J., Nov. 4, 2002 (estimating that a company of 100 employees may generate 7.5 million e-mails per year).

In addition to providing key information, discovery requests seeking electronic data can subject a party to considerable cost and expense. In certain circumstances, these costs can also be outcome-determinative because they may encourage or force a party to settle a claim to avoid such expenses.

Recent decisions also make clear that courts will not accept blind adherence to document retention policies that do not appropriately address electronic data.[65] These factors mandate that in-house counsel, in particular, make electronic data a central part of any records retention program.

The first step in creating an appropriate records retention program addressing electronic data is simply gaining an understanding of what data exists as well as where and how it is stored. Locating electronic data can present a formidable challenge because it can be found on computers, telephones and other electronic devices in the office, as well as, cell phones, personal data assistants and home computers.[66] This process is further complicated because most electronic data is created and saved without the knowledge of the user.[67]

For example, e-mail generated in Microsoft Outlook has approximately 30 fields of information viewable by a user. Yet, Microsoft Outlook generates over 100 fields of data for each e-mail. This "hidden" information, known as "metadata," can be invaluable in the litigation context.[68] Advancements in technology will only further complicate this

---

65. *See, e.g.*, E*Trade Secs. LLC v. Deutsche Bank AG, 02-3711, 02-3682, 2005 U.S. Dist. LEXIS 3021, *14 (D. Minn. Feb. 17, 2005) ("a corporation cannot blindly destroy documents and expect to be shielded by a seemingly innocuous document retention policy"); MOSAID Techs. Inc. v. Samsung Elecs. Co., 348 F. 5(finding Samsung "willfully blinded itself" to its obligation to preserve potentially relevant electronic information and affirming an award of $566,839.97 in sanctions and an adverse inference instruction).

66. As one court noted, the duty to disclose electronic evidence includes the following items: "voice-mail messages and files, backup voice-mail files, e-mail messages and files, backup and archival tapes, temporary files, system history files, website information stored in textual, graphical or audio format, website log files, cache files, cookies, . . . other electronically recorded information . . . (and) any backup copies of files or archival tapes that will provide information about any 'deleted' electronic data." Kleiner v. Burns, 48 Fed. R. Serv. 3d 644 (D. Kan. 2000).

67. *See* THE SEDONA GUIDELINES, *supra* note 14, at v.

68. Gordon M. Shapiro & Brian A. Kilpatrick, *E-Mail Discovery and Privilege*, 23 CORP. COUNS. REV. 201, 201 (2004).

basic search for data because the number of places to store electronic data will continue to expand as the cost of doing so decreases.

For several reasons, electronic data presents special problems between records retention programs and spoliation claims. First, unlike paper documents, a tremendous amount of data and information can be easily stored on computers and backup tapes.[69] The ease and relatively minimal costs of storage heighten the need for appropriate management of this information. Failure to implement and adhere to a records retention program addressing electronic data can subject a party to significant discovery burdens in the event of litigation. By implementing a proper records retention program, a company can effectively determine which information is responsive and discoverable and can produce this information with some assurance that records have not been destroyed improperly.

A detailed discussion of methods and policies for managing electronic information and records is beyond the scope of this text. However, the *Sedona Guidelines* offer a useful and practical starting point for approaching this issue.[70]

E-mail poses other unique problems. Because this mode of communication tends to be more conversational and informal than other business communications, users may be somewhat less thoughtful about content when sending messages.[71] This may result in a proliferation of documents that are less guarded and business-related, which can spell trouble for a company in litigation. Therefore, companies should consider having a separate policy regarding the appropriate use of use of the Internet and e-mail.

Another problem associated with e-mail and other electronic data is that these records are rarely destroyed.[72] Instead, this information can

---

69. One commentator has even argued that "the tremendous capacity and efficiency afforded by electronic instrumentalities could compel the implementation of longer retention periods." Note: *Document Retention Programs for Electronic Records*, 24 Iowa J. Corp. L. 417, 418 (1999).

70. *See* The Sedona Guidelines, *supra* note 14.

71. Comment: *A Wreck on the Info-Bahn: Electronic Mail and the Destruction of Evidence*, 6 CommLaw Conspectus at 76.

72. *See* Steven C. Bennett & Thomas M. Niccum, *Two Views from the Data Mountain,* 36 Creighton L. Rev. 607, 614 (June 2003) (noting it is almost always possible to retrieve data that has been deleted); Armen Artinyan, *Legal Impediments to Discovery and Destruction of E-mail*, 2 Legal Advoc. & Prac. 95, 97 (2000) (noting erased electronic data can often be retrieved because instead of being

be retrieved even though the creator believes it has been deleted or erased.[73] Significantly, several courts have held that "deleted" electronic documents or data is discoverable.[74] Because electronic forms of evidence generally are discoverable,[75] a company may have to produce e-mail that was deleted or erased and forgotten long ago, which can be highly damaging in litigation.

The number of decisions addressing spoliation of evidence involving electronic data continues to increase dramatically.[76] One of

---

deleted, the files are simply moved to another location on the hard drive where the information remains until it is overwritten).

73. *A Wreck on the Info-Bahn*, 6 COMMLAW at 77.

74. *See, e.g.*, Simon Prop. Group L.P. v. mySimon, Inc., 194 F.R.D. 639, 640 (S.D. Ind. 2000) (stating that electronic records including those deleted records are discoverable pursuant to Fed. R. Civ. P. 34); Bills v. Kennecott Corp., 108 F.R.D. 459, 461 (D. Utah 1985) (holding that it is "axiomatic" that electronic data is discoverable).

75. Crown Life Ins. Co. v. Craig, 995 F.2d 1376, 1383-84 (7th Cir. 1993); *A Wreck on the Info-Bahn*, 6 COMMLAW CONSPECTUS at 76.

76. Residential Funding Corp. v. DeGeorge Fin. Corp., 306 F.3d 99 (2d Cir. 2002) (vacating $96.4 million jury verdict based upon negligent delay in producing electronic data); United States v. Philip Morris USA, Inc., 327 F. Supp. 2d 21 (D.D.C. 2004) (imposing $2,750,000 sanction as well as payment of costs for deletion of e-mails despite clear preservation order); Kucala Enters v. AutoWax Co., Inc., No. 02C1403, 2004 U.S. Dist LEXIS 22271 (N.D. Ill. Nov. 2, 2004) (finding no bad faith and limiting spoliation sanction to allowing the plaintiff to argue that the destruction of missing e-mails justified an inference that the public was confused and that the plaintiff's trademark was diluted); Trigon Ins. Co. v. United States, 204 F.R.D. 277, 288-91 (E.D. Va. 2001) (breach of duty to preserve drafts of expert reports warranted sanctions); Danis v. USN Communications, Inc., No. 98C7482, 2000 WL 1694325, at *40-41 (N.D. Ill. Oct. 23, 2000) (finding failure to take reasonable steps to preserve data at the outset of discovery resulted in a personal fine against the defendant's CEO); Lexis-Nexis v. Beer, 41 F. Supp. 2d 950 (D. Minn. 1999) (awarding fees and costs following spoliation of certain electronic data); Procter & Gamble Co. v. Haugen, 179 F.R.D. 622 (D. Utah 1998) (finding no bad faith where e-mails of five individuals were not preserved after litigation filed but imposing fine totaling $10,000); Gates Rubber Co. v. Bando Chem. Indus., 167 F.R.D. 90 (D. Colo. 1996) (imposing sanctions for deleting word-processing files and assessing portion of the plaintiff's fees and costs as damages against defendant); ABC Home Health Servs., Inc. v. Int'l Bus. Machs. Corp., 158 F.R.D. 180 (S.D. Ga. 1994) (issuing an adverse inference where computer files were deleted). *But see* Williams v. Saint-Gobain Corp., No. 00CV0502E, 2002 U.S. Dist. LEXIS 25513 (W.D.N.Y. June 28, 2002) (refusing to issue sanctions in employment action where despite prior statement that no additional responsive documents existed, employer produced e-mails obtained from an executive's computer five days before trial).

the central issues arising with spoliation claims involving electronic data is the scope of the duty to preserve such data. In *Zubulake*, the court addressed the unique issues associated with the duty to retain electronic data and explained:

> A party or anticipated party must retain all relevant documents (but not multiple identical copies) in existence at the time the duty to preserve attaches, and any relevant documents created thereafter. In recognition of the fact that there are many ways to manage electronic data, litigants are free to choose how this task is accomplished.[77]

Discussing the obligation to preserve electronic evidence, including suspending records retention programs and imposing a litigation hold, the *Zubulake* court provided a general rule that described the scope of the records to be retained:

> As a general rule, that litigation hold does not apply to inaccessible backup tapes (*e.g.,* those typically maintained solely for the purpose of disaster recovery), which may continue to be recycled on the schedule set forth in the company's policy. On the other hand, if backup tapes are accessible (*i.e.,* actively used for information retrieval), then such tapes *would* likely be subject to the litigation hold. However, it does not make sense to create one exception to this general rule. If a company can identify where particular employee documents are stored on backup tapes, then the tapes storing the documents of "key players" to the existing or threatened litigation should be preserved if the information contained on those tapes is not otherwise available. This exception applies to *all* backup tapes.[78]

More recently, the *E*Trade* court considered the imposition of sanctions arising from the deletion of e-mails in an action involving allegations of a fraudulent securities lending scheme resulting in the collapse of a broker/lender.[79] The *E*Trade* court explained the obligation to preserve electronic evidence as beginning:

---

77. 220 F.R.D. at 218.
78. *Id.* at 220 (emphasis in original).
79. 2005 U.S. Dist. LEXIS 3021.

[w]hen a party knows or should have known that the evidence is relevant to future or current litigation. If destruction of relevant information occurs before any litigation has begun, in order to justify sanctions, the requesting party must show that the destruction was the result of bad faith. Bad faith need not directly be shown but can be implied by the party's behavior. . . . If, however, the destruction of evidence occurs after litigation is imminent or has begun, no bad faith need be shown by the moving party. When litigation is imminent or has already commenced, "corporation cannot blindly destroy documents and expect to be shielded by a seemingly innocuous document retention policy."[80]

In *E*Trade*, the party had "permanently erased all the company's hard drives in mid-2002," but claimed no resulting prejudice because it had removed and preserved relevant information from certain employees' hard drives. The court disagreed and found that the party's awareness of the potential for litigation at the time the hard drives were erased warranted sanctions. The court found that E*Trade was prejudiced by the "substantial and complete nature of the destruction of the evidence contained in the [destroyed] recorded telephone conversations and hard drives. . . ."[81] Noting that a default judgment could not be entered, the court recommended that the district court issue an adverse inference instruction to the jury.

Courts closely scrutinize a company's actions when imposing a litigation hold or responding to a preservation request.[82] For example, in *MOSAID* the court addressed a request for sanctions and an adverse inference instruction after Samsung failed to preserve and produce potentially relevant e-mail.[83] Samsung never suspended its document retention policy, claiming that MOSAID's discovery requests failed to specify that they sought e-mail and that the absence of intent made the adverse inference instruction unwarranted. The court rejected Samsung's argument and noted that the broad definition of "docu-

---

80. *Id.* at *14.
81. *Id.*
82. *See* Danis v. USN Communications, Inc., No. 98C7482, 2000 U.S. Dist. LEXIS 16900, at 896-100 ("The duty to preserve documents in the face of pending litigation is not a passive obligation. Rather it must be discharged actively.").
83. 348 F. Supp. 2d 332 (D.N.J. 2004).

ment" and the duty to preserve e-mail existed before any discovery requests were served because Samsung knew or reasonably should have known that litigation was foreseeable.

Although the *MOSAID* court found that negligent destruction of evidence could justify an adverse inference, the court found that Samsung's conduct exceeded negligence and constituted knowing and intentional conduct. Specifically, Samsung (1) knew it had a duty to preserve potentially discoverable e-mail; (2) knew how to institute a litigation hold, having done so in a separate litigation; and (3) willfully blinded itself in taking the position that MOSAID's document requests did not seek e-mail.[84]

In addition to monitoring your client's own actions regarding preservation, once litigation has been filed, counsel concerned about the possibility of an opponent's spoliation of electronic data can request a "preservation order" from the court. Federal Rule of Civil Procedure 16 provides for the issuance of orders including those "adopting special procedures for managing potentially difficult or protracted actions that may involve complex issues . . . or unusual proof problems."[85] The issuance of a preservation order can impose severe burdens on parties. For example, in *Madden v. Wyeth*,[86] the plaintiffs sought the following preservation order: (1) preservation of all documents and information, whether in paper or electronic format, pertaining to Children's Advil regardless of the actual trade name used; and (2) suspend all routine destruction of documents, including but not limited to recycling backup tapes. While the court ultimately denied this request, finding no proof that any evidence would be lost or destroyed, it demonstrates the broad scope such orders can possess.

Courts recognize the burdens and special issues surrounding electronic data. As a result, most courts acknowledge that there is generally

---

84. *Id.* at 338-40.

85. Fed. R. Civ. P. 16(c). Courts issue orders pursuant to this provision where a party establishes (1) there is a likelihood of success on the merits; (2) failure to issue the order will inflict irreparable injury; (3) equity is in their favor; and (4) the public interest is served. *See* Smith v. Texaco, 951 F. Supp. 109, 111-12 (E.D. Tex. 1997).

86. Madden v. Wyeth, No. 3-03-CV-0167-R, 2003 U.S. Dist. LEXIS 6427 (N.D. Tex. Apr. 16, 2003).

no duty to retain all documents.[87] Indeed, companies can legitimately destroy electronic data and other records pursuant to the terms of a records retention program.[88] "Courts routinely acknowledge that organizations have the 'right' to destroy (or not track or capture, whether or not it is consciously deleted) electronic information that does not meet the internal criteria of information or records as requiring retention."[89]

ALLOCATING THE COST ASSOCIATED WITH PRODUCTION OF ELECTRONIC DATA

Another issue courts have repeatedly addressed is the allocation of costs associated with the production of electronic data in the context of litigation. The significant costs of producing electronic data can be reduced by a carefully drafted records retention program. While the general rule is that the producing party is responsible for the cost of searching for responsive electronic documents, courts depart from this rule in certain circumstances. For example, in *In re Brand Name Prescription Drugs Antitrust Litigation*,[90] the court considered a request to force the plaintiffs to pay for the production of approximately 30 million pages of backup information at a cost of $50,000-$70,000. In denying the request, the court noted that the producing party's own record-keeping procedure created the cost. As a result, the court ex-

---

87. *See, e.g., Zubulake,* 220 F.R.D. at 217 ("Must a corporation, upon recognizing the threat of litigation, preserve every shred of paper, every e-mail or electronic document, and every backup tape? The answer is clearly, 'no.' Such a rule would cripple large corporations, like UBS, that are almost always unnoticed in litigation."); Wiginton v. Ellis, No. 02 C 6832, 2003 WL 22439865, at *4 (N.D. Ill. Oct. 27, 2003) (organization "does not have to preserve every single scrap of paper in its business"); Concord Boat Corp. v. Brunswick Corp., No. LK-G-95-781, 1997 WL 33352759, at *4 (E.D. Ark. Aug. 29, 1997) 47 n.87("to hold that a corporation is under a duty to preserve all e-mail potentially relevant to any future litigation would be tantamount to holding that the corporation must preserve all e-mail . . . . Such a proposition is not justified.").

88. *See* Redish, *Electronic Discovery and the Litigation Matrix,* 51 Duke L.J. at 621 ("1) Electronic evidence destruction, if done routinely in the ordinary course of business, does not automatically give rise to an inference of knowledge of specific documents' destruction, much less intent to destroy documents for litigation-related reasons, and 2) to prohibit such routine destruction could impose substantial costs and disruptive burdens on commercial enterprises.").

89. The Sedona Guidelines, *supra* note 14, at 24-55

90. No. 94C897, MDL997, 1995 U.S. Dist. LEXIS 8281.

plained that the requesting party "should not be forced to bear a burden caused by [the producing party's] choice of electronic storage."[91]

Sometimes the cost of producing electronically stored information will be shifted to the requesting party.[92] *Rowe Entertainment, Inc. v. William Morris Agency, Inc.* represented the first significant decision addressing analysis of this issue.[93] There, black concert promoters claimed they were frozen out of the market for promoting events with white bands through discriminatory and anticompetitive practices of the defendant booking agents. The booking agents sought an order relieving them from producing e-mails responsive to the concert promoters' requests, claiming the burden and expense involved would far outweigh any possible benefit. The booking agents estimated that it would cost $395,944 to produce eight selected backup tapes and $9.75 million for all backup tapes.[94] The concert promoters disputed this estimate and presented another estimate.[95]

Discussing who would bear the cost of producing the e-mail, the *Rowe* court found the "traditional rule" inapplicable and explained:

> Even if this principle is unassailable in the context of paper records, it does not translate well into the realm of electronic data. The underlying assumption is that the party retaining information does so because that information is useful to it, as demonstrated by the fact that it is willing to bear the costs of retention. That party may therefore be expected to locate specific data, whether for its own needs or in response to a discovery request. With electronic media, however, the syllogism breaks down because the costs of storage are virtually nil. Information is retained not because it is expected to be used, but because there is no compelling reason to discard it. And, even if data is retained for limited purposes, it is not necessarily amenable to discovery.[96]

---

91. *Id.* at *6-7.
92. *See* Zubulake v. UBS Warburg LLC, 217 F.R.D. 309 (S.D.N.Y. 2002).
93. 2002 U.S. Dist. LEXIS 488 (S.D.N.Y. Jan. 16, 2002).
94. *Id.*
95. *Id.*
96. *Id.* at *7.

The *Rowe* court then established eight factors to consider in determing where to place the cost:

1. The specificity of the discovery requests;
2. The likelihood of discovery of critical information;
3. The availability of such information from other sources;
4. The purpose for which the responding party maintains the requested data;
5. The relative benefit to the parties of obtaining information;
6. The total cost associated with production;
7. The relative ability of each party to control costs and its incentive to do so; and
8. The resources available to each party.[97]

Later, the court in *Zubulake v. UBS Warburg LLC*[98] outlined a three-step inquiry for disputes involving the scope and costs of electronic document discovery. First, the court must have a thorough understanding of the responding parties' computer system, including its active and stored data. The usual rules of discovery should be applied to data maintained in an "accessible format,"[99] and the responding party is required to pay for its production.

But when inaccessible data is at issue, the court should consider cost shifting.[100] Since the cost-shifting analysis is fact-intensive, the court must first determine what data may be available from the "inaccessible" media. The *Zubulake* court suggested using a "sampling" approach in most cases.[101] If the court determines there is relevant information in the inaccessible media, then it should consider a cost-shifting analysis using a seven-factor test.[102]

---

97. *Id.* at *8.
98. 217 F.R.D. 309 (S.D.N.Y. 2003).
99. *Id.*
100. *Id.*
101. *Id.*
102. *Zubulake*, 217 F.R.D. at 322 (identifying the following seven factors for cost shifting: (1) the extent to which the request is specifically tailored to discover relevant information; (2) the availability of such information from other sources; (3) the total cost of production, compared to the amount in controversy; (4) the total cost of production, compared to the resources available to each party; (5) the relative ability of each party to control costs and its incentive to do so; (6) the importance of the issues at stake in the litigation; (7) the relative benefits to the parties of obtaining the information).

The *Zubulake* court explained that these seven factors should not be weighed equally. Rather, the first two factors are the most important, and the central inquiry should be, "How important is the sought-after evidence in comparison to the cost of production?"[103]

COUNSEL'S DUTY TO UNDERSTAND THE CLIENT'S DATA STORAGE AND RETRIEVAL SYSTEM

Counsel must also understand the data storage and retrieval systems of their clients. Remaining ignorant to the workings of a client's computer systems and storage practices can result in unanticipated consequences for the client.[104] Not only is a complete understanding of a client's record and data storage system essential to satisfy Rule 26 disclosure obligations, it is critical to responding effectively to arguments regarding the burdens and costs associated with complying with discovery requests.[105]

GTFM, Inc. v. Wal-Mart Stores, Inc.[106] is illustrative. There, the plaintiffs sought electronic data regarding local sales. Without consulting with a representative from the information technology department, Wal-Mart's counsel stated that the data was no longer available and producing it would be unduly burdensome because there was no centralized computer capacity to track it.[107] A year later, the plaintiffs deposed a vice-president from Wal-Mart's management information systems group who testified the sales data could be tracked for up to one year. That meant the information had been available at the time of the plaintiffs' initial request; but because of the delay caused by counsel's misrepresentation, it was no longer available.

The *GTFM* court criticized Wal-Mart's counsel for failure to consult the appropriate personnel, observing, "Whether or not defendant's

---

103. *Id.* at 323.

104. For example, failure to accurately represent these issues can result in courts allowing on-site inspections of computer systems or the imposition of sanctions. *See, e.g., Simon Property Group*, 194 F.R.D. 639 (requiring inspection of hard drive after finding "some troubling discrepancies" in discovery responses); Playboy Enters., Inc. v. Welles, 60 F. Supp. 2d 1050 (S.D. Cal. 1999) 49 n.104(granting access where party testified that relevant e-mails had been deleted and could not be restored).

105. Llewellyn, *supra* note 43 at 10.

106. No. 98 Civ. 7724, 2000 U.S. Dist. LEXIS 3804 (S.D.N.Y. Mar. 30, 2000).

107. *Id.* at *5.

counsel intentionally misled the plaintiffs, counsel's inquiries about defendants' computer capacity were certainly deficient. . . . As a vice president in Wal-Mart's [management information systems] department, she was an obvious person with whom defendant's counsel should have reviewed the computer capabilities."[108] As a result, the court ordered an on-site inspection at Wal-Mart's expense and assessed payment of more than $100,000 toward the legal fees the plaintiffs incurred because of the inaccurate disclosure.

ELECTRONIC OR PAPER—WHAT FORM OF PRODUCTION?

The form of production of electronic data is also important. Recent decisions demonstrate that the production or retention of a hard copy of a document may not be sufficient. As a California appellate court explained: "[t]he hard copy may have contained the same information, but that information was not equally accessible. . . . [T]he computerized records had evidentiary unique value distinct from the hard copy records. They made information accessible."[109]

Considering a motion seeking to compel payment for production of documents, the District Court of New Jersey addressed this issue in *In re Bristol-Myers Squibb Securities Litigation*.[110] There, the parties agreed to allocation of copying costs, but the plaintiffs disputed the charges after delivery of the documents.[111] Bristol-Myers had produced documents it had stored in paper and electronic format. The plaintiffs contested not receiving electronic copies of these documents. The court noted that the plaintiffs "had every opportunity" to request an electronic production, but they did not do so until after receiving the bill for the paper production.[112] Ruling for the plaintiffs, the court found it "somewhat troublesome" that Bristol-Myers had responsive informa-

---

108. *Id.* at *6.

109. Lombardo v. Broadway Stores, Inc., 2002 Cal. App. LEXIS 262, at *22-23 (Cal. Ct. App. Jan. 22, 2002) 50 n.109

110. 205 F.R.D. 437, 441 (D.N.J. 2002). *See also* Anti-Monopoly, Inc. v. Hasbro, Inc., No. 94 Civ. 2120, 1995 U.S. Dist. LEXIS 16355 (S.D.N.Y. Nov. 3, 1995) (finding that production of documents in hard-copy format did not preclude production of same documents in electronic format); *In re* Air Crash Disaster at Detroit Metro Airport, 130 F.R.D. 634, 636 (E.D. Mich. 1989) 50 n.110 (ordering defendant to provide electronic format of documents produced in hard-copy format).

111. 205 F.R.D. at 438-39.

112. *Id.* at 440.

tion in electronic format, but produced it in hard copy. The court held that Bristol-Myers failed to comply with its Rule 26 disclosure obligations by not telling the plaintiffs the information was available in electronic form and did not require them to pay the copying costs.[113]

Yet another issue that may arise is whether a company must retain paper copies of documents after it has recorded them in another form, *e.g.*, on an optical scanning system. Although there do not appear to be any reported cases on this precise issue, at least when a paper copy may not be identical to the computerized documents—for example, if they contain handwritten notes—a company could be held liable for failure to retain these copies.[114]

Practice Tips

A proper records retention policy should be tailored to a company's particular needs, but any well-conceived policy should include the following elements:

- The policy should be reduced to writing, dated, and disseminated to all employees, or, at the very least, to all employees who might be affected by the policy.
- The policy should be written in plain English and kept as simple and straightforward as possible.
- The company should schedule regular audits to ensure compliance with its policy.
- The policy should include at least annual purging periods when employees must review records under their control and dispose of those that have exceeded their retention periods or are otherwise inappropriate for retention.
- The policy should include a procedure for notifying all employees immediately if certain categories of documents are to be exempted from the policy, as when litigation or a government investigation is pending, threatened, or reasonably foreseeable and implicates those documents.

---

113. *Id.* at 440-41.
114. *See generally Demystifying*, 34 TORT INS. L.J. at 779-83.

- The policy should be reviewed and considered for updating regularly as laws governing records retention change.

- Outdated versions of the record retention policy should be permanently retained, as should documents explaining the reasons for the changes and the procedures used to implement the changes.

- The policy should include one or more easy methods—for example, telephone number or e-mail—for employees to contact the records retention officer with questions or concerns.

- The policy should consider applicable federal and state laws and regulations for document retention, as well as company history, litigation experience, and contract obligations that may affect document retention.

Remedies and Sanctions for Spoliation in Pending Litigation

3

Judges must be careful to tailor the remedy to the problem, and to "take pains neither to use an elephant gun to slay a mouse nor to wield a cardboard sword if a dragon looms."[1]

Courts generally have relied upon two methods to remedy spoliation: (1) recognizing an independent cause of action for intentional and/or negligent spoliation,[2] and (2) civil discovery or evidentiary sanctions in pending litigation.[3] Although different remedies are appropriate

---

1. Gates Rubber Co. v. Bando Chem. Indus., Ltd., 167 F.R.D. 90, 106 (D. Colo. 1996) (quoting Anderson v. Beatrice Food Co., 900 F.2d 388, 395 (1st Cir. 1990)).

2. *See* Chapter 4, *infra; see, e.g.,* Smith v. Superior Court, 198 Cal. Rptr. 829, 832 (Cal. Ct. App. 1984) (recognizing action for intentional spoliation); Bondu v. Gurvich, 473 So. 2d 1307, 1312 (Fla. Ct. App. 1984) (recognizing action for negligent spoliation).

3. *See* Hirsch v. General Motors Corp., 628 A.2d 1108, 1127 (N.J. Super. Ct. Law Div. 1993); Welsh v. United States, 844 F.2d 1239, 1246 (6th Cir. 1988); Henderson v. Tyrrell, 910 P.2d 522, 531 (Wash. Ct. App. 1996). *See also* Robert L. Tucker, *The Flexible Doctrine of Spoliation of Evidence: Cause of Action, Defense, Evidentiary Presumption, and Discovery Sanction,* 27 U. TOL. L. REV. 67, 67 (1995). Two commentators have argued that the appropriate method for dealing with spoliation is through the creation of a new

based on the facts of a particular case, courts agree that they should impose the least severe sanction necessary to remedy prejudice to the non-spoliating party.[4]

SOURCES OF AUTHORITY FOR SANCTIONS

Rules of Civil Procedure

Under the federal and state rules of civil procedure that regulate discovery procedures,[5] courts have broad discretion to impose a variety of sanctions against a party that fails to produce evidence in violation of the discovery rules.[6] Further, a court's exercise of this discretion

---

rule of evidence that would provide for an evidentiary presumption against the spoliator. In cases of intentional spoliation, all the sanctions available under Fed. R. Civ. P. 37 would be applicable. *See* Donald H. Flanary, Jr. & Bruce M. Flowers, *Spoliation of Evidence. Let's Have a Rule in Response*, 60 DEF. COUNS. J. 553, 555-56 (Oct. 1993). Others have suggested that courts separate the fault and prejudice analysis and focus solely on remedying prejudice to the non-spoliator. *See* David A. Bell, et al., *Let's Level the Playing Field: A New Proposal for Analysis of Spoliation of Evidence Claims in Pending Litigation*, 29 ARIZ. ST. L.J. 769 (1997).

4. *See, e.g., Gates*, 167 F.R.D. at 106 (explaining that courts "select the least onerous sanction corresponding to the willfulness of the destructive act and the prejudice suffered by the victim") (quoting J. GORELICK, ET AL., DESTRUCTION OF EVIDENCE § 3.16, at 117 (1989)); Patton v. Newmar Corp., 520 N.W.2d 4, 8 (Minn. Ct. App. 1994) (stating that courts should choose least restrictive sanction available), *rev'd on other grounds*, 538 N.W.2d 116, 120 (Minn. 1995); Transamerica Ins. Group v. Maytag, Inc., 650 N.E.2d 169, 171 (Ohio Ct. App. 1994) (noting that, absent bad faith, Ohio courts impose the least restrictive sanction).

5. For example, Fed. R. Civ. P. 37(b)(2) provides that "[i]f a party or an officer, director, or managing agent of a party . . . fails to obey an order to provide or permit discovery . . . the court in which the action is pending may make such orders in regard to the failure as are just. . . ." FED. R. CIV. P. 37. This provision authorizes courts to compel disclosure or discovery or to impose sanctions on the party that has failed to respond to specific discovery requests. Sanctions may include reimbursement of attorneys' fees, recovery of discovery costs, striking an answer, barring the introduction of evidence or expert testimony concerning issues central to the destroyed evidence, or dismissal. *Id.*

6. *See, e.g.*, Petrik v. Monarch Printing Corp., 501 N.E.2d 1312, 1319 (Ill. Ct. App. 1986) (explaining that sanctions for spoliation in violation of discovery rules promote orderly judicial procedures and fair play). *See also Hirsch*, 628 A.2d at 1126 (noting that "district court has wide discretion in imposing discovery sanctions"); Russo v. Goodyear Tire & Rubber Co., 521 N.E.2d 1116, 1120 (Ohio Ct. App. 1987)   54 n.6(noting that determination of the appropriate sanction is exclusively within the trial court's discretion).

will "not be reversed on appeal absent a clear abuse of discretion."[7] Explaining the abuse of discretion standard, one court stated:

We cannot understate the difficulty of the task litigants face when challenging a district court's choice of sanction. They must convince us that the district court abused its discretion in sanctioning them—a burden which is met only when it is clear that no reasonable person would agree [with] the trial court's assessments of what sanctions are appropriate.[8]

One limitation on this authority to impose sanctions for spoliation is that the discovery rules only reach acts of spoliation that occur during the pendency of a lawsuit, or following a court order.[9] Paradoxically, this could encourage parties to destroy evidence before commencement of a lawsuit or discovery proceedings.[10] Therefore, courts also rely on other sources of authority to sanction spoliation, such as a court's inherent power to control the administration of justice.

---

7. *Hirsch*, 628 A.2d at 1126 (citing Hazen v. Pasley, 768 F.2d 226 (8th Cir. 1985)).

8. Marrocco v. General Motors Corp., 966 F.2d 220, 223 (7th Cir. 1992) (citation omitted).

9. *See, e.g.*, Beil v. Lakewood Eng'g & Mfg. Co., 15 F.3d 546, 552 (6th Cir. 1994) (finding that "Rule 37 does not, nor does any procedural rule, apply to actions that occurred prior to the lawsuit"); State Farm Fire & Cas. Co. v. Frigidaire, 146 F.R.D. 160, 162-63 (N.D. Ill. 1992) (finding that the pre-suit duty to preserve evidence is substantive and is controlled by state law rather than federal law, and Rule 37 is inapplicable where destruction occurred pre-commencement); An-Port, Inc. v. MBR Indus., Inc., 772 F. Supp. 1301, 1306 (D. P.R. 1991) (requiring a violation of a court order before sanctions may be imposed). *But see* Bowmar Instrument Corp. v. Texas Instruments, Inc., 25 Fed. R. Serv. 2d 423, 426-27 (N.D. Ind. 1977) (where party requested Rule 37 sanctions prior to filing complaint in response to opposing party's contention that Rule 37 applies only where destruction occurs in defiance of a court order, the court responded that "such a rule would mean the demise of the real meaning and intent of the discovery process . . . some duty must be imposed in circumstances such as these lest the fact-finding process in our courts be reduced to a mockery"). *See also* Fire Ins. Exch. v. Zenith Radio Corp., 747 P.2d 911, 913 (Nev. 1987) (holding that it is "unreasonable to allow litigants, by destroying physical evidence prior to a request for production, to sidestep the district court's power to enforce the rules of discovery").

10. *See* J. Brian Slaughter, Note, *Spoliation of Evidence: A New Rule of Evidence Is the Better Solution*, 18 AM. J. TRIAL ADVOC. 449, 455 (1994).

Court's Inherent Authority

A court's use of its inherent authority is particularly appropriate where litigation has not been commenced, or a specific court order has not been violated, because, under those circumstances, discovery rules generally do not provide for sanctions.[11] One commentator has concluded that in cases of pre-litigation destruction of evidence, "a federal court's inherent authority will generally provide a more efficient method for a court to impose the appropriate remedy."[12] However, the United States Supreme Court has cautioned that this inherent power, although necessary to control parties involved in litigation, must be exercised with restraint.[13]

Several state courts also recognize the inherent power of a trial court to sanction a party for abuse of the judicial process.[14] These states acknowledge that trial courts have the power to take action to aid in the administration of justice and to preserve their independence

---

11. *See* Stevenson v. Union Pac. R.R. Co., 354 F.3d 739, 745 (8th Cir. 2004) (noting court has discretion to impose spoliation sanctions under its inherent authority); Glover v. BIC Corp., 6 F.3d 1318, 1329 (9th Cir. 1993) ("A federal trial court has the inherent discretionary power to make appropriate evidentiary rulings in response to the destruction or spoliation of relevant evidence."); Turner v. Hudson Transit Lines, Inc., 142 F.R.D. 68, 72 (S.D.N.Y. 1991) (finding courts may impose spoliation sanctions relying on their "inherent power to regulate litigation, preserve and protect the integrity of proceedings before [them], and sanction parties for abusive practices"). For a thorough analysis of a federal court's inherent power as a basis for imposing sanctions for pre-litigation destruction of evidence, see Iain D. Johnston, *Federal Courts' Authority to Impose Sanctions for Prelitigation or Pre-Order Spoliation of Evidence*, 156 F.R.D. 313, 319 (1994).

12. *See* Johnston, *supra* note 11, at 325.

13. *See* Roadway Express, Inc. v. Piper, 447 U.S. 752, 764 (1980). Relying on *Roadway Express*, several district courts have imposed sanctions pursuant to their inherent authority. *See, e.g.,* Carlucci v. Piper Aircraft Corp., 775 F.2d 1440, 1447 (11th Cir. 1985); Capellupo v. FMC Corp., 126 F.R.D. 545, 551 (D. Minn 1989). In *Chambers v. NASCO, Inc.*, 501 U.S. 32, 35 (1991), the Supreme Court addressed the question of a federal court's power to sanction a party for bad-faith conduct. Although the *Chambers* Court did not discuss spoliation of evidence, nothing in this decision prevents a federal court from relying on its inherent power to impose sanctions for pre-litigation destruction of evidence. *See, e.g.,* Baliotis v. McNeil, 870 F. Supp. 1285, 1289 (M.D. Pa. 1994) (relying on *Chambers* as authority to sanction spoliation of evidence).

14. *See, e.g.,* Trevino v. Ortega, 969 S.W.2d 950 (Tex. 1998); Richardson v. Sport Shinko, 880 P.2d 69 (Haw. 1994); *In re* Sherman Hollow, Inc., 641 A.2d 753 (Vt. 1993).

and integrity.[15] The destruction of evidence inhibits a court's ability to hear evidence and accurately determine the facts. Therefore, the inherent power to protect against destruction of evidence is necessary to ensure the proper administration of justice.[16]

Absent violation of a court order, courts generally hold that discovery sanctions are inapplicable to spoliation. For example, in *Uniguard Security Insurance v. Lakewood Engineering and Manufacturing Corporation*,[17] the appellate court concluded that the trial court erred in declining to exclude expert testimony as a sanction because the allegedly offending party had not violated any court order. Instead, the trial court should have relied upon its inherent power to make discovery and evidentiary rulings conducive to the conduct of a fair and orderly trial.[18]

Likewise, some federal courts have held that Rule 37 sanctions are inapplicable to pre-litigation destruction of evidence. For instance, in *Beil v. Lakewood Engineering and Manufacturing Company*,[19] an insurer paid a fire claim filed by an estate and acquired subrogation rights. Thereafter, the insurer contacted an independent adjusting firm, which hired an investigator to determine the origin of the fire. The insurer's investigator examined the scene and took possession of several items, including a heater and certain electrical cords. The investigator also photographed the heater and electrical cords.

The insurer's investigator concluded that the heater had caused the fire because, he reasoned, the only heat sources in the area of origin were the heater and its electrical cords. However, the state fire investigator concluded that the fire was caused by a defective extension cord, based on an examination of the fire scene and the extension cord.

---

15. *Trevino*, 969 S.W.2d at 958.
16. *Id.*; *see also* Sacramona v. Bridgestone/Firestone, Inc., 106 F.3d 444 (1st Cir. 1997) (recognizing that courts have the inherent authority to sanction a party for spoliating evidence to prevent prejudice to the non-spoliating party); *Dillon*, 986 F.2d 263, 267 (8th Cir. 1993) (holding that courts have the inherent power to sanction parties for destroying evidence prelitigation that the party knew or should have known was relevant to imminent litigation); Uniguard Sec. Ins. v. Lakewood Eng'g & Mfg. Corp., 982 F.2d 363, 368 n.2 (9th Cir. 1992) 57 n.16 (noting that courts have inherent power to sanction parties who are at fault in destroying evidence prelitigation).
17. 982 F.2d 363 (9th Cir. 1992).
18. *Id.*
19. 15 F.3d 546 (6th Cir. 1994).

Approximately three months after the insurer's fire investigator submitted his report, he discarded the heater and electrical cords. The fire investigator never received express permission from the insurer to discard the items. Six months later, the insurer filed a lawsuit against the heater's manufacturer. After the manufacturer learned that the heater had been discarded, it filed a motion for summary judgment, requesting that the case be dismissed pursuant to Rule 37 because of the "intentional, pre-litigation destruction by an agent" of the insurer.[20] The district court granted the manufacturer's request, under Federal Rule of Civil Procedure 37, and the insurer appealed.

The court of appeals reversed, noting that dismissal is a sanction of last resort that should be imposed only if the court concludes the parties' failure to cooperate in discovery was willful, in bad faith, or due to its own fault.[21] It found that the district court had abused its discretion because, in dismissing the case, it had erroneously applied Rule 37. As the court observed, the heater and electrical cords were not in the insurer's possession or control during the lawsuit. Instead, the investigator discarded these items at least six months prior to litigation. Therefore, had an appropriate Rule 34 request been made, the insurer could have complied with that request and Rule 37 by responding that it could not produce the evidence because it had been destroyed and was not, therefore, in its possession, custody or control.[22]

The Sixth Circuit further observed that its decision was not meant to condone pre-litigation destruction of evidence, but simply to recognize that Rule 37 is a procedural rule and, like similar rules, it governs conduct during the pendency of a lawsuit as opposed to actions that occur before commencement of a lawsuit. In that latter case, the court remarked, a remedy must be found in the substantive law of the case.[23]

FACTORS COURTS CONSIDER TO REMEDY SPOLIATION

Courts have long relied upon discovery and evidentiary sanctions to remedy spoliation that occurs during, or before, litigation. The primary purpose of discovery sanctions is to enforce compliance with

---

20. *Id.* at 549.
21. *Id.* at 552.
22. *Id.*
23. *Id.*

discovery rules rather than to punish the wrongdoer.[24] However, sanctions serve several other purposes, including penalizing those whose conduct warrants sanctions and deterring those who might be "tempted to such conduct in the absence of such a deterrent."[25]

Sanctions also function to compensate victims of spoliation and to promote the accuracy of the fact-finding process. As the Hawaii Supreme Court explained, unintentional spoliation may not implicate the punitive and deterrent purposes of sanctions, but it does "create an unfair disadvantage with respect to the lost evidence."[26] Sanctions, like adverse inferences, provide the necessary mechanism for restoring evidentiary balance[27] and also serve to assist the court in the "management of cases on a crowded docket."[28]

Courts have significant latitude in deciding which discovery sanctions are appropriate.[29] As the District Court for the District of Columbia recently explained, "The choice of sanctions should be guided by the 'concept of proportionality' between offense and sanction."[30] Typically, courts enumerate and attempt to balance a number of factors to ascertain an appropriate sanction for spoliation that occurs during pending litigation.[31] These factors include:

---

24. *See* Robinson v. Transamerica Ins. Co., 368 F.2d 37, 39 (10th Cir. 1966) (explaining that Fed. R. Civ. P. 37(d) secures compliance with discovery rules, rather than punishing parties); *In re* Marriage of Lai, 625 N.E.2d 330, 334 (Ill. App. Ct. 1993) ("The purpose of discovery sanctions is to coerce recalcitrant parties to cooperate in accomplishing the required discovery, not to punish.").

25. Gates Rubber Co. v. Bando Chem. Indus., Ltd., 167 F.R.D. 90, 105-06 (D. Colo. 1996).

26. Stender v. Vincent, 992 P.2d 50, 59 (Haw. 2000).

27. *Id.*

28. *Id.* (citing Ohio v. Crofters, Inc., 75 F.R.D. 12, 22 (D. Colo. 1977) and J. GORELICK, ET AL., DESTRUCTION OF EVIDENCE, § 3.15 at 113 (Wiley 1989)).

29. *See Henderson*, 910 P.2d at 531; *Gates Rubber Co.*, 167 F.R.D. at 102. The latitude given to courts in this area is limited by the requirement that the sanction "must be significantly related to the [discovery dispute at issue]." Insurance Corp. of Ireland v. Compagnie Des Bauxites De Guinee, 456 U.S. 694, 707 (1982).

30. United States v. Philip Morris U.S.A. Inc., 327 F. Supp. 2d 21, 25 (D.D.C. 2004).

31. *See, e.g.*, Ehrenhaus v. Reynolds, 965 F.2d 916, 921 (10th Cir. 1992) (applying a five-factor test); Veloso v. Western Bedding Supply Co., Inc., 281 F. Supp. 2d 743 (D.N.J. 2003) (applying a four-factor test for application of spoliation inference); Jackson v. Fedders Corp., No. 94 -0344, 1996 U.S. Dist. LEXIS 7306, at *29-30 (D.D.C. May 21, 1996) (multi-factor test); Mayes v. Black & Decker (U.S.),

1. The culpability of the spoliating party;
2. The prejudice to the non-offending party;[32]
3. The degree of interference with the judicial process;
4. Whether lesser sanctions will remedy any harm and deter future acts of spoliation;
5. Whether evidence has been irretrievably lost; and
6. Whether sanctions will unfairly punish a party for misconduct by the attorney.[33]

Of course, "these factors do not constitute a rigid test; rather, they represent criteria for the . . . court to consider prior to imposing . . . a sanction."[34] Accordingly, courts will balance a number of factors in attempting to determine whether spoliation should be sanctioned and, if so, what sanction is appropriate in a given case.

Courts generally agree that two factors are most important in assessing whether to impose sanctions, and if so, what types. These two factors "have taken on greater importance in most of the cases on sanctions for spoliation: (1) the culpability of the offender, or the alleged mental state that gave rise to the destruction of evidence, and (2) the degree of prejudice or harm that resulted from the actions of the offender."[35] Therefore, these factors merit further discussion.

Inc., 931 F. Supp. 80, 83 (D.N.H. 1996) (five-factor test); Headley v. Chrysler Motor Corp., 141 F.R.D. 362, 365 n.14 (D. Mass. 1991) (employing five-factor test for sanctioning spoliation); Cabnetware, Inc. v. Sullivan, No. S90313LKK, 1991 U.S. Dist. LEXIS 20329, at *7 (E.D. Cal. July 15, 1991) (four-factor test); *Patton*, 520 N.W.2d at 8 (applying six-factor test and noting that although bad faith is a factor, sanctions can still occur absent bad faith); *Henderson*, 910 P.2d at 532 (applying two-factor test). *See generally* Gorelick, *supra* note 28, at § 3.18 at 88 (noting that "the elements establishing a basis for imposition of sanctions are not settled").

32. One court defined prejudice in this context as "a reasonable possibility that access to the [altered evidence prior to alteration] would have produced evidence favorable to [one of the nonoffending parties] that was not otherwise obtainable." Bright v. Ford Motor Co., 578 N.E.2d 547, 549 (Ohio Ct. App. 1990).

33. *See* Boyd v. Travelers Ins. Co., 652 N.E.2d 267 (Ill. 1995).

34. *Ehrenhaus*, 965 F.2d at 921 (considering whether dismissal was proper based on spoliation). *See also* Martin v. Intex Recreation Corp., 858 F. Supp. 161, 163 (D. Kan. 1994) (explaining that fault is best represented as existing on continuum, without bright lines).

35. 167 F.R.D. at 101-02. *See, e.g.*, McLaughlin v. Denharco, Inc., 129 F. Supp. 2d 32 (D. Me. 2001) (noting conscious wrongdoing and prejudice are two

Culpability of the Offender

Courts look at the mental state of the actor along a continuum of fault; that is, "[n]ondisclosure comes in different shapes and sizes: it may be accidental or inadvertent, or considerably more blameworthy," such as where nonproduction was "knowing and purposeful."[36] Considering degrees of fault, the courts are "unanimous in declaring that a dispositive sanction may be imposed only when the failure to comply with discovery demands is the result of willfulness, bad faith, or some fault of a party other than inability to comply."[37] A "willful failure" has been characterized as "any intentional failure as distinguished from involuntary noncompliance. No wrongful intent need be shown."[38]

Of course, although serious sanctions are appropriate where the court finds a willful or bad-faith failure, dispositive sanctions are not required, since the court's authority to impose such sanctions is permissive.[39] However, where there is a finding of willfulness or bad faith, the trial court can assume that the suppressed evidence would have damaged the non-disclosing party's case and impose sanctions accordingly.[40]

When presented with unintentional conduct, such as recklessness, gross negligence, carelessness, inadvertence or accident, a trial court also has broad discretion to impose sanctions. Appellate review of those sanctions is limited to determining whether the action taken by the court falls within "the universe of suitable alternatives,"[41] which includes a decision to impose no sanction at all.

The Degree of Prejudice Caused by the Spoliator

The selection of an appropriate sanction must be balanced with the other factor that courts most commonly consider, "the degree of preju-

---

key factors in spoliation analysis); Shaffer v. RWP Group, Inc., 169 F.R.D. 19, 25 (E.D.N.Y. 1996) 61 n.35("The two most important factors in determining whether an adverse inference charge is justified are the culpability of the spoliator and the prejudice accruing to the nonspoliator.").

36. *Gates,* 167 F.R.D. at 102 (quoting Anderson v. Cryovac, Inc., 862 F.2d 910, 925 (1st Cir. 1988)).

37. *Id.* at 103 (citing cases).

38. *Id.* (quoting *In re* Standard Metals, 817 F.2d 625, 628-29 (10th Cir. 1987)).

39. *Id.* at 103 (citing cases).

40. *Id.* (citing cases).

41. *Id.* (quoting Jackson v. Harvard Univ., 900 F.2d 464, 468 (1st Cir. 1990)).

dice which has been caused by the conduct of the alleged offender."[42] Prejudice can range from serious to modest to nonexistent. Therefore, in weighing the appropriateness and severity of sanctions, a court must consider the "materiality and value of the suppressed evidence" along with the victim's ability to prepare its case for trial fully and fairly.[43]

The aggrieved party bears the burden of showing that access to the lost evidentiary material would have produced evidence favorable to its case.[44] Professor Wigmore has explained this burden on an aggrieved party:

> The failure or refusal to produce a relevant document, or the destruction of it, is evidence from which alone its contents may be inferred to be unfavorable to the possessor, *provided the opponent, when the identity of the document is disputed, first introduces some evidence tending to show that the document actually destroyed or withheld is the one* as to whose contents it is desired to draw an inference. In applying this rule, care should be taken not to require anything like specific details of contents, but merely such evidence as goes to general marks of identity.[45]

Therefore, before any sanction may be imposed, a trial court must be satisfied that the lost evidentiary material had, or would have had, some relevance and materiality to the case.

REMEDIES AND SANCTIONS FOR SPOLIATION OF EVIDENCE

Adverse Jury Inference

Since the case of *Armory v. Delamirie*,[46] and probably dating back earlier, courts have employed the adverse jury inference, sometimes

---

42. *Gates,* 167 F.R.D. at 104. *See also* Stevenson v. Union Pac. R.R. Co., 354 F.3d 739, 748 (8th Cir. 2004) (stating "there must be a finding of prejudice to the offending party before imposing a sanction for destruction of evidence").

43. *Id.*

44. *Bright,* 578 N.E.2d at 549; Nally v. Volkswagen of America, Inc., 539 N.E.2d 1017 (Mass. 1989).

45. *Gates,* 167 F.R.D. at 104 (citing 2 WIGMORE ON EVIDENCE § 291, at 228 (Little Brown & Co.)) (emphasis in original).

46. 93 Eng. Rep. 664 (K.B. 1722).

called the "spoliation inference," to sanction spoliation of evidence.[47] Under this inference, the jury is instructed that it may assume that the lost evidence, if available, would have been unfavorable to the spoliator.[48] For example, in *Vodusek v. Bayliner Marine Corporation*,[49] the court considered the following adverse inference instruction:

> The defendants contend that their access to relevant and potentially relevant evidence was substantially hindered by the actions of plaintiff's counsel and agents. . . .[I]t is the duty of a party, a party's counsel and any expert witness, not to take action that will cause the destruction or loss of relevant evidence where that will hinder the other side from making its own examination and investigation of all potentially relevant evidence.
>
> If you find in this case the plaintiff's counsel and agents . . . failed to fulfill this duty, then you may take this into account when considering the credibility of [plaintiff's expert] and his opinions and also are permitted to, if you feel justified in doing so, assume that evidence made available to the defendants by acts of plaintiff's counsel or agents, including [plaintiff's expert], would have been unfavorable to the plaintiff's theory in the case.[50]

The basis for an adverse inference like this is "the common sense observation that a party who has notice that [evidence] is relevant to litigation and who proceeds to destroy [it] is more likely to have been threatened by [that evidence] than is a party in the same position who does not destroy the [evidence]."[51] The underlying purpose of this inference is captured in the Latin maxim *omnia presumuntur contra spoliatorem,* "all things presumed against a despoiler or wrongdoer."[52]

---

47. *See Henderson*, 910 P.2d at 531 (explaining that a "common remedy" for spoliation is an adverse inference instruction).
48. *See Baliotis*, 870 F. Supp. at 1292.
49. 71 F.3d 148 (4th Cir. 1995).
50. *Id.* at 155.
51. *Id.* (quoting Nation-Wide Check Corp. v. Forest Hills Distrib., Inc., 692 F.2d 214, 218 (1st Cir. 1982) 63 n.51
52. Wal-Mart Stores, Inc. v. Johnson, 106 S.W.3d 718, 721 (Tex. 2003) (quoting Black's Law Dictionary 980 (5th ed. 1979) 63 n.52

Rationales for Imposing an Adverse Inference

The underlying rationales articulated by courts for the adverse inference instruction include deterrence, remediation, and punishment.[53] One court explained the remediation and punitive purposes of the adverse inference instruction:

> An adverse inference charge serves the dual purposes of remediation and punishment. First, it seeks to put the non-spoliator in a position similar to where it would have been but for the destruction of evidence. Second, it carries a punitive effect; "'the law, in hatred of the spoiler, baffles the destroyer, and thwarts his iniquitous purpose, by indulging a presumption which supplies the lost proof, and this defeats the wrongdoer by the very means he had so confidentially employed to perpetrate the wrong.'"[54]

Thus, the rationale underlying the adverse inference is that deliberate destruction of physical evidence or documents suggests consciousness of guilt.

Level of Culpability Required to Impose an Adverse Inference

Courts are divided on the appropriate level of culpability required in order to give an adverse inference instruction.[55] Some courts require a showing of intent before giving the instruction, reasoning that the inference presupposes that consciousness of wrongdoing motivated the spoliation, and giving the instruction only makes sense if there was an intent to spoliate.[56] Other courts hold that negligence is enough for the in-

---

53. *See Shaffer*, 169 F.R.D. at 25 (explaining that an adverse presumption serves the dual purposes of remediation and punishment); *Turner*, 142 F.R.D. at 75 n.3 (noting that an adverse inference promotes both deterrence and punishment); Pfantz v. Kmart Corp., 85 P.3d 564, 567 (Colo. Ct. App. 2003) (explaining that trial courts may impose sanctions both to punish a party that has spoiled evidence and to remediate the harm to the injured party from absence of that evidence).

54. Shaffer v. RWP Group, Inc., 169 F.R.D. 19, 25 (E.D.N.Y. 1996) (quoting Pomeroy v. Benton, 77 Mo. 64, 86 (1882)) (internal citations omitted).

55. *See Hirsch*, 628 A.2d at 1117 (noting courts disagree on whether bad faith or negligence is required).

56. *See* Hodge v. Wal-Mart Stores, Inc., 360 F.3d 446, 450 (4th Cir. 2004) (holding that spoliation instruction requires intentional conduct and not merely negligent loss or destruction of evidence); Bashier v. Amtrak, 119 F.3d 929, 931

struction, reasoning that the need to deter and punish spoliation is a sufficient basis for giving the instruction and that requiring an innocent litigant to prove fraudulent intent on the part of the spoliator would result in placing too onerous a burden on the aggrieved party.[57]

The two decisions referenced below illustrate these contrasting positions. In *Reilly v. Natwest Markets Group Inc.*,[58] the Second Cir-

---

(11th Cir. 1997) ("mere negligence . . . does not sustain an inference of consciousness of a weak case"); Allen Pen Co. v. Springfield Photo Mount Co., 653 F.2d 17, 22-23 (1st Cir. 1981) (disallowing spoliation inference where destruction not found to be in bad faith); Ricketts v. Eastern Idaho Equip. Co., Inc., 51 P.3d 392 (Idaho 2002) (holding that spoliation requires a state of mind that shows a plan or premeditation); Brumfield v. Exxon Corp., 63 S.W.3d 912, 920 (Tex. Ct. App. 2002) (finding spoliation instruction was not warranted where no evidence that operator had intentionally destroyed evidence at issue); State v. Davlin, 639 N.W.2d 631 (Neb. 2002) (requiring evidence of intentional conduct in bad faith to support adverse inference); Beers v. Bayliner Marine Corp., 675 A.2d 829, 832 (Conn. 1996) (holding spoliation must be intentional for inference); Cherovsky v. St. Luke's Hosp. of Cleveland, No. 68326, 1995 Ohio App. LEXIS 5530, at *23-24 (Ohio Ct. App. Dec. 14, 1995) (explaining adverse inference instruction improper absent intentional, or at least reckless, conduct); Battocchi v. Washington Hosp. Ctr., 581 A.2d 759, 765-66 (D.C. 1990) (holding that an adverse inference may be given either for intentional or reckless spoliation or for failure to preserve evidence within a party's exclusive control even absent intentional or reckless conduct).

57. *See* Kurczy v. St. Joseph Veterans Ass'n, 820 A.2d 929, 947 (R.I. 2003) (holding that negligent destruction of relevant evidence may give rise to adverse inference); *Pfantz*, 85 P.3d 564 (Colo. Ct. App. 2003) (holding that negligent and intentional conduct resulting in spoliation of evidence may warrant an adverse inference); Thomas v. Isle of Capri Casino, 781 So. 2d 125, 123 (Miss. 2001) (holding that requiring intent would encourage parties to "inadvertently" lose particularly damning evidence and then manufacture "innocent" explanations for the loss); Hamann v. Ridge Tool Co., 539 N.W.2d 753, 756-57 (Mich. Ct. App. 1995) (finding exclusion of expert testimony justified even where evidence was lost unintentionally); Glover v. BIC Corp., 6 F.3d 1318, 1329 (9th Cir. 1993) ("Surely a finding of bad faith will suffice [to support an adverse inference], but so will simple notice of potential relevance to litigation.") (citations and internal quotation marks omitted); *Nation-Wide*, 692 F.2d at 219 (showing of bad faith not necessary to establish inference against spoliator); *Baliotis*, 870 F. Supp. at 1291-92 (allowing "spoliation inference" even though evidence did not support a determination that alleged spoliator acted in bad faith); *Turner*, 142 F.R.D. at 364; Sullivan v. General Motors Corp., 772 F. Supp. 358, 364 (N.D. Ohio 1991) (declining to provide an adverse instruction that plaintiff's failure to photograph the defective part prior to repair was either negligent or in bad faith).

58. 181 F.3d 253 (2d Cir. 1999) 65 n.58

cuit Court of Appeals considered the appropriate level of fault necessary to justify an adverse inference instruction. After initially noting the law was unsettled in the circuit, the court acknowledged that failure to produce relevant evidence falls along a continuum of fault—ranging from "innocence through the degrees of negligence to intentionality."[59] Instead of requiring a finding of bad faith, the *Reilly* court stated that trial courts should have the "leeway to tailor sanctions to insure that spoliators do not benefit from their wrongdoing—a remedial purpose that is best adjusted according to the facts and evidentiary posture of each case. . . . [I]t makes little sense to confine promotion of that remedial purpose to cases involving only outrageous culpability, where the party victimized by the spoliation is prejudiced irrespective of whether the spoliator acted with intent or gross negligence."[60] Accordingly, the court held that "a finding of bad faith or intentional misconduct is not a *sine qua non* to sanctioning a spoliator with an adverse inference instruction."[61] Instead, held the court, gross negligence would suffice for the instruction.[62]

In stark contrast, in *Mathis v. John Morden Buick, Inc.*,[63] the Seventh Circuit Court of Appeals noted that to render an adverse inference appropriate, a party must demonstrate that evidence was destroyed in "bad faith."[64] The court explained this meant that the party seeking relief must show that its opponent did more than intentionally destroy evidence; it would have to show the spoliator destroyed evidence "for the purpose of hiding adverse information."[65]

In *Gentry v. Toyota Motor Corporation*,[66] a narrow majority of the court held that sanctions for spoliation were inappropriate absent bad faith by the plaintiff or her attorney and reversed the trial court's dismissal with prejudice based on spoliation. Three judges dissented, rea-

---

59. *Id.* (quoting Welsh v. United States, 844 F.2d 1239, 1246 (6th Cir. 1988)).
60. *Id.* 66 nn.59-62
61. *Id.*
62. *Id.* at 267-68.
63. 136 F.3d 1153 (7th Cir. 1998).
64. *See also* DirecTV, Inc. v. Borow, No. 03C2581, 2005 U.S. Dist. LEXIS 1328 (N.D. Ill. Jan. 6, 2005) 66 nn.64, 65(allowing adverse inference for defendant's bad-faith destruction of relevant electronic documents).
65. *Id.* at 1155.
66. *Gentry v. Toyota Motor Corporation*, 471 S.E.2d 485 (Va. 1996) 66 n.66

soning that even in the absence of bad faith, the prejudice to the defendant required dismissal:

> The fact that the plaintiffs have now focused on an alleged defect not involving the portion of the vehicle removed with a hacksaw by the plaintiff's representative is irrelevant on the issue of prejudice. The manufacturer should not be relegated to merely rebutting some recent theory advanced by the plaintiffs regarding the accident's cause. [The manufacturer] has the right to determine whether there is some cause of the accident related to the now nonexistent part removed by the plaintiffs. The majority has completely disregarded that right to the prejudice of the manufacturer.[67]

As the *Gentry* case demonstrates, even within a particular court, judges disagree about the appropriate level of culpability before sanctioning spoliation.[68]

Alternative Approaches Applying the Adverse Inference

Still other courts have alternative approaches to the application of an adverse inference or presumption. For example, Texas courts recognize two general rules applying to presumptions that arise from the non-production of evidence. The first rule is that failure to produce evidence within a party's control raises the presumption that if produced, it would operate against that party.[69] This rule applies only when one party has introduced evidence harmful to its opponent. Under these circumstances, the opposing party's failure to rebut the harmful evidence with evidence within its control raises a presumption that the unpresented evidence would also be unfavorable to it.

Put another way: Where a party has evidence and does not introduce it, the trial court may take that failure into consideration "not only as strengthening the probative force of the testimony offered to establish the issue, but [also] as itself clothed with some probative

---

67. *Id.* (Compton, J., dissenting).

68. *See also* Tracey v. Tracey, 524 S.E.2d 879 (W. Va. 1999) (analyzing the factors various courts consider before imposing an adverse inference as a sanction. For a more complete discussion of *Tracey* see ch. 7, at West Virginia).

69. Brewer v. Dowling, 862 S.W.2d 156 (Tex. Civ. App. 1993) (citing H. E. Butt Grocery Co. v. Bruner, 530 S.W.2d 340, 343 (Tex. Civ. App. 1975) 67 n.69

force."[70] Courts apply this rule where the party opposing the harmful evidence presents absolutely no evidence to rebut it.[71]

The second rule is that where a party intentionally destroys evidence relevant to a case, that spoliation raises a presumption that the destroyed evidence would have been unfavorable to the cause of the destroyer.[72] When there is no evidence that a party or its agents intentionally destroyed relevant evidence, a trial court properly refuses to instruct the jury regarding spoliation of evidence.[73]

In some jurisdictions, courts will give different types of adverse inference instructions, depending on the circumstances. Once again, Texas courts provide an illustration. There, courts have used two types of instructions, a rebuttable presumption and an adverse presumption. Texas courts consider the rebuttable presumption to be the more severe presumption:

> This is primarily used when the non-spoliating party cannot prove its *prima facie* case without the destroyed evidence. The trial court should begin by instructing the jury that the spoliating party has either negligently or intentionally destroyed evidence and, therefore, the jury should presume that the destroyed evidence was unfavorable to the spoliating party on the particular fact or issue the destroyed evidence might have supported. Next, the court should instruct the jury that the spoliating party bears the burden to disprove the presumed fact or issue. This means that when the spoliating party offers evidence rebutting the presumed fact or issue, the presumption does not automatically disappear. It is not overcome until the fact finder believes that the presumed fact has been overcome by whatever degree of persuasion the substantive law of the case requires. . . . The rebuttable presumption will enable the non-spoliating party to survive summary judgment, directed verdict, judgment notwithstanding the verdict, and the factual legal sufficiency review on appeal.[74]

---

70. *Id.*
71. *Id.* (citing cases).
72. *Id.*
73. *Id.*
74. *Trevino*, 969 S.W.2d at 960-61 (internal citations omitted). *See, e.g.,* RFC Capital Corp. v. EarthLink, No. 03AP-735, 2004 Ohio App. LEXIS 6507 (Ohio Ct.

The other, less severe instruction is merely an adverse presumption that the missing evidence would not have been favorable to the spoliator:

> The presumption itself has probative value and may be sufficient to support the non-spoliating party's assertions. However, it does not relieve the non-spoliating party of the burden to prove each element of its case. Therefore, it is simply another factor used by the factfinder in weighing the evidence.[75]

Maryland courts provide another illustration of alternative adverse inference instructions. In *Anderson v. Litzenberg*,[76] the trial court gave the jury an instruction that did not require a finding of bad faith before the jury could draw a negative inference. Following a verdict for the plaintiff, the defendant appealed, arguing that bad faith should have been required. The court of appeals disagreed and noted that Maryland recognizes two different types of spoliation instructions. If evidence were destroyed due to a spoliator's fraudulent intent, a jury would be instructed that it could infer both that the spoliator's case was weak and that this was the reason for the destruction. If the evidence were destroyed due to negligence or an innocent mistake, however, the jury could still be instructed that the evidence was in an unfavorable condition.

One advantage of the spoliation inference *vis-a-vis* a separate tort claim is that the inference may remedy the harm to the non-spoliator in the existing action without the need for separate litigation. Several state courts have based their decision not to recognize an independent tort for destruction of evidence on the availability of an adverse inference presumption.[77] Commenting on the use of the evidentiary inference, two California practitioners observed:

App. Dec. 23, 2004) (finding that an adverse inference imposes a rebuttable presumption that the spoliating party then has a burden of rebutting by showing that its actions did not deprive the other party of favorable evidence).

75. *Id.*

76. *Anderson v. Litzenberg*, 694 A.2d 150 (Md. 1997) 69 n.76

77. *See, e.g., Temple Community Hosp.*, 976 P.2d 223; *Trevino*, 969 S.W.2d 950; Coletti v. Cudd Pressure Control, 165 F.3d 767 (10th Cir. 1997) 69 n.77

Used properly, an evidentiary instruction of what the fact finder may consider can be a powerful tool in certain circumstances. This instruction gives a jury permission to speculate about evidence that has not been submitted—a notion usually held to be inimical to the U.S. judicial system.[78]

However, because the spoliator is not faced with further sanctions beyond the jury instruction, other courts have suggested that this sanction may not serve as a sufficient disincentive to destroy evidence.[79] Still other courts have commented that the effectiveness of this remedy is difficult to measure given that the jury, and not the judge, determines the impact of the inference.[80]

Courts may also decline to give an adverse inference instruction because it would not cure any prejudice to the non-spoliating party. For example, in *Miller v. Time-Warner Communications, Inc.*,[81] the plaintiff and her counsel acknowledged that before documents were produced during discovery, certain handwritten notes of plaintiff were erased. The plaintiff provided no credible explanation for erasing the notes, rather than simply producing redacted copies. The plain-

---

78. Jerrold Abeles & Robert J. Tyson, *Spoil Sport,* 22 L.A. LAW. 41, 42 (May 1999) 70 n.78

79. *See* Allstate Ins. Co. v. Sunbeam, 865 F. Supp. 1267, 1279 (N.D. Ill. 1994) (dismissing complaint and declining to give limiting instruction because it would not cure the prejudice); *Cf. Uniguard*, 982 F.2d at 369 (upholding district court's exclusion of evidence on the grounds that rebuttable presumption would have been insufficient to cure prejudice).

80. The inference is just that, an inference, and does not "dispens[e] with the necessity of other evidence [by the party in whose favor the inference is offered]." DeLaughter v. Lawrence Cty. Hosp., 601 So. 2d 818, 822 (Miss. 1992) (quoting Bott v. Wood, 56 Miss. 136, 140-41 (1878)). Some courts also hold that where a party has spoliated evidence, a rebuttable presumption may be created, thereby "shifting the burden of proof to a party who destroys, alters, or loses important evidence." *Henderson*, 910 P.2d at 605. This presumption is similar to the adverse inference in that "a rebuttable presumption . . . establishes the missing elements of the [party's] case that could have only been proved by the availability of the missing evidence. . . ." *Hirsch*, 628 A.2d at 1126-27 (quoting *Welsh*, 844 F.2d at 1248). *See also Uniguard*, 982 F.2d at 369 (upholding exclusion of evidence rather than applying rebuttable presumption to cure prejudice to nonspoliating party); *Bright*, 578 N.E.2d at 550 (reversing trial court's decision to exclude evidence and indicating that non-spoliating party should have enjoyed a rebuttable presumption of prejudice).

81. No. 97 Civ. 7286, 1999 U.S. Dist. LEXIS 9689 (S.D.N.Y. June 29, 1999).

tiff argued that the court should impose a sanction short of dismissal. However, the court determined that a lesser remedy, such as an adverse inference instruction, would be impractical. The court reasoned:

> [W]hile we know that there were erasures, we do not know what plaintiff and her counsel erased. Thus, it is hard to conceive what inference the court could ask the jury to draw from the erasure, other than that plaintiff knew that the erased writings would prove that she had no case. This would amount to a directed verdict for the defendant. If the defendant would be entitled to a directed verdict at trial, there is no reason not to dismiss the complaint at this point.[82]

The court instead scheduled a hearing to determine whether dismissal was an appropriate remedy.

Exclusion of Evidence or Expert Testimony

Courts also consider exclusion of evidence as a less drastic alternative to dismissal or entry of a default judgment. This evidentiary sanction often includes the refusal to permit a spoliator to introduce expert or other witness testimony regarding either the spoliated evidence or other evidence.[83]

When a court excludes expert testimony because of spoliation, it also may take the further step of awarding summary judgment against the spoliator, because without such testimony the party cannot prove its case. This does not, however, conflict with the presumption against dismissal. "'[I]n such cases, the judgment itself is not the sanction; rather, the exclusion of evidence is the sanction. 'Judgment only follows because the party cannot otherwise prove its case.'"[84]

---

82. *Id.* at *15.

83. *See Uniguard*, 982 F.2d at 368-69 (upholding exclusion of expert testimony and grant of summary judgment); Cincinnati Ins. Co. v. General Motors Corp., No. 940T017, 1994 Ohio App. LEXIS 4960, at *1415 (Ohio Ct. App. Oct. 28, 1994) (finding exclusion of expert testimony is proper where evidence has been intentionally or negligently destroyed).

84. Simons v. Mercedes-Benz of N. Am., Inc., No. 952705, 1996 U.S. Dist. LEXIS 2695, at *13 (E.D. Pa. Mar. 7, 1996) (quoting Donohoe v. American Isuzu Motors, Inc., 155 F.R.D. 515, 520 (M.D. Pa. 1994)). *See also Uniguard*, 982 F.2d at 368-69; *Cincinnati Ins.*, 1994 Ohio App. LEXIS 4960, at *15 (upholding exclusion of expert evidence and granting of summary judgment). *But see* Howell v. Maytag, 168 F.R.D. 502, 508 (M.D. Pa. 1996) (declining to exclude evidence because it would have the same effect as the outright dismissal of the claim).

For example, in *Unigard Security Insurance v. Lakewood Engineering & Manufacturing Corporation*,[85] a district court granted summary judgment after excluding an insurer's experts as a sanction for the insurer's spoliation of an electric space heater and the remains of a boat destroyed by fire. The court found that the space heater's manufacturer was precluded from "'gaining expert testimony related to whether the heater caused the fire,' and that this case was one in which '[the insurer's] destruction of key evidence renders a full defense impossible.'"[86]

Affirming the exclusion of expert testimony as a sanction, the Ninth Circuit held that "[o]nce the district court excluded 'the testimony of [the insurer's experts] and the evidence from the unavailable heater and vessel,' [the insurer] lacked the ability to put forward . . . any admissible evidence creating a disputed material fact."[87] Accordingly, the court found that summary judgment was proper.[88]

Factors Courts Consider in Determining Whether to Exclude Evidence

Courts look at a number of factors in deciding whether to exclude expert evidence. Some courts consider the probative value of the destroyed evidence to the non-spoliating party as the most important factor in determining whether to exclude expert testimony.[89] Other courts focus on the prejudice to the non-spoliating party's case resulting from the lost evidence.[90]

For example, in *Hirsch v. Superior Court*,[91] the court held that the plaintiff's destruction of a fire-damaged vehicle was intentional, even though the evidence did not show that the vehicle was destroyed "with a view toward precluding examination."[92] The court concluded that "a

---

85. 982 F.2d 363 (9th Cir. 1992).
86. *Id.* at 368.
87. *Id.* at 369.
88. *Id.*
89. *See Bright*, 178 N.E.2d at 549.
90. *See Baliotis*, 870 F. Supp. at 1291-92; *Cincinnati Ins.*, 1994 Ohio App. LEXIS 4960, at *1011.
91. 628 A.2d 1108 (N.J. Super. Ct. Law Div. 1993).
92. *Id.* at 1130. Several spoliation remedies may require intentional conduct. However, "[c]ommentators disagree about the nature of the intentionality requirement." For example, some courts "impose a more stringent intentionality element by requiring proof of fault or 'bad faith.'" *Id.* In *Hirsch*, the court stated that "[f]or

spoliator's intent level does not affect liability for destruction of evidence resulting in interference with discovery. Rather, it has a bearing on the remedy to be administered for that spoliation."[93]

In *Hamann v. Ridge Tool Company*,[94] the Michigan Court of Appeals took a somewhat different approach. There, the trial court admitted expert testimony regarding evidence that the plaintiff had lost inadvertently. The appellate court reversed and remanded for a new trial because it found that the prejudice was the same as if the evidence had been intentionally destroyed, and, therefore, the trial court abused its discretion in admitting the evidence.[95] The court explained:

> We conclude that the trial court erred in permitting plaintiff to offer testimony about evidence that was lost, even though it was unintentionally lost. It would be unfair to permit the negligent party to benefit from his own error. Whether the evidence was destroyed or lost accidentally or in bad faith is irrelevant, because the opposing party suffered the same prejudice; specifically, defendant was unable to challenge the evidence or respond to it. Accordingly, we find defendant is entitled to a new trial because of the unfair prejudice resulting from [the expert] testimony regarding lost evidence.[96]

Some jurisdictions exclude evidence as a sanction for even negligent spoliation. As the court noted in *Indemnity Insurance Company of North America*,[97] spoliation sanctions "are not limited to cases where the evidence was destroyed willfully or in bad faith, since a party's negligent loss of evidence can be just as fatal to the other party's ability to present a defense."[98]

---

the destruction of evidence to be intentional, it need not rise to the level of a malicious or 'evil minded act.'" *Id.* at 1129-30. However, in *Headley v. Chrysler Motor Corp.*, the court stated that "intentional" means that the evidence was destroyed by a party's agent after notice that the evidence should be retained for evidentiary purposes. 141 F.R.D. 361, 364 n.1 (D. Mass. 1991).

93. *Hirsch*, 628 A.2d at 1120.

94. 539 N.W.2d 753 (Mich. Ct. App. 1995) 73 n.94-96

95. *See id.* at 756-57.

96. *Id.*

97. *Indemnity Insurance Company of North America*, No. 96 Civ. 6675 (D.C.), 1998 U.S. Dist. LEXIS 9475 (S.D.N.Y. June 29, 1998) 73 nn.97, 98

98. *Id.* (quoting *Squitieri*, 669 N.Y.S.2d at 59). *See also* Thiele v. Oddy's Auto & Marine, Inc., 906 F. Supp. 158, 162 (W.D.N.Y. 1995) (sanctions for spoliation may

Still other courts hold that a party's bad faith is irrelevant in determining whether to exclude evidence based on spoliation. These courts reason that regardless of the level of culpability, the non-spoliating party has been equally prejudiced. For example, in *Rockwell International Corporation v. Menzies*,[99] the court upheld a default judgment against the defendant for destroying evidence. In reaching this conclusion, the court held that whether the evidence was destroyed in "bad faith or accidentally is irrelevant."[100]

A case involving a lost prosthetic device further illustrates this approach. In *DePuy, Inc. v. Eckes*,[101] a Florida court explained that under the facts and circumstance of that case, fault was irrelevant:

> Whether the prosthesis was destroyed in bad faith or accidentally is irrelevant in the present case. The evidence is unavailable for the plaintiffs' use and they have demonstrated an inability to proceed without it. The second argument of the defendants is equally untenable. While it is true that the plaintiffs had an opportunity to test the prosthesis prior to giving it to the appellants, the [plaintiffs'] failure to run a test does not relieve [defendants] of responsibility for the loss. When they procured the evidence for their inspection, [defendants] did so subject to the plaintiffs' right to the return of the evidence. Having lost the prosthesis, [defendants] are now accountable for the ramifications of their act.[102]

Dismissal and Default Judgment

Dismissal and default judgment are the harshest sanctions that may be imposed for spoliation.[103] Given their severity, as well as the strong presumption that cases should be decided on the merits, these sanc-

---

be imposed when evidence is destroyed "simply through negligent fault"); Brancaccio v. Mitsubishi Motors Co., No. 90 Civ. 7852, 1992 U.S. Dist. LEXIS 11022, *2-3 (S.D.N.Y. July 27, 1992)   74 n.98(sanctions are "warranted where a party fails to comply with discovery willfully, in bad faith, or through fault").
  99. 561 So. 2d 677 (Fla. Ct. App. 1990)   74 nn.99, 100
  100. *Id.* at 679.
  101. 427 So. 2d 306 (Fla. Ct. App. 1983).
  102. *Id.*
  103. *Trevino*, 969 S.W.2d at 959.

tions are rarely imposed.[104] For example, in *Transamerica Insurance Group v. Maytag, Inc.*,[105] an Ohio appellate court reversed an outright dismissal with prejudice based on spoliation. The court held that bad-faith destruction of evidence was a prerequisite to dismissal. Treating the spoliator's action as a mere failure to preserve evidence, rather than deliberate destruction, the court found dismissal to be "disproportionate to the seriousness of the infraction under the facts of the case. . . ."[106] The court also advised that "[w]henever possible, the trial court should impose the least severe sanction which effectively removes the prejudice caused by the sanctioned party's wrongdoing."[107]

Courts appear to be willing to use the sanction of dismissal, particularly where a party demonstrates bad-faith spoliation, or where prejudice is so severe that no other remedy will suffice. Accordingly, in extreme cases, courts will order dismissal or default judgment.[108] For example, in *Computer Associates International v. American*

---

104. *See, e.g.*, Joe Hand Promotions v. Sports Page Cafe, Inc., 940 F. Supp. 102, 104 n.8 (D.N.J. 1996) ("sanction of dismissal is particularly severe and ought to be employed only sparingly"); *In re* Marriage of Lai, 625 N.E.2d at 334 ("[D]efault judgment is the most severe sanction a court can impose on a defendant and is proper only in those cases where actions of a party showed deliberate, contumacious, or unwarranted disregard of a court's authority."); Johnson v. Mountainside Hosp., 488 A.2d 1029, 1031-32 (N.J. Super. Ct. App. Div. 1985) (per curiam) ("Since dismissal with prejudice is the ultimate sanction, it will normally be ordered only when no lessor [*sic*] sanction will suffice to erase the prejudice suffered by the nondelinquent party . . . or when the litigant rather than the attorney was at fault. . . .") (citation omitted). *But see* Kucala Enters., Ltd. v. Auto Wax Co., Inc., No. 02-C-1403, 2003 U.S. Dist. LEXIS 8833 (N.D. Ill. May 23, 2003) (dismissing action as sanction after finding plaintiff acted in bad faith by using computer program to delete documents from his computer and "clean" the hard drive).

105. 650 N.E.2d 169 (Ohio Ct. App. 1994).

106. *Id.* at 171.

107. *Id.*

108. *See Johnson*, 488 A.2d at 1029 (explaining that dismissal with prejudice is a drastic remedy and not to be invoked unless refusal to comply is deliberate and contumacious). *See also* Silvestri v. General Motors Corp., 271 F.3d 583 (4th Cir. 2001) (upholding dismissal as a sanction in an action against a manufacturer involving the failure to preserve a vehicle involved in an accident); Kucala Enters., Ltd., No. 02-C-1403, 2003 U.S. Dist. LEXIS 8833 (dismissing action as sanction after finding plaintiff acted in bad faith by using computer program to delete documents from his computer and "clean" the hard drive).

Fundware,[109] a copyright holder sought a default judgment against a computer software developer that had destroyed portions of the developer's source code during the pendency of the lawsuit. The holder claimed that a comparison of the source codes would show that the developer had violated the copyright in the structure, sequence, organization, and other features of its programs.[110] Granting the holder's motion for a default judgment, the *Computer Associates* court stated:

> One of the most severe sanctions available is default judgment. It is reserved for egregious offenses against an opposing party or a court. Therefore, I have considered default judgment as a last resort to be invoked only if no lesser, yet equally effective, sanction is available. . . .
>
> . . . Destruction of evidence cannot be countenanced in a justice system whose goal is to find the truth through honest and orderly production of evidence under established discovery rules. I hold that nothing less than default judgment on the issue of liability will suffice to both punish this defendant and deter others similarly tempted.[111]

Similarly, in *Cabnetware, Inc. v. Sullivan*,[112] the court adopted the magistrate's recommendation and granted default judgment on the basis of willful destruction of valuable evidence.[113] The court reasoned:

> Defendant's conduct in the instant action, cast in its most charitable light, is an affront to the integrity of the judicial system. Knowing full well the significance of the [evidence] to

---

109. 133 F.R.D. 166 (D. Colo. 1990).
110. *See id.* at 168.
111. *Id.* at 169-70.
112. No. S90313LKK, 1991 U.S. Dist. LEXIS 20329 (E.D. Cal. July 15, 1991).
113. Courts in other jurisdictions also have dismissed claims based on spoliation of evidence. *See, e.g.,* *Allstate*, 865 F. Supp. at 1279 (declining to give limiting instruction because it would not cure the prejudice, since it would not allow defendant to put on evidence it otherwise might have had; court instead dismissed complaint). *See generally* Kenneth R. Lang, et al., *Spoliation of Evidence: The Continuing Search for a Remedy and Implications for Aviation Accident Investigations*, 60 J. Air L. & Com. 997, 1002-14 (1995) (reviewing the requisite level of intent for imposing the sanction of dismissal or default in a spoliation claim); John F. Kuppens, *There Is No Substitute: Spoliation of Evidence in Product Liability Suits*, S.C. Law., Mar./Apr. 1994, at 28.

plaintiff's suit . . . defendant willfully destroyed essential evidence after being served with a request for production. Although I have served many years on the federal bench, this court has never been confronted with such a flagrant example of contempt for the judicial system.[114]

In *Miller v. Time-Warner Communications, Inc.,*[115] the plaintiff not only destroyed evidence willfully and in bad faith, but thereafter perjured herself. The court held that although lesser sanctions such as paying attorneys' fees "might be appropriate" if spoliation alone had occurred, the court found dismissal warranted because plaintiff exacerbated her deliberate attempt to destroy evidence by repeatedly perjuring herself on that subject.[116]

On the other hand, in some jurisdictions courts have entered the extreme sanction of dismissal in cases of negligent spoliation. For example, in *Klein v. Seenauth,*[117] the court discussed the intent requirements regarding the sanction of dismissal. It observed that in New York, "the severe sanction of dismissal was imposed summarily without a hearing in many recent spoliation cases based on the negligent loss of a key piece of evidence."[118] In light of the fact that dismissal may be available as a sanction, even where there has been unintentional spoliation, a careful practitioner will caution clients to take care to retain any evidence and give potentially adverse parties ample opportunity to inspect physical evidence as soon as practicable.

Other Sanctions and Remedies Imposed in Pending Litigation

In addition to the foregoing sanctions, courts also sanction spoliation of evidence by awarding attorney's fees, fines, and punitive dam-

---

114. *Cabnetware*, 1991 U.S. Dist. LEXIS 20329, at *11. *See also* Farley Metals, Inc. v. Barber Coleman Co., 645 N.E.2d 964 (Ill. App. Ct. 1994) (upholding dismissal for destruction of artifacts from fire). One court has concluded that where dismissal or default judgment is contemplated, the burden of proof should be by clear and convincing evidence. *Gates*, 167 F.R.D. at 108.

115. 1999 U.S. Dist. LEXIS 14512 (Sept. 22, 1999).

116. *Id*. at *7.

117. 180 Misc. 2d 213 (Civ. Ct. N.Y. 1999).

118. *Id*. at 220. The court also noted that in a number of other cases, courts had summarily denied the imposition of sanctions. *Id*.

ages.[119] The imposition of monetary sanctions and fines is becoming more common in the context of spoliation of electronic documents.[120] Some courts imposing monetary sanctions require bad faith or intentional conduct.[121]

Procter & Gamble Company v. Haugen[122] provides an example of a factual situation in which a court imposed a monetary sanction for destruction of evidence. There, a defendant sought sanctions against a soap manufacturer for violating its duty to preserve relevant information, namely, corporate e-mail communications created during the pendency of a certain litigation. Even after having been ordered to do so, defendant claimed, the manufacturer failed either to search for or to save certain e-mail communications that it had identified as having relevant information. Discussing its inherent authority and its power under Federal Rule of Civil Procedure 37(b)(2), the court observed that it could sanction a litigant who has notice that information in its possession is relevant to litigation or potential litigation.

The *Procter & Gamble* court acknowledged that Rule 37 sanctions are appropriate only if a party violates a discovery order, and no such discovery order existed. Therefore, the court considered imposition of a fine under its inherent authority.[123] Finding that mere negligence in losing or destroying a document will not support an

---

119. Kawamata Farms, Inc. v. United Riga Products, 948 P.2d 1055 (Haw. 1997) (imposing $1.5 million punitive sanction and requiring the spoliator to pay plaintiff's attorneys' fees and costs incurred as a result of discovery abuse, where a party intentionally withheld information and documents); Moskovitz v. Mt. Sinai Med. Ctr., 635 N.E.2d 331 (Ohio 1994) (approving punitive damage award where a doctor altered medical records to avoid liability); Medical Billing, Inc. v. Med. Mgmt. Service, Inc., No. 1:96CV1015 (N.D. Ohio Oct. 16, 1996) (sanctioning an attorney for involvement in destroying evidence).

120. *See, e.g.*, MOSAID Techs. Inc. v. Samsung Elecs. Co., 348 F. Supp. 2d 332 (D.N.J. 2004) (affirming $566,839.97 sanctions award where party "willfully blinded itself" to its obligation to preserve potentially relevant electronic information); United States v. Philip Morris USA Inc., 327 F. Supp. 2d 21 (D.D.C. 2004) (imposing $2.75 million in sanctions plus costs following failure to comply with preservation order).

121. *Stevenson*, 354 F.3d 739 (requiring bad faith to assess attorneys' fees as sanction for destruction of evidence).

122. 179 F.R.D. 622 (D. Utah 1998).

123. *Id.*

inference that a party was conscious of a weakness in its case, the *Procter & Gamble* court declined to impose an adverse inference instruction, despite defendant's contention that the court could infer bad faith from the manufacturer's refusal to save certain e-mail.

The court stated that it could not determine that the manufacturer acted in bad faith and observed that there was no court order that would have delineated the scope of the manufacturer's duties to preserve evidence. However, because it found that the manufacturer itself identified the e-mail communications of five individuals as having relevant information, the court held that the failure to preserve that evidence constituted a sanctionable breach of the soap manufacturer's discovery duties.[124] Because the soap manufacturer had identified the e-mails itself, which belied any claim these e-mails were not relevant, the court ordered the soap manufacturer to pay defendants a $10,000 sanction.[125]

Practice Tips

To avoid imposition of sanctions for destruction of evidence in pending lawsuits, consider the following:

- Take the opportunity to inspect evidence, if offered by the opposing party. Courts will not sanction exclusion of evidence or otherwise assist a party that demonstrates it had no intention of inspecting evidence later destroyed by the opposing party.[126]

- Be certain to advise adverse parties or likely adverse parties and offer them an opportunity to inspect any physical

---

124. *Id.*

125. *Id.*

126. One appellate court considered whether a trial court had properly declined to give a rebuttable presumption instruction, which would have shifted the burden of proof to a spoliating party for the destruction of evidence. In that case, the allegedly prejudiced party did not request an inspection of the treadmill until four years after the injury. During that same time period she also failed to request that the treadmill be preserved. The appellate court held that because the non-spoliating party "had ample opportunity to obtain the evidence she now claims is essential to her case," the request for such an instruction was properly denied. Marshall v. Bally's Pacwest, Inc., 972 P.2d 475 (Wash. 1999).

object in its post-accident condition.[127] Keep a record of any offers to inspect and the responses received.

- If it is necessary to discard or destroy physical evidence before a potential opponent has had an opportunity to inspect it, make a careful photographic or video record. Although some courts may not accept such evidence as a substitute, an effort to minimize any prejudice the destruction may cause can be considered when determining the spoliator's culpability.

- Take all reasonable steps to locate missing evidence, including tracing it to third parties, before seeking judicial intervention. As the injured party, in many jurisdictions, the movant bears the burden of demonstrating that the absence of the destroyed evidence will cause it prejudice and it did all it could to locate the missing evidence.

- Do not assume that the absence of a pending lawsuit leaves your client free to discard or destroy potentially relevant evidence without adverse consequences.

- Bear in mind that when analyzing requests for sanctions for spoliation, a court generally focuses on culpable conduct and prejudice to the innocent party.

- Carefully consider the law of the appropriate jurisdiction when requesting a sanction or other remedy for spoliation. Many states vary the sanctions based on the degree of the spoliator's culpability and the extent of the prejudice to the non-spoliator.

---

127. *Beers v. Bayliner Marine Corp.*, 675 A.2d 829, discusses the efforts a party seeking an inference must make to ensure it uses all appropriate means to have evidence produced, including placing the spoliator on notice that certain evidence should be produced and, if necessary, obtaining a pre-litigation, court-ordered inspection. *See also* Chapman v. Auto Owners Ins. Co., 469 S.E.2d 783 (Ct. App. Ga. 1996) (finding photographs of the destroyed evidence an inadequate substitute given plaintiff's expert's testimony regarding tests he would have performed if the evidence were available).

Independent Causes of Action for Spoliation 4

> *New and nameless torts are being recognized constantly . . .*[1]

Courts in virtually every jurisdiction impose appropriate sanctions for spoliation that occurs during pending litigation. Yet, only a minority of state high courts have recognized an independent tort claim for spoliation of evidence. The high court in six states and the district court in the District of Columbia have recognized a cause of action for spoliation of evidence.[2]

Other state courts recognize that spoliation may be remedied through existing tort remedies.[3] Even those states that

---

1. Smith v. Superior Court, 198 Cal. Rptr. 829 (Cal. Ct. App. 1984).

2. Smith v. Atkinson, 771 So. 2d 429 (Ala. 2000); Hazen v. Anchorage, 718 P.2d 456 (Alaska 1986); Nichols v. State Farm Fire and Cas. Co., 6 P.3d 300 (Alaska 2000); Holmes v. Amerex Rent-A-Car, 710 A.2d 846, 847 (D.C. 1998); Oliver v. Stimson, 991 P.3d 11 (Mont. 1999); Coleman v. Potash, 905 P.2d 185, 189 (N.M. 1995); Torres v. El Paso Elec. Co., 987 P.2d 386, 401 (N.M. 1999); Smith v. Howard Johnson Co., 615 N.E.2d 1037 (Ohio 1993). *See also* Hannah v. Heeter, 584 S.E.2d 560, 567 n.8 (W. Va. 2003) (adopting the spoliation tort and noting more than 26 jurisdictions have addressed this issue).

3. *See, e.g.,* Builder's Square, Inc. v. Shaw, 755 So. 2d 721 (Fla. Ct. App. 1999); Cook v. Dep't of Transp., 985 P.2d 1150 (Idaho 1999); Boyd v. Travelers Ins. Co., 652 N.E.2d 267 (Ill. 1995); Broadnax v. ABF Freight Sys., Inc., No. 96C1674, 1998 U.S. Dist. LEXIS 4662, at *10-11 (N.D. Ill. Mar. 30, 1998).

recognize a cause of action for spoliation may limit the tort to intentional causes of action or to a cause of action against a third party.[4]

The highest courts in Alaska,[5] New Mexico,[6] Ohio,[7] and West Virginia[8] have recognized a cause of action for intentional spoliation. Courts in at least four jurisdictions have recognized a cause of action for negligent spoliation: Indiana,[9] Montana,[10] Alabama,[11] and the District of Columbia.[12] The District of Columbia has recognized a cause of action for negligent *or* reckless spoliation.[13]

Courts in Illinois,[14] Idaho,[15] Louisiana,[16] New Jersey,[17] and Pennsylvania[18] have not recognized an independent spoliation tort. Instead, these courts have found that a cause of action for negligent

---

4. *See, e.g., Atkinson*, 771 So. 2d 429 (limiting claims to negligent spoliation against third parties); Hannah v. Heeter, 584 S.E.2d 560 (limiting claims against parties to a civil action to intentional spoliation and adopting negligent and intentional spoliation as to third parties).

5. *Hazen*, 718 P.2d 456; *Nichols*, 6 P.3d 300.

6. *Coleman*, 905 P.2d at 189; *Torres*, 987 P.2d at 401.

7. *Smith*, 615 N.E.2d 1037.

8. *Hannah*, 584 S.E.2d 560.

9. Glotzbach v. Froman, No. 45A03-0307-CV-264, 2005 Ind. App. LEXIS 797 (Ind. Ct. App. May 11, 2005) (recognizing the continuing viability of a negligent or intentional spoliation claim against third parties owing a duty to the person bringing the claim after the Indiana Supreme Court declined to recognize a first-party spoliation as an independent tort in *Gribben v. Wal-Mart Stores*, 824 N.E.2d 349, 355 (Ind. 2005)).

10. *Oliver*, 991 P.3d 11.

11. *Smith*, 771 So. 2d 429.

12. *Holmes*, 710 A.2d 846.

13. *Id.* at 847. *See generally* Thomas G. Fischer, Annotation, *Intentional Spoliation of Evidence, Interfering with Prospective Civil Action, as Actionable*, 70 A.L.R. 4th 984 (1999).

14. Boyd v. Travelers Ins. Co., 652 N.E.2d 267 (Ill. 1995); Dardeen v. Kuehling, 821 N.E.2d 227 (Ill. 2004).

15. Yoakum v. Hartford Fire Ins. Co., 923 P.2d 416 (Idaho 1996); Ricketts v. Eastern Idaho Equip. Co., 51 P.3d 392 (Idaho 2002).

16. Bethea v. Modern Biomedical Servs., Inc., 704 So. 2d 1227 (La. Ct. App. 1997).

17. Rosenbilt v. Zimmerman, 766 A.2d 749, 758 (N.J. 2001) (finding the tort of fraudulent concealment provides an adequate remedy for litigants faced with destruction of evidence by a party to a lawsuit).

18. Elias v Lancaster Gen. Hosp., 710 A.2d 65, 67-69 n.2 & 3 (Pa. Super. Ct. 1998).

spoliation can be stated under general negligence principles and similar existing causes of action.[19] But a majority of the states considering the issue have concluded that existing case law and available civil sanctions provide an adequate remedy for spoliation.[20]

The first decision to expressly recognize the tort of spoliation was the 1984 California case of *Smith v. Superior Court*.[21] In that case, the plaintiff suffered permanent injuries following an accident in which an oncoming truck's wheel crashed into her windshield. After the accident, the truck was taken to the dealership that had customized the truck's wheels. The plaintiff's attorney notified the dealership of the truck's evidentiary importance and explained it would be subject to testing by experts. Subsequently, the dealership disposed of the truck with knowledge and understanding of its importance.[22]

The court began its analysis by explaining how new torts evolve:

> New and nameless torts are being recognized constantly, and the progress of the common law is marked by many cases of first impression, in which the court has struck out boldly to create a new cause of action, where none had been recognized before. . . . *When it becomes clear that the plaintiff's interests are entitled to legal protection against the conduct of the defendant*, the mere fact that the claim is novel will not itself operate as a bar to a remedy.[23]

---

19. *Boyd,* 652 N.E.2d 267; *Yoakum,* 923 P.2d 416; Elias v. Lancaster Gen. Hosp., 710 A.2d 65; *Rosenbilt,* 766 A.2d at 758.

20. *See Atkinson,* 771 So. 2d at 433 n.2 (citing cases); *Hannah,* 584 S.E.2d 560 (declining to recognize first-party spoliation because the adverse inference instruction and civil rules provide sufficient remedies); *Gribben,* 824 N.E.2d 349 (refusing to recognize first-party spoliation tort because existing remedies and sanctions outweighed the potential disadvantages of the tort).

21. 198 Cal. Rptr. 829 (Cal. Ct. App. 1984). Prior to 1984, scattered courts had recognized the tort of spoliation of wills, and language in certain decisions suggested the existence of such a tort. J. Gorelick, et al., Destruction of Evidence § 4.2, at 140 (1994). The California Supreme Court has since overruled *Smith. See* ch. 7, at California.

22. *Smith,* 198 Cal. Rptr. at 831-32.

23. *Id.* at 832 (emphasis in original). The *Smith* court compared spoliation of evidence with the tort of intentional interference with prospective business advantage. *See id.* at 836. The court explained that this analogy was necessary in the adoption of a spoliation tort because of the uncertainty of damages. *See id.* at 837.

The *Smith* court explained that "a large part of what is most valuable in modern life depends upon 'probable expectancies'; [and] as social and industrial life become more complex the courts must do more to discover, define and protect [expectancies] from undue interference."[24] The court declared that "the primary function of the tort of intentional spoliation is to compensate for the destruction of evidence even though the probative value of the evidence is not known, because the accuracy of the facts related to the evidence will never be restored."[25]

In delineating the boundaries of this new tort, the *Smith* court further likened it to the tort of interference with prospective business advantage. The court concluded "that a prospective civil action in a product liability case is a valuable 'probable expectancy' that the court must protect from the kind of interference alleged herein."[26]

The underlying premise for recognition of this new tort is that a victim of spoliation is entitled to recover compensatory, and possibly punitive, damages for the loss of a prospective lawsuit.[27] The ineffectiveness of judicial sanctions in deterring spoliation prompted, in part, the recognition of this tort.[28] Courts also point to the integrity of the judicial system[29] and deterrence as important policy goals sup-

---

24. *Id.* at 836 (quoting WILLIAM L. PROSSER, HANDBOOK OF THE LAW OF TORTS, § 130, at 950 (4th ed. 1971)).

25. *Id.*; *see also* Russell W. Welsh & Andrew C. Marquardt, *Spoliation of Evidence*, 23 WTR BRIEF 9, 11 (1994).

26. *Smith*, 198 Cal. Rptr. at 837.

27. *See* Hirsch v. General Motors Corp., 628 A.2d 1108, 1126 (N.J. Super. Ct. Law Div. 1993).

28. *See* Charles C. Cohn, *Tort and Other Remedies for Spoliation of Evidence*, 81 ILL. B.J. 128, 134 (1993) (citing Marrocco v. General Motors Corp., 966 F.2d 220, 225 (7th Cir. 1992) (arguing a tort remedy provides redress to litigants whose expectancy of recovery is injured by a spoliator who cannot be reached by sanctions in the underlying action)); Steffen Nolte, *The Spoliation Tort: An Approach to Underlying Principles*, 26 ST. MARY'S L.J. 351, 355 (1995) ("traditional procedural and nonprocedural remedies are flawed by their limited scope, their inadequate preventive effect, and their failure to provide the victim with just compensation"); *see, e.g., Hannah*, 584 S.E.2d 560 (adopting spoliation tort because of the ineffectiveness of other remedies).

29. Sean R. Levine, Note, *Spoliation of Evidence in West Virginia: Do Too Many Cooks Spoil the Broth?*, 104 W. VA. L. REV. 419 (Winter 2002) (hereinafter *Too Many Cooks*) (citing Stephen Ruben, *Tort Reform: A Call for Florida to Scale Back Its Independent Tort for Spoliation of Evidence*, 51 FLA. L. REV. 345 (1999)).

porting recognition of the tort.[30]

"The spoliation tort protects a litigant's interest in bringing a prospective cause of action" by "compensat[ing] the non-spoliating litigant for uninvited interference with the prospective lawsuit resulting from destroyed evidence."[31] Courts recognizing a cause of action for intentional spoliation generally emphasize the inadequacy of traditional remedies to compensate the nonspoliating party.[32]

Since the *Smith* decision in California in 1984, courts in numerous jurisdictions have either declined to recognize the new tort or have found it unnecessary to resolve the issue on the facts before it.[33] Perhaps the chief concern courts articulate is the uncertainty of damages, given that there is no way to establish with certainty what the missing evidence would have shown and the "inherent difficulty of proving the fact of injury."[34] Even the *Smith* court, which first recognized the tort, noted that the uncertainty of damages due to destroyed or altered evidence was the "most troubling aspect" of the new tort.[35]

The majority of jurisdictions that have addressed the issue have declined to recognize a cause of action for intentional spoliation of evidence. These courts articulate a variety of reasons for refusing to do so, including that this new tort is unnecessary because existing remedies can adequately address the spoliation problem.[36]

---

30. *Too Many Cooks, supra* note 29 (citing Bart S. Wilhoit, *Spoliation of Evidence: The Viability of Four Emerging Torts,* 46 UCLA L. Rev. 631 (1998)).

31. *Hirsch,* 628 A.2d at 1119. *See also* Federated Mut. Ins. Co. v. Litchfield Precision Components, Inc., 456 N.W.2d 434, 437 (Minn. 1990) ("The rationale for this new tort is that a potential civil action is deemed an interest worthy of protection from undue interference.") (citation omitted).

32. *See, e.g., Oliver,* 991 P.2d 11; *Hannah,* 584 S.E.2d 560.

33. *Gribben,* 824 N.E.2d 349; *Hannah,* 584 S.E.2d 560, 567 n.8 (noting that more than 26 jurisdictions have addressed the issue) (citing *Too Many Cooks, supra* note 29); Lucas v. Christiana Skating Ctr., Ltd., 722 A.2d 1247, 1248 (Del. Super. 1998).

34. *Too Many Cooks, supra* note 29, at 438.

35. *Smith,* 198 Cal. Rptr. at 835.

36. *See* Miller v. Montgomery County, 494 A.2d 761, 768 (Md. Ct. Spec. App. 1985) (asserting spoliation inference represents a satisfactory remedy). One commentator has explained that "courts are reluctant to award damages that are purely speculative, as spoliation damages almost always are. The jury faces the paradox of having to measure the impact of evidence it has never seen." RICHARD J. HEAFEY &

In *Federated Mutual Insurance Company v. Litchfield Precision Components, Inc.,*[37] the Minnesota Supreme Court examined the is-

---

DON M. KENNEDY, PRODUCT LIABILITY & WINNING STRATEGIES AND TECHNIQUES, § 11.06 (1996). However, in those "rare circumstances where the ability to pursue civil litigation has been effectively nullified by the alleged spoliation of evidence, courts have been willing to recognize the tort. . . ." Medical Billing, Inc. v. Medical Mgt. Sciences, Inc., No. 1:96CV1015, slip op. (N.D. Ohio Oct. 16, 1996) at 9 (noting that the spoliation tort has not been "widely embraced").

For a lively dissent from a decision holding that plaintiff stated a claim for negligent spoliation, see *County of Solano v. Delancy*, 264 Cal. Rptr. 721, 731-37 (Cal. Ct. App. 1989) (Anderson, J., dissenting), *opinion withdrawn*, No. S013565, 1990 Cal. LEXIS 488 (Feb. 1, 1990).

Those critical of the spoliation tort may wish to consider the remarks of one commentator who points out that the practical effect of the tort may do less to expand the available remedies than first appears:

> Even in those jurisdictions that recognize the tort, its incremental practical effect may be more modest than first appears. Consider, for example, the central case of intentional spoliation by a party opponent. At first glance, the tort seems greatly to expand the set of remedies and sanctions by offering monetary compensation—beyond fee reimbursement—to the victim of the spoliation. But in a sense the set of procedural and evidentiary remedies for foul play do already compensate the victim, albeit in a procedural and evidentiary currency. Such remedies include, for example, taking certain facts as given or allowing an adverse inference instruction. These remedies translate into monetary awards by increasing the chance of a favorable verdict in the underlying case or increasing the level of damages awarded. In principle, then, the spoliation tort, which compensates for expected favorable verdicts foregone, covers the same injury as procedural and evidentiary remedies. It would seem, therefore, that the curative effects of procedural and evidentiary remedies would have to be subtracted in calculating spoliation tort damages. Possibly, in the spirit of the contractual duty to mitigate, or the tort doctrine of avoidable consequences, attempting to secure pre-verdict remedies would be a prerequisite for later recovery. Thus, the incremental effect of the spoliation tort must lie in the narrow intersection between those injuries that procedural and evidentiary sanctions could not cure, and those injuries that are nonetheless concrete enough to be compensable in tort.

Chris William Sanchirico, *Evidence Tampering*, 53 DUKE L. J. 1215, 1282 (2004) (internal citations omitted).

37. 456 N.W.2d 434 (Minn. 1990). *See also* Met Life Auto & Home Co. v. Joe Basil Chevrolet, Inc., 809 N.E.2d 865 (N.Y. 2004) (identifying the difficulty of assessing damages as among its reasons for declining to recognize the tort).

sue of whether the uncertainty of damages precluded recognition of the tort. The court noted that "mere negligence 'in the air' is not a tort and does not become actionable until the force of the wrongful conduct impinges on a person."[38] The court further explained:

> Speculation is a prime concern in the context of a spoliation claim because it is impossible to know what the destroyed evidence would have shown. It would seem to be pure guess-work, even presuming that the evidence went against the spo-liator, to calculate what it would have contributed to the plaintiff's success on the merits of the underlying lawsuit. Given the plaintiff has lost the lawsuit without the spoliated evidence, it does not follow that he would have won it with the evidence.[39]

Courts have expressed other concerns as well with the spoliation tort, including concerns about "rank speculation" regarding whether a plaintiff could have recovered in the primary action and, "if so, the speculative nature of the damages."[40] Courts have also raised con-cerns about the scope of the new duty that would be created and about intruding on the property rights of individuals who lawfully dispose of their property.[41]

Another concern of courts is that recognition of a new tort could lead to generation of endless litigation.[42] As one commentator noted:

> Much of this concern stems from what courts refer to as "de-rivative tort" actions, or those premised on the idea that the conclusion of one lawsuit [permits the filing of another]. De-rivative tort actions are perceived as a threat to the finality of

---

38. 456 N.W.2d at 437.

39. *Id.* (internal citation omitted).

40. 456 N.W.2d 434.

41. *Koplin*, 734 P.2d at 1183. *See also* Bush v. Thomas, 888 P.2d 936, 939 (N.M. Ct. App. 1994); Trevino v. Ortega, 969 S.W.2d 950 (Tex. 1998); Temple Comm. Hosp. v. Superior Court, 976 P.2d 223, 233 (Cal. 1999).

42. *Trevino*, 969 S.W.2d 950; *Temple Comm. Hosp.*, 976 P.2d at 233; *Meyn*, 594 N.W.2d 31; Timber Tech Engineered Bldg. Prods. v. Home Ins. Co., 55 P.3d 952 (Nev. 2002); Dowdle Butane Gas Co. v. Moore, 831 So. 2d 1124 (Miss. 2002); *Gribben*, 824 N.E.2d 349.

judgments, and the limited resources of the court system strongly favor an end to litigation.[43]

Courts also have voiced concerns about imposing additional duties upon litigants as a result of this new tort. As one court explained, tort liability for spoliation "involves the recognition of a duty on the part of the owner or custodian of the evidence to preserve it for the use of the plaintiff, which would outweigh the owner or custodian's general right to use, modify, or destroy his own property as he chooses."[44] Moreover, there may be good reasons—for example, safety concerns—to destroy what might be regarded as potential evidence that is relevant to litigation.[45]

THE TORT OF INTENTIONAL SPOLIATION OF EVIDENCE

Although no uniform body of case law has developed regarding the precise contours of this tort,[46] most states that have adopted the tort agree that the elements of intentional spoliation consist of:

(1) pending or probable litigation involving the plaintiff, (2) knowledge on the part of defendant that litigation exists or is probable, (3) willful destruction of evidence by defendant designed to disrupt the plaintiff's case, (4) disruption of the

---

43. *Too Many Cooks*, *supra* note 29, at 445 (citing Cedars-Sinai Med. Ctr. v. Superior Court, 954 P.2d 511 (Cal. 1998)).

44. Ortega v. Trevino, 938 S.W.2d 219, 222 (Tex. App. 1997), *reversed*, Trevino v. Ortega, 969 S.W.2d 950 (Texas 1998). *See also Met Life Auto & Home Co.*, 809 N.E.2d 865.

45. Foster v. Lawrence Mem'l Hosp., 809 F. Supp. 831, 837 (D. Kan. 1992) ("destruction of the property may be reasonable under the facts of a specific case, *i.e.,* destroying property for safety reasons"); Coley v. Arnot Ogden Mem'l Hosp., 107 A.D.2d 67, 69-70 (N.Y. App. Div. 1985) (observing that a defective ladder had been destroyed so that others would not be injured by using it again).

46. *See* Edwards v. Louisville Ladder Co., 796 F. Supp. 966, 968 (W.D. La. 1992) (finding that "no general consensus has developed as to the basis, essential elements, or even existence of such a tort") (citations omitted); *Coleman*, 905 P.2d at 188 ("In general . . . the tort of spoliation of evidence has not been widely adopted . . . nor has much agreement emerged on its contours and limitations.").

plaintiff's case, and (5) damages proximately caused by the defendant's acts. . . .[47]

Although there has been general agreement on the first two elements of the tort, the last three elements have been somewhat problematic for courts and will be discussed below.

THE TORT OF NEGLIGENT SPOLIATION OF EVIDENCE

The tort of negligent spoliation generally requires:

(1) existence of a potential civil action; (2) a legal or contractual duty to preserve evidence which is relevant to the potential civil action; (3) destruction of that evidence; (4) significant impairment in the ability to prove the lawsuit; (5) a causal relationship between the evidence destruction and the inability to prove the lawsuit; and (6) damages.[48]

Only Alabama, Montana, Indiana, some Pennsylvania courts and the District of Columbia presently recognize this tort.[49] As with intentional spoliation of evidence, a number of courts have refused to recognize the tort, on various grounds, including the availability of adequate remedies under a state's existing law.[50]

---

47. *Smith,* 615 N.E.2d at 1038. The Ohio Supreme Court's decision in *Smith* offers limited guidance for the application of these elements. The *Smith* court did not apply these elements to the facts of the case, it simply responded to a question that had been certified from an Ohio federal district court posed in the abstract. *See, e.g., Hannah,* 584 S.E.2d 560; *Coleman,* 905 P.2d 185; *Oliver,* 993 P.2d 11.

48. *Holmes,* 710 A.2d 846.

49. *Elias,* 710 A.2d 65 (suggesting parties may recover for spoliation under traditional negligence principles); Pirocchi v. Liberty Mut. Ins. Co., 365 F. Supp. 277, 281 (E.D. Pa. 1973) (finding a Pennsylvania court would likely recognize such a tort); *but see* Olson v. Grutza, 631 A.2d 191, 195 (Pa. Super. Ct. 1993) (declining to determine whether spoliation is a viable tort in Pennsylvania).

For a list of jurisdictions that decline to recognize the spoliation tort, see *Gribben,* 824 N.E.2d 349; *Hannah,* 584 S.E.2d 560; Willard v. Caterpillar, Inc., 48 Cal. Rptr. 2d 607, 618 (Cal. Ct. App. 1995); *Federated Mut. Ins. Co.,* 456 N.W.2d at 437; *Coleman,* 905 P.2d at 189.

50. *See Atkinson,* 771 So. 2d 429; *Oliver,* 993 P.2d 11.

Once again, California led the way in recognizing this cause of action. In *Velasco v. Community Building Maintenance Company*,[51] the plaintiff sustained injuries when a bottle exploded.[52] The plaintiff's attorney placed the bottle's remains in a paper bag and left it on his desk. Subsequently, a janitor discarded the bag while cleaning the desk. In determining whether to recognize a cause of action for negligent spoliation, the *Velasco* court examined the following factors:

> (1) the extent to which the transaction was intended to affect the plaintiff; (2) the foreseeability of harm to the plaintiff; (3) the degree of certainty that the plaintiff suffered injury; (4) the closeness of the connection between the defendant's conduct and the injury suffered; (5) the moral blame attached to the defendant's conduct; and (6) the policy of preventing future harm.[53]

Applying these factors, the *Velasco* court found that the janitor could not reasonably have foreseen that in throwing away the bottle remains, he was destroying valuable evidence. Thus, the court dismissed the action, finding that the janitor's actions were reasonable.[54]

Some courts that have addressed the issue have declined to recognize a cause of action for negligent spoliation, instead preferring to treat such claims under existing tort law. For example, in *Boyd v. Travelers Insurance Company*,[55] the court held that "an action for negligent spoliation can be stated under existing negligence law without creating a new tort."[56] Other courts have suggested that a cause of action for intentional or negligent interference with prospective business advantage,[57] or an action for intentional interference with a prospective civil action,[58] may offer an adequate remedy.

---

51. 215 Cal. Rptr. 504, 506 (Cal. Ct. App. 1985).

52. *Id.*

53. *Id.* at 506 (quoting J'Aire Corp. v. Gregory, 598 P.2d 60 (Cal. 1979)).

54. *Id.* at 507.

55. 652 N.E.2d 267 (Ill. 1995).

56. *Id.* at 270 (citation omitted). *Accord Federated Mut. Ins. Co.*, 456 N.W.2d at 436; *Hirsch*, 628 A.2d at 1119; *Elias*, 710 A.2d at 67. *Compare Atkinson*, 771 So. 2d 429 (changing the burden of proof for ordinary negligence and creating a rebuttable presumption in cases of spoliation).

57. *See, e.g., Federated Mut. Ins. Co.*, 456 N.W.2d at 439.

58. *Yoakum*, 923 P.2d 416; *Ricketts*, 51 P.3d 392.

PROBLEMATIC ELEMENTS OF THE SPOLIATION TORT

Willful Destruction Designed to Disrupt Plaintiff's Case

One issue addressed by courts is the type of intent required for an actionable intentional tort. In *Torres v. El Paso Electric Company*,[59] the court considered this issue, analogizing spoliation to the so-called *prima facie* tort. The *Torres* court concluded that a mere intent to do the act, that is, to destroy evidence, was insufficient. Rather, to be actionable, a despoiling party has to destroy evidence with "a level of culpability that is particularly egregious in civil actions: a malicious intent to harm."[60]

Analogizing to the tort of intentional interference with prospective business relations, the *Torres* court reasoned that intent to disrupt or defeat the opposing party's lawsuit must be the sole motivation for destruction of evidence to satisfy the prerequisites for an intentional tort.[61] The court also noted that even if the spoliator's actions did not manifest the requisite malicious conduct, a non-spoliating party still might be entitled to an adverse inference instruction.

Other courts have held that the required intent "contemplates not only an intentional commission of the act, but also a wrongful commission of the act."[62] These courts look at willful or purposeful conduct designed to disrupt or deter litigation.[63]

---

59. 987 P.2d 386 (N.M. 1999).

60. *Id.*

61. *Id.*

62. Owca v. Federal Ins. Co., 02-3981, 2004 U.S. App. LEXIS 1369 (6th Cir. Jan. 27, 2004) (quoting Drawl v. Cornicelli, 706 N.E.2d 849, 852 (Ohio Ct. App. 1997)).

63. Boggs v. Scotts Co., 04AP-425, 2005 Ohio App. LEXIS 1238 (Ohio Ct. App. Mar. 22, 2005) (observing that because employee negligently destroyed records before she knew about a lawsuit and because Ohio does not recognize negligent spoliation, the plaintiff-employee failed to show deliberate destruction of documents designed to disrupt pending or probable litigation). *Compare* Bugg v. Am. Standard, Inc., No. 84829, 2005 Ohio App. LEXIS 2485 (Ohio Ct. App. 2005) (finding no factual allegations that any insurer defendant "destroyed" or altered any relevant documents as a means to disrupt the present litigation where insurer defendants had destroyed or discarded documents in other litigation).

Disruption of Plaintiff's Case

Another issue that has been addressed by courts applying the elements of a spoliation claim is whether a party's case has been "disrupted." Considering whether a doctor could maintain a claim against a hospital for spoliation arising out of its alteration of evidence, a district court illustrated the type of evidence that may establish the "disruption" element.[64] The court explained that to establish this element, the doctor must show that the hospital willfully altered the evidence, which "contemplates not only an intentional commission of the act, but also a wrongful commission of the act."[65]

To support his spoliation claim, the doctor introduced evidence that the hospital altered his privilege application, which had been in the sole possession of the hospital, by showing that thecheck mark for the box indicating he was applying for certain privileges was completed in a different-colored ink, and the hospital did not dispute that the application had been altered. The doctor also pointed out that the hospital had reason to alter the application because it could then make it appear he had the qualifications to administer sedation so that liability in the underlying action could be shifted to him. The district court held a reasonable jury could conclude that the hospital had willfully altered the application to disrupt the underlying medical malpractice action.[66]

Two decisions illustrate the analysis that Ohio courts employ in determining whether a party's case has been "disrupted." First, in *Sheets v. Norfolk Southern Corporation*,[67] plaintiffs sued a railroad for wrongful death arising out of a train accident. Plaintiffs also brought a claim for spoliation of evidence because the railroad had destroyed the train's "black box," a device that recorded communications between the train and the dispatcher. At trial, a railroad employee testified that the railroad routinely pulled and preserved the "black box" following an accident, but offered no explanation as to why the railroad did not produce the evidence at trial.[68] Affirming

---

64. Hicks v. Bryan Med. Group, Inc., 287 F. Supp. 2d 795 (N.D. Ohio 2003).
65. *Id.* (quoting *Drawl*, 706 N.E.2d at 851).
66. *Id.*
67. 671 N.E.2d 1364 (Ohio Ct. App. 1996).
68. *See id.* at 1368.

the denial of the railroad's motions for summary judgment and directed verdict on the spoliation claim, the *Sheets* court explained that the device was the only record of communication between the train crew and the dispatcher.[69] The court held the plaintiffs had satisfied their burden of establishing a *prima facie* case of spoliation because the absence of the device disrupted their case.[70]

In another case, *Tittle v. Rent-A-Wreck*,[71] the plaintiff lost control of a rental car and struck a bridge. He then sued the car rental agency for negligence and spoliation of evidence because parts from the car were missing when the plaintiff's expert examined it. The court of appeals found that because the plaintiff's expert asserted that the missing parts were integral to determining whether the vehicle had a defect, a fact finder could determine that the defendant's spoliation of the evidence disrupted the plaintiff's case, resulting in damages.[72]

Disruption of a party's case is a critical element of the intentional spoliation tort. One district court characterized the required showing as having a common thread, explaining that in cases where a party has proceeded on a spoliation theory, "a common thread exist[ed]—by loss of the evidence that was allegedly destroyed, [the party's case was] rendered virtually speculative."[73] In those cases, destruction or loss of evidence left a plaintiff without "the direct evidence necessary to establish [its] liability claims . . . or from which an opinion regarding defects or causation could be rendered. . . ."[74]

Damages Proximately Caused by Spoliation
Causation

The purpose of an independent cause of action for destruction of evidence "lies in the inability of the plaintiff to prove proximate causation to the proper degree of certainty required in the underlying

---

69. *See id.*

70. *See id.*

71. No. 92B51, 1993 Ohio LEXIS 4563 (Ohio Ct. App. Sept. 24, 1993).

72. *See id.* at *4.

73. *Medical Billing*, No. 1:96CV1015, at *9.

74. *Id. Compare Hazen*, 718 P.2d at 463 (finding no evidence to support or refute the parties' competing versions of the events at issue) *with Hannah*, 584 S.E.2d 560 (holding "it must be shown that the evidence was destroyed with the specific intent to defeat a pending or potential lawsuit").

lawsuit."[75] Discussing proximate cause in the context of a spoliation tort, one court found that although proximate cause generally requires a "reasonable causal connection between the conduct and the resulting injury," such a standard does not protect the interests of a plaintiff in a third-party spoliation claim.[76]

In *Holmes v. Amerex Rent-a-Car*,[77] the court identified three approaches taken by different jurisdictions with regard to proximate cause in spoliation cases. First, the *Holmes* court agreed with an Illinois appellate court, which decided it would place too heavy a burden on a plaintiff to show that it would have won the underlying case with the missing evidence. The *Holmes* court considered such a showing nearly impossible, since a fact finder cannot evaluate evidence it cannot see.[78] In addition, it would be "an inequity" to prevent a plaintiff from recovering because of its inability, allegedly caused by the defendant, to prove the underlying claim.[79] Therefore, the *Holmes* court held that a plaintiff should not be required to make a showing of causation by a preponderance of the evidence, since such a standard would be both impractical and inequitable for this tort.[80]

On the other hand, a defendant should not be required to pay damages to a plaintiff in the complete absence of proof of causation, such as where a plaintiff had only a frivolous underlying lawsuit. Therefore, a plaintiff must make some threshold showing of causation and damage.[81] As the *Holmes* court explained:

> [t]his adds a unique characteristic to the tort. Not only must the plaintiff show that an expectancy of recovery was harmed, but also that such an expectancy realistically existed. Specifically, proximate cause must include two showings. First, it must be shown that the defendant's actions proximately caused some level of impairment to the plaintiff's ability to

---

75. *Holmes*, 710 A.2d 846.
76. *Id.*
77. 710 A.2d 846.
78. *Id.*; *see also* Petrick v. Monarch Printing, 501 N.E.2d 1312, 1322 (Ill. App. Ct. 1986).
79. 710 A.2d 846.
80. *Id.*
81. *Id.*

prove an existing underlying civil claim. Second, in order to show that the defendant's actions proximately caused any damages, it must be shown that the plaintiff's underlying claim was, at some threshold level, meritorious.[82]

The *Holmes* court contrasted this approach to proximate causation with the approach taken by Ohio courts, observing that under the Ohio rule, a plaintiff must generally attempt and lose the underlying lawsuit to demonstrate that its claim has been precluded by the destruction of evidence at issue.[83] Therefore, under this approach, a plaintiff's expectancy must be eliminated to make a threshold showing of causation.[84] The second prong of this approach to proximate cause requires a spoliation plaintiff to show it was more probable than not that the plaintiff would have succeeded on the underlying claim.[85] That is, "plaintiff's burden is to present evidence from which it reasonably could infer that it is more probable" than not that the underlying lawsuit would have been successful.[86] The plaintiff must also show that the defendant's destruction of that particular evidence had an impact on the merits of the underlying case.[87] Accordingly, there must be some proximate relationship between the failure to succeed in the underlying action and the unavailability of the spoiled evidence.

"[S]peculation based on possibilities is too tender a reed upon which to base a claim for relief."[88] Thus, explained the *Holmes* court, this approach sets a high standard for protecting the interest of a defendant by requiring a plaintiff to show a causal link between the

---

82. *Id.*

83. *Id.*; *see* Tomas v. Nationwide Mut. Ins. Co., 607 N.E.2d 944, 947-48 (Ohio App. 1992); *compare Petrick*, 501 N.E.2d at 1317 (observing "a spoliation claim could not be brought until after the underlying lawsuit was lost").

84. 710 A.2d 846. In Davis v. Wal-Mart Stores, Inc., 756 N.E.2d 657, 660 (Ohio 2001), the Ohio Supreme Court held that a separate, subsequent claim for the spoliation of evidence may be allowed "only when evidence of spoliation is not discovered until after the conclusion of the primary action." That decision does not appear to alter the manner in which Ohio courts treat the causation element because a litigant may bring both claims in the same lawsuit).

85. *Tomas*, 607 N.E.2d at 948.

86. *Id.*

87. 710 A.2d 846.

88. *Id.* (quoting *Tomas*, 607 N.E.2d at 949-50).

destroyed evidence and the impairment or preclusion of the underlying claim.[89]

Still another approach to causation was the one taken by the California and Florida courts that addressed this issue when those states
recognized the spoliation tort.[90] The California approach required
that a plaintiff show "a reasonable probability" it would have successfully litigated the underlying case with access to the spoiled evidence.[91] But California courts have no clear requirement that plaintiffs
establish that the destruction of evidence impaired their ability to
succeed in the underlying lawsuit.[92]

In contrast, Florida courts did not require a plaintiff to demonstrate that its underlying suit had some degree of merit. Rather, Florida
required a plaintiff to show "a significant impairment" in its ability
to successfully prosecute the underlying case.[93] Thus, the Florida
approach focused on the first prong of causation, that the underlying
claim be impaired by the spoliation, to the exclusion of the second
prong, that the underlying claim was meritorious.[94]

The *Holmes* court found each of these separate approaches inadequate, but "[t]aken together, . . . they create an effective approach
to the tort."[95] In crafting its own standard for proximate cause, the
court modified the "reasonable probability" standard from the California court's terminology because it found this standard came too
close to requiring a plaintiff to show causation by a preponderance
of the evidence. Rather, the *Holmes* court required the plaintiff to

---

89. *Id.*

90. California courts had this proximate cause requirement until the California Supreme Court declined to recognize the tort of spoliation in *Cedar Sinai,
infra,* and *Temple Hospital, infra.* Some Florida appellate courts had recognized
the spoliation tort until the Florida Supreme Court refused to recognize that tort
in *Martino v. Wal-Mart Stores, Inc., infra.*

91. *Smith,* 198 Cal. Rptr. at 835-36.

92. 710 A.2d 846.

93. *Id. See also* Strasser v. Yalamanchi, 783 So. 2d 1087 (Fla. Ct. App. 2001)
(affirming judgment for claimant on both breach of contract and spoliation claims
because "Florida law does not require that it be impossible for a party to prove its
case in order to recover damages on a spoliation claim. A party significantly
impaired by the destruction of evidence may still be able to prevail in an action
for breach of contract on the basis of existing evidence, albeit to a lesser extent
and for reduced damages.").

94. 710 A.2d 846.

95. *Id.*

show that the underlying lawsuit "enjoyed a significant probability of success."[96] Accordingly, in the District of Columbia, a plaintiff must show a substantial and realistic possibility of success on the merits of the underlying claim. The District of Columbia also requires a plaintiff to show a "nexus between the spoliated evidence and the impairment of the underlying lawsuit."[97]

Damages

Among the reasons many courts have declined to adopt the tort of spoliation is the speculative nature of damages.[98] Calculation of damages is the most difficult aspect of a spoliation of evidence claim because the tort "does not allow for standard calculations of damages to the proper degree of certainty."[99] One court observed that a plaintiff must generally establish both the fact of damages and the amount with reasonable certainty. However, where the tort itself precludes determination of the amount of damages with certainty, it would pervert fundamental notions of justice to deny relief to an injured person, thereby relieving the wrongdoer from making amends for his act.[100]

Courts have taken a number of approaches to consider damages for a claim of spoliation. The court in *Holmes v. Amerex Rent-A-Car* discussed several possible ways in which it could measure damages. Among the possibilities considered were: (1) awarding the plaintiff the entire amount of damages that it would have received had the original lawsuit been pursued successfully; (2) awarding the plaintiff costs and fees incurred in pursuit of the original lawsuit; and (3)

---

96. *Id.*

97. 710 A.2d 846. *Compare* Brown v. City of Delray Beach, 652 So. 2d 1150 (Fla. Ct. App. 1995) (holding that a party seeking to prove a negligent destruction of evidence claim need not prove it would have succeeded, but only need establish that the destruction of evidence "cost him an opportunity to prove his lawsuit").

98. *See* 710 A.2d 846. *See also Koplin*, 734 P.2d at 1183; *Bush*, 888 P.2d at 939; *Trevino*, 969 S.W.2d 950; *Temple Comm. Hosp.*, 976 P.2d at 233.

99. 710 A.2d 852.

100. Story Parchment Co. v. Paterson Parchment Paper Co., 282 U.S. 555, 563, 51 S. Ct. 248 (1931).

attempting a balance of interests in light of the uncertainties of proof relevant to this tort.

After analyzing the strengths and weaknesses of each of these approaches to damages, the *Holmes* court decided to adopt the method suggested by the Illinois court in *Petrik v. Monarch Printing Corporation*[101] and held that

> in an action for negligent or reckless spoliation of evidence, damages arrived at through just and reasonable estimation based on relevant data should be multiplied by the probability that the plaintiff would have won the underlying suit had the spoliated evidence been available.[102]

However, if the spoliator acted "willfully or wantonly in the destruction of evidence, then punitive damages can be levied against the spoliator in an amount adequate to punish the spoliator . . . and to deter others. . . ."[103]

In a decision discussing the appropriate measure of damage for spoliation, the West Virginia Supreme Court explained that determining damages in a spoliation claim is "generally considered to be a task fraught with uncertainty and speculation." In fact, one of the principle reasons for not recognizing the tort in the first instance "'is the inherent difficulty of proving the fact of injury in a spoliation suit.'" The *Hannah* court addressed the problem of damages, guided by "'the general rule in awarding damages [which] is to give compensation for pecuniary loss; that is, to put the plaintiff in the same position, so far as money can do it, as he would have been if . . . the tort [had] not [been] committed.'" The court adopted the approach used by the Alabama court in *Smith* [*v. Atkinson*],[104] where the court explained:

> under the [rebuttable presumption] approach we adopt today, the risk of a windfall to the plaintiff has been minimized.

101. 501 N.E.2d 1312 (Ill. App. Ct. 1986).

102. 710 A.2d 846. For an example of how to determine the amount of a plaintiff's damages based on this "formula," see *id*. *See also Atkinson*, 771 So. 2d 479; *Oliver*, 993 P.2d 11.

103. *Id*.

104. *Hannah*, 584 S.E.2d at 571 (citing *Atkinson*, 771 So. 2d 490).

We decline to gauge damages on the plaintiff's probability of success on the merits. We conclude that without the spoliated evidence, the plaintiff's probability of success is too tenuous a measure to be consistently applied and that any attempt to apply it would constitute pure speculation. Therefore, in determining damages, we reject the use of probability of success as a benchmark, in favor of the use of compensatory damages that would have been awarded on the underlying cause of action, if the defendant cannot overcome the rebuttable presumption.[105]

UNAVAILABILITY OF TORT CLAIM TO DEFENDANTS

Generally, a defendant cannot avail itself of a claim for intentional spoliation because the defendant cannot establish that it lost a potential cause of action as a result of spoliation by the plaintiff or a third party. For example, in *Hewitt v. Allen Canning Company*,[106] the plaintiff filed a lawsuit claiming he became ill as a result of consuming a grasshopper contained in a can of spinach. While the can of spinach was in the possession of the plaintiff's law firm, it was discarded. The defendants sought to file a third-party complaint against the law firm based on spoliation of evidence. The trial court denied the motion and the defendants appealed. The court of appeals affirmed, reasoning:

> Both the spoliation and concealment torts are designed to remediate tortious interference with a prospective economic advantage. . . . The prospective economic advantage being protected is a plaintiff's opportunity to bring a cause of action for which damages may be awarded.

In such cases, the plaintiff's remedy is money damages. The spoliation and concealment tort remedy of money damages is inapplicable, however, where the destruction of evidence, or its concealment, occurs in the context of a defendant's ability to defend against a

---

105. *Id.* (quoting *Atkinson*, 771 So. 2d 479) (internal citations omitted).
106. 728 A.2d 319 (N.J. Super. Ct. Law Div. 1999).

plaintiff's cause of action. In such cases, "the rules of court provide more than sufficient remedy."[107]

Even though damages are not ordinarily available to a defendant prejudiced by spoliation, when a third party deprives a defendant of the ability to defend an action brought by a plaintiff because the third party destroyed evidence it had a duty to retain, then a defendant may have an action for money damages against the third-party spoliator.[108] Of course, such an action is available only in those states where the courts have recognized a claim for third-party spoliation.

WHEN AND WHERE SPOLIATION CLAIMS SHOULD BE BROUGHT

Another important issue that arises in this area is whether a spoliation claim should be tried with the underlying claim or in a separate trial. Courts generally hold that for various reasons, a single trial is preferable. As one court explained:

> Spoliation, at least spoliation that is discovered prior to trial, should be tried in conjunction with the underlying claim rather than in a bifurcated or separate trial. A single trier of fact would be in the best position to resolve all the claims fairly and consistently. If a plaintiff loses the underlying suit, only the trier of fact who heard the case would know the real reason why.[109]

When a party is aware that evidence has been destroyed, some courts have suggested that spoliation claims must be raised during pending litigation or the doctrine of *res judicata* can be raised to

---

107. *Id.* at 321-22 (internal citation omitted). *See also* Restaurant Mgt. Co. v. Kidde-Fenwal, Inc., No. 19, 137, 1999 N.M. App. LEXIS 71, at *18 (N.M. Ct. App. June 24, 1999) (same). *See* Christopher B. Major, *Where's the Evidence? Dealing With Spoliation by Plaintiffs in Product Liability Cases,* 53 S.C. L. Rᴇᴠ. 415 (Winter 2002) ("[N]o jurisdiction has made an independent tort cause of action available to defendants.").

108. *See* Kolanovic v. Pak Gida A/S (Turkey), 77 F. Supp. 2d 595 (D.N.J. 1999).

109. *Boyd*, 652 N.E.2d 267; William v. General Motors Corp., No. 93C6661, 1996 U.S. Dist. LEXIS 10555 (N.D. Ill. July 25, 1996) (action for negligent spoliation should be tried concurrently with underlying suit).

defeat a later claim. For example, in *Williamson v. Rodenberg*,[110] an employee filed an age discrimination lawsuit against her employer based on her termination during a company restructuring. Before trial, the employee learned of allegations that the employer had instructed the hiring managers to destroy interview notes, but she did not seek leave to amend her complaint to add a claim for spoliation. The jury returned a verdict for the defendants.[111]

Subsequently, the employee filed a new complaint for spoliation of evidence. The employer argued that the doctrine of *res judicata* barred the second lawsuit. The employee claimed that *res judicata* did not apply because, among other things, the spoliation issue was not actually litigated in the first lawsuit.[112]

The court of appeals affirmed the trial court's grant of summary judgment to the employer, noting, under applicable state law, a "valid, final judgment rendered upon the merits bars all subsequent actions based upon any claim arising out of the transaction or occurrence that was the subject matter of the previous action."[113] Because the plaintiff learned of the alleged spoliation before trial, and because such a claim "shares the same nucleus of facts as the common age discrimination case," *res judicata* barred the spoliation claim.[114]

In *Davis v. Wal-Mart Stores, Inc.*,[115] the Ohio Supreme Court rejected a supermarket's claim that *res judicata* precluded an action for spoliation because the plaintiff did not discover the evidence of spoliation until after the primary action, an intentional tort, had been concluded. Finding sufficient evidence that the primary action and the alleged spoliation claim did not arise out of a "common nucleus of operative facts," the court rejected the supermarket's *res judicata*

---

110. No. 96APE10-1395, 1997 Ohio App. LEXIS 2855 (Ohio Ct. App. June 30, 1997).

111. *Id.* at *2-4.

112. *Id.* at *7-9.

113. *Id.* at *6 (quoting Grava v. Parkman Twp., 653 N.E.2d 226, syllabus (Ohio 1995)).

114. *Id.* at *10-11. *But see* Rodgers v. St. Mary's Hosp. of Decatur, 556 N.E.2d 913 (Ill. Ct. App. 1990) (spoliation claim not barred by earlier judgment on negligence claim; because elements of negligence against hospital in treating plaintiff's decedent are not crucial element of claim against hospital for losing evidence, two actions are not "based on a common core of operative facts").

115. 756 N.E.2d 657 (Ohio 2001).

defense. The court also held that "claims for spoliation of evidence may be brought after the primary action has been concluded *only* when evidence of spoliation is not discovered until after the conclusion of the primary action."[116]

Still, other courts have held that tort claims for spoliation are premature until a party actually loses in the underlying action.[117] Of course, where the parties to the underlying claim are different from those to the spoliation claim, as in the case of third-party spoliation, it will be impossible to resolve all issues in a single trial.

RECENT DEVELOPMENTS

Since 1998, a number of jurisdictions have declined to recognize an independent tort claim for spoliation of evidence. For example, in *Trevino v. Ortega*,[118] the Supreme Court of Texas refused to recognize this type of claim. The court determined that although more than 20 states have considered whether to adopt the spoliation tort, only six have adopted the tort of either negligent or intentional spoliation. The court explained:

While the law must adjust to meet society's changing needs, we must balance that adjustment against boundless claims in an already crowded judicial system. We are especially averse to creating a tort that would only lead to duplicative litigation, encouraging inefficient re-litigation of issues, better handled within the context of the core cause of action. We

116. *Id.* (emphasis added)

117. Kent v. Construzione Aeronautiche Giovanni Agusta, S.P.A., No. 90-2233, 1990 U.S. Dist. LEXIS 12583 (E.D. Pa. Sept. 20, 1990) ("Not until there is a disposition with respect to the underlying civil action can it be determined whether the destruction of evidence has prejudiced plaintiff."); *Federated Mut. Ins. Co.*, 456 N.W.2d 434 (finding plaintiff's underlying claim must first be resolved to demonstrate cognizable injury, if Minnesota decided to recognize such a tort); Fox v. Cohen, 406 N.E.2d 178 (Ill. Ct. App. 1980) (cause of action for negligent spoliation of evidence is premature until plaintiff actually loses her medical malpractice action due to lost EKG, as damages are otherwise "purely speculative and uncertain").

118. 969 S.W.2d 950 (Tex. 1998).

thus decline to recognize evidence spoliation as an independent tort.[119]

The court further analogized its refusal to recognize this claim to the refusal by other courts to create separate causes of action for civil perjury and civil embracery.[120]

In a pair of significant decisions, the Supreme Court of California overturned the long-standing position of its lower courts and held that California does not recognize the tort of intentional spoliation either by a party to litigation[121] or by a third party.[122] In effect, these two decisions reversed more than a decade of spoliation law in California. The reasoning of the court in these decisions remains instructive.

In *Cedars-Sinai Medical Center v. The Superior Court of Los Angeles County,*[123] the court rejected a tort remedy for first-party spoliation, reasoning that other adequate remedies existed to both compensate victims of spoliation and deter acts of spoliation. Further, the court found that recognition of the tort would not promote the important principle of finality in litigation and would impose significant burdens on parties and the judicial system.

In *Temple Community Hospital v. The Superior Court of Los Angeles County,*[124] the Supreme Court of California extended its earlier decision to third-party claims for spoliation. Again, the court voiced its concern that to recognize such a tort would inundate the judicial system with claims.[125] The court further reasoned that although "occasional miscarriages of justice" might result from the unavailability of this tort remedy, the absence of finality in litigation would be, on balance, an even worse result.[126]

After these decisions, several state high courts rejected calls to recognize a spoliation tort based on the reasoning in *Cedars-Sinai*

---

119. *Id.* at 951.
120. *Id.* at 953.
121. *Cedars-Sinai,* 954 P.2d 511.
122. *Temple Community,* 976 P.2d 223.
123. 954 P.2d 511 (Cal. 1998).
124. 976 P.2d 223 (Cal. 1999).
125. *Id.* at 233.
126. *Id.* at 229.

Medical Center and *Temple Community.*[127] These decisions, and others decided within the past couple of years,[128] may signal a trend away from adopting spoliation of evidence as a separate tort.[129] It appears that, although spoliation is a significant problem in litigation, the increasing willingness of courts to remedy spoliation through the use of sanctions during pending litigation may moderate against the perceived need for separate tort remedies.[130]

Despite the trend against recognizing the spoliation tort, the Supreme Court of New Mexico reaffirmed its recognition of the spoliation tort in *Torres v. El Paso Electric Company.*[131] There, the court first reviewed the grounds articulated by courts for declining to recognize a cause of action for spoliation, including such factors as the adequacy of alternative remedies, the lack of any remedies for other "litigation-related wrongs such as perjury, and 'procedural' complications, such as jury confusion, duplicative litigation, or arbitrarily inconsistent results."[132] The court went on to recognize that "these considerations, while important, are outweighed by the strong public policy in New Mexico disfavoring unjustifiable, intentional wrongs that cause harm to others."[133]

More recently, in response to two certified questions regarding the viability of independent torts for spoliation, the West Virginia Supreme Court recognized intentional spoliation as an independent tort in both the first- and third-party context in *Hannah v. Heeter.*[134] The court recognized the tort because "intentional spoliation of evidence is misconduct of such a serious nature, [that] the existing remedies are not a sufficient response."[135]

---

127. *Gribben,* 824 N.E.2d 349; *Goff,* 27 S.W.3d 387; *Timber Tech,* 55 P.3d 952.

128. *See, e.g., Meyn,* 594 N.W.2d 31 (declining to adopt tort of negligent spoliation); Sharpnack v. Hoffinger Indus., Inc., 499 S.E.2d 363 (Ga. Ct. App. 1998) (declining to consider whether to adopt tort on facts before it).

129. *But see Hannah,* 584 S.E.2d 560; *Atkinson,* 771 So. 2d 429.

130. *See, e.g.,* Martino v. Wal-Mart Stores, Inc., 908 So. 2d 342 (Fla. 2005).

131. 987 P.2d 386 (N.M. 1999).

132. *Id.* at 402.

133. *Id.*

134. 584 S.W.2d 560.

135. *Id.* Discussing its rationale for recognizing the tort, the *Hannah* court quoted extensively from the *Cedars-Sinai Med. Ctr., supra,* decision.

In contrast to this trend in first-party spoliation cases, at least three post–*Cedars-Sinai* and *Temple Community* decisions have recognized a claim against third parties for spoliation.[136] For instance, the Supreme Court of Alabama declined to recognize a new cause of action for first-party spoliation of evidence. Instead, it recognized a claim against a third party for spoliation of evidence under the traditional doctrine of negligence, but shifted the burden of proof from where it is ordinarily placed in a negligence claim.[137] To prevail on a claim against a third party for negligent spoliation of evidence in Alabama, a plaintiff not only must prove a duty, a breach, proximate cause, and damage, but also must show that:

1. The defendant spoliator had actual knowledge of pending or potential litigation;
2. A duty was imposed upon the defendant through a voluntary undertaking, an agreement, or a specific request; and
3. The missing evidence was vital to the plaintiff's pending or potential action.[138]

Once a plaintiff establishes these three elements, a rebuttable presumption arises that, but for the spoliation of evidence, the plaintiff would have recovered in the pending or potential litigation. To escape liability, a defendant then must overcome that rebuttable presumption.[139]

Likewise, the Montana Supreme Court, in *Oliver v. Stimson Lumber Company*,[140] noted that the various sanctions available to trial court judges are inapplicable when evidence is the possession of third parties. Accordingly, the court recognized the torts of intentional and negligent spoliation of evidence against third parties, but only where such a party has notice that certain evidence should be preserved.[141]

---

136. *Hannah*, 584 S.E.2d 560; *Smith*, 771 So. 2d 429; *Oliver*, 993 P.3d 11. *See also Holmes*, 710 A.2d 846.
137. *Smith*, 771 So. 2d 429.
138. *Id.*
139. *Id.*
140. 991 P.3d 11 (1999).
141. *Id.*

West Virginia also recognized claims for intentional and negligent spoliation by third parties as stand-alone torts after California abandoned those torts. In *Hannah v. Heeter,*[142] the court observed that, unlike a party to litigation, if a third party destroys evidence, it is not subject to sanctions like an adverse inference instruction or discovery sanctions. Therefore, the injured party does not have the benefit of the remedies available to the injured party in an ongoing lawsuit. The *Hannah* court emphasized that the third party must have "actual knowledge of the pending or potential litigation" because constructive knowledge alone is insufficient to impose a duty to preserve evidence.[143]

Practice Tips

Here are some issues to consider with regard to independent tort claims for spoliation:

- If you believe your client has been prejudiced by destruction of evidence, be prepared to argue that the trial court should recognize a claim for spoliation of evidence, unless that cause of action has been rejected by that state's highest court.

- Raise spoliation claims that come to light in pending litigation during the litigation, because a later court may conclude that *res judicata* bars a subsequent claim for spoliation and/or decline to allow a party a "second bite" at making a claim.

- Bear in mind, when situations arise involving spoliation by third parties, there is a recent trend favoring recognition of a cause of action against third-party spoliators.

---

142. 584 S.E.2d 560.
143. *Id.*

- In states where courts have yet to address the issue of an independent tort action for spoliation, consider similar claims, like intentional interference with a prospective civil action or other claims available under the state's existing tort law.

Criminal Sanctions for Spoliation

5

Premised on the notion that nothing concentrates the mind like the prospect of a hanging, Sarbanes-Oxley added strong penalties for corporate wrong-doing . . .[1]

Federal and state laws providing for criminal penalties for the destruction of evidence have long existed.[2] Notwith-

---

1. WALL STREET JOURNAL EUROPE (Aug. 6, 2002).

2. For a discussion of criminal statutes that are potentially applicable to spoliation of evidence, see chapter 7, which identifies, for each state, statutes that may prohibit destruction of evidence. A detailed discussion of sanctions and penalties for spoliation of evidence that occur in the context of federal and state criminal prosecutions is beyond the scope of this book. *See also* Joseph V. DeMarco, *A Funny Thing Happened on the Way to the Courthouse: Mens Rea, Document Destruction, and the Federal Obstruction of Justice Statute,* 67 N.Y.U. L. REV. 570 (1992) (observing "criminal sanctions for the spoliation of evidence in a civil case are flatly inadequate, due to the fact that there are no cases where a party was criminally convicted for the spoliation of evidence in civil litigation"); Note, *Tort Reform: A Call for Florida to Scale Back Its Independent Tort for the Spoliation of Evidence,* 51 FLA. L. REV. 345, 365 (1999) (criminal statutes prohibiting spoliation are "uncommon," often provide only misdemeanor penalties, and serve merely as "mild deterrence"); P. Wilson, *Doctrinal Malfunction—Spoliation and Products Liability Law in Pennsylvania,* 69 TEMP. L. REV. 899, 915-16 (1996) (criminal statutes prohibiting evidence destruction "do little to deter spoliation in the civil context" as "prosecutions for civil spoliation are rare and the burden of proof is high").

standing changes to the legal landscape that resulted from the Enron and Arthur Andersen debacles, "the proposition that destroying documents may have criminal consequences is nothing new."[3] Among the federal statutes that were applicable to the destruction of evidence before Congress enacted the Sarbanes-Oxley Act of 2002[4] are the following:

- 18 U.S.C. § 1503, which prohibits obstruction of justice;
- 18 U.S.C. § 1505, which governs obstruction of agency and congressional proceedings;
- 18 U.S.C. § 1512, which governs witness tampering;[5] and
- 18 U.S.C. § 2071, which criminalizes willful destruction of records filed or deposited with federal courts or public offices, or by one having custody of such records.

In the wake of accounting and corporate fraud scandals, the high-profile collapse of Enron and Worldcom, and a falling stock market, Congress passed the Sarbanes-Oxley Act of 2002 (the Act).[6] The Act makes civil, criminal, and administrative reforms that alter practices in corporate governance and in the securities and accounting industries.[7] In the Act, Congress created new criminal laws and penalties and amended existing federal statutes and penalties criminalizing the destruction of evidence.

For example, Section 802 of the Act creates a new offense, codified at 18 U.S.C. § 1519, which provides:

---

3. Gary G. Grindler & Jason A. Jones, *Please Step Away From the Shredder and the "Delete" Key: §§ 802 and 1102 of the Sarbanes-Oxley Act*, 41 Am. Crim. L. Rev. 67 (Winter 2004).

4. Sarbanes-Oxley Act of 2002, Pub. L. No. 107-204, 116 Stat. 745 (2002).

5. *See* Arthur Andersen, LLP v. United States, 125 S. Ct. at 5 (2005) (reversing conviction of an accounting firm for obstruction of an SEC official investigation based on its directives to firm personnel to destroy or conceal documents). *See also* Bethany McLean & Peter Elkind, *The Smartest Guys in the Room: The Amazing Rise and Scandalous Fall of Enron*, 381-83 (Portfolio 2003) (discussing Arthur Andersen's document shredding, which ended only after it received a subpoena from the SEC).

6. For a summary of the Act's criminal provisions, *see* William S. Duffey, Jr., *Corporate Fraud and Accountability: A Primer on Sarbanes-Oxley Act of 2002*, 54 S.C. L. Rev. 405 (2002).

7. *Recent Legislation: Corporate Law—Congress Passes Corporate and Accounting Fraud Legislation*, 116 Harv. L. Rev. 728 (December 2002).

> Whoever knowingly alters, destroys, mutilates, conceals [or] alters . . . any record, document, or tangible thing with the intent to impede, obstruct, or influence the investigation or proper administration of any matter within the jurisdiction of any department or agency of the United States or any case filed under title 11, or in relation to or contemplation of any such matter or case, shall be fined . . . , imprisoned not more than 20 years, or both.[8]

The amended provisions regarding document destruction in 18 U.S.C. §§ 1512(b), 1519, and 1520 "cast a wider net, reaching persons who shred documents even where a proceeding or investigation does not yet exist."[9]

The Act also amends an existing obstruction of justice offense, 18 U.S.C. § 1512(c), by adding a provision punishing alteration, destruction, mutilation or concealment of records. Unlike 18 U.S.C. § 1519, this amendment only applies to official proceedings and not to acts taken in "contemplation" of such proceedings.[10]

Section 802 also creates another new criminal offense, 18 U.S.C. § 1520(a)(1), which requires accountants to "retain corporate 'audit or review work papers for a period of 5 years . . .'" and makes it a crime to "knowingly and willfully violate § 1520(a)(2) or any rules or regulations promulgated by the Securities and Exchange Commission under § 1520(a)(2) relating to the retention of relevant records."[11]

---

8. Section 802(a) of the Sarbanes-Oxley Act of 2002, 18 U.S.C. § 1519 (2002).

9. Grindler & Jones, *supra* note 3, at 68. *See also* Dana E. Hill, *Anticipatory Obstruction of Justice: Pre-Emptive Document Destruction Under The Sarbanes-Oxley Anti-Shredding Statute,* 18 U.S.C. § 1519, 89 CORNELL L. REV. 1519 (Sept. 2004) (discussing the consequences of anticipatory document shredding under the Sarbanes-Oxley Act). The Supreme Court's decision in *Arthur Andersen* interpreted 18 U.S.C. § 1512(b) before the amendments made by the Sarbanes-Oxley Act. Like the provision in that case, newly enacted 18 U.S.C. § 1519 requires a knowing conduct. Therefore, with regard to anticipatory document destruction, it would appear that the government must show a defendant anticipated a particular official proceeding and chose to shred relevant documents despite that knowledge. *See Arthur Andersen,* 125 S. Ct. 2129.

10. *Recent Legislation: Corporate Law—Congress Passes Corporate and Accounting Fraud Legislation, supra* note 7, at 729 (quoting 18 U.S.C. § 1519 (2002)).

11. *Id.* (citing 18 U.S.C. § 1520(b) (2002)).

As one commentator noted, many of the criminal provisions in the Act "duplicate the conduct and intent terms of existing provisions" of the federal criminal code.[12] For instance, Section 802(a), the new obstruction of justice offense codified at 18 U.S.C. § 1519, is nearly identical to 18 U.S.C. § 1505, which prohibits obstruction in any "pending proceeding."[13] Both acts appear to have the same requisite intent. Section 802(a), 18 U.S.C. § 1519, requires intent to impede, obstruct, or influence, while the intent required in 18 U.S.C. § 1505 is for "the purpose of obstructing justice."[14]

The new obstruction statute also appears to make unlawful only "slightly more types of conduct" than 18 U.S.C. § 1505.[15] Although section 802(a) extends to acts taken in "contemplation of federal investigations, the courts have already defined 'pending proceedings' quite broadly under [18 U.S.C. §] 1505."[16]

Likewise, although the newly enacted 18 U.S.C. § 1520 looks like a "novel offense targeting accountants," it is likely that the proscribed conduct will also fall under pre-Sarbanes-Oxley obstruction of justice statutes.[17] And, given their limited resources, it seems unlikely that prosecutors will use such resources to pursue "negligent or sloppy recordkeeping" absent other criminal conduct that will also fall under preexisting obstruction of justice laws.[18] Therefore, 18 U.S.C. § 1520(b) is more likely to serve as an additional penalty for obstruction of justice by accountants rather than a new federal crime.[19]

In addition to federal criminal laws, a number of states' laws provide criminal sanctions for tampering with or destroying evidence to obstruct justice.[20] However, there is considerable variation from state

---

12. *Id.* (citing 18 U.S.C. § 1505 (2000)).

13. *Id.*

14. *Id.*

15. *Id.*

16. *Id. See also Arthur Andersen,* 125 S. Ct. 2129 (noting that to be a knowingly corrupt persuader, a defendant must at least foresee a particular official proceeding).

17. *Id.*

18. *Id.*

19. *Id.*

20. *See, e.g.,* ALA. CODE § 13A-10-129 (2004); CAL. PENAL CODE § 135 (Mathew Bender 2003); COLO. REV. STAT. § 18-8-610 (2004); MINN. STAT. ANN. § 609.63 (7) (2004); W. VA. CODE § 61-5-27(f) (2005); *see also* S. Katz, *Spoilage of Evidence: Crimes, Sanctions, Inferences, and Torts,* 29 TORTS & INS. L.J. 51 n.17 (1993) (listing state statutes that criminalize destruction of evidence).

to state in the scope of criminal statutes that reach destruction of evidence. A substantial majority of states have statutes that specifically prohibit destruction of evidence, while a minority of states have statutes that prohibit tampering with or destroying evidence generally (that is, an obstruction of justice statute) or do not have any clearly applicable statutes.[21]

Criminal sanctions have been imposed for destruction of evidence in the context of criminal proceedings, such as grand jury proceedings.[22] However, although criminal sanctions theoretically are available as well for destruction or concealment of documents during civil litigation, "there are no reported criminal convictions for evidence destruction in civil litigation."[23]

One reason for the unavailability of criminal sanctions in civil litigation is that criminal sanctions "cannot restore the accuracy of the original fact finding proceeding, nor do they compensate the victim of evidence destruction for its loss in the civil suit."[24] Moreover, "[s]carce prosecutorial resources simply do not permit prosecution of spoliation in private lawsuits."[25] In addition, many state statutes that provide for criminal penalties for spoliation are inapplicable to civil proceedings.[26]

---

21. JAMIE S. GORELICK ET AL., DESTRUCTION OF EVIDENCE 189-94 (1994); *see also* ch. 7, *infra,* identifying criminal statutes by state.

22. *Id.* at 174; *see generally* M. Bester, *A Wreck on the Info-Bahn: Electronic Mail and the Destruction of Evidence,* 6 COMM. L. CONSPECTUS 75, 80-81 (discussing available criminal sanctions for destruction of documents).

23. *Id.* at 198; *see also* L. Solum & S. Marzen, *Truth and Uncertainty: Legal Control of the Destruction of Evidence,* 36 EMORY L.J. 1085, 1087 (1987); Comment, *A Funny Thing Happened on the Way to the Courtroom: Spoliation of Evidence in Illinois,* 32 J. MARSHALL L. REV. 325, 346 (1999) (hereinafter *A Funny Thing*); J. Kinsler & A. MacIver, *Demystifying Spoliation of Evidence,* 34 TORT & INS. L.J. 761, 774 n.92 (1999). *See, e.g.,* Coley v. Arnot Ogden Mem'l Hosp., 485 N.Y.S.2d 876 (3d Dept. 1985) (rejecting an employee's civil claim for destruction of evidence under New York Penal Law § 215.40 because the alleged destruction appeared to be innocent and because "it appears that Penal Law § 215.40 was enacted to protect the courts, our system of justice and society . . . in general rather than to benefit any specific class, and, therefore, plaintiff cannot seek civil redress thereunder").

24. GORELICK, *supra* note 21, at 198; *A Funny Thing, supra* note 23, at 346.

25. *Id. See also* Eric Lent & Melinda Williams, *Obstruction of Justice,* 39 AM. CRIM. L. REV. 865, 873-74 (Spring 2002).

26. *Id.*

More than one court has recognized that criminal penalties may be applied for spoliation of evidence that occurs during civil litigation.[27] For instance, in *United States v. Lundwall*,[28] the U.S. District Court in New York refused to dismiss an indictment against two former officials of an oil company. The indictment charged conspiracy to obstruct justice by destroying documents relevant to a class-action lawsuit against an oil company. The former officials moved to dismiss the case, arguing the obstruction of justice statute, 18 U.S.C. § 1503, had never been used against individuals for destruction or concealment of documents during civil litigation.[29] The court denied the motion, reasoning, "[n]othing in the legislative history [of the statute] demonstrates that its broad language was not intended to cover allegedly 'corrupt' conduct in civil litigation that impedes the due administration of justice."[30]

The court observed that good reasons exist for prosecutors' reluctance to bring criminal charges relating to conduct occurring during civil litigation, one being that "[p]rosecutorial resources would risk quick depletion if abuses in civil proceedings—even the most flagrant ones—were the subject of criminal prosecutions rather than civil remedies."[31] However, "the panoply of tools used to address civil discovery problems such as monetary sanctions, orders of preclusion, or dismissal of claims or defenses might at times be insufficient."[32] Therefore, although civil sanctions may not be adequate in every instance,

---

27. There are few reported decisions imposing criminal sanctions for destruction of documents in civil litigation. Margaret A. Egan, *Spoliators Beware, but Fear Not an Independent Civil Suit*, 24 U. ARK. LITTLE ROCK L. REV. 233 (Fall 2001).

28. 1 F. Supp. 2d 249 (S.D.N.Y 1998). *But see* Rafferty v. Halprin, No. 90 CIV 2751(CSH), 1991 U.S. Dist. LEXIS 10344 (S.D.N.Y. 1991) (holding that in light of the extensive framework of rules and remedies provided for the resolution of civil discovery disputes, it would decline to stretch the definition of obstruction of justice to include the concealment or withholding of discovery documents); Richmark Corp. v. Timber Falling Consultants, 730 F. Supp. 1525, 1532 (D. Or. 1990) (finding that in light of the extensive remedies available in civil disputes, 18 U.S.C. § 1503 should not be extended to spoliation in civil cases). *See also* Sarah Roadcap, *Obstruction of Justice*, 41 AM. CRIM. L. REV. 911 (2004).

29. 1 F. Supp. 2d at 251.

30. *Id.*

31. *Id.* at 254.

32. *Id.* at 255.

the court stated that "[t]he case law demonstrates that [section] 1503 has been repeatedly applied in a wide variety of civil matters."[33]

The *Lundwall* court determined that those circumstances existed in the case of the oil company officials, because they carried out the alleged destruction against the direction of their employer and counsel, who had cautioned them that relevant documents should be preserved.[34] The court concluded that "[u]nder these unusual circumstances, the government's contention that civil remedies are inadequate seems to us to be correct."[35] As *Lundwall* demonstrates, although it is rarely used, prosecutors have the power to prosecute criminal claims for destruction of evidence in a civil matter and will do so under the appropriate circumstances.[36]

In a civil case involving criminal sanctions for destruction of evidence, the Fourth Circuit Court of Appeals reversed a fine for contempt pursuant to its authority under Federal Rule of Civil Procedure 37.[37] There, the district court ordered a manufacturer to produce certain products and threatened to impose criminal contempt sanctions for failure to provide discovery as ordered. Before the court imposed those sanctions, the parties settled the lawsuit. Three years later, the settling homeowners sought to reopen the case, seeking sanctions against the manufacturer for continuing to dispose of the products before and after the settlement. Relying on its inherent authority and its authority under Rule 37, the district court imposed a $300,000 fine on the manufacturer payable to the court and ordered it to pay the homeowners' fees and expenses.[38]

Finding that the "weighty fines" were intended to punish the manufacturer rather than to compensate the homeowners, the court of appeals held that under Rule 37, a fine is essentially a criminal contempt sanction. Vacating the district court's decision, the *Bradley* court explained:

---

33. *Id.* at 253.
34. *Id.*
35. *Id.* The *Lundwall* defendants were ultimately acquitted.
36. *Cf.* Roberts v. United States, 239 F.2d 467, 470 (9th Cir. 1956) (obstruction of justice covers attempted corruption of witness in civil actions in federal court).
37. Bradley v. American Household, Inc., 378 F.3d 373 (4th Cir. 2004).
38. *Id.*

[W]e have previously made clear "that a Rule 37 fine is effectively a criminal contempt sanction, requiring notice and the opportunity to be heard." "Criminal contempt is a crime in the ordinary sense," and "criminal penalties may not be imposed on someone who has not been afforded the protections that the Constitution requires of such criminal proceedings." At a minimum, criminal contempt defendants have the right to receive notice of the criminal nature of the charges, and to be prosecuted by an independent prosecutor, and to have their guilt determined "beyond a reasonable doubt." Perhaps because the district court did not believe it was conducting criminal contempt proceedings, it failed to provide any of these basic procedural protections.[39]

The *Bradley* case teaches that where courts decide to impose criminal sanctions for destruction of evidence in a civil proceeding, even under the authority granted to district courts by Rule 37, basic criminal procedural protections must be afforded to the alleged spoliator.

Practice Tips

When advising clients in the context of civil litigation:

- Consider the enhanced focus by the media, shareholders, and employees on destruction of records and documents caused by the recent rash of corporate scandals and bankruptcies.
- Review the new federal obstruction of justice crimes and increased penalties for preexisting federal obstruction of justice crimes enacted in the Sarbanes-Oxley Act of 2002.
- Keep in mind that in a high-profile case, when the prosecutor has weak evidence, he or she may use the Sarbanes-Oxley Act's increased penalty to secure a plea bargain or leverage the enhanced penalties to secure cooperation from lower-level criminals for the purpose of ob-

---

39. *Id.* (internal citations omitted).

taining tougher sentences against higher-profile defendants.[40]

- Be aware that given the limited resources of prosectors, it
  is unlikely they will waste precious resources pursuing
  "negligent or sloppy recordkeeping."[41]

- Remember that absent extraordinary circumstances, the
  range of civil sanctions available against a person who
  destroys evidentiary material in a civil action gives courts
  little reason to impose criminal sanctions.

---

40. *Recent Legislation: Corporate Law—Congress Passes Corporate and
Accounting Fraud Legislation, supra* note 7, at 729.
   41. *Id.*

Statutory Record-keeping Obligations | 6

There is no good reason to destroy documents during the period when the statutes or regulations require employers to maintain them.[1]

The existence of pending, threatened, or reasonably foreseeable litigation is not the only basis for a duty to preserve evidence. Federal and state laws also can require a party to preserve documents or other types of potential evidence. A failure to retain such records may result in the imposition of an adverse inference or, alternatively, may shift the burden of proof under the applicable law. The rationale for imposing such sanctions is that "[t]here is no good reason to destroy documents during the period when the statutes or regulations require employers to maintain them."[2]

A comprehensive listing of federal and state statutes that impose record-keeping requirements is beyond the scope of this book.[3] For a more detailed treatment of record retention requirements, the reader may wish to consult the publication titled *Guide to Records Retention in the Code*

---

1. GORELICK, J., ET AL., DESTRUCTION OF EVIDENCE (1994 and Supp. 2005).

2. *Id.*

3. For a discussion of the applicability of criminal statutes to civil spoliation, see ch. 5, *supra.*

of Federal Regulations[4] as well as the treatise by Jamie S. Gorelick, et al., titled *Destruction of Evidence.*[5]

By way of illustration, however, such statutes and accompanying regulations include Title VII of the Civil Rights Act of 1964,[6] the Family and Medical Leave Act,[7] the Fair Labor Standards Act,[8] the Employee Retirement Income Security Act of 1974,[9] and the Occupational Safety and Health Act (OSHA).[10] These laws can require companies to retain documents for periods of time that can range up to 30 or 40 years, in the case of OSHA. Although the duty to preserve documents is "more narrow in scope than under the federal discovery rules,"[11] these laws often contain explicit requirements for what must be preserved and for how long.

The Private Securities Litigation Reform Act of 1995 (Reform Act),[12] for example, contains a provision that prohibits parties with actual notice of litigation from destroying or altering evidence. The Reform Act provides for a stay of discovery during the pendency of a motion to dismiss the complaint. Under 15 U.S.C. § 78u-4(b)(3)(C), during a stay in discovery pending ruling on a motion, "any party to the action with actual notice of the allegations contained in the complaint shall treat all documents . . . and tangible objects that are in the custody or control of such person and that are relevant to the allegations, as if they were the subject of a continuing request for production of documents. . . ."[13] The purpose of this provision is to ensure that evidence is retained pending a ruling on a motion to dismiss.[14]

For example, in *In re Tyco International, Ltd. Securities Litigation,*[15] the plaintiff sought an order requiring the defendants to preserve documents pending discovery as required by 15 U.S.C. § 78u-4(b)(3)(C). Re-

---

4. RICHARD L. CLAYPOOLE & GLADYS QUEEN RAMEY, GUIDE TO RECORDS RETENTION IN THE CODE OF FEDERAL REGULATIONS (Diane Pub. Co. 2004).

5. (1989 & Supp. 2005).

6. 29 C.F.R. § 1602.14 (2005).

7. 29 C.F.R. § 825.110(c) (2005).

8. 29 U.S.C. § 211(c) (2005).

9. 29 U.S.C. § 1027 (2005).

10. 29 U.S.C. § 654 (2005).

11. R. Kahn & K. Vaiden, *If the Slate Is Wiped Clean (Spoliation: What It Can Mean for Your Case)*, BUS. L. TODAY (May/June 1999).

12. 15 U.S.C. § 78 U-4 (2005).

13. 15 U.S.C. § 78 U-4(b)(3)(C) (2005).

14. Powers v. Eichen, 961 F. Supp. 233, 236 (S.D. Cal. 1997).

15. MDL No. 00-MD-1335-B, 2000 U.S. Dist LEXIS 11659 (D.N.H. 2000).

fusing to issue a preservation order, the court held that "[a]bsent a showing that defendants are not acting in accordance with their statutory duty, the preservation provisions of [the Act are] sufficient to ensure preservation of the documents in the defendants' custody or control."[16] The court pointed out that the statute provided sanctions for "willful failure" to comply with this statutory obligation.[17]

Similarly, employment discrimination statutes, such as Title VII, impose on employers the duty to preserve documents that are relevant to discrimination claims.[18] The failure to do so can result in a "[rebuttable] presumption that the destroyed documents would have bolstered [the plaintiff's] case."[19] However, this rule may be inapplicable where the destruction of records does not manifest bad faith.[20]

For instance, in *Favors v. Fisher*,[21] an employer destroyed test records in violation of 29 C.F.R. § 1602.14. The employer's representative testified he had not destroyed the test records because they showed something contrary to its position. Rather, he was unaware that federal regulations required retention of the records and he discarded them because he planned to use similar test questions in future promotion decisions. The *Favors* court held that "the destruction of the ten-question test and answers entitled [the employee] to a presumption of pretext, which imposed upon [the employer] the burden of showing the documents were destroyed in good faith." Finding sufficient evidence to show that the employer met its burden, the court affirmed the employer's favorable judgment.[22]

---

16. *Id.*

17. *Id.*

18. *See* 29 C.F.R. § 1602.14.

19. Lombard v. MCI Telecomm. Corp., 13 F. Supp. 2d 621, 627-28 (N.D. Ohio 1998) (internal citation omitted); Coates v. Johnson & Johnson, 756 F.2d 524, 551 (7th Cir. 1985).

20. Park v. City of Chicago, 297 F.3d 606 (7th Cir. 2002) (requiring a showing of "bad faith" before an adverse inference may be drawn from the destruction of records an employer is required to retain under 29 C.F.R. § 1602.14);Vick v. Texas Employment Comm'n, 514 F.2d 734, 737 (5th Cir. 1975). *See also* Rich v. Delta Air Lines, Inc., 921 F. Supp. 767, 772 (N.D. Ga. 1996) (if an employer fails to maintain accurate records to establish whether employee has worked requisite number of hours to be covered under FMLA, burden shifts to employer to prove employee has not worked required number of hours).

21. 13 F.3d 1235 (8th Cir. 1994).

22. *Id.*

In contrast, in *Byrnie v. Town of Cromwell*,[23] the court considered whether the trial court should have imposed an adverse inference as a sanction for the destruction of records an employer had a statutory duty to retain and whether an adverse inference would have allowed a finding of unlawful discrimination. The court held it did not matter that the school board usually destroyed such records at the conclusion of the interview process, because a federal regulation required it to "retain all records pertaining to employment decisions for a period of two years."[24]

A similar obligation to maintain records also exists under ERISA. Under 29 U.S.C. § 1059, an employer must retain certain records regarding employees' entitlement to plan benefits. At least three circuit courts have held that "an employer's failure to comply with its statutory duty to maintain adequate records shifts the burden to the employer to prove the number of hours worked."[25] For example, in *Stanton v. Larry Fowler Trucking, Inc.,* the court held that this rule also operates to shift the burden of proof to the plan administrator to prove that proper notice was given under the Consolidated Omnibus Budget Reconciliation Act (COBRA). The court reasoned:

> [T]he administrator is in a better position to prove the COBRA notice was given. It is only fitting to place the burden of proving notice was given on the party required to give notice, the administrator. To hold otherwise would place the employee in the untenable position of proving a negative and would reward shoddy recordkeeping practices by the administrator and the employer.[26]

---

23. 243 F.3d 93 (2d Cir. 2001).

24. *Id.* (citing 29 C.F.R. 1602.40).

25. Stanton v. Larry Fowler Trucking, Inc., 52 F.3d 723, 727 (8th Cir. 1995) (citing decisions from the Sixth, Ninth, and Eleventh Circuits). *See* Starr v. Metro Sys., Inc., No. 01-1122, 2004 U.S. Dist. LEXIS 15744 (D. Minn. 2004) (observing that employer had a duty to retain records sufficient to show it provided notice to employee of employee's rights under COBRA, distinguishing *Stanton* and holding the former employee was not entitled to summary judgment when the dispute involved whether employee received COBRA notice, not whether employer had produced a record of the actual notice it sent).

26. *Id.* at 728.

Despite these statutory obligations to retain records, courts considering the question have determined that there is no private cause of action for enforcement violations of these statutes. Interpreting record-keeping requirements under the Fair Labor Standards Act, the Sixth Circuit held that there is no private cause of action for record-keeping violations in *Elwell v. University Hospitals Home Care Services.*[27] There, a home health care nurse alleged violations of the FLSA overtime provisions and contended the district court erred by refusing to allow the jury to consider the defendant's record-keeping violations on the issue of whether the defendant's acts were willful.[28] The *Elwell* court held that the "authority to enforce the Act's recordkeeping provisions is vested exclusively in the Secretary of Labor" and concluded that the district court had properly refused to give a jury instruction stating that a violation of the record-keeping requirement constituted a "willful" disregard of the FLSA requirements. But the court also held the district court should have allowed the nurse to offer evidence of violations of record-keeping provisions to corroborate her allegations that the employer willfully failed to compensate for overtime.[29]

Practice Tips

To avoid violation of statutory record-keeping laws and related regulations:

- Any company document retention policy should include an appropriate retention schedule based on the requirements of applicable federal and state statutes and regulations.

- Bear in mind that some statutes and regulations mandate penalties for violation of record-keeping obligation that shift the burden of proof to and/or impose a rebuttable presumption on the spoliator.

---

27. 276 F.3d 832 (6th Cir. 2002). *See also* Catoire v. Caprock Telcomm. Corp., No.: 01-3577 Section: "J"(2), 2003 U.S. Dist. LEXIS 8812 (E.D. La. May 21, 2003) (finding there is no private cause of action under 29 C.F.R. § 1602.14); *Lombard*, 13 F. Supp. 2d 621 (same).

28. 276 F.3d at 841.

29. *Id.* at 843-44.

The Developing Law of Spoliation in State Civil Courts

7

This chapter surveys the law of independent tort claims for destruction of evidence and the available remedies and sanctions for spoliation in pending civil litigation throughout the United States. Most states sanction deliberate spoliation, and many courts impose sanctions for negligent or reckless destruction of relevant evidence. In a minority of states, the highest court has recognized independent tort claims that an injured party may bring when another person destroys evidence relevant to the injured party's civil claim.

The following summary highlights the current law in all 50 states and the District of Columbia. It is not intended to be an exhaustive statement of the law for each state and should not be relied upon as such.

ALABAMA

Independent Causes of Action for Destruction of Evidence

The Alabama Supreme Court has declined to recognize an independent cause of action for spoliation of evidence when the spoliator is a defendant in the action.[1] However, the Supreme Court recognized a remedy in negligent spoliation of evidence if evidence is lost or destroyed by a third party in *Smith v. Atkinson*.[2] Although the court declined to recognize a new cause of action in *Smith*, it announced a three-part test for determining whether a third party could be held liable for negligent spoliation, which, when established by a plaintiff, creates a rebuttable presumption that "but for" the defendant's action, the plaintiff would have recovered in the underlying claim.[3]

Civil and Evidentiary Sanctions for Destruction of Evidence

Alabama recognizes a wide range of civil and evidentiary sanctions. For example, Alabama Rule of Civil Procedure 37 gives trial courts the power to impose discovery sanctions when a party to litigation destroys evidence. The trial court may require the spoliating party, among other things, to reimburse attorneys' fees and costs, strike a pleading, bar introduction of evidence or expert testimony and/or dismiss the action, or enter a default judgment. Alabama courts are prepared to impose the harshest sanctions, dismissal or default judgment, where those sanctions are deemed appropriate.[4]

Trial courts determine the severity of the sanction by balancing the culpability of the spoliator against the prejudice to the non-spoliating party.[5] For instance, in *Cincinnati Insurance Company v. Synergy Gas, Inc.*,[6] the Alabama Supreme Court affirmed a trial court's entry of summary judgment in favor of a gas company on a subrogated

---

1. Christian v. Chandler Construction Co., 658 So. 2d 408 (Ala. 1995). The Alabama Supreme Court also decided two other cases based on the same set of facts the same day. Rouse v. Chandler, 658 So. 2d 405 (Ala. 1995); Peek v. State Auto Mut. Ins. Co., 661 So. 2d 737 (Ala. 1995).

2. 771 So. 2d 429, 432-33 (Ala. 2000).

3. *Id.* For a more detailed discussion of the court's analysis of *Smith, see supra* chapter 5.

4. *See, e.g.*, Capitol Chevrolet, Inc. v. Smedley, 614 So. 2d 439 (Ala. 1993) (finding that trial court abused its discretion by not dismissing an action where relevant evidence had been irreparably lost by the actions of an insurer, reversing the insurer's favorable judgment and remanding the case with instructions to dismiss the case).

5. E. M. Wilson, *The Alabama Supreme Court Sidesteps a Definitive Ruling in Christian v. Kenneth Chandler Construction Co.: Should Alabama Adopt the Independent Tort of Spoliation?* 47 ALA. L. REV. 971, 984 (Spring 1996).

6. 585 So. 2d 822 (Ala. 1991).

insurer's claim charging that an alleged malfunction of a gas system caused a fire. Considering whether the insurer's claim should be dismissed as a sanction for allowing destruction of the fire artifacts, the trial court looked at the importance of the destroyed evidence, the culpability of the offending party, fundamental fairness, and alternative sources of information from which causes of the blaze could be determined.[7]

On appeal, the Alabama Supreme Court analyzed the standard of review applicable to a trial court's decision to impose sanctions, noting that a trial court is the more "suitable arbiter" for determining a party's culpability for destruction of evidence.[8] Accordingly, the court held it will show "great deference" toward a trial court's choice of civil sanctions.[9] The court then reaffirmed its decision in *Iverson v. Xpert Tune, Inc.,*[10] and held that a trial court's decision regarding sanctions will not be disturbed absent a gross abuse of discretion.

Alabama courts also permit a fact finder to draw an adverse inference against a litigant who destroys relevant evidence.[11] A party may introduce evidence of another party's purposeful or wrongful destruction of evidence that it knows supports the interests of the opposing party, even if the destruction occurred before litigation commenced. Further, spoliation of evidence or an attempt to suppress evidence favorable to an adverse party is "sufficient foundation for an inference of [the spoliator's] guilt or negligence."[12]

A divided Alabama Supreme Court discussed when a trial court may give an adverse inference instruction, similar to the instruction contained in the Alabama Pattern Jury Instructions,[13] in *Alabama Power Company v. Murray.*[14] There, the majority upheld the trial court's de-

---

7. *Id.* at 824.

8. *Id.* at 826.

9. *Id.* at 826-27.

10. 553 So. 2d 82 (Ala. 1989); *see also Ex parte* Seaman Timber Co., 850 So. 2d 246, 257 (Ala. 2002); *Ex parte* Maple Chase Co., 840 So. 2d 147, 149 (Ala. 2002).

11. May v. Moore, 424 So. 2d 596 (Ala. 1982); *see also* Smith v. Atkinson, 771 So. 2d 429 (Ala. 2000); WalMart Stores, Inc. v. Goodman, 789 So. 2d 166, 176 (Ala. 2000).

12. *Id.* at 603.

13. ALABAMA PATTERN JURY INSTRUCTION, Civil 15, 13 (2d., 1998 cum supp.).

14. Alabama Power Co. v. Murray, 751 So. 2d 494, 496 (Ala. 1999).

cision to give an adverse inference instruction, despite the dissenting justices' concern about the lack of evidence that the power company purposefully and wrongfully destroyed material evidence. In his dissenting opinion, Justice Lyons explained that a spoliation instruction is not precluded every time a spoliator asserts, "Oops, I dropped it."[15] However, the victim of the spoliation must do more than simply show that the evidence was destroyed; it must introduce evidence that would be "sufficient for a jury to infer the commission of an intentional act."[16]

Criminal Statutes

Alabama permits a court to impose criminal sanctions for tampering with evidence where the person destroying the evidence believes that a proceeding was pending or would be filed.[17] There are no reported cases of prosecution under this statute arising from destruction of evidence in a civil action.[18]

ALASKA

Independent Causes of Action for Destruction of Evidence

The Alaska Supreme Court recognized the tort of intentional interference with a prospective civil action by spoliation of evidence in *Hazen v. Municipality of Anchorage*.[19] In Alaska, "[I]ntentional spoliation claims can be made against parties to the original action, called 'first-party spoliators,' and non-parties to the original action, called 'third-party spoliators.'"[20]

---

15. *Id.* at 503 (Lyons, J., dissenting).

16. *Id. Compare* Vesta Fire Ins. Corp. v. Milan & Co., 2004 Ala. LEXIS 217, at *36 (Aug. 27, 2004) (reversing summary judgment based on alleged spoliation because other less onerous sanctions were available and the alleged destroyers' culpability was of "'relatively low range' along a continuum of fault").

17. ALA. CRIM. CODE § 13A-10-129 (2004); E. M. Wilson, *supra* note 5, at 983.

18. E. M. Wilson, *supra* note 5, at 983 n.98.

19. 718 P.2d 456 (Alaska 1986).

20. Nichols v. State Farm Fire & Cas. Co., 6 P.3d 300, 303-04 (Alaska 2000). *See also* Hibbits v. Purvis, 34 P.3d 327, 330 (Alaska 2001) (quoting Temple Cmty. Hosp. v. Superior Court, 976 P.2d 223, 237 (Cal. 1999) (recognizing third-party spoliation and observing that third parties will not be held liable if "the missing evidence has simply been discarded or misplaced in the ordinary course of events")).

The *Hazen* litigation that led to recognition of the independent tort arose out of a massage parlor owner's civil action for false arrest and malicious prosecution following her arrest for prostitution. Municipal police officers tape-recorded their encounter with the owner and produced the tape to her lawyers during the criminal proceedings. The owner's attorneys listened to the arrest tape and claimed it was "very clear" and demonstrated the owner's innocence. Prosecutors apparently recognized that the tape did not help their case, but argued it was not particularly clear.[21]

At a tape-recorded hearing on a motion to dismiss the criminal charges, the owner asked that the arrest tape be preserved or that she be given a copy of it because she was contemplating a civil suit. The prosecutor agreed to preserve the tape. Immediately after that, the recorded record reflected a male voice at the prosecutor's table whispering, "Wait 'til you hear what is on the tape now."[22]

Subsequently, the massage parlor owner filed a civil suit against the police officers, the prosecutor, and the city. During discovery, she requested and received the arrest tape. When they listened to the tape, the owner and her counsel found it inaudible and found it was not as clear as it had been at the dismissal hearing two years earlier. They then listened to the record of the criminal proceedings and heard the whispered remark for the first time. The massage parlor owner amended her complaint to assert a claim for violation of state and federal civil rights by destruction or alteration of evidence. Because no common-law cause of action existed for the alleged alteration of the tape, the trial court fashioned an implied cause of action for deliberate violation of due process under the Alaska Constitution.[23]

Challenging, among other things, the trial court's directed verdict on her claim that the city, the prosecutor, and its officers altered the arrest tape, the owner argued there was sufficient evidence that these defendants knew about the possibility of a civil suit, and that each had access to the tape, to allow the claim to go to the jury.[24] The Supreme Court agreed, but only in regard to the prosecutor and the city. It then held the massage parlor owner had a common-law cause of action for

---

21. *See Hazen*, 718 P.2d at 458.
22. *Id.* at 459.
23. *See id.*
24. *See id.* at 463.

the tort of intentional interference with a prospective civil action by spoliation of evidence, noting that the owner's prospective false arrest and malicious prosecution actions were "valuable probable expectancies."[25]

The Alaska Supreme Court also has addressed whether the tort of spoliation can stand as "its own tort." In *Estate of Day v. Willis*,[26] the court explained that the "tort of spoliation is meritless unless it can be shown that a party's underlying cause of action has been prejudiced by the spoliation."[27] Therefore, to prevail on an intentional spoliation claim, a party must establish a viable underlying cause of action.[28]

In *Sweet v. Sisters of Providence*,[29] the Alaska Supreme Court declined to recognize an independent cause of action for negligent spoliation of evidence—in this case, the destruction of medical records. There, the court observed that the remedy of burden shifting was a sufficient response to the loss or destruction of the missing records. The *Sweet* court did not decide whether recognition of a separate tort for negligent spoliation would be appropriate under any set of circumstances.[30]

Civil and Evidentiary Sanctions for Destruction of Evidence

Alaska courts also may impose sanctions for withholding, destroying or altering relevant documents or evidence under Alaska Rule of Civil Procedure 37(b).[31] The test for validity of a discovery sanction, such as dismissal of a claim or an order that certain facts or issues be taken as established, is whether claims or issues are "'elements of the dispute that cannot be determined on the merits without disclosure of the evidence the Court has ordered the party to produce.'"[32]

On review, the *Hazen* court found that the trial court abused its discretion by dismissing the massage parlor owner's false arrest and malicious prosecution claims as a sanction for failure to produce certain records. The Alaska Supreme Court reversed the dismissal of the

---

25. *Id.* at 464.
26. 897 P.2d 78 (Alaska 1995).
27. *Id.* at 81.
28. *See id.*
29. 895 P.2d 484 (Alaska 1995); *see also Nichols*, 6 P.3d 300.
30. *See Sweet*, 895 P.2d at 493.
31. *See Hazen*, 718 P.2d at 460; *see also* ALASKA R. CIV. P. 37 (2004).
32. *Id.* (citing Bachner v. Pearson, 479 P.2d 319, 324 (Alaska 1970)).

false arrest and malicious prosecution claims, explaining that the documents the owner had failed to produce to the police defendants had no bearing on the question of probable cause to arrest.[33]

Alaska courts also have imposed an adverse inference or presumption to remedy loss or destruction of evidence or records a party has a duty to maintain. For instance, in *Sweet*, the court discussed claims by the parents of a brain-damaged child that a hospital's destruction of certain medical records stripped them of their ability to prosecute a medical malpractice claim. The parents claimed that the hospital breached its duty to create and preserve required medical records, and the hospital's breach entitled them to a judgment as a matter of law on their spoliation claims. The trial court disagreed and, instead, shifted the burden of proof to the hospital on the issues of its duty and breach on the parents' medical malpractice claim.[34]

On appeal, the parents asserted that the hospital should have borne the burden of proving that its negligence did not cause the child's injuries. The Supreme Court agreed, holding the trial court should have adopted a rebuttable presumption that the hospital was medically negligent in treating the child and this negligence legally caused the child's injury "absent a jury finding that [the hospital's] failure to maintain [the child's] records was excused."[35]

Criminal Statutes

Alaska law prohibits tampering with evidence.[36] A person may be charged with this crime for destroying or removing physical evidence with the intent to impair its use in an official proceeding. It appears that the charge is usually brought in connection with other criminal charges or to prevent another from being charged with a crime.[37]

---

33. *See id.* at 460-61.
34. *See Sweet*, 895 P.2d at 490.
35. *Id.* at 492.
36. *See* ALASKA STAT. § 11.56.610 (2004).
37. *See, e.g.,* Gargan v. State, 805 P.2d 998 (Alaska Ct. App. 1991); Williamson v. State, 692 P.2d 965 (Alaska Ct. App. 1984).

ARIZONA

Independent Causes of Action for Destruction of Evidence

The Arizona Supreme Court considered and refused to recognize a tort for destruction of evidence in *La Raia v. Superior Court.*[38] The court explained that a landlord's failure to provide a complete and accurate list of the pesticides it used on a tenant's apartment could be remedied "within the realm of existing tort law"[39] and accordingly, a separate tort claim is unnecessary. The *La Raia* court noted that providing correct information on the type of pesticide used on an apartment when requested by a tenant and her doctors was within what could reasonably be expected, especially since the landlord possessed information. However, in failing to provide it, and intentionally providing false information, the landlord did not spoil the evidence; rather, the landlord caused a new or further injury to the tenant.[40]

Although it did not recognize a cause of action for intentional or negligent spoliation, the *La Raia* court adopted the *Restatement (Second) of Torts* § 322 (1965) analysis. Section 322 imposes a duty to exercise reasonable care to prevent further harm on an actor who knows or has reason to know his conduct has caused bodily harm to another such that it makes the person helpless and in danger of further harm.

Civil and Evidentiary Sanctions for Destruction of Evidence

In *Souza v. Fred Carries Contracts, Inc.,*[41] an Arizona court addressed, for the first time, the effect of unintentional destruction of relevant evidence. There, a plaintiff charged a used car dealer with negligent repair and maintenance following an accident that the plaintiff claimed resulted from improper repairs. The plaintiff's car was totaled and towed to a storage facility. Unbeknownst to the parties, the storage facility owner obtained title to the vehicle and transferred it to a recycler. The

---

38. 722 P.2d 286 (Ariz. 1986). *See* Tobel v. Travelers Ins. Co., 988 P.2d 148 (Ariz. Ct. App. 1999) (denying motion to amend complaint to add spoliation of evidence claim because Arizona has not recognized spoliation of evidence as a separate tort). *See also* Monica L. Klug, Note, *Torts—Arizona Should Adopt the Tort of Intentional Spoliation of Evidence—La Raia v. Superior Court*, 150 Ariz. 118, 722 P.2d 286 (1986), 19 ARIZ. ST. L.J. 371 (1987).

39. *La Raia*, 722 P.2d at 289.

40. *Id.* at 290.

41. 955 P.2d 3 (Ariz. Ct. App. 1997).

recycler destroyed the vehicle before either party had an opportunity to inspect it. The used car dealer moved for summary judgment, arguing that the permanent loss of the vehicle precluded the plaintiff from establishing a *prima facie* case and irreparably prejudiced its ability to defend.[42] The dealer requested the sanction of dismissal of the plaintiff's case under Arizona Rule of Civil Procedure 37(A) and (B) for inadvertent failure to preserve the vehicle. The trial court dismissed the plaintiff's case.

Reviewing the trial court's decision for abuse of discretion, the appellate court evaluated the totality of the circumstances and concluded that dismissal was too harsh a sanction. The court declined to adopt any bright-line rule, instead preferring to analyze issues concerning destruction of evidence and appropriate sanctions on a case-by-case basis.[43]

Analyzing the parties' conduct in *Souza*, the court also noted there was no evidence that plaintiff willfully destroyed the evidence or even knew it was about to be destroyed. Nor did the case involve the failure to comply with a court order or abuse of discovery or disclosure requirements. In addition, the car dealer had not requested that the plaintiff preserve the vehicle or make it available for inspection, even though, as a lienholder, it had the right, opportunity, and ability to retrieve and preserve the vehicle if it so chose. The court also observed that the used car dealer knew where the car was being stored.[44]

The court found it significant that loss of the vehicle did not render the dealer incapable of mounting a defense or irreparably prejudice its ability to defend. Finally, the record did not demonstrate that the lower court had "thoroughly considered other, less severe, sanctions before resorting to the most extreme."[45] Accordingly, the appellate court reversed the trial court's decision to dismiss the plaintiff's case and remanded the case for a hearing to determine the availability of any lesser sanctions without limiting the trial court's alternatives on remand.[46] Therefore, it appears that before imposing sanctions, Arizona courts will consider the alleged spoliator's conduct, the injured

42. *Id.*
43. *Id.*
44. *Id.*
45. *Id.* at 11.
46. *Id.*

party's effort to preserve or ensure the evidence is preserved, and the harm to the injured party caused by the loss of evidence before it selects an appropriate sanction.

Criminal Statutes

Arizona prohibits destruction, mutilation, and/or alteration of physical evidence by a person who knows that an official proceeding is pending or about to be instituted.[47] There is no reported case in which this statute has been used to impose criminal penalties for destruction of evidence in a civil case.

ARKANSAS

Independent Causes of Action for Destruction of Evidence

In *Goff v. Harold Ives Trucking Company*,[48] the Arkansas Supreme Court found it "unnecessary and unwise" to recognize first-party spoliation of evidence as an independent tort.[49] After a head-on collision with a tractor-trailer driven by an employee of the defendant, the plaintiff filed suit alleging spoliation of evidence because some of the driver's logs had either negligently or intentionally been lost or destroyed. The plaintiff was successful on the underlying negligence claim.

Ultimately, the plaintiff refiled the spoliation claim in a county circuit court, and it was dismissed for failure to state a claim. In reviewing the trial court's decision, the court held:

> [T]here are sufficient other avenues, short of creating a new cause of action, that serve to remedy the situation for a plaintiff. Most significant, an aggrieved party can request that a

---

47. ARIZ. REV. STAT. § 13-2809 (2003).
48. 27 S.W.3d 387 (Ark. 2000). Prior to this decision, the Arkansas Supreme Court had not addressed whether it would recognize an independent cause of action for destruction of evidence or intentional interference with a prospective civil action by spoliation of evidence. However, in *Wilson v. Beloit Corporation*, 921 F.2d 765 (8th Cir. 1990), the Eighth Circuit Court of Appeals applied Arkansas law and found spoliation is not a cognizable claim. The *Wilson* court observed that "the general rule is that there is no duty to preserve possible evidence for another party to aid that other party in some future legal action against a third party." *Id.* at 767.
49. *Id.* at 391.

jury be instructed to draw a negative inference against this spoliator. Additionally, and as discussed earlier, the plaintiff can ask for discovery sanctions or seek to have a criminal prosecution initiated against the party who destroyed relevant evidence.[50]

In reaching this conclusion, the *Goff* court relied heavily on the reasoning employed by the California Supreme Court in *Cedars-Sinai Medical Center v. Superior Court*.[51] Specifically, the court identified the strong policy concerns that weigh against the adoption of spoliation as a new tort, including the speculative nature of damages.[52] In refusing to recognize the claim, the court emphasized that the plaintiff won the underlying negligence claim despite the absence of the driver logs. Moreover, there was no allegation that if the spoliation claim was permitted, there would have been no way for the jury to tell what the logs would have shown and what injury, if any, the plaintiff had suffered as a result of the destruction of the logs.[53]

Civil and Evidentiary Sanctions for Destruction of Evidence

In *Stevenson v. Union Pacific Railroad Co.*,[54] the Eighth Circuit Court of Appeals held "there must be a finding of prejudice to the opposing party before imposing a sanction for destruction of evidence."[55] The defendant railroad company destroyed a tape of conversations between the train crew and dispatcher at the time of the accident and track maintenance records predating the accident. The Eighth Circuit allowed an adverse inference jury instruction, but also held that a permissive inference is subject to reasonable rebuttal.[56] The court also reviewed the standard to award attorneys' fees and held "a bad faith finding is specifically required in order to assess attorneys' fees."[57] Applying this analysis, the absence of a bad-faith finding made an

---

50. *Id.*
51. 954 P.2d 511 (Cal. 1998).
52. 27 S.W.3d at 389.
53. *Id.* at 391.
54. 354 F.3d 739 (8th Cir. 2004).
55. *Id.* at 748.
56. *Id.* at 750.
57. *Id.* at 751.

award of attorneys' fees based on prelitigation destruction of evidence unwarranted.[58]

Affirming a $25 million punitive damage award in another railroad-crossing accident case, the Arkansas Supreme Court noted that an adverse inference instruction is appropriate when intentional destruction of evidence has been established.[59] There, the jury was given the following instruction with regard to the railroad's failure to preserve evidence:

> In this case, the plaintiffs contend that by intentional conduct the defendant railroad failed to preserve voice tapes and track inspection records that should have been preserved. Therefore, you may, but you are not required to, infer that the contents of the voice tapes and track inspection records would have been unfavorable to the defendant.[60]

Criminal Statutes

Arkansas maintains statutory provisions prohibiting tampering with evidence.[61] In *Goff*, the Arkansas Supreme Court noted that Arkansas Code Annotated section 5-53-111 makes it a Class B misdemeanor if a person "alters, destroys, suppresses, removes, or conceals any record, document, or thing with the purpose of impairing its verity, legibility, or availability in any official proceeding or investigation." Moreover, a federal district court considered whether these statutes imposed a duty to preserve evidence in *Wilson v. Beloit Corporation.*[62] There, the court rejected an injured employee's claim that these statutes required his employer to preserve certain machine parts the employee needed to sustain a claim against the machine manufacturer.[63]

There are no reported cases imposing criminal penalties under these statutes on civil litigants.

---

58. *Id.*

59. Union Pac. R.R. Co. v. Barber, 149 S.W.3d 325 (Ark.), *cert. denied*, 160 L. Ed. 249, 125 S. Ct. 320 (2004).

60. *Id.* at 345-46.

61. 27 S.W.3d at 390. *See also* Ark. Code Ann. §§ 5-53-110 and 5-53-111 (2004).

62. 725 F. Supp. 1056 (W.D. Ark. 1989), *aff'd*, 921 F.2d 765 (8th Cir. 1990).

63. *Id.*

CALIFORNIA

Independent Causes of Action for Destruction of Evidence

In two decisions in 1998 and 1999, the California Supreme Court "wiped out 14 years of judicial precedent supporting the tort of intentional spoliation of evidence by holding that such claims may no longer be brought under California law."[64]

In the first decision, *Cedars-Sinai Medical Center v. Superior Court,*[65] the court rejected creating a tort remedy for first-party spoliation because it found that: (1) strong and effective remedies existed to correct destruction of evidence by party litigants; (2) those remedies worked to compensate victims of spoliation for their losses; and (3) a tort created to remedy first-party spoliation would undermine the finality of litigation.[66]

One year later, in *Temple Community Hospital v. Superior Court,*[67] a divided supreme court refused to recognize an independent tort in cases of third-party spoliation. The majority emphasized its reluctance to expand tort liability for litigation-related misconduct beyond malicious prosecution, explaining:

> Our decisions have stressed the importance of encouraging parties to make their best effort to investigate and litigate their claims in a single proceeding, and have observed that "[t]o allow a litigant to attack the integrity of evidence after the proceedings have concluded, except in the most narrowly cir-

---

64. Jerrold Abeles & Robert J. Tyson, *Spoil Sport*, 22 L.A. Law. 41 (May 1999); *see also* Temple Comm. Hosp. v. Superior Court, 976 P.2d 223 (Cal. 1999) (holding that no tort cause of action will lie for intentional third-party spoliation of evidence); Cedars-Sinai Med. Ctr. v. Superior Court, 954 P.2d 511 (Cal. 1998) (refusing to recognize a tort cause of action for intentional spoliation of evidence against a party when the destruction was or should have been discovered before the conclusion of the litigation).

65. 954 P.2d 511.

66. One commentator has suggested that *Hernandez v. Garcetti*, 68 Cal. App. 4th 675 (1998), provides a "possible open door" for revival of the spoliation tort "especially if the actions of the spoliator prevented the victim from learning of the spoliation until after a final judgment was reached in the underlying cause of action." JAMIE S. GORELICK ET AL., DESTRUCTION OF EVIDENCE, 2005 CUMULATIVE SUPPLEMENT 194-95 (Aspen Publishers 2004). *See also* Abeles & Tyson, *supra* note 64.

67. 976 P.2d 223.

cumscribed situations, such as extrinsic fraud, would imper-
missibly burden, if not inundate, our justice system."[68]

Detailing the sanctions available to remedy spoliation in pending
litigation, the *Temple Community* court acknowledged that its decision not to recognize an independent tort could leave some potential
litigants without a remedy. However, the majority concluded that
"'[e]ndless litigation, in which nothing was ever finally determined,
would be worse than occasional miscarriages of justice.'"[69] This decision also acknowledged that a court may sanction a third party who
fails to respond as required to a subpoena seeking production of evidentiary materials the third party destroyed.[70] The court also pointed
out that imposing liability for first-party spoliation could place significant burdens on parties and the judicial system "disproportionate to
the merit of a particular claim or to the effectiveness of the tort remedy
as a deterrent."[71]

In dissent, the minority argued in favor of "a narrowly drawn tort
remedy for the intentional destruction of evidence by someone not a
party to the underlying cause of action . . . when the evidence is destroyed with the intent of affecting the outcome of the underlying action."[72] In reaching this conclusion, the dissenters considered other
non-tort remedies ineffective to deter third-party spoliation.

Although the California Supreme Court has yet to consider whether
a cause of action will lie for negligent spoliation of evidence,[73] several
California appellate courts have refused to recognize such a cause of
action. For example, in *Farmers Insurance Exchange v. Superior
Court*,[74] the court applied the reasoning in *Temple Community* and
found that the same policy considerations that came to bear in *Temple
Community* were present in the analysis of whether to recognize a

---

68. *Id.* at 228 (quoting Silberg v. Anderson, 786 P.2d 365 (Cal. 1990)).
69. *Id.* at 229 (quoting *Cedars-Sinai*, 954 P.2d at 517).
70. *Id.*; *see also* Waicis v. Superior Court, 276 Cal. Rptr. 45, 48 (Ct. App. 1990).
71. *Temple Comm. Hosp.*, 976 P.2d at 228.
72. *Id.* at 235.
73. *Id.* at 228 n.3.
74. 95 Cal. Rptr. 2d 51 (Ct. App. 2000).

negligent spoliation claim. The *Farmers Insurance* court therefore declined to recognize a tort for negligent spoliation of evidence.

More recently, one California court went even further and found that in light of the California Supreme Court's decision in *Temple Community*, "like night follows day . . . courts *cannot* recognize a tort cause of action for negligent spoliation of evidence."[75]

Despite the absence of tort remedies in California, one California appellate court has held there may be a remedy in contract.[76] The court based is decision on language in *Temple Community*, where the court commented, "[t]o the extent third parties may have a contractual obligation to preserve evidence, contract remedies. . . may be available for breach of the contractual duty."[77] In *Coprich v. Superior Court*,[78] the court held that "the policy considerations concerning intentional spoliation discussed by [the California Supreme Court] . . . do not preclude a cause of action for breach of a contractual duty to preserve evidence."[79]

Civil and Evidentiary Sanctions for Destruction of Evidence

Among the principal reasons for the Supreme Court's decisions in *Cedars-Sinai* and *Temple Community* is the availability of adequate non-tort remedies to "punish and deter spoliation of evidence."[80] In particular, the *Cedars-Sinai* court pointed to the "evidentiary inference that evidence which one party has destroyed or rendered unavailable was unfavorable to that party."[81] The court referenced Evidence Code section 413, which provides that "in determining what inferences to draw from the evidence of facts in the case against a party, the trier of fact may consider, among other things, the party's failure to explain or to deny by his testimony such evidence or facts in

---

75. Lueter v. State of California, 115 Cal. Rptr. 2d 68, 79 (Ct. App. 2002) (emphasis added).

76. *See Temple Community*, 976 P.2d at 232; Coprich v. Superior Court, 95 Cal. Rptr. 884 (Ct. App. 2000); *see generally* JAMIE S. GORELICK ET AL., DESTRUCTION OF EVIDENCE, 2005 CUMULATIVE SUPPLEMENT 194-96 (Aspen Publishers 2004).

77. *Temple Community*, 976 P.2d at 232.

78. 95 Cal. Rptr. 884.

79. *Id.* at 885.

80. *Cedars-Sinai*, 954 P.2d at 517.

81. *Id.*

the case against him, or his willful suppression of evidence relating thereto, if such be the case."[82]

California litigants also may rely on Code of Civil Procedure section 2023. As suggested by the *Cedars-Sinai* court, sanctions may issue against a party who destroys evidence in anticipation of, or in response to, discovery requests. Among other things, the statute permits a trial court to impose monetary sanctions, issue contempt sanctions, order that designated facts be taken as established, prohibit introduction of designated matters into evidence, and preclude a party from supporting or opposing designated claims or defenses.[83] Section 2023 also allows a court to impose sanctions, including "striking part or all of the pleadings, dismissing part or all of the action, or granting a default judgment against the offending party."[84]

Discovery sanctions are limited to remedying misconduct that occurs during litigation or in anticipation of discovery. Therefore, if a party destroys evidence before litigation is commenced, even with malicious intent, discovery sanctions will likely be unavailable.[85]

A court also may sanction a third party who has destroyed evidence. A third party may be fined or found in contempt of court for failure to respond as required to a subpoena seeking production of evidentiary materials that the third party destroyed.[86]

It is interesting to note that one California court allowed a client to bring a legal malpractice claim against her former counsel because he failed to arrange for a vehicle inspection or secure an automobile as evidence.[87] The court held that the former client asserted sufficient facts to shift the burden of proof to her counsel and required the former attorney to show that his negligence did not cause his client to lose her case.[88]

---

82. *Id.* (quoting CAL. EVID. CODE § 413).
83. CAL. CODE CIV. PROC. § 2023 (2005).
84. R.S. Creative, Inc. v. Creative Cotton, Ltd., 89 Cal. Rptr. 2d 353, 360 (Ct. App. 1999) (quoting *Cedars-Sinai*, 954 P.2d at 517-518); *see also* CAL. CODE CIV. PROC. § 2023.
85. *Id.* § 2023.
86. *See, e.g., Waicis*, 276 Cal. Rptr. 45.
87. Galanek v. Wismar, 69 Cal. App. 4th 1417 (1999).
88. *Id.*

Criminal Statutes

California Penal Code section 135 makes it a misdemeanor to willfully Sdestroy or conceal evidence. The California Supreme Court has twice suggested that this statute is among the available deterrents to spoliation of evidence by civil litigants.[89] To date, there is no reported case in which this statute has been imposed on a party to a civil lawsuit.

COLORADO

Independent Causes of Action for Destruction of Evidence

The Colorado Supreme Court has not considered whether a cause of action exists for intentional or negligent destruction of evidence.

Civil and Evidentiary Sanctions for Destruction of Evidence

A Colorado court may impose sanctions for destruction of evidence under Colorado Rule of Civil Procedure 37 when a party first obtains an order compelling production of that evidence.[90] But sanctions need not be based on Rule 37 alone.

Like courts elsewhere, Colorado trial courts have certain inherent powers, including those necessary to enable the court to perform "its judicial functions, to protect its dignity, independence, and integrity, and to make its lawful actions effective."[91] Among other sanctions, a trial court may impose an adverse inference where there is a showing of intentional destruction of evidence.[92]

For example, in *The Lauren Corporation v. Century Geophysical Corporation*, the court considered, for the first time, whether a Colorado trial court has the discretion to impose attorneys' fees as a sanction for the destruction or spoliation of evidence. There, the court held that a trial court may impose attorneys' fees and costs as a sanction for the "bad faith and willful destruction of evidence, even in the absence of a specific discovery order."[93] In a strongly worded concurring opinion,

---

89. *See Temple Comm. Hosp.*, 976 P.2d 223; *Cedars-Sinai*, 954 P.2d 511.

90. Colo. R. Civ. P. 37; The Lauren Corp. v. Century Geophysical Corp., 953 P.2d 200 (Colo. Ct. App. 1998).

91. *Id.* at 203 (quoting Pena v. District Court, 681 P.2d 953, 956 (Colo. 1984)).

92. *Id.* at 204.

93. *Id.*

Judge Metzger observed that Colorado Revised Statute 13-17-102 (1997) requires assessment of attorneys' fees against a party who defends an action that lacks substantial justification or unnecessarily expands proceedings by improper conduct, such as by destruction of evidence.[94]

More recently, a Colorado appellate court imposed sanctions on a department store for reckless destruction of a bench left in its possession.[95] During the two years after the claimant's counsel requested that the bench be preserved as evidence, it remained in use at the store. After removing the bench from use, store employees disassembled and discarded it. When the store learned the bench had been discarded, a manager located it, but by then it had been substantially destroyed. Although the bench had never been requested in discovery, the bench manufacturer's expert could not examine the bench to determine whether the store had made pre-accident modifications to it.

The trial court held the store's actions in this case were either intentional or so reckless that it must be held accountable.[96] The court of appeals upheld the trial court's imposition of sanctions for less than intentional conduct, stating:

> No Colorado case has addressed whether the inherent power to impose punitive sanctions extends to spoliation that is more serious than negligence, but less serious than willful or intentional. Nevertheless, we are persuaded by Colorado cases involving discovery violations, as well as more recent federal precedent, that conduct between negligent and intentional which results in spoliation of evidence may warrant a punitive sanction as a discretionary exercise of inherent power.[97]

The Colorado Supreme Court has also accepted review of two issues in *Alio v. Union Pacific Railroad Company*[98] relating to whether a trial court had given appropriate adverse inference instructions to a jury as a sanction for a railroad's destruction of evidence.

---

94. *Id.* at 205.
95. Pfartz v. Kmart Corp., 85 P.3d 564 (2003).
96. *Id.*
97. *Id.* at 568.
98. 2004 Colo. LEXIS 934 (Nov. 22, 2004).

Criminal Statutes

Colorado prohibits tampering with evidence.[99] Among other things, that statute prohibits destruction, mutilation, concealment, and removal or alteration of physical evidence with the intent to make it unavailable in an official proceeding.

An "official proceeding" includes civil trial proceedings, depositions given under oath, and responses to interrogatories.[100] Thus, it appears that Colorado's prohibition on tampering with evidence may be applicable to the intentional destruction of evidence in a civil lawsuit, although no reported case addresses this question.

CONNECTICUT

Independent Causes of Action for Destruction of Evidence

The Connecticut Supreme Court has not addressed whether negligent or intentional destruction of evidence constitutes an actionable tort. But several lower courts in Connecticut have considered and requested independent causes of action for spoliation.[101]

Civil and Evidentiary Sanctions for Destruction of Evidence

In *Beers v. Bayliner Marine Corporation*,[102] Connecticut joined the "rule of the majority of jurisdictions that have addressed the issue in

---

99. Colo. Rev. Stat. § 18-8-610 (2004).
100. People v. Chaussee, 847 P.2d 156 (Colo. Ct. App. 1994).
101. *See, e.g.*, Massaro v. Yale New Haven Hosp., No. CV020459379, 2003 Conn. Super. LEXIS 1513 (Conn. Super. Ct. May 14, 2003) (striking spoliation of evidence claim on the authority of Beers v. Bayliner Marine Corp., 675 A.2d 829 (Conn. 1996) and noting that spoliation should be viewed as a rule of evidence and not a cause of action); Langlais v. Donovan, No. CV000271417S, 2002 Conn. Super. LEXIS 525 (Conn. Super. Ct. Feb. 19, 2002) (finding no entitlement to adverse inference where failure to prove intentional conduct and requisite notice on part of alleged spoliator); Butler v. Buchanan Marine Inc., No. CV950149347, 1998 Conn. Super. LEXIS 1542 (Conn. Super. Ct. May 29, 1998) (striking spoliation claims and stating under both state procedural law and admiralty substantive law there is no cause of action for spoliation of evidence). *See also* Fontanella v. Liberty Mut. Ins. Co., No. 369092, 1998 Conn. Super. LEXIS 2414 (Conn. Super. Ct. Aug. 26, 1998) (discussing negligent spoliation); Moisei v. Pilkington Barnes-Hind, Inc., No. 960561712S, 1997 Conn. Super. LEXIS 2293 (Conn. Super. Ct. Aug. 21, 1997) (striking claims for negligent and intentional spoliation).
102. 675 A.2d 829 (Conn. 1996).

a civil context" and held that "the trier of fact may draw an inference from the intentional spoliation of evidence. . . ."[103] In *Beers*, a boat owner sued following an accident that, he claimed, resulted from a defect in the boat. The boat owner conceded that following the accident, he removed the motor from the boat and gave it away. The parties disputed whether the manufacturer had an opportunity to inspect the boat. Claiming the spoliation had stripped it of the ability to defend itself, the manufacturer moved for and obtained summary judgment.

The Supreme Court of Connecticut reversed, concluding that summary judgment was inappropriate. However, it stated that summary judgment may be appropriate in a different factual scenario when, as the result of innocent or intentional destruction of evidence, a plaintiff cannot establish its burden of proving liability. In such a case, summary judgment would be appropriate—not as a penalty, but because the plaintiff cannot sustain the burden of proving liability.[104]

Instead, the *Beers* court found that an adverse inference may be drawn against a party who has destroyed evidence, if the trier of fact is satisfied that the party who seeks the adverse inference has shown that:

1. The spoliation was intentional—that is, the party destroyed the evidence intentionally, not inadvertently;
2. The destroyed evidence is relevant to the issue or matter for which the party seeks the inference; and
3. The party who seeks the inference must have acted with due diligence with respect to the destroyed evidence.[105]

In addition, the trial court must instruct the jury that it is not required to draw an adverse inference, but it may do so if these conditions have been met. Although the *Beers* court required the moving party to show the evidence was intentionally destroyed, the court declined to determine the appropriate remedy when a spoliator acted in bad faith or with conscious awareness that it was destroying evidence.

The *Beers* court also discussed the efforts a party seeking an inference must take, stating it must use all appropriate means to have the evidence produced. This may include placing the spoliator on notice

---

103. *Id.* at 832.
104. *Id.*
105. *Id.*

that the evidence should be preserved and, if necessary, obtaining a court-ordered inspection.[106]

Criminal Statutes

Connecticut General Statute section 53a-155 makes it a crime for a person to tamper with evidence with knowledge that an official proceeding is pending or about to be instituted.[107] There are no reported decisions applying this statute in the context of a civil suit.

DELAWARE

Independent Causes of Action for Destruction of Evidence

A Delaware Superior Court declined to recognize a cause of action for intentional or negligent spoliation of evidence in *Lucas v. Christiana Skating Center, Ltd.*[108]

Civil or Evidentiary Sanctions for Destruction of Evidence

Delaware recognizes the general rule that when a litigant intentionally destroys or suppresses relevant evidence, an inference arises that such evidence could have been adverse to his case.[109] Some Delaware courts have suggested that application of the "spoliation rule" requires a showing of intentional or reckless destruction of evidence.[110] But other Delaware courts have held a finding of negligent destruction sufficient where there is a showing of prejudice.[111]

---

106. *Id. See also* Leonard v. Comm'r Revenue Services, 823 A.2d 1184 (2003) (affirming trial court's refusal to draw an adverse inference when a taxpayer destroyed records because the inference is a permissive one).

107. CONN. GEN. STAT. § 53a-155 (2003).

108. 722 A.2d 1247 (Del. Super. Ct. 1998).

109. Collins v. Throckmorton, 425 A.2d 146 (Del. 1980); Equitable Trust Co. v. Gallagher, 102 A.2d 538, 541 (Del. 1954) (noting the maxim that "everything will be presumed against the despoiler" and citing Armory v. Delamirie, 93 Eng. Rep. 664).

110. Leslie v. Jones, No. 98C-10-345-VAB, 2000 Del. Super. LEXIS 423, at *4 (Del. Super. Ct. Oct. 16, 2000) (noting Delaware's spoliation rule requires a showing of intentional or reckless destruction of evidence).

111. Lucas v. Christiana Skating Center, Ltd., 722 A.2d 1247 (Del. Super. Ct. 1998); McMillan v. Masten Lumber & Supply Co., No. 97C-01-089, 2000 Del. Super. LEXIS 307 (Del. Super. Ct. Jan. 19, 2000) (finding a party may be entitled to a spoliation instruction based on negligent conduct provided there is a showing of prejudice).

In *Collins v. Throckmorton*,[112] the court declined to reverse the trial court's judgment denying an adverse inference based on allegedly destroyed documents. While recognizing the existence of the adverse inference instruction as a remedy when a party has intentionally destroyed evidence, the court found the non-spoliating party had not exercised the necessary diligence to obtain the allegedly destroyed documents. The non-spoliating party had not moved to compel or otherwise sought court assistance in obtaining the documentary evidence.[113] The court reiterated this general rule in *Lucas*, holding that when a party produces evidence of negligent or intentional destruction of evidence, the proper remedy is for the court to instruct the jury about the permissible inferences from that act.[114]

A request for an adverse inference based on spoliation may also arise when a test is not performed with the applicable standard of care.[115] In *Welsh*, the court held that the lack of a toxicology test as part of an autopsy did not constitute negligent spoliation of evidence unless the standard of care for an autopsy required such testing.[116]

Criminal Statutes

Under Delaware law, a person shall not tamper with physical evidence when that person believes certain evidence is about to be produced or used in an official or prospective proceeding and when that person intends to prevent the evidence from being used.[117] The Delaware Supreme Court referenced this statute in the *Lucas* decision as one of the bases for its decision not to recognize an independent spoliation tort.[118]

---

112. 425 A.2d 146.

113. *Id.*; *see also Leslie*, 2000 Del. Super. LEXIS 423 (holding spoliation rule regarding the adverse inference is not applicable where the evidence in question is requested after the expiration of the discovery cutoff date).

114. 722 A.2d 1247; *see also* McMillan v. Masten Lumber and Supply Co., No. 97C-01-089, 2000 Del. Super. LEXIS 307 (Del. Super. Ct. Jan. 19, 2000).

115. Welsh v. Delaware Clinical Lab. Assoc., No. 98C-06-0003, 2000 Del. Super. LEXIS 420 (Del. Super. Ct. Nov. 9, 2000).

116. *Id.* at *3.

117. Del. Code Ann. tit. 11, § 1269 (2004).

118. 722 A.2d at 1250.

DISTRICT OF COLUMBIA

Independent Causes of Action for Destruction of Evidence

In 1998, in *Holmes v. Amerex Rent-A-Car*,[119] the District of Columbia Court of Appeals recognized a cause of action for negligent or reckless spoliation of evidence. In *Holmes*, the plaintiff alleged that injuries suffered in a car accident were due to a defective engine. Following the accident, Amerex took possession of the car. The plaintiff's lawyer attempted to ensure that Amerex would retain possession of the car until it could be inspected by the plaintiff's representative. Amerex subsequently agreed to sell the car to a salvage yard, which severed the front of the car and removed the engine. The plaintiff was not informed of its destruction until a week later. The plaintiff's expert testified that, as a result, it was "impossible to determine within a reasonable degree of certainty whether or not the vehicle had design, manufacturing and/or maintenance defects which proximately caused Plaintiff's injuries."[120]

Afterward the case was removed from state to federal court. The district court granted summary judgment for Amerex, holding that even if the District of Columbia were to recognize a claim for spoliation, the plaintiff would not be able to recover on those facts.[121] On appeal, the U.S. Court of Appeals for the District of Columbia Circuit certified to the District of Columbia Court of Appeals two questions:

1. Whether the District of Columbia recognizes a claim for negligent or reckless spoliation; and
2. If so, the appropriate standards for proximate causation.

On certification, the District of Columbia Court of Appeals held that a cause of action is available for negligent or reckless spoliation. The court especially noted the appropriateness of this tort where evidence is destroyed while in the possession of third parties:

> Some remedy, therefore, should be available to those whose expectancy of recovery has been eliminated or severely hampered throughout the negligent or reckless act of another. In

---

119. 710 A.2d 846 (D.C. 1998).
120. *Id.* at 848.
121. *Id.*

the third-party defendant scenario presented in this case, however, the already recognized remedy of permitting an adverse inference against the spoliator would serve no purpose. Because sanctions may not be levied on a disinterested, independent third party, an independent tort action for negligent spoliation of evidence is the only means to deter the negligent destruction of evidence and to compensate the aggrieved party for its destruction.[122]

The court further held that no general duty exists on the part of a third party to preserve evidence. "Absent some special relationship or duty rising by reason of an agreement, contract, statute, or other special circumstance, the general rule is that there is no duty to preserve possible evidence for another party to aid that other party in some future legal action against a third party."[123] For purposes of answering the certified question, the court assumed that such a duty existed.

Next, the court turned to the issue of proximate cause. It held that "a plaintiff must show, based on reasonable inferences derived from both existing and spoliated evidence, that the underlying lawsuit was significantly impaired, that the spoliated evidence was material to that impairment and that the plaintiff enjoyed a significant possibility of success in the underlying claim."[124] The court surveyed different approaches to proximate causation adopted by Ohio, California, and Florida courts. The court fashioned a standard for proximate causation that combined the "reasonable probability" of success standard (California) with the "significant impairment" of plaintiff's case due to spoliation standard (Florida).[125]

Finally, turning to damages, the court reasoned:

We . . . hold that in an action for negligent or reckless spoliation of evidence, damages arrived at through just and reasonable estimation based on relevant data should be multiplied by the probability that the plaintiff would have won the underlying suit had the spoliated evidence been available. For example, hypo-

---

122. *Id.* at 849 (internal quotations omitted).
123. *Id.* at 850.
124. *Id.*
125. *Id.* at 852.

thetically, if a jury determined that the expected recovery in an underlying suit was $200,000.00, and that there was an estimated sixty percent probability that a plaintiff would have recovered that amount if the underlying suit had not been impaired or precluded due to the spoliated evidence, then the award of damages would be $120,000 or sixty percent of $200,000.00.[126]

Civil and Evidentiary Sanctions of Destruction of Evidence

In *Battocchi v. Washington Hospital Center*,[127] the District of Columbia Court of Appeals reviewed a defense verdict in favor of a hospital and a physician in a medical malpractice action. The trial court had declined to give a missing evidence instruction as a sanction for the hospital's failure to preserve an attending nurse's notes.[128] However, the trial court did not make a finding regarding whether the evidence had been destroyed recklessly or merely negligently. The court of appeals held that it "is well settled that a party's bad faith destruction of a document relevant to proof of an issue at trial gives rise to a strong inference that production of the document would have been unfavorable to the party responsible for its destruction."[129] The court defined the requisite bad faith to include either deliberate destruction or destruction done in "reckless disregard" of the relevance of evidence.[130] Because the trial court had not made an express finding on this issue, the case was remanded for the court to make such a finding.[131]

The court in *Lebron v. Powell*[132] dealt with a plaintiff-employee's failure to provide honest, truthful answers and to correct previously incomplete or inaccurate disclosures regarding her treatment for emotional distress and her efforts to find post-termination employment. Although not a spoliation case, the sanction imposed by the court merits mention. After it analyzed the employee's failure to comply with her discovery obligations, the *Lebron* court observed that the damage done by her conduct centered on her claimed damages. Therefore, the court

---

126. *Id.* at 853-54.
127. 581 A.2d 759 (D.C. 1990).
128. *Id.*
129. *Id.* at 765.
130. *Id.* at 766.
131. *Id.*
132. 217 F.R.D. 72 (D.D.C. 2003).

precluded the employee from seeking damages for emotional distress or from recovering back pay for the two-year delay caused by her actions. The court also noted that before the employee would be permitted to introduce any witness or document, the government-employer would be permitted to challenge the evidence by showing that the employee's delay prejudiced its ability to meet "the probative force of the testimony or exhibit."[133] If the government made that showing, the court would exclude such evidence.[134]

In a case involving destruction of electronic mail, the court in *United States v. Phillip Morris USA, Inc.*[135] imposed a significant monetary and evidentiary sanction. There, the court had entered a preservation order for all documents and other records relevant to the litigation. Despite the order, at least 11 high-level executives and officers failed to follow the company's document preservation procedures, and as a result, some relevant electronic mail was lost or destroyed.

The court rejected the government's request for an adverse inference instruction because it "simply casts too wide a net."[136] Instead, the court precluded the tobacco company from calling as a fact or expert witness any individual who failed to comply with the company's internal document retention program. In addition, the court imposed a $2,750,000 monetary sanction—that is, a $250,000 sanction on each of the 11 corporate officers or managers who failed to comply with the company's retention policy.[137]

Criminal Statutes

The District of Columbia Code[138] provides that a person commits the crime of tampering with evidence when, knowing an official proceeding has begun or is likely to be instituted, that person "alters, destroys, mutilates, conceals, or removes a record, document, or other object, with intent to impair its integrity" or its availability in the official proceeding.[139] However, there is no case law to support whether destruction of evidence in a civil proceeding is a violation of this statute.

---

133. *Id.* at 78.
134. *Id.*
135. 327 F. Supp. 2d 21 (D.D.C. 2004).
136. *Id.* at 25.
137. *Id.*
138. D.C. CODE ANN. § 22-723 (2004).
139. *Id.* at § 22-723(a).

FLORIDA

Independent Causes of Action for Destruction of Evidence

The Florida Supreme Court resolved a split among the Florida appellate districts on the existence of a claim for negligent spoliation by a party to the underlying cause of action in *Martino v. Wal-Mart Stores, Inc.*[140] Addressing a conflict between appellate districts, the *Martino* court refused to recognize an independent cause of action for first-party spoliation of evidence

There, a customer brought a negligence claim for injuries arising from a collapsed shopping cart. The customer amended her complaint to add a spoliation claim when Wal-Mart could not produce the defective shopping cart or a videotape of the incident. The appellate court had upheld dismissal of the spoliation claim because it found that there were other sanctions available to remedy the wrong suffered by the customer as a result of the destruction of evidence.[141]

The Florida Supreme Court agreed. Pointing to its earlier decision in *Public Health Trust of Dade County v. Valcin*,[142] the court found that the remedy for negligent spoliation by a first party should be a rebuttable presumption of negligence for the underlying tort action. The court explained that this presumption is available only "when the absence of the records [or thing] hinders the plaintiff's ability to establish a *prima facie* case."[143] The *Martino* court expressly disapproved of the decision of the Third Appellate District in *Bondu v. Gurvich*,[144] to the extent that it conflicted with the supreme court's decision.

As for claims for third-party spoliation, at least one Florida court has held that, absent a contractual or statutory duty, there is no duty for a third party to retain evidence. In *Royal & Sunalliance v. Lauderdale Marine Center*,[145] the court rejected an insurer's attempt to hold a marina operator responsible for discarding evidence related to a fire that damaged two yachts docked there. The court held that even if it

---

140. 908 So. 2d 342 (Fla. 2005).
141. *Id.* at 1256. *See also* Jost v. Lakeland Reg'l Med. Ctr., Inc., 844 So. 2d 656 (Fla. Dist. Ct. App. 2003).
142. 507 So. 2d 596 (Fla. 1987).
143. No. SC03-334, 2005 Fla. LEXIS 1457, at *13 (internal citations and quotations omitted).
144. 473 So. 2d 1307 (Fla. Dist. Ct. App. 1984).
145. 877 So. 2d 843 (Fla. Dist. Ct. App. 2004).

had reason to anticipate that litigation would be instituted, the marina operator had no duty to preserve the evidence because it had not been served with a discovery request, and in Florida there is no general common-law duty to preserve evidence in anticipation of litigation.[146]

Civil and Evidentiary Sanctions for Destruction of Evidence

Florida courts have held that civil and evidentiary sanctions for spoliation or destruction of evidence are appropriate. These sanctions include the striking of pleadings, entry of a default judgment, exclusion of expert testimony, imposition of an adverse inference or evidentiary presumption, and dismissal of a claim.[147]

Some Florida courts have held that when a spoliator loses evidence, its intent is irrelevant.[148] These courts tend to focus on whether the destroyed or missing evidence is so important to the non-spoliating party's case that the case cannot proceed without it.[149]

However, other Florida courts have been reluctant to impose sanctions absent a showing of bad faith.[150] For example, in *Federal In-*

---

146. *Id.* at 846.

147. *See, e.g.,* DePuy, Inc. v. Eckes, 427 So. 2d 306 (Fla. Dist. Ct. App. 1983) (upholding trial court's decision to strike answer and affirmative defenses of defendant who lost a crucial piece of a plaintiff's prosthesis); Sponco Mfg., Inc. v. Alcover, 656 So. 2d 629 (Fla. Dist. Ct. App. 1995) (affirming entry of default judgment where manufacturer lost allegedly defective ladder in the absence of evidence of willful intent); *see also* Figgie Int'l, Inc. v. Dennis, 698 So. 2d 563 (Fla. Dist. Ct. App. 1997) (striking the pleadings and entering a default for noncompliance with discovery obligations); FLA. R. CIV. P. 1.380(b)(2).

148. *See, e.g., DePuy,* 427 So. 2d 306.

149. *Id.*

150. *See, e.g.,* Federal Ins. Co. v. Allister, 622 So. 2d 1348 (Fla. Dist. Ct. App. 1993); Metropolitan Dade Cty. v. Bermudez, 648 So. 2d 197 (Fla. Dist. Ct. App. 1994) (stating that appropriate sanctions depend on the willfulness or bad faith of the spoliating party); Tramel v. Bass, 672 So. 2d 78 (Fla. Dist. Ct. App. 1996) (affirming entry of a default judgment against the sheriff and his office for "willfully and intentionally" omitting a crucial portion of a videotape); Derosier v. Cooper Tire & Rubber Co., 819 So. 2d 143, 144 (Fla. Dist. Ct. App. 2003) (holding appropriateness of sanctions for loss of evidence depends upon the willfulness or bad faith of the spoliating party); Fleury v. Biomet, Inc. 865 So.2d 537 (Fla. Dist. Ct. App. 2003) (reversing spoliation sanction in the absence of a showing of fault by the alleged spoliator or prejudice to the non-spoliating party).

surance Company v. Allister,[151] the evidence showed that the plaintiff's loss of a garage door opener occurred while it was in the possession of the plaintiff's expert. Since there was other evidence available to the defendant, the *Allister* court reversed the trial court's sanction, which was equivalent to a dismissal. The appellate court suggested that on remand the trial court consider other, less onerous sanctions, including exclusion of the testimony of the expert who lost the evidence and/or an adverse inference instruction.[152]

In addition to these discovery and pleading sanctions, the Florida Supreme Court set forth criteria for imposing an evidentiary presumption when a party negligently or intentionally destroys hospital records.[153] If a hospital is unable to produce records, a plaintiff must show that the absence of the record hinders the plaintiff's ability to establish a *prima facie* case. If the plaintiff makes this showing, then a rebuttable presumption of liability arises. This rebuttable presumption is not overcome until the fact finder believes the presumed fact has been overcome by the degree of persuasion required by the substantive law of the case.[154] Mere negligent destruction of records is sufficient to impose liability on a hospital; however, further sanctions are available upon a showing of intentional destruction.[155]

Criminal Statutes

Florida Statute section 918.13 prohibits a person from tampering with evidence knowing that a "criminal trial or proceeding or an investigation" by a "prosecuting authority, law enforcement agency, grand jury or legislative committee of this state" is pending or is about to be instituted.[156] Criminal liability is only imposed in cases involving criminal proceedings or investigations.[157]

---

151. 622 So. 2d 1348.
152. *Id.*
153. Public Health Trust of Dade Cty. v. Valcin, 507 So. 2d 596 (Fla. 1987).
154. *Id.*
155. *Id.*
156. Fla. Stat. § 918.13 (2004).
157. *Id.*

GEORGIA

Independent Causes of Action for Destruction of Evidence

Georgia has not recognized spoliation of evidence as an independent cause of action.[158] In *Sharpnack v. Hoffenger Industries, Inc.*, the court declined to address whether to recognize an independent tort because it determined the alleged spoliation of evidence did not affect the outcome of the underlying claims.

Civil and Evidentiary Sanctions for Destruction of Evidence

Georgia courts have upheld a number of sanctions as appropriate to remedy destruction of evidence, including the use of an adverse inference instruction. For example, in *American Casualty Co. v. Schafer*,[159] two insurers brought claims for failure to pay premiums against an individual and a Georgia construction company. The construction company had once been incorporated in Louisiana, but later reincorporated in Georgia. The individual and his spouse were the sole shareholders for both the Louisiana and Georgia companies. Both the individual and the Georgia company asserted that they had no contractual relationship with one insurer. The trial court agreed and granted all defendants summary judgment, and the insurers appealed.[160]

The insurers argued there was an issue of fact regarding whether the Georgia company and the Louisiana company were each other's alter ego and sought to pierce the corporate veil. In discovery, one insurer had requested certain financial records of the defunct Louisiana company from the individual defendant. When the company failed to provide the records, the insurer moved to compel their production.

---

158. *See* Sharpnack v. Hoffenger Indus., Inc., 499 S.E.2d 363, 364 (Ga. Ct. App. 1998) ("a fresh look at the issue of whether Georgia should recognize an independent tort of [spoliation] may be appropriate. Nonetheless, this is not an appropriate case in which to conduct such a re-examination of Georgia law."). *See also* Owens v. American Refuse Systems, Inc., 563 S.E.2d 782, 784 (Ga. Ct. App. 2000) (declining to recognize spoliation of evidence as a tort claim); Gardner v. Blackston, 365 S.E.2d 545, 546 (Ga. Ct. App. 1988) ("Georgia law does not recognize spoliation of evidence as a separate tort."); Richardson v. Simmons, 538 S.E.2d 830 (Ga. Ct. App. 2000) (same).
159. 420 S.E.2d 820 (Ga. Ct. App. 1992).
160. *Id.*

The court of appeals reversed the Georgia company's favorable judgment and held there were genuine issues of material fact regarding the individual defendant's failure to produce the Louisiana company's financial records, including whether the records were in the individual defendant's control. If the records were found to be within the individual's control, then there would be a presumption raised against him,[161] because "[s]poliation of evidence raises a presumption against the spoliator."[162]

Georgia courts have also excluded evidence, including expert testimony, as a sanction for spoliation of evidence. In *Chapman v. Auto Owners Insurance Company*,[163] an insurer sued Robert Chapman for fire damage allegedly caused by one of his employees. Chapman moved to dismiss the complaint or to exclude testimony because a company hired by the insurer to investigate the fire destroyed items recovered from the fire shortly after the company filed the lawsuit. The insurer argued, and the trial court agreed, that the only available sanction under Georgia law for spoliation was an adverse inference instruction. But on interlocutory appeal, the court of appeals disagreed. It held:

> Chapman cites no Georgia cases and we have found none which address any other remedy available to the trial court when evidence has been destroyed. However, we find persuasive the reasoning in cases from foreign jurisdictions which have upheld the exclusion of testimony about the destroyed evidence in circumstances such as those presented by this case. Those decisions reason that a jury charge is insufficient to counter the prejudice resulting to a party who, because of the destruction of evidence, was unable to put on a full defense of its case.[164]

The court also reasoned that the availability of photographs of the destroyed evidence was an inadequate substitute for the evidence itself, particularly given testimony by Chapman's expert regarding

---

161. *Id.*

162. Greer v. Andrew, 75 S.E. 1050, 1051 (Ga. 1912); *see also* Cavin v. Brown, 538 S.E.2d 802, 803 (Ga. Ct. App. 2000) (same); Lane v. Montgomery Elevator Co., 484 S.E.2d 249, 251 (Ga. Ct. App. 1997) (same).

163. 469 S.E.2d 783 (Ga. Ct. App. 1996).

164. *Id.* at 784.

the tests it would have performed on the evidence if it had been available.[165]

Citing to *Northern Assurance Co. v. Ware*,[166] the *Chapman* court noted that the following factors are relevant in determining whether to exclude evidence: (1) whether the defendant was prejudiced by spoliation; (2) whether it could be cured; (3) the practical importance of the evidence; (4) whether the plaintiff acted in good or bad faith; and (5) the potential for abuse if expert testimony regarding the spoliated evidence were not excluded.[167]

Accordingly, where spoliation of evidence has prejudiced a party, the trial court has the discretion either to give an adverse inference instruction or to exclude testimony, including expert testimony.[168]

Criminal Statutes

Georgia law provides that "a person commits the crime of hindering the apprehension or punishment of a criminal when, with intent to hinder the apprehension or punishment of a person whom he knows or has reasonable grounds to believe has committed a felony or to be an escaped inmate or prisoner, he . . . [c]onceals or destroys evidence of the crime."[169] Although it appears that no Georgia court has directly addressed the issue, in *Baker v. State*,[170] the Georgia Court of Appeals noted, in affirming a conviction under the statute, that "purloining, destruction, or substitution of evidence needed or used in the prosecution of a criminal offense" would constitute a violation of the statute.[171] Accordingly, it appears that intentional destruction of evidence to prevent apprehension or punishment of one believed to be a felon for purposes of hindering his apprehension or punishment would constitute obstruction of justice under Georgia law.

---

165. *Id.*
166. 145 F.R.D. 281 (D. Me. 1993).
167. *Chapman*, 469 S.E.2d at 785; *see also* Bridgestone/Firestone N. Am. Tire v. Campbell Nissan N. Am., 574 S.E.2d 923, 926 (Ga. Ct. App. 2002) (same).
168. R.A. Siegel Co. v. Bowen, 539 S.E.2d 873 (Ga. Ct. App. 2000) (excluding defendant's expert witness as a sanction for destruction of evidence in violation of a preservation order).
169. Ga. Code Ann. § 16-10-50(A)(2) (2004).
170. 178 S.E.2d 278 (Ga. Ct. App. 1970).
171. *Id.* at 279.

HAWAII

Independent Causes of Action for Destruction of Evidence

The Hawaii Supreme Court accepted a certified question asking whether Hawaii law recognized a first-party civil action for intentional and/or negligent spoliation of evidence in *Matsuura v. E.I. du Pont de Nemours & Company*.[172] But the court declined to answer the question, because the facts alleged in the case before it could not support a spoliation claim.[173] Therefore, whether there is a cause of action for intentional or negligent spoliation of evidence under Hawaii law remains an open question.

Civil and Evidentiary Sanctions for Destruction of Evidence

The Hawaiian Supreme Court has considered whether and under what circumstances a Hawaiian trial court may impose sanctions for the destruction or concealment of relevant evidence. In *Kawamata Farms, Inc. v. United Agri Products*,[174] the court analyzed a contentious discovery dispute between plaintiffs and a chemical manufacturer. The parties had obtained 54 discovery orders and 27 court-imposed sanctions for discovery violations. Five of these orders dealt with intentionally withholding or destroying material evidence.[175] The trial court imposed, and the supreme court upheld, a variety of discovery sanctions, including a monetary sanction of $1.5 million and lifting protective orders concerning the confidentiality of the manufacturer's documents, declaring that it would give the jury remedial instructions reflecting the discovery misconduct and explaining the basis on which certain witnesses would be called regarding withheld or destroyed documentary evidence.[176] In addition, the court prevented the chemical manufacturer's experts from offering rebuttal testimony in response to testimony by plaintiff's expert. Thus, *Kawamata Farms* teaches that a trial court in Hawaii may impose a variety of civil and evidentiary sanctions to remedy intentional destruction of evidence.

The Hawaiian Supreme Court also recognizes that courts may impose a preclusion sanction as a penalty for tampering with or destroy-

---

172. 73 P.3d 687 (Haw. 2003).
173. *Id.* at 706.
174. 948 P.2d 1055 (Haw. 1997).
175. *Id.*
176. *Id.*

ing evidence. In *Wong v. City & County of Honolulu*,[177] an automobile hit a pedestrian while the pedestrian was crossing an intersection controlled by a malfunctioning traffic light. The pedestrian brought suit against the city, claiming its negligent failure to properly maintain the traffic light proximately caused the accident. Despite formal and informal requests for the production of the traffic signal, city employees removed and destroyed it. Accordingly, the trial court imposed a preclusion sanction that estopped the city from arguing that the malfunctioning traffic lights were caused by anything other than its own negligence.[178]

The key to the supreme court's holding in *Wong* was (1) the city's culpability in destroying a piece of potentially critical evidence that had been formally requested in discovery; (2) the resulting prejudice to the plaintiff's case; and (3) the inequity that would occur in allowing the city to accrue benefit from its conduct.[179] The court imposed this sanction because "[I]t is only fair that sanctions be imposed so that the city does not benefit from its destruction of potentially significant evidence."[180]

The court in *Richardson v. Sport Shinko* held that Hawaiian courts have inherent equity, supervisory, and administrative powers, as well as the inherent power to control the litigation process before them. Among the courts' inherent powers is the power to "create a remedy for a wrong even in the absence of specific statutory remedies."[181] The court observed that trial courts have the inherent power to curb abuses and provide a fair process, which extends to precluding evidence and, in severe circumstances, dismissal.[182]

Because a trial court has the inherent power to impose the ultimate sanction of dismissal, it follows that the court may take all reasonable steps short of dismissal, depending on the equities of the case. Thus, the Hawaiian Supreme Court has authorized trial courts to fashion a remedy to cure prejudice suffered by one party as a result of another

---

177. 665 P.2d 157 (Haw. 1983).

178. *Id.*

179. *Id. See also* Richardson v. Sport Shinko, 880 P.2d 169, 182 (Haw. 1994) (citing *Wong, supra*).

180. *Id.* at 161.

181. *Richardson*, 880 P.2d at 182 (quoting Peat, Marwick, Mitchell v. Superior Court, 200 Cal. App. 3d 272, 288 (1988)).

182. *Id.*

party's loss or destruction of critical evidence.[183]

Criminal Statutes

Hawaii prohibits tampering with physical evidence with the intent to impair its verity in a pending or prospective official proceeding.[184] Tampering with such evidence is a misdemeanor. It does not appear that a Hawaiian court has imposed any criminal sanction against a party for tampering with physical evidence in a civil matter.

IDAHO

Independent Causes of Action for Destruction of Evidence

The Idaho Supreme Court has not expressly adopted the tort of spoliation of evidence.[185] However, in *Yoakum v. Hartford Fire Insurance Company*,[186] the court discussed the "intentional interference with [a] prospective civil action by spoliation of evidence."[187] There, the court stated that to establish such a claim, the plaintiff must show that the defendant either had an improper motive to harm the plaintiff or used wrongful means to cause injury to the plaintiff's prospective advantage.[188] To be actionable, the means used by the defendant must be wrongful based on a statute, regulation, common-law rule, or established standard of a trade or profession.[189] Criticizing the majority for failing to recognize or reject the tort of spoliation, in dissent, Chief Justice Schroeder stated that whatever the title, "there should be recognized a cause of action for intentionally depriving a party of the value of a cause of action by improper means."[190]

Civil and Evidentiary Sanctions for Destruction of Evidence

In Idaho, spoliation is a "rule of evidence applicable at the discretion

---

183. *Id.*
184. HAW. REV. STAT. § 710-1076 (2003).
185. Yoakum v. Hartford Fire Ins. Co., 923 P.2d 416 (Idaho 1996); *see also* Ricketts v. Eastern Idaho Equip. Co., Inc., 51 P.3d 392 (Idaho 2002).
186. *Id.*
187. *Id.* at 423.
188. *Id.*
189. *Id.*
190. *Id.* at 427 (Schroeder, C.J., dissenting).

of the trial court."[191] The spoliation doctrine recognizes that a party will not usually destroy favorable evidence. Therefore, the doctrine provides that "when a party with a duty to preserve evidence intentionally destroys it, an inference arises that the destroyed evidence was unfavorable to that party."[192]

Criminal Statutes

Idaho Code section 18-2603[193] prohibits the willful destruction, alteration or concealment of evidence that is about to be produced, used or discovered as evidence upon any trial, proceeding, inquiry or investigation with the intent to prevent it from being produced, discovered or used. If the proceeding, inquiry or investigation is criminal in nature and involves a felony offense, the spoliation offense is a felony.[194] Otherwise, the offense is a misdemeanor.[195] No Idaho courts have applied the statute in a civil context.

ILLINOIS

Independent Causes of Action for Destruction of Evidence

The Illinois Supreme Court declined to recognize the tort of spoliation of evidence in *Boyd v. Travelers Insurance Company.*[196] Rather, the court held that a claim for negligent spoliation can be stated under existing negligence law. That claim also may be heard along with the underlying suit on which it is based. This allows a single trier of fact to resolve all claims "fairly and consistently."[197] The *Boyd* court considered it important that a single trier of fact resolve all claims because:

---

191. Bromley v. Garey, 979 P.2d 1165, 1170 (Idaho 1999); *see also* Ricketts v. Eastern Idaho Equip. Co., Inc., 51 P.3d 392 (Idaho 2002) (holding denial of adverse inference instruction appropriate in the absence of intentional conduct); Murray v. Farmers Ins. Co., 796 P.2d 101 (Idaho 1990) (holding denial of adverse inference appropriate in a malpractice action where the jury determined that plaintiffs had failed to prove that their attorney's malpractice had caused them to lose a right to recover).

192. *Id.*

193. Idaho Code § 18-2603 (2004).

194. *Id.*

195. *Id.*

196. 652 N.E.2d 267 (Ill. 1995). *See also* Miller v. Gupta, 672 N.E.2d 1229 (Ill. 1996).

197. 652 N.E.2d at 272.

[i]f a plaintiff loses the underlying suit, only the trier of fact who heard the case would know the real reason why. Therefore, a spoliator may be held liable in a negligence action *only* if its loss or destruction of evidence caused a plaintiff to be unable to prove the underlying suit.[198]

Under *Boyd*, to prevail in a negligence action involving the loss or destruction of evidence, a plaintiff must plead the existence of a duty owed by a defendant to it, a breach of that duty, an injury proximately resulting from that breach, and damages.[199] A defendant owes a duty of care to preserve evidence if a reasonable person in the defendant's position should have foreseen that the evidence was material to a potential civil action. A plaintiff must allege facts describing conduct in its pleadings.[200] A plaintiff also must plead sufficient facts to support a claim that, but for the defendant's loss or destruction of the evidence, it had a reasonable probability of succeeding on the merits.[201] Illinois courts refers to these two elements as the "relationship" and the "foreseeability prong[s]."[202]

In December 2004, the Illinois Supreme Court reversed an appellate court decision that took an expansive view of the duty to preserve evidence, holding that a defendant need not have possession of the evidence before a duty to preserve will be imposed.[203]

In that case, a newspaper delivery man fell in a hole on a brick sidewalk and injured his elbow. Because it was not yet daylight, the delivery man bent down close to the hole to get a good look at it. He later returned with a neighbor to look at the brick walk and obtained the name of the homeowner's insurance company.

---

198. *Id.* (emphasis in original).

199. *Id.*

200. Anderson v. Mack Trucks, Inc., 793 N.E.2d 962 (Ill. App. 2003) (citing Jackson v. Michael Reese Hosp. & Med. Ctr., 689 N.E.2d 205 (Ill. App. 1998)). *See also* Kelly v. Sears Roebuck & Co., 720 N.E.2d 683 (Ill. App. 1999).

201. *Id. See also* Thornton v. Shah, 777 N.E.2d 396 (Ill. App. 2002).

202. Dardeen v. Kuehling, No. 97999 (Ill. Dec. 2, 2004); Anderson v. Mack Trucks, Inc., 793 N.E.2d 962 (Ill. App. 2003). In December 2004, the Illinois Supreme Court stated that "*Boyd* remains our watershed pronouncement on spoliation of evidence." Dardeen v. Kuehling, No. 97999.

203. Dardeen, No. 97999 (Ill. S. Ct. Dec. 2, 2004), *reversing* 801 N.E.2d 960 (Ill. App. 2003).

The homeowner reported the accident to her insurer, explaining that the bricks were "cocked up" in the area where the plaintiff fell. She asked the insurer if she could remove the bricks so that no one else would be injured and, according to the homeowner, the insurer told her she could remove them. Neither the delivery man nor the homeowner photographed the accident site, but the delivery man did have his injuries photographed.

The delivery man brought suit claiming that a hole in the walk caused his injuries, and the homeowner defended by denying that a hole existed. The delivery man then amended his complaint to include a claim for spoliation against the homeowner and the insurer. The trial court granted the insurer summary judgment, the delivery man appealed, and the appellate court reversed, stating that the insurer should have directed the homeowner to photograph or videotape the walk before removing the bricks.[204]

In the Illinois Supreme Court, the insurer argued that it satisfied its burden of showing that the insured had a duty to preserve the sidewalk because the insurance contract "somehow created a special circumstance that satisf[ied] the relationship prong."[205] Rejecting that assertion, the *Dardeen* court observed, "No Illinois court has held that a mere opportunity to exercise control over the evidence at issue is sufficient to meet the relationship prong" and held that because the insurer had neither possession nor control over the sidewalk, it had no duty to preserve it.[206]

Other recent decisions by Illinois courts have focused on the duty to preserve evidence and when that duty may arise. For example, in *Jones v. O'Brien Tire & Battery Service Center,*[207] the court focused on when the duty to preserve evidence attached, commenting that the existence of a potential lawsuit was irrelevant. Rather, the court found that the critical factor is what the defendant knew or should have known under the facts and circumstances of the case. The court then found that there were sufficient special circumstances

---

204. Dardeen v. Kuehling, 801 N.E.2d 960, 967 (Ill. App. 2003).
205. Dardeen v. Kuehling, No. 97999.
206. *Dardeen*, 801 N.E.2d at 967.
207. 752 N.E.2d 8 (Ill. App. 2001). *See also Andersen*, 793 N.E.2d 962 (rejecting a spoliation claim where plaintiff failed to allege that a contract, agreement, statute or regulation created the duty to preserve evidence).

to establish a landscaper's duty to preserve a tire assembly for any potential party's benefit.[208]

Civil and Evidentiary Sanctions for Destruction of Evidence

Illinois courts may impose a variety of sanctions for spoliation that occurs during pending or threatened litigation. These include dismissal, exclusion of evidence, and the giving of an adverse inference instruction to the jury.[209]

Illinois Supreme Court Rule 219(c) permits a trial court to impose sanctions, including dismissal of a particular claim or cause of action, on any party who unreasonably refuses to comply with discovery rules or orders entered under those rules.[210] The trial court has discretion to select a particular sanction, and its decision will not be reversed absent an abuse of discretion.[211]

In *Shimanovsky v. General Motors Corporation*,[212] the Illinois Supreme Court addressed whether a trial court has authority under Illinois Supreme Court Rule 219(c) to impose a sanction for destruction of evidence that occurs before commencement of a lawsuit. There, the owners of a vehicle claimed that a defect in the power-steering mechanism of their automobile caused a crash resulting in injury. Before filing the lawsuit, the owners' expert performed destructive testing on a portion of the power-steering mechanism without notifying the defendant-manufacturer. Shortly before trial, the manufacturer sought and obtained an order dismissing the owners' claims as a sanction under Supreme Court Rule 219(c). The owner challenged the dismissal, arguing, among other things, that before imposing the sanction of dismissal, the trial court should have held an evidentiary hearing to determine the extent to which the manufacturer had been prejudiced.[213]

---

208. *Id. See also* Note, *Spoiling an Illinois Personal Injury Plaintiff's Spoliation Claim for Routinely Maintained Items*, 28 S. ILL. U. L.J. 455 (Winter 2004).

209. *See* Kambylis v. Ford Motor Co., 788 N.E.2d 1 (Ill. Ct. App. 2003); American Family Ins. Co. v. Village Pontiac-GMC, Inc., 585 N.E.2d 1115 (Ill. Ct. App. 1992); Thomas v. Bombardier-Rotax Motorefabrik, GmbH, 909 F. Supp. 585, 587 (N.D. Ill. 1996).

210. *See* Lekkas v. Mitsubishi Motors Corp., No. 97C6070, 2002 U.S. Dist. LEXIS 18390 (N.D. Ill. 2002).

211. Shimanovsky v. General Motors Corp., 692 N.E.2d 286 (Ill. 1998).

212. 692 N.E.2d 286 (Ill. 1998).

213. *Id.*

Acknowledging that dismissal and default judgment are drastic sanctions that should only be invoked when a party's actions show "deliberate, contumacious or unwarranted disregard of the court's authority,"[214] the Illinois Supreme Court held that reversing a trial court's choice of a particular sanction is justified only when the record shows a clear abuse of discretion. It identified the factors that courts should consider in imposing a particular sanction as (1) surprise to the adverse party; (2) the prejudicial effect of the proffered evidence; (3) the nature of the testimony or evidence; (4) the diligence of the adverse party in seeking discovery; (5) the timeliness of the adverse party's objection to the evidence; and (6) the good faith of the party offering the evidence.[215]

The *Shimanovsky* court explained that when imposing sanctions, the court's purpose is to coerce compliance with discovery rules and orders, not to punish the dilatory party:

> Dismissing [the owners'] cause of action solely because evidence was altered, without regard to the unique factual situation or the relevant factors which should be considered in determining an appropriate sanction, is a sanction which serves only to punish the party and does nothing to further object to discovery.[216]

The Illinois Supreme Court then applied the six factors discussed above and remanded the case to the trial court with instructions to impose lesser sanctions on the owners if the court so chose, but not the sanction of dismissal.[217]

Criminal Statutes

An Illinois criminal statute prohibits obstruction of justice. Among other things, the statute defines obstruction as destroying, altering, concealing, or disguising physical evidence with the intent to prevent its use by the prosecution or the defense.[218] The statute does not appear to have been applied in a civil lawsuit.

---

214. *Id.* at 291.
215. *Id. See also Lekkas*, 2002 U.S. Dist. LEXIS 1839.
216. *Shimanovsky*, 692 N.E.2d at 293.
217. *Id.*
218. 720 ILL. COMP. STAT. 5/31-4 (West 2003).
§ 2023.

INDIANA

Independent Causes of Action for Destruction of Evidence

Answering a question certified from the United States District Court for the Southern District of Indiana in *Gribben v. Wal-Mart Stores, Inc.*,[219] the Indiana Supreme Court refused to recognize a claim for first-party intentional or negligent spoliation. The court found the availability of existing remedies, like sanctions, outweighed the disadvantages, like continuous litigation, of recognizing the tort.

The *Gribben* court discussed the narrow rejection of a spoliation claim by the court in *Murphy v. Target Products*.[220] There, an employee filed a complaint against several defendants, alleging defective manufacture and design of a power saw. Thereafter, he sought leave to add his employer as another defendant. The basis for the claim against the employer was that it allegedly spoliated evidence relevant to plaintiff's lawsuit.[221]

The *Murphy* court granted the employer's motion to dismiss for failure to state a claim. On appeal, the court affirmed. Although the court noted that two jurisdictions had recognized the tort of intentional spoliation of evidence, it further reasoned as follows:

> Carefully considering the issue, we conclude that in Indiana there is no common law duty on the part of an employer to preserve, for an employee, potential evidence in an employee's possible third party action. We therefore hold that at least in the absence of an independent tort, contract, agreement, or special relationship imposing a duty to the particular claimant, the claim of negligent or intentional interference with a person's prospective or actual civil litigation by the spoliation of evidence is not and ought not be recognized in Indiana.[222]

The *Murphy* court concluded that because the employee had failed to allege any basis for the existence of an independent tort, contract, agreement, or special relationship with the employer, no duty ex-

---

219. 824 N.E.2d 349 (Ind. 2005).
220. 580 N.E.2d 687 (Ind. Ct. App. 1991).
221. *Id.* at 689.
222. *Id.* at 690.

isted on the part of the employer to preserve the allegedly spoliated evidence.[223]

The *Gribben* court also discussed *Thompson v. Owensby*,[224] where the plaintiffs filed suit against owners of a dog that had disfigured their six-year-old child. They also sued the manufacturer of the dog-restraining cable and the dog owners' landlords. The landlords' insurance company investigated the claim and took possession of the restraining cable, which it subsequently lost. The plaintiffs thereupon sued the insurance company for negligence, and an Indiana appellate court ruled that although courts can sanction spoliation in pending litigation using other remedies (e.g., an adverse inference), the plaintiffs were entitled to pursue their tort action as an alternative remedy. The court also noted that an insurer has a duty to retain items that are entrusted to it in connection with possible litigation, and reversed.[225]

The *Gribben* court distinguished *Thompson*. It emphasized that the claim involved third-party spoliation by a liability insurer and pointed out that the *Thompson* court had declined to address whether there would be a duty to maintain evidence outside that context.

The *Gribben* court further noted that its response to the certified question was limited to "first party" spoliation. It observed that a tort remedy may be needed in cases of third-party spoliation.[226]

Civil and Evidentiary Sanctions for Destruction of Evidence

Indiana courts will impose sanctions for spoliation of evidence during pending litigation. This can include giving an adverse inference instruction against the party who lost the evidence.[227] It appears that courts in Indiana require evidence of intentional destruction of evidence before they will give an adverse inference or spoliation instruction to a jury.[228]

---

223. *Id.*

224. 704 N.E.2d 134 (Ind. Ct. App. 1998).

225. *Id.*

226. 824 N.E.2d 349 (Ind. 2005).

227. *Thompson*, 704 N.E.2d at 140. The Indiana Supreme Court has held the spoliation rule applies to altered as well as destroyed documents. *See* Cahoon v. Cummings, 734 N.E.2d 535, 545 (Ind. 2000).

228. *See* Estate of Curtis Underwood v. Gale Tschuor Co., 799 N.E.2d 1122 (Ind. Ct. App. 2003).

In more extreme situations, dismissal with prejudice may be warranted.[229] Alternatively, a party may seek to exclude evidence based on spoliation.[230] But in any case, Indiana courts limit sanctions for spoliation of evidence, whether as an evidentiary inference or as a tort, to the destruction or alteration of physical evidence.[231]

Criminal Statutes

The Indiana Code[232] provides that a person tampers with evidence when the person "alters, damages, or removes any record, document, or thing, with intent to prevent it from being produced or used as evidence in any official proceeding or investigation."[233] Indiana courts have not clarified whether an "official proceeding" includes both a criminal and a civil proceeding and whether criminal sanctions are available for spoliation of evidence during a civil proceeding.

IOWA

Independent Causes of Action for Destruction of Evidence

In *Meyn v. Iowa*,[234] the Supreme Court of Iowa declined to adopt a cause of action for negligent spoliation of evidence in a third-party context. There, the spoliation occurred while evidence was in possession of a third-party hospital, which had no connection to litigation between plaintiff and the manufacturer of an allegedly defective product. The court analyzed several rationales articulated by other courts for refusing to adopt this tort theory, including that recognition of a new tort would

---

229. Greco v. Ford Motor Co., 937 F. Supp. 810, 815 (S.D. Ind. 1996) ("a dismissal with prejudice is a harsh sanction which should usually be employed only in extreme situations, where there is a clear record of delay or contumacious conduct, or when less drastic sanctions have proven unavailable") (internal citation omitted).

230. *Id.* at 816 (considering and rejecting an argument that evidence should be excluded and summary judgment granted).

231. *See, e.g., Cahoon*, 734 N.E.2d at 545; Loomis v. Ameritech Corp., 764 N.E.2d 658 (Ind. Ct. App. 2002) (denying claim for spoliation of testimonial evidence).

232. IND. CODE § 35-44-3-4 (2004).

233. *Id.* at § 35-44-3-4(a)(3).

234. 594 N.W.2d 31 (Iowa 1999).

spawn further litigation, lead to a lack of finality, potentially impose new duties on strangers to litigation, and lead to speculation.[235]

Moreover, reasoned the court, Iowa already provided a number of remedies for spoliation of evidence, including "discovery sanctions, barring duplicative evidence where fraud or intentional disruption is indicated and instructing on an unfavorable inference to be drawn from the fact that evidence was destroyed."[236] Finally, the *Meyn* court concluded that the fact that the evidence was in the possession of the third party also weakened the argument in favor of adopting a negligent spoliation of evidence tort.[237] Accordingly, the court declined to adopt the new tort on the facts before it.

Civil or Evidentiary Sanctions for Destruction of Evidence

As noted, Iowa courts can impose a variety of remedies for spoliation of evidence, including discovery sanctions, precluding evidence, and giving an adverse inference instruction.[238] Iowa courts generally allow a spoliation inference "when the destruction of relevant evidence was intentional, as opposed to merely negligent or the evidence was destroyed as the result of routine procedure."[239]

For example, in *Gamerdinger v. Schaefer*,[240] the plaintiff sued the defendants for damages allegedly sustained as a result of a collision between a motorized cart driven by one of the plaintiffs and a forklift driven by one of the defendants. Following a jury verdict for the plaintiff, which was reduced by her percentage of fault, the plaintiff successfully moved for a new trial. The plaintiff raised certain evidentiary issues, including that the trial court had erred in declining to give a spoliation instruction based on photographs taken of the accident scene by the defendants. During discovery, the plaintiff requested copies of photographs, but the defendants responded there were none.

---

235. *Id.* at 33-34.
236. *Id.* at 34.
237. *Id.*
238. *Id.*
239. Lynch v. Saddler, 656 N.W.2d 104, 111 (Iowa 2003); Carter v. Cedar Rapids Bowl, Inc., 2002 Iowa App. LEXIS 498, *4 (Iowa Ct. App. 2002); Phillips v. Covenant Clinic, 625 N.W.2d 714, 721 (Iowa 2001); Hendricks v. Great Plains Supply Co., 609 N.W.2d 486, 491 (Iowa 2000).
240. 603 N.W.2d 590 (Iowa 1999).

On appeal, the Iowa Supreme Court held that the trial court's failure to give this instruction was reversible error. It reasoned that "the court is required to give a requested instruction when it states a correct rule of law having application to the facts of the case, and the concept is not otherwise embodied in other instructions."[241] Moreover, "[i]t stands without argument that where relevant evidence is within the control of a party whose interest would naturally call for its production, and he failed to do so without satisfactory explanation, it may be inferred such evidence would be unfavorable to him."[242] Accordingly, the Iowa Supreme Court held that the trial court erred by not giving the requested instruction.[243]

Despite its endorsement of the adverse reference, the Iowa Supreme Court has observed that the spoliation inference "should be used prudently and sparingly."[244] That is, unless a party can show "both intentional destruction and control of evidence," he is not entitled to such an instruction.[245]

Criminal Statutes

Under the Iowa Code, a person is guilty of preventing apprehension, obstructing prosecution, or obstructing defense when the person "[d]estroys, alters, conceals, or disguises physical evidence that would be admissible in the trial of another."[246] Iowa courts have not clarified whether "trial courts" refers to both criminal and civil proceedings or only to criminal proceedings.

KANSAS

Independent Causes of Action for Spoliation of Evidence

In *Koplin v. Rosel Well Perforators, Inc.*,[247] the Supreme Court of Kansas addressed whether to recognize the tort of intentional interference

---

241. *Id.* at 595.
242. *Id.* (quoting Quint-Cities Petroleum Co. v. Maas, 143 N.W.2d 345, 348 (Iowa 1966)).
243. *Id.*
244. 656 N.W.2d 104, 111.
245. *Id.*
246. Iowa Code § 719.3(1) (2003).
247. 734 P.2d 1177 (Kan. 1987).

with prospective civil action by spoliation of evidence. In that case, the defendant allegedly failed to preserve a T-clamp that injured an employee in a workplace accident. After recovering workers' compensation benefits, the employee sued the manufacturer and the seller of the T-clamp. The employee also alleged spoliation of evidence against his employer.

The district court certified the spoliation question to the Supreme Court of Kansas, which declined to recognize a claim on the facts before it. The court noted there was no duty on the part of the employer to preserve the T-clamp, since it was not involved in pending or contemplated litigation with the employee at the time.[248] The *Koplin* court declined to impose a duty on the employer to retain the T-clamp, stating that "to adopt such a tort and place a duty upon an employer to preserve all possible physical evidence that might somehow be utilized in a third-party action by an injured employee would place an intolerable burden on every employer."[249]

The court distinguished two earlier spoliation cases, *Smith v. Superior Court*[250] and *Hazen v. Municipality of Anchorage*,[251] on the basis that in those cases, unlike the present case, "the defendants or potential defendants in the underlying case destroyed the evidence to their own advantage."[252] The court left open whether it would recognize a claim for spoliation of evidence on facts similar to those in *Smith* and *Hazen*.[253]

One federal district court sitting in Kansas has held that the Kansas Supreme Court may recognize the tort of spoliation when there was some independent duty to preserve evidence. In *Foster v. Lawrence Memorial Hospital*,[254] the court concluded that Kansas would recognize a tort of spoliation in some circumstances and noted the following language from the *Koplin* decision: "We conclude that absent some independent tort, contract, agreement, voluntary assumption of duty, or special relationship of the parties the new tort of 'intentional inter-

248. *Id.*
249. *Id.* at 1182.
250. 198 Cal. Rptr. 829 (1984).
251. 718 P.2d 456 (Alaska 1986).
252. *Koplin*, 734 P.2d at 1182.
253. *Id.*
254. 809 F. Supp. 831 (D. Kan. 1992).

ference with a prospective civil action by spoliation of evidence' should not be recognized in Kansas."[255]

Based on this language, the *Foster* court concluded that the Kansas Supreme Court would recognize a spoliation tort if the alleged spoliator already owes an independent duty to the non-spoliating party to preserve the evidence.[256] The district court concluded, on the facts before it, that the issue of whether the defendant doctor had a duty to plaintiff to preserve his personal notes was a question of fact, precluding summary judgment on the spoliation issue. Later, the district court determined that the non-spoliating party could not assert a claim for spoliation of evidence because it did not claim any damages that were distinct from the underlying claim.[257]

Civil and Evidentiary Sanctions for Destruction of Evidence

Kansas courts have the "inherent authority" to "sanction counsel for bad faith conduct."[258] Accordingly, Kansas courts have the authority to impose sanctions for spoliation of evidence. In *Kansas v. Folks*,[259] the court held: "Generally, the destruction of evidence without satisfactory explanation gives rise to an inference unfavorable to the spoliator and he who destroys such evidence is thereby held to admit the truth of the allegations of the opposing party."[260] Kansas courts also have authority to impose sanctions for misconduct under the civil discovery rules.[261]

---

255. *Id.* at 837.

256. *Id.* at 838.

257. Foster v. Lawrence Mem'l Hosp., 818 F. Supp. 319, 322 (D. Kan. 1993).

258. Knutson Mortgage Corp. v. Coleman, 951 P.2d 548, 550-51 (Kan. Ct. App. 1997).

259. No. 58,471, 1986 Kan. App. LEXIS 1617 (Kan. Ct. App. Dec. 24, 1986).

260. *Id.* at *8. *See also* Armstrong v. Salina, 507 P.2d 323, 339 (Kan. 1973) ("Failure of a party to an action to throw light upon an issue peculiarly within his own knowledge or reach, raises a presumption that the concealed information is unfavorable to him.").

261. Shay v. Kansas Dep't of Transp., 959 P.2d 849, 851 (Kan. 1998) (discovery sanctions available under KAN. STAT. ANN. § 60-237); Canaan v. Bartee, 35 P.3d 841 (Kan. 2001) (holding imposition of sanctions for failure to comply with discovery orders is a matter within the court's sound discretion).

Criminal Statutes

Under Kansas statute,[262] a person commits the crime of "[o]bstructing legal process or official duty" by:

> knowingly and intentionally obstructing, resisting, or opposing any person authorized by law to serve process in the service or execution or in the attempt to serve or execute any writ, warrant, process, or order of a court in the discharge of any official duty.[263]

The statute does not specifically address whether destruction of evidence would constitute obstructing legal process or official duty.

KENTUCKY

Independent Causes of Action for Destruction of Evidence

In *Monsanto Company v. Reed*,[264] the Kentucky Supreme Court declined to recognize a new cause of action for spoliation of evidence. In this products liability case, the court chose to "remedy the matter through evidentiary rules and 'missing evidence' instructions," rather than by recognizing a new tort.[265]

Civil and Evidentiary Sanctions for Destruction of Evidence

The Supreme Court of Kentucky has sanctioned the use of a "missing evidence instruction" as a remedy for the loss or destruction of evidence in a civil context. Such an instruction is a matter left to the trial court, and its purpose is to "eliminate the prejudice resulting from the unavailability of . . . evidence."[266]

In *Sanborn v. Commonwealth of Kentucky*,[267] the Kentucky Supreme Court approved an instruction allowing a jury to draw an infer-

---

262. KAN. STAT. ANN. § 21-3808 (2005).
263. *Id.* at § 21-3808(a).
264. 950 S.W.2d 811 (Ky. 1997).
265. *Id.* at 815 (citing Tinsley v. Jackson, 771 S.W.2d 331 (Ky. 1989)); Sanborn v. Commonwealth, 754 S.W.2d 534 (Ky. 1988).
266. *Tinsley,* 771 S.W.2d at 332; Kentucky Dep't of Corrections v. McCullough, No. 1998-CA-001403-MR, 2000 Ky. App. LEXIS 57 (Ky. App. Ct. May 26, 2000).
267. 754 S.W.2d 534 (Ky. 1988).

ence favorable to a defendant from destruction of evidence by a prosecutor. Nine years later, the Kentucky Supreme Court cited *Sanborn* with approval as the method trial courts should use to remedy spoliation of evidence in civil matters.[268]

Criminal Statutes

Under Kentucky statute,[269] a person commits a crime of tampering with physical evidence when that person destroys, mutilates, conceals, removes or alters evidence or potential evidence, with the intent to impair its availability in an official proceeding.

LOUISIANA

Independent Causes of Action for Destruction of Evidence

The Louisiana Supreme Court has not addressed whether Louisiana recognizes an independent cause of action for spoliation of evidence. However, at least two federal district courts have addressed how they believe the Louisiana Supreme Court would rule on the facts before those courts. In addition, some Louisiana appellate courts have acknowledged tort claims for intentional spoliation, but not for negligent spoliation.

In *Edwards v. Louisville Ladder Company*,[270] a products liability action arising from an employee's fall from a ladder, the employer disposed of the ladder before the defendants had an opportunity to examine it. The defendants brought a tort action for spoliation against the third-party employer.[271]

The *Edwards* court observed that the Louisiana Supreme Court has been cautious about expanding tort liability and emphasized the policy considerations weighing against recognizing spoliation as a tort. The court discussed the difficulty in determining the actual value or

---

268. *See Monsanto Co.*, 950 S.W.2d at 815. Although it considered the issue in a criminal case, the Kentucky Supreme Court has held that "absent some degree of 'bad faith,' the defendant is not entitled to an instruction that the jury may draw an adverse inference from [the loss or destruction of exculpatory evidence]." Roark v. Commonwealth, 90 S.W.3d 24 (Ky. 2002) (citation omitted).

269. Ky. Rev. Stat. Ann. § 524.100 (2003).

270. 796 F. Supp. 966 (W.D. La. 1992).

271. *Id.*

detriment of the destroyed evidence to either party and the potential to interfere with another's right to dispose of his own property, especially where the evidence is in the possession of a third party. The court also questioned whether the spoliation tort would give parties a "second bite of the apple" to retry a case if they received an unfavorable result in the first trial.[272]

The *Edwards* court also noted that in Louisiana, adequate remedies exist to deal with spoliation, including Federal Rule of Civil Procedure 37 and Louisiana Code of Civil Procedure Article 1471, which may effectively address problems of spoliation. Explaining that the employee had not alleged a special relationship, statute, contract or affirmative agreement to preserve the missing evidence, the court found that the employee failed to state a claim for spoliation of evidence. The *Edwards* court also found insufficient authority to establish the existence of an independent tort of spoliation.[273]

Courts in Louisiana also have considered spoliation in the context of a claim for intentional or negligent impairment of a civil action. For example, in *Bethea v. Modern Biomedical Services, Inc.,*[274] a Louisiana appellate court analyzed a plaintiff's claim for impairment of a civil claim and spoliation of evidence where the plaintiff had been electrocuted while plugging in an intravenous pump. After her injury, the plaintiff asked the defendant to preserve the plug, receptacle, and cover plate; however, the defendant lost or destroyed the evidence.

The *Bethea* court addressed whether Louisiana recognizes a cause of action for intentional or negligent impairment of a civil action in the absence of a contractual or statutory duty to preserve evidence. The court held that a duty to preserve evidence and to avoid hindering a plaintiff's claim arises under Louisiana Civil Code Article 2315, which states: "[E]very act whatever of man that causes damage to another obliges him by whose fault it happened to repair it."[275] The court determined this article should be read broadly to encompass all the unfore-

---

272. *Id.* at 971.
273. *Id.; see also* Bell v. CSX Transp., Inc., 1997 U.S. Dist. LEXIS 17843, at *6 (E.D. La. Nov. 7, 1997) (noting that following a thorough study of the doctrinal, codal, and jurisprudential authority, it did not believe the Louisiana Supreme Court would recognize an independent tort for spoliation).
274. 704 So. 2d 1227 (La. Ct. App. 1997).
275. *Id.* at 1233 (quoting LA. CIV. CODE ANN. § 2315).

seen civil actions that may harm people. As such, the *Bethea* court held that Article 2315 imposes liability on one who spoliates evidence even if the spoliator does not have a specific statutory duty to preserve it. It also found "a viable cause of action for impairment of a civil claim and spoliation of evidence stands against the defendants in this case."[276]

Two earlier Louisiana courts also recognized a cause of action for impairment of a civil claim. In each of these cases, courts found that the defendants had a statutory duty to preserve evidence and assist in the investigation of the case.[277]

Carter v. Exide Corporation[278] considered whether an employer may be held liable for spoliation of evidence in a case arising out of an employee's injury from a battery explosion. The employer disposed of the battery before the employee could determine the cause of the explosion.

The court first noted that an employer's statutory immunity from tort liability to its employee for work-related injuries does not, standing alone, shield it from a claim for economic injury as a result of post-accident conduct that prevents its employee from recovering tort damages. However, to impose liability for the destruction of evidence, the employee must show the employer had a "duty to preserve the evidence for the plaintiff, whether arising from a statute, a contract, a special relationship between the parties, or an affirmative agreement or undertaking to preserve the evidence."[279] Because there was evidence that the employee had asked his employer to retain the battery, the court of appeals remanded this case to allow the employee to allege his spoliation claim against his employer with greater particularity.[280]

Although some earlier Louisiana appellate court decisions had suggested that a Louisiana court may permit a claim for negligent spoliation, recent authorities suggest otherwise. For instance, in a slip-and-fall case, a pedestrian filed suit against a property owner after she fell while crossing a sidewalk abutting the landowner's property.[281]

---

276. 704 So. 2d at 1233.
277. *See* Fischer v. Travelers Ins. Co., 429 So. 2d 538 (La. Ct. App. 1983); Duhe v. Delta Airlines, Inc., 635 F. Supp. 1414 (E.D. La. 1986).
278. 661 So. 2d 698 (La. Ct. App. 1995).
279. *Id.* at 704 (citing *Edwards*, 796 F. Supp. 966).
280. *Id.* at 706.
281. Quinn v. Riso Investments, Inc., 869 So. 2d 922 (La. Ct. App. 2004).

After the pedestrian fell, the landowner repaired the sidewalk because a city employee told her the property owner had responsibility to make such repairs. While the repairs were under way, a friend of the pedestrian took photographs of the condition of the sidewalk.[282]

Eleven months later the pedestrian filed a lawsuit asserting that, among other things, the landowner spoiled the evidence relative to her case by repairing the sidewalk. The trial court denied summary judgment to the landowner on the spoliation claim, and the court of appeals agreed. The appellate court observed that "[r]ecognizing a claim in tort for spoliation presents a relatively new concept in Louisiana jurisprudence and has been the subject of recent consideration in our courts."[283] The court held that to establish spoliation, the pedestrian must show that the property owners destroyed evidence "to intentionally deprive [her] of its use at trial."[284]

Acknowledging that a state tort claim requires a showing of intentional destruction, the court in *Desselle v. Jefferson Parish Hospital*[285] held that allegations of negligent spoliation are insufficient to establish the tort.[286] The court stated, "[w]here suit has not been filed and there is no evidence that a party knew suit would be filed when the evidence was discarded, the theory of spoliation of evidence does not apply."[287]

Civil and Evidentiary Sanctions for Destruction of Evidence

Louisiana has long permitted use of an adverse evidentiary presumption against a party who fails to produce evidence within its con-

---

282. *Id.*

283. *Id.* at 992 (citing Guillory v. Dillard's Dep't Store, Inc., 777 So. 2d 1, 3 (La. Ct. App. 2001)).

284. *Id.* Since summary judgment is rarely appropriate for determination of questions of subjective facts such as intent and motive, there were issues of fact for a jury to consider regarding the landowner's motives and knowledge. *See, e.g.*, Catoire v. Caprock Telcomm. Corp., No. 01-3577 Section: "J"(2), 2003 U.S. Dist. LEXIS 8812 (E.D. La. 2003) (dismissing state law claim for negligent spoliation because it appears that Louisiana requires a showing of intentional conduct to state a claim for spoliation).

285. 887 So. 2d 524 (La. Ct. App. 2004).

286. *Id.*; *see also* Pham v. Contico Int'l Inc., 759 So. 2d 880, 882 (La. Ct. App. 2000); Smith v. Jitney Jungle of Am., 802 So. 2d 988, 995 (2002), *writ denied*, 811 So. 2d 913 (2002).

287. *Id.* at 534.

trol.[288] However, Louisiana courts have been reluctant to impose this inference absent evidence the spoliator had a duty to preserve the evidence. Therefore, courts allow a spoliator the opportunity to make a "reasonable explanation" to avoid imposition of an adverse presumption.[289]

For example, the court in *Randolph v. General Motors Corporation*[290] allowed an employer the opportunity to make a "reasonable explanation" to avoid an adverse inference or presumption. There, an employee had suffered injuries when an engine pulling a drag line caused him to fall. Prior to litigation, the employer had disposed of the allegedly defective part. The employer appealed the trial court's decision, which held that its destruction of evidence rendered it partially liable.

Reversing, the court of appeals found there was no evidence of intentional destruction. Acknowledging that a litigant's failure to produce evidence within his control raises a presumption that such evidence is unfavorable to him, the court observed that "[t]he presumption of spoliation is not applicable when the failure to produce the evidence has a reasonable explanation."[291] The court explained that the employer in this case had a reasonable explanation: It threw away the defective part because it was broken and before it anticipated litigation.

In *Kammerer v. Sewerage & Water Board*,[292] the trial court declined a plaintiff's request for a spoliation instruction because the defendant destroyed a manhole cover, a relevant piece of evidence, pursuant to company policy. A divided court of appeals held that a spoliation instruction was not warranted because the defendant company provided a reasonable explanation—the company policy of routinely destroying all broken manhole covers it replaced.

The *Kammerer* dissent noted that under Louisiana law, when a litigant fails to produce available evidence and fails to give a reason-

---

288. Maria A. Losavio, *Synthesis of Louisiana Law on Spoliation of Evidence—Compared to the Rest of the Country, Did We Handle It Correctly?*, 58 LA. L. REV. 837, 869 (1998).

289. *Id.* at 870-71; *see also* Babineaux v. Black, 396 So. 2d 584 (La. Ct. App. 1981).

290. 646 So. 2d 1019 (La. Ct. App. 1994).

291. *Id.* at 1026 (citing *Babineaux*, 396 So. 2d 584).

292. 633 So. 2d 1357 (La. Ct. App. 1994).

able explanation for its destruction, there is a presumption that such evidence would have been unfavorable to that party. However, no such presumption exists where the litigant explains his failure to produce evidence.[293] The dissent found the defendant's explanation spurious and criticized the majority for providing the spoliator with an incentive to routinely destroy crucial evidence. The dissent stated, "The decision to immediately destroy, as a matter of policy . . . , every manhole cover that is defective, even if that manhole cover is relevant to a civil action, is contrary to sound public policy."[294]

In addition to the availability of an adverse inference to remedy spoliation, Louisiana Code of Civil Procedure Article 1471, a rule comparable to Federal Rule of Civil Procedure 37, permits courts to impose various sanctions for violation of discovery orders. In addition, Louisiana Code of Civil Procedure Article 191 gives Louisiana state courts inherent power to impose sanctions for spoliation of evidence.

Criminal Statutes

The Louisiana statute prohibits tampering with evidence, which may include spoliation of evidence.[295] However, it is only applicable in a criminal investigation or proceeding.

MAINE

Independent Causes of Action for Destruction of Evidence

It does not appear that any state court in Maine has determined whether or under what circumstances Maine would recognize an independent tort for the loss or destruction of evidence.

Civil and Evidentiary Sanctions for Destruction of Evidence

Although there are no reported opinions in which a Maine court has imposed sanctions for destruction of evidence, it appears that Rule 37 of the Maine Rules of Civil Procedure provides a court with such authority. Maine Rule of Civil Procedure 37 permits a superior court, in

---

293. *Id.* (citing Boh Bros. Constr. Co. v. Luber-Finer, Inc., 612 So. 2d 270, 274 (La. Ct. App. 1992)).

294. *Id.* at 1368 (Plotkin, J., dissenting).

295. La. Rev. Stat. Ann. § 14:130.1 (2004).

the exercise of its discretion, to impose sanctions for failure to comply with discovery orders.[296]

In addition, the Maine Supreme Court has recognized the inherent power of a court to sanction a party for abuse of the litigation process.[297] However, as the *Linscott* court observed:

> [A]uthority to sanction parties and attorneys for abuse of the litigation process "should be sparingly used and sanctions imposed only when the abuse of process by the parties or counsel is clear."[298]

Therefore, Maine courts may award sanctions,[299] such as attorney's fees, where there is a showing of bad faith by a litigant.

Criminal Statutes

Under Maine criminal law, when a person alters, destroys, conceals or removes anything relevant to an official proceeding with the intent to impair its verity, authenticity or availability, that person has committed the crime of falsifying physical evidence.[300] There are no reported cases in which this statute has been applied to the destruction of evidence in a civil case.

MARYLAND

Independent Causes of Action for Destruction of Evidence

The Maryland Supreme Court has not considered whether to recognize an independent cause of action for spoliation of evidence. However, it does not appear that Maryland courts favor recognizing an independent cause of action for spoliation. In a frequently cited case, *Miller v. Montgomery County,*[301] a Maryland appellate court stated, in

---

296. *See* Ricci v. Delehanty, 719 A.2d 518 (Me. 1998).
297. Linscott v. Foy, 716 A.2d 1017 (Me. 1998); *see also* State v. Grant, 510 A.2d 240 (Me. 1986) (noting the inherent power of a trial court to sanction lawyer conduct that is inimical to the integrity of the judicial process).
298. 716 A.2d at 1021.
299. *Id.*
300. ME. REV. STAT. ANN. tit. 17A, § 455 (1999).
301. 494 A.2d 761 (Md. Ct. Spec. App. 1985).

dicta, that the remedy for alleged spoliation would be an appropriate jury instruction, "not a separate and collateral action."[302]

Civil and Evidentiary Sanctions for Destruction of Evidence

Maryland courts have the power to sanction destruction of evidence and to impose sanctions appropriate under the circumstance of each case. This power exists regardless of whether that authority is derived from the civil rules regarding discovery sanctions or from the court's inherent power.[303]

Klupt v. Krongard illustrates the use of this power. There, the inventor of a disposable cardboard videocassette licensed the exclusive rights to produce that invention to one party. Believing the licensee had breached its agreement, the inventor licensed the rights to a third party and accepted payments from that party. The second licensee sued the inventor for fraud, and the inventor filed a counterclaim, asserting various causes of action. The inventor surreptitiously tape-recorded his telephone conversations and prepared typewritten memoranda about them.[304]

During discovery, plaintiffs requested all written and oral records relating to the transactions. The inventor falsely affirmed that all documents and oral records had been provided. After a deposition during which the existence of the tapes became known, the inventor destroyed the tapes. The trial court dismissed the inventor's counterclaim as a sanction for his intentional destruction of discoverable evidence, and the inventor appealed.[305]

Affirming the trial court's dismissal, the *Klupt* court held:

[T]he Rules [of Civil Procedure] do not deal explicitly with the destruction of discoverable evidence. But they do clearly allow for the dismissal of a party's claims for failure to respond to a request for production and for failure to obey an order compelling such a response or the actual production itself. Destruction of evidence such as was found in this case would

---

302. *Id.* at 768.
303. Klupt v. Krongard, 728 A.2d 727 (Md. Ct. Spec. App. 1999) (citing Turner v. Hudson Transit Lines, Inc., 142 F.R.D. 68, 72 (S.D.N.Y. 1991)).
304. *Id.*
305. *Id.*

render hollow any response to a request for production, even if timely filed, just as it would render an order to compel moot. If dismissal is permissible in those cases, it would seem to be *a fortiori* permissible in a case of destruction of evidence.[306]

The court then enumerated four elements a court should consider before imposing a spoliation sanction: whether there is (1) an act of destruction, (2) discoverable evidence, (3) an intent to destroy the evidence, and (4) an act of destruction at a time after suit has been filed, or, if before, at a time when the filing is fairly perceived as imminent.[307]

Maryland courts also recognize the use of an adverse inference or presumption to remedy spoliation. Discussing the adverse inference or evidentiary presumption, the court in *Anderson v. Litzenberg*[308] observed:

> The destruction or alteration of evidence by a party gives rise to inferences or presumptions unfavorable to the spoliator, the nature of the inference being dependent upon the intent or motivation of the party. Unexplained and intentional destruction of evidence by a litigant gives rise to an inference that the evidence would have been unfavorable to his cause, but would not in itself amount to substantive proof of a fact essential to his opponent's cause. The maxim, *Omnia praesumuntur contra spoliatem*, "all things are presumed against the spoliator," rests upon the logical proposition that one would ordinarily not destroy evidence favorable to himself.[309]

As *Anderson v. Litzenberg* illustrates, Maryland courts do not require a showing of bad faith before imposing an adverse inference. Rather, courts impose a different type of adverse inference instruction depending upon the spoliator's intent. If evidence is destroyed negligently or innocently, the jury may presume that the evidence was un-

---

306. *Id.* at 734.

307. *Id.* at 737 (citing JAMIE S. GORELICK, ET AL., DESTRUCTION OF EVIDENCE §§ 3.8-312, at 88-109 (1989)). *See also* White v. Office of the Public Defender, 170 F.R.D. 138, 147-48 (D. Md. 1997).

308. 694 A.2d 150 (Md. Ct. Spec. App. 1997).

309. *Id.* at 155-56 (citing *Miller*, 494 A.2d 761 (Md. Ct. Spec. App. 1985)).

favorable. If the spoliator destroyed the evidence with fraudulent intent, the jury may also infer that the spoliator had a weak case and destroyed the evidence for that reason.[310]

Criminal Statutes

Maryland Criminal Statutes do not appear expressly to bar destruction or alteration of evidence. One Maryland court upheld a charge for obstruction of justice under Maryland Criminal Law Code Annotated section 9-306[311] where a defendant removed a knife at a crime scene and substituted a different weapon.[312] However, this statute has not been applied based on destruction of evidence in a civil suit.

MASSACHUSETTS

Independent Causes of Action for Destruction of Evidence

The Supreme Judicial Court of Massachusetts considered and refused to recognize an action in tort for intentional or negligent spoliation of evidence in *Fletcher v. Dorchester Mutual Insurance Company*.[313] This case arose after a house fire resulted in the death of three children. The insurance company's expert removed wiring components and fixtures from the house approximately two weeks after the fire. Thereafter, the parents of several children filed an action that included a separate count for spoliation of evidence. The court held that allowing a separate cause of action for spoliation would recognize a claim that could not be proved "without resort to multiple levels of speculation" and opined the state had a range of other remedies for spoliation.[314]

The Massachusetts high court also declined to recognize a cause of action for spoliation of evidence as a deceptive or unfair trade practice under Massachusetts General Law ch. 93A.[315] Quoting its deci-

---

310. *Id.; see also* DiLeo v. Nugent, 592 A.2d 1126 (Md. Ct. Spec. App. 1991) (instructing jury the destruction could give rise to an unfavorable presumption or inference, with the nature of the inference depending upon its finding about the spoliator's motivation).

311. MD. CODE ANN. § 9-306 (2002) is derived without substantive change from former MD. CODE ANN. Art. 27, § 27, as it related to obstructing justice.

312. *See* Mayne v. Maryland, 414 A.2d 1, 4 (1980).

313. 773 N.E.2d 420 (Mass. 2002).

314. *Id.* at 426.

315. *Of Jeffrey Gath*, 802 N.E.2d 521 (2003).

sion in *Fletcher,* the court explained: "Our view is that 'appropriately tailored sanctions imposed in the underlying action are a more efficacious remedy for spoliation than allowing a separate, inherently speculative cause of action for such litigation misconduct.'" [316]

Civil and Evidentiary Sanctions for Destruction of Evidence

Massachusetts law affords a greater range of remedies for spoliation than the majority of jurisdictions.[317] Sanctions for spoliation considered by Massachusetts courts include dismissal or default judgment, exclusion of evidence or expert testimony, and an adverse jury inference.[318] A court has discretion to impose cumulative remedies as appropriate.[319]

Sanctions may be imposed on a party if that party, or its expert, destroys or alters evidence.[320] For example, in *Nally v. Volkswagen of America, Inc.,* the court excluded testimony of a plaintiff's accident reconstruction expert because, when the expert destroyed certain evidence, it knew an item might be material to the litigation. The *Nally* court explained that:

> unfair prejudice may result from allowing an expert deliberately or negligently to put himself or herself in the position of being the only expert with first-hand knowledge of the physical evidence on which expert opinions as to defects and causation may be grounded.[321]

---

316. *Id.* at 534 (quoting Fletcher, 773 N.E.2d at 551).

317. *Of Jeffrey Gath,* 802 N.E.2d 521.

318. Mass. R. Civ. P. 37(b)(2) (providing sanctions for failure to comply with discovery obligations imposed by rule or court order, including orders designating certain facts as established, refusing to allow introduction of evidence supporting certain claims or defenses, striking a pleading, and/or dismissing the action); *see also* Linnen v. A.H. Robins Co., Inc., No. 97-2307, 1999 Mass. Super. LEXIS 240 (Mass. Dist. Ct. June 16, 1999) (discussing available sanctions for destruction of evidence during pending civil litigation).

319. *Of Jeffrey Gath,* 802 N.E.2d 521.

320. Nally v. Volkswagen of America, Inc., 539 N.E.2d 1017 (Mass. 1989).

321. *Id.* at 1021. *See also* Johnson v. Harvard Univ., No. 93-04622, 1996 Mass. Super. LEXIS 399 (Mass. Dist. Ct. Sept. 27, 1996) (excluding evidence of the pre-accident condition of an allegedly smooth terrazzo floor, which the property owner claimed had a "roughed up" surface, where the owner knew or should have known that plaintiff's photographs of the floor surface would not be as persuasive as the actual surface).

When considering civil and evidentiary sanctions for spoliation of evidence in pending litigation, Massachusetts courts consider:

1. whether the non-spoliating party has been or will be prejudiced as a result of the alteration or destruction of the item of evidence;
2. whether any such prejudice can be remedied;
3. whether the altered or destroyed item has practical importance to the case;
4. the good faith of the party who altered or destroyed the item of evidence; and
5. whether any abuse may result if the evidence is not excluded.[322]

Significantly, Massachusetts courts require a showing of wrongful intent before they will consider imposing civil or evidentiary remedies for spoliation.[323] As the Supreme Judicial Court of Massachusetts explained in *Kippenhan v. Chaulk Services, Inc.*, a negligence action against the manufacturer of an ambulance stretcher, excluding evidence as a sanction for spoliation of evidence is a minority position.[324] The court reasoned that most jurisdictions have adopted a less severe rule, holding that the trier of fact may draw an inference from the intentional spoliation of evidence. Reversing a trial court's entry of summary judgment and noting that the plaintiff had no fault in the loss of the stretcher, the court explained that the plaintiff should not have

---

322. Jackson v. Harvard Univ., 900 F.2d 464, 469 (1st Cir. 1990). *See also Nally*, 539 N.E.2d 1017 (stating the spoliation doctrine applies, at the request of a "potentially prejudiced" party, when an expert or a party to an action has caused a change in or removed an item which is material to litigation, and when a party knew or reasonably should have known the item was possibly relevant to litigation); Bolton v. Mass. Bay Transp. Auth., 593 N.E.2d 248 (Mass. App. Ct. 1992) (excluding evidence destroyed by a party's expert inspectors after litigation had commenced); Munsinger v. Berkshire Med. Ctr., No. 95-239, 1998 Mass. Super. LEXIS 689 (Mass. Dist. Ct. Oct. 7, 1998) (applying MASS. R. CIV. P. 37(b)(2)(A) to prelitigation destruction of evidence and ruling certain facts would be taken as established where spoliator knew or should have known suit was possible at the time it destroyed evidence).
323. Kippenhan v. Chaulk Services, Inc., 697 N.E.2d 527 (Mass. 1998) (noting spoliation of evidence may result from the intentional or negligent destruction or loss of evidence, but not from fault-free destruction or loss).
324. *Id.* at 531.

been barred on spoliation principles from using testimony concerning the pre-accident condition of the stretcher.[325]

Sanctions may be imposed even where evidence is destroyed or discarded before litigation is commenced if a litigant knows, or reasonably should know, that it might be relevant to a possible lawsuit. But the threat of a lawsuit "must be sufficiently apparent . . . that a reasonable person in the spoliator's position would realize, at the time of the spoliation, the possible importance of the evidence to the resolution of the potential dispute."[326]

Criminal Statutes

Massachusetts has no statute that criminalizes the destruction or spoliation of evidence in a civil matter.

MICHIGAN

Independent Causes of Action for Destruction of Evidence

It does not appear that the Supreme Court of Michigan has addressed whether to recognize an independent tort for destruction of evidence or intentional interference with a prospective civil action by spoliation of evidence. In 1989, a Michigan court of appeals declined to recognize such a cause of action in *Panich v. Iron Wood Products Corporation*.[327] In that case, the court declined to create an independent cause of action for spoliation of evidence because there was no evidence that the missing evidence had been destroyed by the adverse party, or that the party had assumed a duty to preserve the destroyed evidence.[328]

At least one Michigan appellate court has observed that the *Panich* court did not expressly reject the spoliation tort and that in some medi-

---

325. *Id.*; *compare* Tammy Paradis v. Congress Mgt. Co. L.P., No. 92-2053-G, 1995 Mass. Super. LEXIS 498 (Mass. Dist. Ct. May 1, 1995) (denying motion for a new trial where plaintiff produced no evidence that defendant, who removed lock hardware it manufactured during post-fire demolition, knew the lock was at issue in the case).

326. Kippenhan v. Chaulk Services, Inc., 697 N.E.2d 527 (Mass. 1998). *See also* Stull v. Corrigan Racquetball Club, 17 Mass. L. Rep. 388 (2004) (denying request for default judgment as a sanction for defendant's negligent post-accident destruction of a spring-clip, but allowing an instruction on the inferences the jury could draw from its loss).

327. 445 N.W.2d 795 (Mich. 1989).

328. *Id.* at 798.

cal malpractice cases, the tort may be "ripe for recognition as an independent tort."[329]

Civil and Evidentiary Sanctions for Destruction of Evidence

Under Michigan law, a trial court has the authority, under discovery rules and under its inherent power, to sanction a party for failing to preserve evidence it knows or should know is relevant to potential litigation.[330] The court may impose a sanction "regardless of whether the evidence is lost as a result of a deliberate act or simple negligence, [as] the other party is unfairly prejudiced because it is unable to challenge or respond to the evidence."[331] The decision to impose sanctions for spoliation of evidence is left to the sound discretion of the trial judge.[332] However, since dismissal of a case for spoliation of evidence is a drastic step, before imposing such a sanction, Michigan courts require the trial court to consider lesser sanctions, including the exclusion of evidence that is unfairly prejudicial to defendants as a result of a plaintiff's failure to preserve evidence.[333]

As the court in *Brenner* explained, a trial court should:

[c]arefully fashion a sanction that denies the party the fruits of the party's misconduct, but that does not interfere with the party's right to produce other relevant evidence. An appropriate sanction may be the exclusion of evidence that unfairly prejudices the other party or an instruction to the jury that it may draw an inference adverse to the culpable party from the absence of the evidence.[334]

In *Brenner*, the court determined that because Michigan courts have the inherent power to sanction litigation misconduct, even when there

---

329. Wilson v. Sinai Grace Hosp., No. 24345, 2004 Mich. App. 1099 (Mich. Ct. App. Apr. 29, 2004).

330. Bloemendaal v. Town & Country Sports Ctr. Inc., 659 N.W.2d 684 (Mich. 2002); Roskam Baking Co. v. Lanham Mach. Co., Inc., 71 F. Supp. 2d 736 (W.D. Mich. 1999) (citing MASB-SEG Property/Casualty Pool v. Matalux, 586 N.W.2d 549, 553 (Mich. Ct. App. 1998)).

331. *Roskam,* 71 F. Supp. 2d at 749 (quoting Brenner v. Kolk, 573 N.W.2d 65, 70 (Mich. Ct. App. 1997)).

332. *Id.*

333. *Id.* (citing *MASB-SEG Property*, 586 N.W.2d at 553).

334. 573 N.W.2d at 65, 70 (Mich. Ct. App. 1997) (internal citations omitted).

is no statute or rule addressing the particular form of misconduct, a court also may sanction a party, pursuant to its inherent power for the loss or destruction of evidence.[335] The *Brenner* court reasoned that a court must be able to make such rulings as are necessary to promote fairness and justice. If a court were denied the power to sanction parties in such circumstances, it would only encourage "unscrupulous parties to destroy damaging evidence before a court order had been issued."[336] Therefore, whether evidence has been intentionally or negligently lost or destroyed, the other party is unfairly prejudiced because it is unable to respond to the evidence. Accordingly, the *Brenner* court held that a trial court has authority, pursuant to its inherent power, to sanction a party for failing to preserve evidence "that it knows or should know is relevant before litigation has commenced."[337]

Among the sanctions suggested by the *Brenner* court was the exclusion of evidence that might unfairly prejudice another party.[338] Or, alternatively, the court may instruct the jury to draw an inference adverse to the culpable party.[339]

In Michigan, there are two pattern jury instructions available for use under the appropriate circumstances. SJI 2d 6.01(D) reads in relevant part:

> You may infer that this evidence would have been adverse to the [plaintiff/defendant] if you believe that the evidence was under the control of the [plaintiff/defendant] and could have been produced by [him/her] and no reasonable excuse for [plaintiff's/defendant's] failure to produce evidence has been shown. SJI 2d 6.01 simply permits an inference that would have been adverse; the jury is free to decide for itself.[340]

335. *Id.*
336. *Id.*
337. *Id.* at 71.
338. *See, e.g.*, Hamann v. Ridge Tool Co., 539 N.W.2d 753 (Mich. Ct. App. 1995) (finding trial court abused its discretion by admitting expert opinion testimony regarding a lost piece of physical evidence because the expert's testimony was based upon observations made of a piece of evidence not available to the adverse party).
339. *Brenner,* 573 N.W.2d 65.
340. Lagalo v. Allied Corp., 592 N.W.2d 786 (Mich. Ct. App. 1999).

In *Lagalo v. Allied Corporation*,[341] the court distinguished the use of this instruction from the case where there is evidence of intentional spoliation, explaining that the intentional spoliation or destruction of evidence raises a presumption against the spoliator. Generally, Michigan courts have only applied such a presumption where there is intentional conduct indicating fraud and a desire to destroy and thereby suppress the truth.[342] Thus, the presumption that non-produced evidence would have been adverse applies only where there is evidence of intentional fraudulent conduct and the intentional destruction of evidence.[343]

The appellate court decision in *Bryson v. VTS*[344] exemplifies this approach. Affirming the trial court's dismissal for failure to make service of process, the *Bryson* court rejected the plaintiff's contention that the trial court should have drawn an inference of service because the defendant's insurer had destroyed its investigation file. The court found that the plaintiff failed to show intentional destruction of evidence for the purpose of preventing its use in litigation. The insurer explained that it closed its file because it had no record that the plaintiff had filed suit within the limitations period, which the court considered a reasonable excuse for not producing its file.[345]

Criminal Statutes

Under the recently enacted Michigan Anti-Terrorism Act, it is a felony to hinder prosecution of terrorism by suppressing the "alteration, or destruction [of] any physical evidence that might aid in the discovery, apprehension, or prosecution of [a terrorist or suspected terrorist]."[346]

---

341. 592 N.W.2d 786 (Mich. Ct. App. 1999).

342. Ward v. Consol. Rail Corp., No. 234619, 2003 Mich. App. LEXIS 1865 (Mich. Ct. App. Aug. 7, 2003) (citing Johnson v. Sec'y of State, 280 N.W.2d 9 (1979)). *See also* Ritter v. Meijer, Inc., 341 N.W.2d 220 (Mich. 1983).

343. In contrast, SJI 2d 6.01(D) allowed only for a permissible inference. *Lagalo*, 592 N.W.2d at 789 (citing Trupiano v. Cully, 84 N.W.2d 747 (Mich. 1957)).

344. No. 239841, 2003 Mich. App. LEXIS 951 (Mich. Ct. App. Apr. 15, 2003).

345. *Id.* at *3.

346. MICH. COMP. LAWS §§ 750.543b(f) and 750.543(h)(2004).

MINNESOTA

Independent Causes of Action for Destruction of Evidence

Minnesota has not recognized a cause of action for intentional or negligent spoliation of evidence.[347]

Civil and Evidentiary Sanctions for Destruction of Evidence

In *Patton v. Newmar Corporation*,[348] plaintiffs heard a pop that sounded like a blown tire while driving their motor home. After they pulled over to the side of the road, they noticed that the vehicle was on fire. While exiting the vehicle, one of the plaintiffs sustained an injury to her back. Thereafter, the plaintiffs commenced an action, and the defendant requested to inspect the vehicle. The plaintiffs informed the defendant that they no longer knew the location of the motor home, and the parts their expert had removed had been lost.[349]

The defendant moved for summary judgment on a number of grounds, including that the action should be dismissed as a sanction for spoliation of evidence. The trial court granted the motion and dismissed. The court of appeals reversed, holding that the sanction was excessive. The Supreme Court of Minnesota reversed and held that because failure to preserve evidence precluded the plaintiffs from proving the alleged defect, summary judgment had been properly granted for defendant.[350]

The Minnesota Supreme Court noted that a trial court has the inherent power to impose sanctions for spoliation. It approved of what had been called "a reasonable and workable standard by which to test the impact of the spoliation—the prejudice to the opposing party."[351] The court further reasoned that the trial court's choice of a sanction would be affirmed unless the trial court abused its discretion, "a burden which is met only when it is clear that no reasonable person would agree [with] the trial court's assessment of what sanctions are appro-

---

347. Federated Mut. Ins. Co. v. Litchfield Precision Components, Inc., 456 N.W.2d 434, 436 (Minn. 1990).
348. 538 N.W.2d 116 (Minn. 1995).
349. *Id.* at 118.
350. *Id.* at 120.
351. *Id.* at 119. *See also* Dodd v. Leviton Mfg. Co., No. CX-02-1570, 2003 Minn. App. LEXIS 626 (2003) (applying an abuse of discretion standard to a trial court's decision on spoliation sanctions).

priate."[352] The Minnesota Supreme Court upheld the trial court's exclusion of expert testimony and, in particular, noted that photographic evidence was not an adequate substitute for the missing evidence.[353]

Like other jurisdictions, Minnesota courts have noted that it is proper to impose the least restrictive sanction appropriate under the circumstances.[354] The relevant factors in determining the appropriate sanctions include the degree of fault or willfulness and the degree of prejudice suffered by the opposing party.[355] Where a party destroys evidence deliberately but without bad faith, and prejudice to a non-spoliating party is not severe, the trial court properly exercises its discretion by allowing evidence of the spoliation to be introduced at trial and imposing a moderate, monetary sanction.[356] However, to hold a party liable for spoliation, the allegedly missing evidence must have been within the "exclusive control and possession" of that party.[357] And "the propriety of a sanction for the spoliation of evidence is determined by the prejudice resulting to the opposing party."[358]

Where a party destroyed documents under circumstances that demonstrate "a deliberate, willful and contumacious disregard of the judicial process and the rights of [the] opposing part[y]," one court ruled that monetary sanctions were appropriate.[359] Accordingly, it required the spoliating party to reimburse the other party for all expenditures resulting from document destruction. Furthermore, the court doubled the fees and costs given the egregious nature of the conduct, and also

---

352. *Id.* (quoting Marrocco v. General Motors Corp., 966 F.2d 220, 223 (7th Cir. 1992)).

353. *Id.*

354. State Farm Fire & Cas. Co. v. Burns, No. C9-94-735, 1994 Minn. App. LEXIS 1112 (Minn. Ct. App. Nov. 15, 1994). *See also* State Farm Ins. Co. v. Chase, No. C6-01-969, 2002 Minn. App. LEXIS 68, at *10-11 (2002) (reversing trial court's sanction because "the power to sanction must be tempered by 'the duty to impose the least restrictive sanction available under the circumstances'") (citations omitted).

355. *State Farm Fire & Cas. Co.*, 1994 Minn. App. LEXIS 1112, at *2-3.

356. *Id.* at *3.

357. Wright v. Romfo, No. C4-95-1818, 1996 Minn. App. LEXIS 340, at *11 (Minn. Ct. App. Mar. 26, 1996).

358. Spaise v. Dodd, No. A03-1430, 2004 Minn. App. LEXIS 607, at *29 (2004) (quoting Hoffman v. Ford Motor Co., 587 N.W.2d 66, 71 (Minn. Ct. App. 1998)).

359. Capellupo v. FMC Corp., 126 F.R.D. 545, 551 (D. Minn. 1989).

required the spoliating party to bear the other party's attorneys' fees and costs in connection with document destruction.[360]

Criminal Statutes

Under Minnesota law, a person destroying a "writing or object to prevent it from being produced at trial, hearing, or other proceeding authorized by law" has committed the crime of forgery.[361] There is no Minnesota case law to support whether this statute would apply to the destruction of evidence in a civil case.

MISSISSIPPI

Independent Causes of Action for Destruction of Evidence

The Mississippi Supreme Court considered and refused to recognize a tort for intentional spoliation of evidence against both first- and third-party spoliators in *Dowdle Butane Gas Company v. Moore.*[362] There, an underground propane tank exploded and injured a property owner. After the utility company removed the tank, the property owner alleged that the gas company deprived him of the ability to discover the cause of the explosion when it conducted destructive testing on the tank.

Refusing to recognize an independent tort, the *Dowdle* court reviewed decisions of other courts and noted the existing remedies for spoliation in Mississippi, including Mississippi Code Annotated section 97-9-44 and Mississippi Rule of Civil Procedure 37.[363] The *Dowdle* court emphasized that creating a tort would "lead to duplicative litigation, [and] encourage inefficient relitigation of issues better handled within the context of the core cause of action."[364]

The court further observed the enormous costs that recognizing such a tort could impose. It weighed, in particular, "the risks of erroneous determinations of liability due to the uncertainty of the harm and from the extraordinary measures required to preserve for indefinite periods items for the purpose of avoiding potential spoliation liability in future litigation. . . ."[365]

---

360. *Id.* at 553-54.
361. Minn. Stat. § 609.63(7) (2004).
362. 831 So. 2d 1124 (Miss. 2002).
363. *Id.* at 1133.
364. 831 So. 2d at 1135.
365. *Id.*

The *Dowdle* court left the question of whether to recognize a claim for negligent spoliation for another day, and in *Richardson v. Sara Lee Corporation*,[366] the Mississippi high court refused to recognize that claim as well. Pointing out that non-tort remedies for spoliation are sufficient in the majority of cases, the court stated that the benefits of recognizing the tort were outweighed by the burdens it imposed.[367]

Civil and Evidentiary Sanctions for Destruction of Evidence

Mississippi Rule of Civil Procedure 37 empowers a trial court to impose sanctions upon parties to pending litigation for the "failure to make or cooperate in discovery."[368] Trial courts are afforded great discretion under this rule to impose sanctions to resolve specific problems created by failures in discovery.[369] This broad grant of authority gives a trial court the power to impose sanctions for destruction of evidence during pending litigation.[370]

Mississippi also has adopted the "spoliation inference" to remedy problems with destruction of evidence, recognizing it as a remedy for spoliation as early as 1878.[371] In *DeLaughter v. Lawrence County Hospital*,[372] the Mississippi Supreme Court considered a lower court's refusal to give an instruction regarding a hospital's loss of certain medical records relevant to a wrongful death claim. Although the hospital had attempted to reconstruct the file, important documents remained missing at the time of trial.[373]

The *DeLaughter* court held the lower court erred by refusing to give a spoliation instruction that shifted to the hospital the burden of showing that it did not lose or destroy the records. The court further found that the jury should have been told the original hospital records had been lost or destroyed, as well as the reason these records were missing. The court also noted, "[t]he doctrine is, that unfavorable presumption and intendment shall be against the party who has destroyed

---

366. 847 So. 2d 821 (Miss. 2003).
367. *Id.*
368. Miss. R. Civ. P. 37(b).
369. Cunningham v. Mitchell, 549 So. 2d 955, 958 (Miss. 1989).
370. *See* Maurice L. Kervin, *Spoliation of Evidence: Why Mississippi Should Adopt the Tort*, 63 Miss. L.J. 227, 230-31 (Fall 1993).
371. Bott v. Wood, 56 Miss. 136 (1878).
372. 601 So. 2d 818 (Miss. 1992).
373. *Id.*

an instrument which is the subject of inquiry, in order that he may not gain by his wrong."[374]

The *DeLaughter* court observed that the records could be missing for a variety of reasons, ranging from intentional destruction to an innocent loss. The court, therefore, held that the trial court should have given an instruction that would have allowed the jury to determine whether the hospital lost the medical records intentionally or negligently, and, if so, "infer" that the missing records contained information unfavorable to the hospital.[375]

The instruction endorsed by the *DeLaughter* court creates a rebuttable presumption that the information contained in lost, destroyed or missing documents would be unfavorable to the party responsible for retention of the records. This instruction places the burden on the record keeper to show that it did not destroy or misplace the record and, unless that party overcomes the presumption, the presumption will operate against it.[376]

Criminal Statutes

Although Mississippi does not have a criminal statute that specifically addresses destruction of evidence as a crime, a Mississippi court may impose criminal sanctions for obstruction of justice.[377] Mississippi Code Annotated section 97-9-55 provides for criminal sanctions for those who destroy evidence.[378] However, there do not appear to have been any criminal convictions in Mississippi for destroying evidence in a civil case.[379]

MISSOURI

Independent Causes of Action for Destruction of Evidence

At least one Missouri court has declined to recognize an independent

---

374. *Id.* at 822 (quoting *Bott*, 56 Miss. 136).

375. *Id.* at 823.

376. *Id. See also* Thomas v. Isle of Capri Casino and CDS Systems, 781 So. 2d 125 (Miss. 2001) (holding the negligent destruction of a slot machine, the most probative evidence in the case, raised a rebuttable presumption against the spoliators).

377. Miss. Code Ann. § 97-9-55 (2004).

378. *Dowdle*, 831 So. 2d at 1133.

379. Kervin, *supra* note 369, at 229.

tort for spoliation of evidence.[380] In *Baugher v. Gates Rubber Company*, the court reviewed the basis on which a California court first recognized the tort.[381] The court noted that California's intentional interference action requires only acts that would disrupt a business relationship and subsequent disruption. In a similar context, Missouri courts require a "but for" relationship. Based on Missouri's higher causation standard, the court concluded that Missouri would not recognize an independent tort for spoliation of evidence.[382]

Furthermore, because Missouri does not recognize an action for negligent interference with a prospective business advantage, the *Baugher* court also declined to recognize the independent tort of negligent spoliation. However, the *Baugher* court based its refusal to recognize an independent tort in part on the fact that the plaintiff in the underlying lawsuit had not yet resolved its claim.[383]

Commentators have called for Missouri to recognize an independent tort action for spoliation only against third parties, noting that Missouri's current scheme for addressing spoliation encourages destruction or loss of evidence and insulates third parties from prosecution for spoliation of evidence, thereby allowing such parties to evade liability.[384]

Civil and Evidentiary Sanctions

For more than a hundred years, when a Missouri court has been faced with a claim of spoliation or destruction of evidence, it has applied an evidentiary inference.[385] In *Pomeroy v. Benton*, the court that first recognized the doctrine permitting an evidentiary inference for spoliation observed:

> The law, in hatred of the spoiler, baffles the destroyer, and
> thwarts his iniquitous purpose, by indulging a presumption

---

380. *Baugher v. Gates Rubber Co., Inc.*, 863 S.W.2d 905 (Mo. Ct. App. 1993).
381. *Id.* (citing Smith v. Superior Court, 198 Cal. Rptr. 829, 836 (Cal. Ct. App. 1984)).
382. *Id.*
383. *Id.*
384. Kathleen Kedigh, *Spoliation: To the Careless Go the Spoils*, 67 Mo. UMKC L. Rev. 597, 603 (Summer 1999); *see also* Benjamin T. Clark, *The License to Spoliate Must Be Revoked: Why Missouri Should Welcome a Tort for Third-Party Spoliation*, 59 J. Mo. Bar 308 (Nov./Dec. 2003).
385. Pomeroy v. Benton, 77 Mo. 64 (Mo. 1882).

which supplies the lost proof, and thus defeats the wrong-doer by the very means he had so confidently employed to perpetrate the wrong.[386]

Missouri courts apply the adverse inference against a party for the "intentional destruction of evidence, indicating fraud and the desire to suppress the truth."[387] However, courts require more than the mere loss or destruction of evidence, and will only give a spoliation inference if the spoliator fails to provide a satisfactory explanation for the loss or destruction of the evidence.[388] The proponent of the inference may show that the spoliator had a duty or should have recognized a duty to preserve evidence, and the evidence must be within the party's power to produce.[389] However, the adverse inference does not prove the opposing party's case; it simply allows the jury to assume that the destroyed evidence is adverse to the spoliator's position.[390]

Criminal Statutes

Under Missouri law, a person commits the crime of tampering with evidence when such person alters, destroys, suppresses or conceals any record, document or thing with the intent to impair its availability in an official proceeding or investigation.[391] The absence of case law imposing criminal sanctions in a civil context suggests that Missouri courts will only apply this sanction in the criminal context. Also, the legislature has specifically omitted any reference in the tampering statute to proceedings that are only prospective.[392] Therefore, it appears unlikely that Missouri would impose criminal sanctions in a civil case for destruction of evidence.

---

386. *Id.* at 86.
387. Brown v. Hamid, 856 S.W.2d 51, 56-57 (Mo. 1993); *see also* DeGraffenreid v. R. L. Hannah Trucking, 80 S.W.3d 866 (Mo. Ct. App. 2002).
388. *Brown* at 57.
389. Morris v. JC Penney Life Ins. Co., 895 S.W.2d 73, 77 (Mo. Ct. App. 1995); Brissett v. Milner Chevrolet Co., 479 S.W.2d 176, 182 (Mo. Ct. App. 1972).
390. Schneider v. G. Gilliams, Inc., 976 S.W.2d 522, 526 (Mo. Ct. App. 1998).
391. Mo. Rev. Stat. § 575.100 (2004).
392. State v. Carver, 888 S.W.2d 411 (Mo. Ct. App. 1994).

MONTANA

Independent Causes of Action for Destruction of Evidence

In *Oliver v. Stimson Lumber Company,*[393] the Supreme Court of Montana recognized the torts of both intentional and negligent spoliation of evidence. However, the court limited these torts to situations in which the evidence is in the possession of third parties. The court explained:

> We see no reason to recognize a new tort theory to provide relief to litigants when evidence is intentionally or negligently destroyed by a party to the litigation. Trial judges are well equipped under the Montana Rules of Civil Procedure to address the problem as it occurs and deal with it accordingly, even entering default when the circumstances justify such relief.

> When evidence is in the possession of a third party, however, the various sanctions available to the trial judge are inapplicable and other considerations arise. For instance, the property in question may be owned by the third party. A property owner normally has the right to control and dispose of his property as he sees fit. The owner of the property may legitimately question what right a plaintiff has to direct control over such property. Yet, the importance of evidence preservation and the critical importance it plays in the civil justice system cannot be ignored.[394]

With regard to the issue of negligent spoliation, the court held that a factual issue existed regarding whether the defendant had a duty to preserve evidence. To establish a duty to preserve evidence, the requesting party had to put the party in possession of the evidence on notice that it should be preserved. Moreover, the party being requested to preserve evidence had a right to seek from the requesting party reasonable costs of preservation.[395] In the case before the court, since

393. 993 P.2d 11 (Mont. 1999).
394. *Id.* at 17-18.
395. *Id.* at 20.

there was a material dispute regarding whether a proper request to preserve evidence had been received, the supreme court reversed the trial court's grant of summary judgment for the defendant.[396]

The Stimson court next determined that a threshold showing of both causation and damages was required to make out a spoliation claim. The court adopted the standard set forth in *Holmes v. Amerex Rent-A-Car*.[397] To prove causation, the plaintiff had to show that (1) the underlying claim was significantly impaired due to the spoliation of evidence; (2) a causal relationship existed between failure of the underlying action and the unavailability of spoliated evidence; and (3) the underlying action would have a "significant possibility of success" if the evidence still existed.[398] Finally, with regard to damages, the court held:

> [D]amages arrived at through reasonable estimation based on relevant data should be multiplied by the significant possibility that the plaintiff would have won the underlying suit had the spoliated evidence been available. For example, if a jury determined that the expected recovery in the underlying suit was $200,000 and that there was an estimated 60% possibility that the plaintiff would have recovered that amount in the underlying suit had it not been impaired by the spoliated evidence, then the award of damages would be $120,000 (60 percent of $200,000).[399]

Finally, the court upheld summary judgment in favor of the defendant on the intentional spoliation of evidence claim, holding that there were no facts to support that any evidence had been destroyed for the purpose of disrupting the plaintiff's third-party suit.[400]

Civil and Evidentiary Sanctions for Destruction of Evidence

Montana courts have the power, under the Montana Rules of Civil Procedure, to sanction spoliation that occurs during pending litiga-

---

396. *Id.* at 23.
397. 710 A.2d 846 (D.C. 1998).
398. 993 P.2d at 21 (citing *Holmes*, 710 A.2d at 851-52).
399. *Id.*
400. *Id.* at 23.

tion. As the court noted in *Oliver v. Stimson Lumber Company*, trial judges have authority under the Rules of Civil Procedure to deal with spoliation by parties to litigation, up to and including entering default judgment under the appropriate circumstances.[401]

Criminal Statutes

Under Montana statute,[402] a person commits the crime of tampering with evidence when "believing that an official proceeding or investigation is pending or about to be instituted," the person "alters, destroys, conceals, or removes any record, document, or thing with the purpose to impair its verity or availability."[403] The Montana legislature has defined "an official proceeding" to mean "a proceeding heard . . . before a legislative, a judicial, an administrative, or another governmental agency or official authorized to take evidence under oath."[404]

Although the statute arguably suggests that criminal sanctions may apply to destruction of evidence in a civil proceeding, there does not appear to be any case law supporting the use of criminal sanctions for spoliation that occurs in a civil proceeding.

NEBRASKA

Independent Causes of Action for Destruction of Evidence

Nebraska courts have not addressed whether an independent cause of action exists for intentional or negligent spoliation of evidence.

Civil and Evidentiary Sanctions

The Nebraska Court of Appeals has held that a trial court has the inherent power to exclude testimony based on spoliation of evidence. In *Estate of Schindler v. Walker*,[405] the plaintiff filed suit on behalf of the decedent, alleging that the defendants were negligent in treating the decedent following a neck injury. The plaintiff also sought recovery for wrongful death and negligent infliction of emotional distress. Two weeks prior to trial, without notifying the defendants, the plaintiff dis-

---

401. *Id.* at 17.
402. MONT. CODE ANN. § 45-7-207 (2004).
403. *Id.* at § 45-7-207(1)(a).
404. MONT. CODE ANN. § 45-2-101(50).
405. 582 N.W.2d 369 (Neb. Ct. App. 1998), *aff'd*, 592 N.W.2d 912 (Neb. 1999).

interred the decedent's body and had an autopsy performed. During that autopsy, the performing physician allegedly destroyed evidence and, as a result, his findings could not be confirmed or disproved by the defendants.[406]

On the defendants' motion, the district court excluded testimony regarding the autopsy as a sanction for spoliation. The jury rendered a verdict in favor of the defendants on all claims except the negligent infliction of emotional distress claim. On appeal, the court of appeals upheld the exclusion of evidence as within the discretion of the trial court. It further noted the court has the inherent power to exclude evidence under Nebraska law.[407] Applying a multifactor test derived from *Lewis v. Darce Towing Company, Inc.*,[408] the court noted that the conduct of the plaintiff, her counsel, and the expert resulted in the destruction of evidence, and, further, the plaintiff's failure to timely amend discovery responses also violated Nebraska Rule 26(e). Accordingly, analyzing and applying the five factors set forth in *Lewis*, the court concluded that the trial court had properly excluded this evidence.[409]

The Supreme Court of Nebraska considered the application of the adverse inference in *State v. Davlin*.[410] There, the court explained as follows:

> An instruction on the inference that may be drawn from spoliation of evidence may be appropriate only where substantial evidence exists to support findings that the evidence had been in existence, in possession or under the control of the party against whom the inference may be drawn; that the evidence would have been admissible at trial; and that the party responsible for the destruction of the evidence did so intentionally and in bad faith.[411]

In *Davlin*, the defendant requested jury instructions for an adverse inference against the state, based on evidence that was destroyed ac-

---

406. *Id.* at 376.
407. *Id.* at 377.
408. 94 F.R.D. 262 (W.D. La. 1982).
409. 582 N.W.2d at 376.
410. 639 N.W.2d 631 (Neb. 2002).
411. *Id.* at 649.

cording the hospital's routine procedure. But the *Davlin* court found no evidence that the destruction of evidence was intentional or in bad faith. Since the destruction of the evidence was a matter of routine for the hospital, it did not support an inference that the destroyed evidence would have been unfavorable. The lower court did not err in refusing the jury instruction for the adverse inference.[412]

Criminal Statutes

Under Nebraska law,[413] a person commits the crime of tampering with physical evidence when, believing that an official proceeding is pending or about to be instituted, a person "[d]estroys, mutilates, conceals, removes or alters physical evidence with the intent to impair its verity, authenticity, or availability."[414] Nebraska courts have not addressed whether the statute would cover spoliation of evidence during a civil proceeding.

NEVADA

Independent Causes of Action for Destruction of Evidence

Addressing a question of first impression in Nevada in *Timber Tech Engineered Building Products v. The Home Insurance Company,*[415] the Supreme Court of Nevada declined to recognize an independent cause of action for intentional destruction of evidence. There, a restaurant roof collapsed and several patrons were injured. The building owner and contractor retained some ceiling debris for three years but eventually discarded it. After settling with the injured patrons, a subcontractor brought a claim against the building owner and its insurers for destruction of evidence.

The *Timber Tech* court followed the reasoning of the California Supreme Court in *Temple Community Hospital v. The Superior Court of Los Angeles,*[416] concluding it would not recognize an independent

---

412. *Id.*; *see also* Triewieler v. Sears, 689 N.W.2d 807, 841 (Neb. 2004) (observing that an adverse inference instruction should be predicated on "bad conduct").

413. NEB. REV. STAT. § 28-922(1) (2004).

414. *Id.* at § 28-922(1)(a).

415. 55 P.3d 952 (Nev. 2002).

416. 976 P.2d 223 (Cal. 1999).

tort for spoliation of evidence regardless of whether a first or third party committed the alleged spoliation.[417] The *Timber Tech* court explained that "the benefits of recognizing a tort cause of action . . . are outweighed by the burden to litigants, witnesses, and the judicial system that would be imposed by endless litigation over a speculative loss, and by the cost to society of promoting onerous record and evidence retention policies."[418]

The *Timber Tech* court also held that the subcontractor could not recover from the building owner for negligent spoliation under the circumstances of that case. The court explained that the owner never owed the subcontractor a duty to preserve the ceiling debris at issue.[419]

Civil and Evidentiary Sanctions for Destruction of Evidence

The Nevada Supreme Court has considered both civil and evidentiary sanctions in connection with a party's destruction of evidentiary material. In *Reingold v. Wet'N Wild Nevada, Inc.*,[420] the Nevada Supreme Court addressed giving an adverse inference instruction in a case involving a slip-and-fall accident at a water park. In *Reingold*, the water park owner claimed that all first-aid logs it maintained were routinely destroyed at the end of every season and, therefore, the logs for the year of the plaintiff's accident would have been destroyed well before the water park received a complaint commencing suit.[421]

At trial, the plaintiff requested a jury instruction that allowed the jury to infer that those first-aid logs would have been unfavorable to the water park. The district court declined to give the instruction, since it found no evidence that the water park willfully suppressed the logs.[422] The trial court apparently believed that "willful suppression" under NEVADA REVISED STATUTE section 47.250(3)[423] required more than simply following the company's routine record destruction policy.[424]

---

417. 55 P.3d at 954.
418. *Id.* (citing *Temple Cmty. Hosp.*, 976 P.2d at 233).
419. 55 P.3d at 954.
420. 944 P.2d 800 (Nev. 1997).
421. *Id.* at 802.
422. *Id.*
423. NEV. REV. STAT. § 47.250(3) (2004) provides for a rebuttable presumption that "evidence willfully suppressed would be adverse if produced."
424. 944 P.2d at 802. *See also* Bohlmann v. Printz, 96 P.3d 1155, 1158 (Nev. 2004) (observing that "whether the evidence was willfully suppressed or destroyed is highly factual in nature").

The Nevada Supreme Court disagreed, finding that the records were willfully or intentionally destroyed—that is, the water park owner intended to destroy the records at the end of the season. The *Reingold* court criticized the water park for destroying these records "even before the statute of limitations had run on any potential litigation for that season,"[425] suggesting that the records destruction policy was designed to prevent production of records in subsequent litigation. The court held that if the water park chose to have such a record retention policy, it was obliged to accept the adverse inferences of that policy.[426]

Nevada also sanctions the destruction or loss of evidence under Nevada Rule of Civil Procedure 37. These sanctions may only be imposed where there has been "willful noncompliance with a court order or where the adversary process has been halted by the actions of the unresponsive party."[427] The *GNLV* court observed, "[e]ven when an action has not been commenced, and there is only potential for litigation, a litigant is under a duty to preserve evidence which it knows or reasonably should know is relevant to an action."[428] Sanctions imposed by the court are reviewed by Nevada courts for abuse of discretion, unless the sanction is that of dismissal with prejudice, in which case "a somewhat heightened standard of review applies."[429]

Nevada Rule of Civil Procedure 37 offers a panoply of sanctions including, among other things, an order that designated facts shall be taken as established, an order refusing to allow the disobedient party to support or oppose a designated claim, an order prohibiting a party from introducing designated matters in evidence, or an order dismissing the action or proceedings or any part thereof.[430] Before a Nevada court may dismiss an action with prejudice as a discovery sanction, it

---

425. 944 P.2d at 802.

426. In dissent, Judge Young remarked, "The majority seemingly superimposes its judgment over that of the district court by concluding that simple 'housecleaning' removal of apparently unimportant first aid logs is a 'willful suppression' of documents." *Id.* at 803-04. *See also* Douglas Spencer & Assocs. v. Las Vegas Sun, Inc., 439 P.2d 473 (Nev. 1968) (finding failure of defendant to produce checks allowed the court to rely on the presumption that this evidence would have been adverse to the defendant if produced).

427. GNLV Corp. v. Service Control Corp., 900 P.2d 323, 325 (Nev. 1995) (citing Fire Ins. Exch. v. Zenith Radio Corp., 747 P.2d 911, 913 (Nev. 1987)).

428. *GNLV Corp.*, 900 P.2d at 325 (quoting *Fire Ins. Exch.*, 747 P.2d at 914).

429. 900 P.2d at 325.

430. Nev. R. Civ. P. 37 (2004).

may properly consider the factors set forth by the Nevada Supreme Court in *Young v. Johnny Ribeiro Building, Inc.*:[431]

1. The degree of willfulness of the offending party;
2. The extent to which the non-offending party would be prejudiced by a lesser sanction;
3. The severity of dismissal relative to the severity of the abusive conduct;
4. Whether evidence has been irreparably lost;
5. The feasibility and fairness of alternative and less severe sanctions;
6. The policy favoring adjudication on the merits;
7. Whether sanctions unfairly operate to penalize a party for the misconduct of his or her attorney; and
8. The need to deter both the parties and future litigants from similar abuses.[432]

Nevada courts will permit dismissal for failure to obey a discovery order; however, this sanction should only be used in "extreme situations."[433] If less drastic sanctions are available, Nevada trial courts are expected to employ them.[434]

Criminal Statutes

Under Nevada law, a person commits the crime of destroying evidence if that person willfully destroys, alters, erases, obliterates, or conceals any book, record, writing or thing with the intent to hinder or delay the administration of the law or to prevent the production thereof at any time in any court.[435] There is no reported case imposing criminal sanctions under this statute for destroying evidence in a civil proceeding.

---

431. 787 P.2d 777 (Nev. 1990).
432. *Id.* at 780.
433. Nevada Power Co. v. Fluor Ill., 837 P.2d 1354, 1359 (Nev. 1992).
434. *Id.* at 1359. The *Fluor Illinois* court also noted that Nevada has previously recognized that Rule 37 sanctions may also be imposed where the complaining party has destroyed evidence relating to the lawsuit before filing the suit. *Id.* at 1359 n.7.
435. NEV. REV. STAT. § 199.220 (2004).

NEW HAMPSHIRE

Independent Causes of Action for Destruction of Evidence

The New Hampshire Supreme Court has not decided whether it will recognize an independent tort for the negligent or intentional destruction of evidence. In its most recent ruling on the question, *Rodriguez v. Webb*,[436] a plaintiff suffered injuries while crushing aluminum cans in a metal baling machine. Shortly after the accident, the owner destroyed the baler and sold it as scrap metal.

The plaintiff brought a lawsuit against the owner of the baler, asserting a negligent failure to warn claim and claims for negligent and intentional spoliation of evidence. At the close of plaintiff's case, the trial court dismissed the claim for negligent spoliation but refused to dismiss the claim that the owner intentionally destroyed the baler.[437] The trial court instructed the parties that it would bifurcate the jury's deliberations, permitting it to consider the intentional spoliation claim only after it had resolved the negligent failure to warn claim. The court allowed the parties to address the intentional spoliation claim in closing, where the plaintiff argued that the owner destroyed the baler to hide evidence that would support his negligence claim.[438] The jury returned a verdict for the plaintiff on the negligent failure to warn claim, and the plaintiff dropped his claim for intentional spoliation.

The owner appealed, challenging the trial court's recognition of the tort of intentional spoliation of evidence. The owner also argued that the court improperly admitted evidence of the destruction of the baler, claiming it was not relevant to the negligence claim.[439]

The New Hampshire Supreme Court did not decide whether to recognize intentional spoliation as an independent tort. Instead, it found that any error in recognizing this tort was harmless, because evidence of the owner's destruction of the baler was appropriately considered on the negligent failure to warn claim.[440]

Civil and Evidentiary Sanctions

Rodriguez provides some insights into how New Hampshire courts

---

436. 680 A.2d 604 (N.H. 1996).
437. *Id.*
438. *Id.*
439. *Id.*
440. *Id.*

might analyze the issue. As noted above, the trial court permitted the destruction of the baler to be admitted into evidence and allowed the operator to argue that the owner destroyed it to hide evidence of the operator's claim.[441]

On appeal, the owner challenged the admissibility of evidence of the destruction of the baler on relevance grounds, arguing that there was no evidence of bad faith or wrongful intent. The owner's testimony, that he did not believe a lawsuit was imminent and that he destroyed the baler to prevent further injury, was uncontroverted. Affirming the operator's favorable judgment, the court observed that the owner admitted he destroyed the baler intentionally. Therefore, the jury could assess his credibility and decide whether he destroyed it to hide evidence or for innocent reasons.[442]

Rodriguez foreshadowed the New Hampshire Supreme Court's decision in *Murray v. Developmental Services*[443] regarding use of an adverse inference where there is evidence of intentional destruction. There, plaintiffs, severely developmentally disabled adults who lived in group homes, alleged they were physically and sexually assaulted by another resident while in the group home operator's care. The residents claimed that the group home operator omitted certain documents from its discovery response. The group home operator challenged the scope and wording of the trial court's jury instruction:

> Evidence has been presented that certain records or documents may have been intentionally lost or destroyed by the [group home operator.] The [group home operator] denies that any records or documents were intentionally lost or destroyed, and to the extent documents or records are missing, the [group home operator] has presented evidence suggesting innocent explanations.
>
> If you find that those records or documents would have been relevant to this case, and that the [group home owner] intentionally lost or destroyed them to keep the information secret, you may draw an inference on account of there being missing documents or records. However, if you find there was

---

441. *Id.*
442. *Id.* at 607 (citing Pittsfield v. Barnstead, 40 N.H. 477, 496 (1860) (finding it proper for a jury to consider evidence of fraudulent alteration of records)).
443. 818 A.2d 302 (N.H. 2003).

an innocent explanation for the missing records or documents, or if you find these records or documents would not have been relevant to this case, you may not draw such an inference.[444]

The *Murray* court rejected the group home owner's argument that, because there was no evidence of document destruction after the residents filed their lawsuit, an adverse inference "can be drawn only when the evidence is destroyed deliberately with a fraudulent intent." [445] Instead, the court held that an adverse inference can be drawn even when the evidence is destroyed before a claim is made because "the timing of the document destruction is not dispositive on the issue of intent."[446]

Criminal Statutes

New Hampshire imposes criminal liability on a person who alters, destroys or removes "any thing with the purpose to impair its verity or availability" in an official proceeding or investigation that is "pending or about to be instituted."[447] This statute is applicable only in the context of an official investigation; it does not appear to have any applicability in civil matters.[448]

NEW JERSEY

Independent Causes of Action for Spoliation of Evidence

New Jersey does not recognize an independent cause of action for intentional spoliation. Instead, the New Jersey Supreme Court has held that the tort of fraudulent concealment provides litigants with adequate protection against intentional spoliation of evidence.[449]

The court considered the viability of a spoliation claim in a medical malpractice lawsuit in *Rosenblit v. Zimmerman*,[450] when a doctor deliberately altered the plaintiff's medical records and then destroyed the originals. The court discussed an earlier New Jersey appellate court

444. *Id.* at 309-10.
445. *Id.* at 309.
446. *Id.*
447. N.H. REV. STAT. ANN. § 641:6 (2004).
448. *Id.*
449. Rosenblit v. Zimmerman, 766 A.2d 749, 758 (N.J. 2001).
450. *Id.*

decision, *Viviano v. CBS, Inc.*,[451] explaining that though some have identified that case as recognizing an independent tort, the *Viviano* court simply identified fraudulent concealment as a preexisting tort remedy for spoliation.

The *Rosenblit* court approved the approach taken by the *Viviano* court, but differed slightly on the elements of fraudulent concealment of evidence in the litigation context. It held that in such a context, a plaintiff must show the following:

1. The defendant in the fraudulent concealment action had a legal obligation to disclose evidence in connection with an existing or pending lawsuit;
2. The evidence was material to the litigation;
3. The plaintiff could not reasonably have obtained access to the evidence from another source;
4. The defendant intentionally withheld, altered or destroyed the evidence with purpose to disrupt the litigation; and
5. The plaintiff was damaged in the underlying action by having to rely on an evidential record that did not contain the evidence concealed.[452]

New Jersey courts also appear to be employing an existing tort cause of action to remedy alleged cases of negligent spoliation.[453] In two recent decisions, New Jersey appellate courts have declined to recognize a separate tort for negligent spoliation and instead have applied "traditional negligence principles."[454]

Earlier decisions by New Jersey appellate courts and federal courts applying New Jersey law had been split on this issue, with at least one court recognizing the tort of negligent spoliation,[455] one court recognizing the analogous tort of fraudulent concealment of evidence,[456] and a

---

451. 597 A.2d 543 (N.J. Super. Ct. App. Div. 1991).
452. *Rosenblit*, 766 A.2d at 758.
453. *See, e.g.*, Swick v. New York Times, 815 A.2d 508 (N.J. Super. Ct. App. Div. 2003); Gilleski v. Cmty. Med. Ctr., 765 A.2d 1103 (N.J. Super. Ct. App. Div. 2001).
454. *Swick*, 815 A.2d at 512; *Gilleski*, 765 A.2d at 1104.
455. Callahan v. Stanley Works, 703 A.2d 1014 (N.J. Super. Ct. Law Div. 1997).
456. *Viviano*, 597 A.2d 543.

number of courts either declining to reach the issue on the facts before them[457] or expressly refusing to recognize such a cause of action.[458]

Civil and Evidentiary Sanctions for Destruction of Evidence

New Jersey courts will impose sanctions for spoliation occurring during pending litigation. These sanctions include exclusion of expert evidence, the giving of an adverse inference instruction, and an award of attorney fees or punitive damages.[459] A trial court can impose such sanctions under its inherent power to manage cases.[460]

A New Jersey superior court in *Hirsch v. General Motors Corporation* thoroughly analyzed the available sanctions for spoliation.[461] In that case, the plaintiffs had purchased a new Cadillac, which they brought in for repair of an air conditioner, new front brakes, and rear brake cleaning and adjustment two years later. Less than two months after the repairs, the vehicle caught fire and was destroyed while parked in the owner's driveway. The insurance company settled with the vehicle owners. Thereafter, an inspector for the insurance company examined the vehicle and concluded that a ruptured brake fluid line caused the fire. The vehicle was sold and was never seen again.

Approximately five months later, the insurance company notified the manufacturer of the vehicle that it held the manufacturer responsible for the damage. The manufacturer denied liability. The owner's insurer filed suit, alleging claims including breach of contract, negli-

---

457. *See, e.g.,* Proske v. St. Barnabas Med. Ctr., 712 A.2d 1207 (N.J. Super. Ct. App. Div. 1998); Allis-Chalmers Corp. Prod. Liability Trust v. Liberty Mut. Ins. Co., 702 A.2d 1336 (N.J. Super. Ct. App. Div. 1997); Marinelli v. Mitts & Merrill, 696 A.2d 55 (N.J. Super. Ct. App. Div. 1997).

458. *See, e.g.,* Kolanovic v. Pak Gida A/S (Turkey), 77 F. Supp. 2d 595 (D.N.J. 1999); Trump Taj Mahal Assoc. v. Aeronautiche Giovanni Agusta, S.P.A., 761 F. Supp. 1143 (D.N.J. 1991).

459. *See, e.g., Rosenblit,* 766 A.2d at 760 (explaining innocent party entitled to a spoliation instruction when spoliation discovered before or at the time of trial).

460. Manorcare Health Services, Inc. v. Osmose Wood Preserving, Inc., 764 A.2d 475, 482 (N.J. Super. Ct. App. Div. 2001) (quoting Aetna Life & Cas. Co. v. Imet Mason Contractors, 707 A.2d 180, 183 (N.J. Super. Ct. App. Div. 1998)); Larison v. City of Trenton, 180 F.R.D. 261, 266 (D.N.J. 1998) (rejecting tort claim and reasoning that preclusion of evidence and jury instructions are favored methods).

461. 628 A.2d 1108 (N.J. Super. Ct. Law Div. 1993).

gent design, and negligent manufacture of the car. The manufacturer moved to dismiss based on spoliation of evidence.

The trial court extensively analyzed the law of spoliation in New Jersey, noting that New Jersey had recognized a tort analogous to intentional spoliation of evidence, but not a separate tort for negligent spoliation of evidence.[462] The court determined that negligent spoliation could be properly remedied by excluding evidence at trial.[463] It then held that the owner's insurer had a duty to preserve evidence based on its investigation, and this duty extended to allowing the manufacturer reasonable time after receiving an incident report from the owner or the owner's insurer to access the vehicle.

Next, the *Hirsch* court examined available remedies for spoliation, including recognition of a tort claim, civil discovery sanctions, and a spoliation inference.[464] Evaluating the prejudice to the manufacturer, the level of culpability of the owner's insurer, and the range of available sanctions, the court concluded that exclusion of all evidence regarding the insurer's inspection of the vehicle was the appropriate sanction.[465]

Criminal Statutes

New Jersey law provides that a person commits the crime of hindering apprehension or prosecution if, with purpose to hinder, that person suppresses "by way of concealment or destruction, any evidence of the crime or tampers with a . . . document or other source of information, regardless of its admissibility in evidence, which might aid in the discovery or apprehension of such a person. . . ."[466]

The New Jersey Supreme Court suggested that the New Jersey falsification statute[467] may also provide criminal sanctions for spoliation.[468] The authors have not found a reported New Jersey decision imposing criminal sanctions for the destruction of evidence during a civil proceeding.

---

462. *Id.* at 1115 (citing *Viviano*, 597 A.2d 543).
463. *Id.* at 1119-20.
464. *Id.*
465. *Id.*
466. N.J. STAT. ANN. § 2C:29-3(a)(3) (2004).
467. N.J. STAT. ANN. § 2C:28-6(1) (2004).
468. *Rosenblit*, 766 A.2d at 754.

NEW MEXICO

Independent Causes of Action for Destruction of Evidence

In *Coleman v. Eddy Potash, Inc.*,[469] the New Mexico Supreme Court recognized a claim for intentional spoliation of evidence. The elements of that tort are: (1) the existence of a potential lawsuit; (2) the defendant's knowledge of the potential lawsuit; (3) the destruction, mutilation, or significant alteration of potential evidence; (4) intent on the part of the defendants to disrupt or defeat the lawsuit; (5) a causal relationship between the act of spoliation and the inability to prove the lawsuit; and (6) damages.[470] To prevail, a plaintiff must show that the defendant had the actual intent to harm the plaintiff's economic interests.[471]

In *Torres v. El Paso Electric Company*,[472] the court examined the scope of this tort and the meaning of the intent element of that claim. It held that the "element of an intent to disrupt or defeat a lawsuit refers not to a mere intentional act but to a level of culpability that is particularly egregious in civil actions: a malicious intent to harm."[473] The court further noted that the tort it recognized in *Coleman*[474] seeks to remedy actions taken with the sole intent to maliciously defeat or disrupt a lawsuit.

Civil and Evidentiary Sanctions for Destruction of Evidence

The *Torres* court also discussed the remedy for the action of a spoliator when its actions did not rise to the level of malicious conduct or otherwise meet the element of an intentional tort. The court determined that "a more appropriate remedy would be a permissible adverse evidentiary inference by the jury in the underlying claim."[475]

The court identified the factors a trial court should consider in determining whether to give such an instruction as whether the spoliation was intentional, whether the spoliator knew that a lawsuit involving the spoiled object was reasonably possible, whether the party requesting the adverse inference acted with due diligence in seeking

---

469. 905 P.2d 185, 189 (N.M. 1995)
470. *Id.*
471. *Id.* at 193.
472. 987 P.2d 386 (N.M. 1999).
473. *Id.* at 405.
474. *Id.*
475. *Id.* at 406.

the spoiled evidence, and if the evidence would have been relevant to a material issue in the case. The court did not find it necessary that the spoliator act with malice or bad faith before a sanction, like an adverse inference, could be imposed.

Criminal Statutes

New Mexico prohibits tampering with evidence, which includes destroying, changing, hiding or fabricating any physical evidence with the intent to prevent apprehension, prosecution or conviction of any person of a crime.[476]

NEW YORK

Independent Causes of Action for Destruction of Evidence

In an apparent case of first impression, the New York Court of Appeals refused to recognize a claim for third-party spoliation of evidence in *MetLife Auto & Home Company v. Joe Basil Chevrolet, Inc.*[477] There, a manufacturer's insurer destroyed a vehicle that allegedly caused a fire that damaged a home insured by another insurer. The homeowner's insurer claimed that even though the manufacturer's insurer was not a party to the lawsuit, it assumed an independent duty to preserve the vehicle when it agreed in a telephone conversation to preserve it, and the homeowner's insurer relied on that agreement to its detriment.

Rejecting the homeowner's insurer's claim, the court observed that no relationship existed between the two insurers, and the homeowner's insurer made no effort to preserve the evidence by obtaining a court order or written agreement or volunteering to cover the cost of preserving the damaged vehicle. The court concluded that "[t]he burden of forcing a party to preserve evidence when it has no notice of an impending lawsuit, and the difficulty of assessing damages militate against establishing a cause of action for spoliation in this case, where there was no duty, court order, contract or special relationship."[478]

---

476. N.M. STAT. ANN. § 30-22-5 (2003).

477. 807 N.E.2d 865 (N.Y. App. Div. 2004). The court of appeals acknowledged that New York appellate courts had recognized that spoliation of evidence may support a common-law cause of action when it impairs an employee's right to sue a third-party tortfeasor, discussing and distinguishing *DiDomenico v. C&S Aeromatik Supplies, Inc.*, 682 N.Y.S.2d 452 (N.Y. App. Div. 1998).

478. *Id.* at 868.

Civil and Evidentiary Sanctions for Destruction of Evidence

New York courts have held that "[w]hen a party alters, loses or destroys key evidence before it can be examined by the other party's expert, the court should dismiss the pleadings of the party responsible for the spoliation."[479] For example, in *Squitieri v. The City of New York*,[480] a city sanitation worker's street sweeper filled up with carbon monoxide fumes while he was operating it, allegedly leaving him with serious physical and psychological injuries. The city worker filed suit against the City of New York in March of 1985. Notwithstanding that litigation was pending, on September 8, 1985, the city discarded the sweeper. Several years later, the city filed a third-party claim against the distributor and manufacturer of the sweeper.

The manufacturer and the distributor moved for summary judgment against the city, arguing that the spoliation of evidence had severely prejudiced them. The trial court denied the motion, reasoning that dismissal was too harsh a remedy, since the city worker could still prove design defect without the product. The court of appeals reversed and ordered the third-party complaint dismissed. It reasoned that harsh sanctions such as dismissal and preclusion of evidence "are not limited to cases where the evidence was destroyed willfully or in bad faith, since a party's negligent loss of evidence can be just as fatal to the other party's ability to present a defense."[481]

The court also rejected the city's argument that dismissal was inappropriate because the design could be evaluated and any design defect "proved circumstantially."[482] However, the court also noted, "Although the absence of the sweeper would prevent [the manufacturer] from countering the design defect claim with evidence, the [city's] misuse, alteration, or poor maintenance of this particular sweeper was a proximate cause of [the city's worker's] injuries."[483]

New York courts may impose other sanctions in addition to dismissal of a claim. For example, if a party discards evidence without

---

479. Squitieri v. City of New York, 669 N.Y.S.2d 589, 590 (N.Y. App. Div. 1998); *see also* DiDomenico v. C & S Aeromatik Supplies, Inc., 682 N.Y.S.2d 452 (N.Y. App. Div. 1998).

480. 669 N.Y.S.2d 589 (N.Y. App. Div. 1998).

481. *Id.* at 590.

482. *Id.* (quoting Kirkland v. New York City Hous. Auth., 666 N.Y.S.2d 609, 613 (N.Y. App. Div. 1997)).

483. *Id.*

moving for a protective order, an adverse inference instruction may be given.[484]

Where the non-spoliating party is unable to show it has been prejudiced by the destruction of evidence, particularly where spoliation is not shown to be willful, dismissal of claims or preclusion of evidence may be considered too harsh a sanction. In *Anderson v. Avis Rent-A-Car System, Inc.*,[485] for example, the plaintiff suffered a severe head injury during a car accident while operating a vehicle owned by the rental company. Less than two months after the accident, the rental company sold the vehicle for scrap, after retaining its own expert to inspect the vehicle and render a report, but without informing the plaintiff.[486] The company did not disclose that the vehicle had been scrapped until several years later in response to a court order mandating disclosure.

The plaintiff moved to strike the company's answer or to preclude its use of a seat-belt defense. Although the court was troubled by the fact that "[the company] routinely scraps automobiles that have been in serious accidents before an injured party could realistically be expected to be thinking in terms of litigation or preservation of evidence,"[487] it declined to impose the requested sanctions. Instead, because it believed the spoliation of evidence was not "innocent," the court held that the plaintiff would have the opportunity to depose the company's seat-belt expert before trial and review any reports or notes by the expert. Additionally, the plaintiff would have the opportunity after this examination to obtain his own expert or experts. The court reasoned that this remedy would enable the plaintiff to overcome any prejudice resulting from the destruction of the vehicle.[488]

Criminal Statutes

Under New York Penal Law section 215.40,[489] a person commits the crime of tampering with physical evidence when "[b]elieving that certain physical evidence is about to be produced or used in an official

---

484. *DiDomenico*, 682 N.Y.S.2d at 459.
485. 667 N.Y.S.2d 220 (N.Y. Sup. Ct. 1997).
486. *Id.*
487. *Id.* at 222.
488. *Id.* at 223.
489. (Consol. 1999).

proceeding or prospective proceeding," and intending to prevent its production or use, suppresses it by "act of concealment, alteration, or destruction."[490] An "official proceeding" is defined as "any action or proceeding conducted by or before a legally constituted judicial, legislative, administrative, or other governmental agency or official, in which evidence may be properly received."[491]

In *Coley v. Arnot Ogden Memorial Hospital*,[492] the court rejected an employee's civil claim for violation of New York Penal Law section 215.40 because the alleged destruction appeared to be innocent. The *Coley* court also held, "There is nothing to support the conclusion that defendant's employees intended to prevent the use of the ladder in an official proceeding. . . . It appears that Penal Law § 215.40 was enacted to protect the courts, our system of justice and society in general rather than to benefit any specific class, and, therefore, plaintiff cannot seek civil redress thereunder. . . ."[493]

New York courts also will impose sanctions against lawyers who are convicted of tampering with physical evidence, which is a felony and can result in disbarment.[494]

NORTH CAROLINA

Independent Causes of Action for Destruction of Evidence

North Carolina courts have not addressed whether spoliation of evidence should be recognized as an independent tort claim.

Civil and Evidentiary Sanctions for Destruction of Evidence

The traditional remedy for spoliation of evidence in civil litigation is an adverse inference instruction.[495] In *McLain v. Taco Bell Corporation*,[496] an employee filed a lawsuit for, among other things, wrongful

---

490. *Id.* at § 215.40(2).
491. N.Y. PENAL LAW § 215.35(2) (1999).
492. 485 N.Y.S.2d 876 (3d Dep't 1985).
493. *Id.* at 879.
494. *See, e.g.*, In the Matter of Decious, 512 N.Y.S.2d 115, 116 (2d Dep't 1987).
495. *See* Red Hill Hosiery Mill, Inc. v. Magnetek, Inc., 530 S.E.2d 321 (N.C. App. 2000) (reversing and remanding grant of summary judgment on product liability claim and noting spoliation issue proper for development at trial following remand).
496. 527 S.E.2d 712 (N.C. App. 2000).

discharge against her employer and its managers, claiming they sexually harassed her. According to the employee, she left notes in the manager's log book regarding the alleged harassment. The log book was purportedly kept locked in the restaurant office and made available for review only by the store management team, which included the complaining employee. The employee contended no manager ever contacted her regarding her notes about the alleged harassment.

After a co-worker assaulted the complaining employee, the store manager discharged her for alleged work rule violations. Taco Bell's district manager investigated and, as a result, terminated the alleged harassers and reinstated the employee, who resigned shortly thereafter and filed suit.

During discovery, the employee observed that the log book was missing entries she had given to the district manager. Although the district manager conceded that he had destroyed some parts of the log book, he denied that any "pertinent" material was missing.[497] The trial court declined to give the adverse inference instruction requested by the employee.

The *McLain* court reversed, holding that an adverse inference instruction should have been given under established North Carolina law. The court reasoned that a showing that evidence was destroyed in bad faith or in anticipation of trial was not essential, but such a showing may warrant a stronger instruction.[498] The court further determined that there was sufficient evidence to require an adverse inference instruction because the employer gave no satisfactory explanation for the destruction of evidence, was aware that the log book contained relevant evidence, and knew "of circumstances that were likely to give rise to future litigation."[499]

North Carolina courts have held that a trial court has authority, under both North Carolina Civil Rule 37 and its inherent authority, to impose sanctions for discovery violations.[500] This includes the author-

---

497. *Id.* at 717.
498. *Id.*
499. *Id.* at 718 (quoting Blinzler v. Marriott Int'l, Inc., 81 F.3d 1148, 1158-59 (1st Cir. 1996)). *See also* Jones v. GMRI, Inc., 551 S.E.2d 867 (N.C. App. 2001) (suggesting that a party could assert spoliation as grounds for a directed verdict under proper circumstances).
500. *See, e.g.*, Bumgarner v. Reneau, 422 S.E.2d 686, 689 (N.C. 1992).

ity to "refus[e] to permit the disobedient party to introduce the matters in question into evidence."[501] Accordingly, it appears that North Carolina trial courts may impose the full range of sanctions available under Rule 37 to punish a party who has spoliated evidence.

Criminal Statutes

Under North Carolina statute,[502] a person commits the crime of "altering, destroying, or stealing evidence of criminal conduct" if the person "alters, destroys, or steals any evidence relevant to any criminal offense or court proceeding."[503] There is no case law to support that courts would impose criminal sanctions for the destruction of evidence in a civil proceeding.

OHIO

Independent Causes of Action for Destruction of Evidence

Ohio is among the minority of states that recognize an independent tort claim for spoliation of evidence. In *Smith v. Howard Johnson Company, Inc.*,[504] the Supreme Court of Ohio recognized intentional spoliation as providing the basis for an independent cause of action. In that case, accepted as a certified question from the District Court for the Northern District of Ohio, the court set out the elements of the tort of intentional destruction of evidence:

1. Pending or probable litigation involving the plaintiff;
2. Knowledge on the part of the defendant that litigation exists or is probable;
3. Willful destruction of evidence by the defendant designed to disrupt the plaintiff's case;
4. Actual disruption of the plaintiff's case; and
5. Proximately caused damages.[505]

---

501. *Id.* at 690.
502. N.C. Gen. Stat. § 14-221.1 (2004).
503. *Id.*
504. 615 N.E.2d 1037 (Ohio 1993).
505. *Id.* at 1038. The *Smith* court did not recognize a claim for negligent spoliation although the question was presented to the court. White v. Ford Motor Co., 755 N.E.2d 954 (Ct. App. Ohio 2001).

In *Davis v. Wal-Mart Stores, Inc.,*[506] the Ohio Supreme Court clarified *Smith* and held that "[independent tort] claims for spoliation of evidence may be brought after the primary action has been conducted *only* when evidence of spoliation is not discovered until after the conclusion of the primary action."[507]

Since *Smith*, a number of Ohio courts have analyzed an independent tort claim for spoliation. These courts have focused on evidence of "willful" withholding, alteration, falsification or destruction of evidence, and disruption of the complaining party's case.[508] Ohio courts have been reluctant to allow recovery unless the plaintiff shows egregious conduct and also that, as a result of that conduct, the plaintiff's case has been rendered virtually speculative.[509]

The Ohio Eleventh District Court of Appeals' decision in *Drawl v. Cornicelli*[510] is illustrative. There, a plaintiff-patient had sued her former employer for sexual harassment. The defendant-employer subpoenaed certain medical records related to her treatment for psychological problems resulting from the harassment. Unbeknownst to the patient, the doctor's office altered the patient's medical records after it produced the records to her former employer. The alterations became apparent at the trial on the patient's sexual harassment case and, according to the patient, resulted in the loss of her case against her former employer. The patient then sued her doctor for intentional spoliation. The doctor testified that in the normal course of her record keeping she updated patient records to reflect the patient's condition and treatment. Despite expert testimony that the doctor's procedure failed to comply with standards for medical record keeping, the court affirmed sum-

---

506. 756 N.E.2d 657 (Ohio 2001).
507. *Id.* at 660 (emphasis added).
508. *See, e.g.,* Tate v. Adena Regional Med. Ctr., 801 N.E.2d 930 (Ohio Ct. App. 2003) (rejecting spoliation claim where claimant offered no evidence to show a hospital destroyed evidence to harm her case); Miller v. Wire One Techs., Inc., 2004-Ohio-2038, 2004 Ohio App. LEXIS 1776 (Ohio Ct. App. 2004) (same). *See also* Keen v. Hardin Mem. Hosp., 2003-Ohio-6707, 2003 Ohio App. LEXIS 6076 (Ohio Ct. App. 2003); Pratt v. Payne, 794 N.E.2d 723 (Ohio Ct. App. 2003); Sheets v. Norfolk Southern Corp., 671 N.E.2d 1364 (Ohio Ct. App. 1996); Tittle v. Rent-A-Wreck, No. 92-B-51, 1993 Ohio App. LEXIS 4563 (Ohio Ct. App. Sept. 24, 1993).
509. *Sheets,* 671 N.E.2d at 1364.
510. 706 N.E.2d 849 (Ohio Ct. App. 1997).

mary judgment for the doctor, finding nothing "sinister or wrongful" in the doctor's actions.[511]

In other independent spoliation tort cases, Ohio courts also have looked carefully at the intent of the spoliator and have consistently required evidence of "wrongful" intent. For example, in *Sheets v. Norfolk Southern Corporation*,[512] following an accident resulting in a wrongful death action, plaintiffs brought a claim for spoliation of evidence because a railroad had destroyed the train's "black box." A railroad employee testified that the railroad routinely preserved the black box after an accident, but the railroad offered no explanation for not producing the black box at trial. Affirming denial of a directed verdict motion, the appellate court held that the plaintiffs met their *prima facie* burden because the absence of the box disrupted their case.[513]

Civil and Evidentiary Sanctions for Destruction of Evidence

Sanctions for spoliation considered by Ohio courts include dismissal or default judgments, exclusion of evidence or expert testimony, monetary sanctions, and adverse jury inferences.[514] Generally, Ohio courts follow the policy of imposing the least severe sanction, or at least a sanction short of outright dismissal of the action with prejudice, unless the spoliator's conduct evidences bad faith.[515] Thus, when considering civil and evidentiary sanctions for spoliation in pending litigation, Ohio courts have taken a balanced approach, weighing the intent of the offending party, the degree of prejudice, and the reasonableness of the offending party's action.[516]

Even though Ohio requires a showing of wrongful intent when considering civil or evidentiary remedies for spoliation, some Ohio

511. *Id.* at 853. *See also* McGuire v. Draper, Hollenbaugh & Briscoe Co., *L.P.A.*, 2002-Ohio-6170, 2002 Ohio App. LEXIS 6003 (Ohio Ct. App. 2002) (refusing to find willful destruction of evidence where the evidence revealed that the offending party possessed a good-faith belief that it was entitled to withhold a client file and stating "[c]arelessness [...] is insufficient to establish willfulness.").
512. 671 N.E.2d 1364 (Ohio Ct. App. 1996).
513. *Id.*
514. *Keen,* 2003-Ohio-6707 at ¶¶ 10-19.
515. Transamerica Ins. Group v. Maytag, Inc., 650 N.E.2d 169 (Ohio Ct. App. 1994) (citing Evans v. Smith, 598 N.E.2d 1287, 1288-89 (Ohio Ct. App. 1991)).
516. *Keen,* 2003-Ohio-6707 at ¶ 16 (citing Hubbard v. Cleveland, Columbus & Cincinnati Hwy., Inc., 76 N.E.2d 721 (Ohio Ct. App. 1947)).

courts have held that inadvertent destruction of evidence is sufficient to trigger sanctions where the loss disadvantages the opposing party. In *American States Insurance Company v. Tokai-Seike (H.K.), Ltd.,*[517] for instance, the court found no evidence of wrongful intent by a homeowner and its insurer, who failed to preserve the entire scene following a fire supposedly caused by a defective lighter. Rather than dwell on the absence of wrongful intent, the court instead focused on the relative importance of certain portions of the fire scene evidence and the reasonableness of the conduct by the homeowners and their insurer in preserving that evidence. In order to place the parties on a "level playing field," the court ordered that, at trial, the jury would be given an adverse inference instruction.[518]

Criminal Statutes

Under Ohio Revised Code section 2921.12, it is a crime for a person to tamper with or destroy physical evidence knowing that an official proceeding or investigation is in progress.[519] Although no Ohio court appears to have applied this provision in a civil lawsuit, at least two Ohio courts referenced section 2921.12 as, at least in part, a basis for the tort of intentional spoliation, before Ohio recognized the tort.[520]

OKLAHOMA

Independent Causes of Action for Destruction of Evidence

In *Patel v. OMH Medical Center, Inc.,*[521] the Supreme Court of Oklahoma declined to address recognition of a civil action for spoliation because the conduct complained of in the action before it did not present such a case. However, the court remarked that apart from remedies available in a pending litigation, such as discovery and other sanctions, where litigation-related misconduct occurs, a party aggrieved by such misconduct may invoke sanctions available under criminal

---

517. 704 N.E.2d 1280 (Ohio C.P. 1997).

518. *Id.* at 1285.

519. Ohio Rev. Code § 2921.12 (Anderson 2003).

520. *See* Tomas v. Nationwide Mut. Ins. Co., 607 N.E.2d 944 (Ohio Ct. App. 1992); Williams v. Dunagan, No. 15870, 1993 Ohio App. LEXIS 2430 (Ohio Ct. App. May 5, 1993).

521. 987 P.2d 1185 (Okla. 1999).

law, or, in cases of attorney misconduct, by disciplinary measures to the bar association.

The Oklahoma Supreme Court also has observed that there is no civil action that may be maintained for damages caused by perjury, reasoning that perjurious testimony constitutes a fraud or deceit upon the finders of fact and on the judicial system as a whole, but not on an individual litigant.[522] Therefore, it is unlikely that the Supreme Court will recognize an independent tort for destruction of evidence.

Civil and Evidentiary Sanctions

An Oklahoma appellate court addressed the question of civil or evidentiary sanctions in the context of lost or destroyed evidence in pending litigation in a worker' compensation case. In *Manpower Inc. v. Brawdy*,[523] the court suggested that the use of an adverse inference would be a proper remedy to destruction of evidence unless there was a satisfactory explanation for its loss.[524] But the *Manpower* court refused to sanction an employee who had surgery that an employer's insurer claimed to have destroyed evidence it could have used to defeat the case. It held that "[m]edical treatment is generally not sought for the purpose of prejudicing the rights of those who may later be found liable for the treatment."[525]

Explaining the sanctions available for noncompliance with notice to a party regarding court-ordered discovery, in *Payne v. Dewitt*,[526] the Oklahoma Supreme Court discussed section 3237(B)(2) of the Oklahoma Discovery Code. The court observed that this provision authorizes a broad spectrum of sanctions for abuse of the discovery process. The court relied on a five-factor test employed by the Tenth Circuit Court of Appeals to provide lower courts with guidance for imposing sanctions: (1) the quantum of prejudice noncompliance has caused the moving party; (2) the extent of interference with the judicial process; (3) the culpability of the litigant; (4) where a dismissal or default is being considered, whether the court warned the party in advance

522. Cooper v. Parker-Hugey, 894 P.2d 1096 (Okla. 1995).
523. 62 P.3d 391 (Okla. Ct. App. 2002).
524. *Id.*
525. 62 P.3d 391.
526. 995 P.2d 1088 (Okla. 1999).

that noncompliance could lead to dismissal or default judgment; and (5) the efficacy of lesser sanctions.[527]

Oklahoma courts will only consider the harshest of sanctions, dismissal or default, where a party's failure to comply with a discovery order results from fault, willfulness or bad faith.[528] A court's decision to impose sanctions will be reviewed for abuse of discretion. A sanction must be both fair and related to the particular claim or defense at issue in the discovery order.[529]

However, even following entry of a default judgment as a sanction, a default declaration imposed as a section 3237(B)(2) sanction cannot extend beyond imposing liability on the wrongdoer and imposing punitive damages. The sanctioning court must allow the defaulted party to have a meaningful opportunity to inquire into actual and punitive damages without stripping him of basic truth-testing devices. Accordingly, in *Payne*, the trial court's decision to strip the defendant of the right to cross-examine witnesses, object to testimony, and otherwise participate in the damage portion of the case constituted an abuse of discretion.[530]

Criminal Statutes

Under Oklahoma law, a person commits the crime of destruction of evidence if that person, "knowing that any book, paper, record instrument in writing, or other matter or thing, is about to be produced" in a trial proceeding inquiry or investigation, willfully destroys the item with intent to "prevent the same being produced."[531] Although this language suggests that an Oklahoma court would impose criminal sanctions in a case, we found no reported case in which a prosecutor has pursued such a claim that arose from destruction of evidence in a civil proceeding.

---

527. *Id.* at 1092.

528. *See, e.g.*, Beverly v. Wal-Mart Stores, Inc., 3 P.3d 163 (Okla. 1999) (affirming grant of summary judgment in product liability action where product was destroyed but noting that loss of evidence was not result of willful or fraudulent destruction).

529. 995 P.2d 1088.

530. *Id. See also* Goldman v. Goldman, 883 P.2d 181 (Okla. Ct. App. 1992) (reversing trial court's entry of dismissal of a cross-claim as a sanction for destruction of certain evidentiary tapes as a result of a flooded basement because the court failed to afford the party an opportunity for a hearing as to its reasons for noncompliance).

531. OKLA. STAT. tit. 21, § 454 (2003).

OREGON

Independent Causes of Action for Destruction of Evidence

Oregon courts have not recognized a cause of action for intentional or negligent spoliation of evidence.[532]

Civil and Evidentiary Sanctions for Destruction of Evidence

There do not appear to be any reported Oregon cases addressing the appropriateness of sanctions for spoliation of evidence in civil litigation.[533] In *Pamplin v. Victoria*,[534] the Supreme Court of Oregon reversed the trial court's dismissal of the plaintiffs' complaint as a sanction for failure to provide discovery. It held that prior to dismissing a case as a sanction under Rule 46, the trial court must explain why the sanction is just.[535] Moreover, a finding of "willfulness, bad faith, or fault of a similar degree" is required; however, finding prejudice to the party seeking discovery is not required.[536]

Based on *Pamplin*, it appears the Supreme Court of Oregon probably would recognize the propriety of sanctions for spoliation of evidence. Further, given its requirement of a finding of willfulness, bad faith, or similar fault, the court arguably would require a similar level of culpability prior to the imposition of sanctions for spoliation.[537] However, the court in *Pamplin* reasoned that the only prejudice required under Federal Rule of Civil Procedure 37, as well as Oregon Rule 46, is prejudice to the operation of the legal system rather than the party seeking discovery. It is unclear whether prejudice to the non-

---

532. Fox v. Country Mut. Ins. Co., 7 P.3d 677 (Or. Ct. App. 2000) (observing that purpose of the tort of tortious interference with a prospective economic advantage is to protect the integrity of voluntary economic relationships and that no court has recognized such a claim in the spoliation context because litigation is not a voluntary relationship).
533. Pamplin v. Victoria, 877 P.2d 1196 (Ore. 1994).
534. 877 P.2d 1196 (Ore. 1994).
535. *Id.* Oregon Rule of Civil Procedure 46(B)(2)(c) is virtually identical to FED. R. CIV. P. 37(b)(2)(C).
536. *Pamplin,* 877 P.2d at 1201.
537. The court in *Pamplin* based its fault requirement on the U.S. Supreme Court decision of *Societe Internationale v. Rogers*, 357 U.S. 197 (1958), in which the Court required a finding of willfulness, bad faith, or similar fault prior to sanctions under FED. R. CIV. P. 37.

spoliating party would be a factor in determining whether sanctions are applicable for spoliation of evidence.[538]

Criminal Statutes

Oregon Revised Statute section 162.295 provides that a person who commits the crime of tampering with physical evidence, "with intent that it be used, introduced, rejected, or unavailable in an official proceeding" that is pending or about to be instituted, "destroys, mutilates, alters, conceals, or removes physical evidence impairing its verity or availability."[539] There is no case law to support whether Oregon would apply this statute to destruction of evidence in a civil case.

PENNSYLVANIA

Independent Causes of Action for Destruction of Evidence

Neither the Supreme Court nor any appellate court in Pennsylvania has recognized a separate cause of action for intentional or negligent spoliation of evidence. A few Pennsylvania Common Pleas courts have embraced spoliation as a separate claim, and appellate courts have considered the question on several occasions.[540]

For example, in *Elias v. Lancaster General Hospital*,[541] the court considered whether Pennsylvania should recognize a cause of action in tort against a third party who discards relevant evidence in an existing or probable civil case where a special relationship exists between the plaintiff and the alleged spoliator. The court did not find it necessary to create an entirely new and separate cause of action for third parties' negligent spoliation. As the court explained, traditional negligence principles are available, and adequate remedies

538. *Pamplin*, 877 P.2d at 1200.
539. OR. REV. STAT. §162.295(1) (2003).
540. Elias v. Lancaster General Hosp., 710 A.2d 65, 67 nn. 2, 3 (Pa. Super. Ct. 1998); *see also* Doe v. Curran, 45 Pa. D.& C.4th 544 (2000) (noting reluctance to recognize separate spoliation tort but explaining possibility of adverse inference upon demonstration of intentional destruction of records); Olson v. Grutza, 631 A.2d 191 (Pa. Super. Ct. 1993) (declining to consider a cause of action for spoliation of evidence); Kelly v. St. Mary's Hosp., 694 A.2d 355 (Pa. Super. Ct. 1997) (declining to consider whether Pennsylvania recognizes a cause of action for spoliation).
541. 710 A.2d 65.

exist under those principles to redress the negligent destruction of potential evidence.[542]

The *Elias* court also considered whether a patient could sustain a viable negligence claim against a third-party hospital for negligent destruction of wires from a pacemaker surgically removed from his heart. There, the court focused on whether the hospital owed a duty to the patient to preserve evidence relevant to existing or probable litigation, weighing the relationship of the parties, the nature of the risk, and the public interest in the proposed solution. The court held that absent a statutory or contractual duty, it would not place on hospitals the added burden of protecting patients' financial interest when hospitals are already charged with the vital burden of dispensing healthcare. Under these facts, the court found that the patient failed to present a viable cause of action for spoliation.[543]

The *Elias* court declined to express a view on whether a separate tort is needed where an adverse party to litigation spoils evidence. However, the court observed that traditional evidentiary remedies more than adequately protect the non-spoiling party when the spoiling party is party to the underlying action.[544]

Civil and Evidentiary Sanctions for Destruction of Evidence

In *Schroeder v. Commonwealth of Pennsylvania, Department of Transportation*,[545] the Pennsylvania Supreme Court adopted the Third Circuit Court of Appeals' approach in fashioning the appropriate sanction for spoliation of evidence in a civil case.[546] Under this approach, the court considers fault, prejudice, and whether other available sanctions will discourage intentional destruction, and then balances each of these elements based on the facts of each case.[547]

---

542. *Id.*
543. *Id.*
544. *Id.*
545. 710 A.2d 23 (Pa. 1998). *See also* Cecilia Hallinan, Comment: *Balancing the Scales After Evidence Is Spoiled: Does Pennsylvania's Approach Sufficiently Protect the Injured Party?* 44 VILL. L. REV. 947 (1999).
546. *Id.* at 26 (citing Schmid v. Milwaukee Elec. Tool Corp., 13 F.3d 76 (3d Cir. 1994)).
547. Eichman v. McKeon, 824 A.2d 305 (Pa. Super. Ct. 2003); Tenaglia v. Procter & Gamble, Inc., 737 A.2d 306 (Pa. Super. Ct. 1998).

The Pennsylvania Supreme Court adopted the spoliation inference at the turn of the last century.[548] The court considered the question again in *Pia v. Perrotti,*[549] discussing the propriety of the adverse inference as a remedy for spoliation. Applying the *Schmid v. Milwaukee Electric Tool* [550] test, the court concluded that the trial judge acted appropriately when it told the jury it could draw an adverse inference against a property owner based on an electrical contractor's inability to inspect certain fire scene evidence. Pennsylvania courts continue to apply the adverse inference instruction as the sanction of choice when dealing with spoliation.[551]

Criminal Statutes

Pennsylvania prohibits concealing or destroying evidence to hinder apprehension, prosecution, conviction, or punishment of another for a crime.[552] However, this statute is not applicable in civil actions.[553]

RHODE ISLAND

Independent Causes of Action for Destruction of Evidence

Rhode Island courts have not considered whether an independent cause of action of any kind exists for destruction of evidence.

Civil and Evidentiary Sanctions for Destruction of Evidence

The Superior Court Rule of Civil Procedure 37(b) permits a court to make such orders as are just when a party fails to provide discovery. Available sanctions include dismissal or default, striking pleadings or

---

548. McHugh v. McHugh, 40 A. 410 (Pa. 1898) (affirming admission of evidence that party had attempted to procure false testimony as inference of falsity of a claim).
549. 718 A.2d 321 (Pa. Super. Ct. 1998).
550. 13 F.3d 76 (3rd Cir. 1994).
551. *See, e.g.,* Oxford Presbyterian Church v. Weil-McLain Co., 815 A.2d 1094 (Pa. Super. Ct. 2003) (holding the adverse inference instruction is a common remedy for spoliation compared to the more severe sanction of striking testimony); Mount Olivet Tabernacle Church v. Edwin L. Wiegand Div., 781 A.2d 1263, 1273 (Pa. Super. Ct. 2001) (noting courts should select the "least onerous sanction commensurate with the spoliator's fault and the other party's prejudice").
552. 18 PA. CONS. STAT. § 5105(A)(3) (2004).
553. *Id.*

parts thereof, and/or refusing to allow the offending party to support or oppose designated claims or defenses.[554]

Presumably, Rule 37(b) is applicable when a party fails to produce evidentiary material because it has been destroyed or discarded.[555] However, it is unclear whether Rule 37(b)(2) permits dismissal with prejudice for spoliation where the inability to produce the requested evidence is not the result of "any willful or intentional conduct on the part of the litigant."[556]

In addition, the Rhode Island Supreme Court has observed that "[d]estruction of potentially relevant evidence obviously occurs along a continuum of fault—ranging from innocence through the degrees of negligence to intentionally."[557] It appears, therefore, that a Rhode Island trial court should impose the least onerous sanction that will eliminate prejudice to the non-spoliating party.

Rhode Island courts have also considered exclusion of evidence and use of the spoliation inference where critical evidence is destroyed. Considering whether a trial court abused its discretion by excluding certain evidence in a products liability case, in *Farrell v. Connetti Trailer Sales, Inc.,*[558] the Supreme Court of Rhode Island noted with approval the trial court's consideration of five factors before it determined the appropriate sanction for the spoliation of evidence. These factors included: "1) prejudice to the non-spoliating party; 2) whether the prejudice can be cured; 3) the practical importance of the evidence; 4) the good or bad faith of the spoliator; and 5) the potential for abuse if the evidence is not excluded."[559]

The Rhode Island Supreme Court also has considered whether destruction of evidence warrants an adverse inference instruction. In *Mead v. Papa Razzi Restaurant,*[560] defendants argued that their failure to preserve an incident report did not constitute spoliation because,

---

554. S. Ct. R. Civ. P. 37 (b).

555. *See* Sampson v. Marshall Brass Co., 661 A.2d 971 (R.I. 1995).

556. *Id.*

557. Rhode Island Hosp. Trust Nat'l Bank v. Eastern Gen. Contractors, Inc., 674 A.2d 1227, 1234 (R.I. 1996) (quoting Welsh v. United States, 844 F.2d 1239, 1246 (6th Cir. 1988)); *see also* Kurczy v. St. Joseph Veteran's Ass'n, Inc., 820 A.2d 929 (R.I. 2003).

558. 727 A.2d 183 (R.I. 1999).

559. *Id.* at 187.

560. 840 A.2d 1103 (R.I. 2004).

despite a policy requiring preparation of such a report, there was no evidence the report had ever been prepared or destroyed. The court "decline[d] to allow defendants to benefit from [their] own unexplained failure to preserve and produce responsive and relevant information during discovery."[561] The *Mead* court reasoned that without a satisfactory explanation that such a report never existed, the jury should be allowed to "infer that its production would have adverse consequences for defendants."[562]

Criminal Statutes

Rhode Island does not have a statute that recognizes destruction of evidence in a civil case as a crime. However, Rhode Island Rule of Professional Conduct section 3.4 forbids a lawyer from unlawfully obstructing another party's access to evidence or unlawfully altering, changing, destroying or assisting another to do any such act.

SOUTH CAROLINA

Independent Causes of Action for Spoliation of Evidence

South Carolina courts have not addressed whether that state recognizes independent tort claims for intentional or negligent spoliation of evidence.

Civil and Evidentiary Sanctions for Spoliation of Evidence

In South Carolina, when evidence has been destroyed, adverse inference instruction has long been considered the appropriate sanction. The leading case in South Carolina on this issue is *Kershaw County Board of Education v. United States Gypsum Company.*[563] There, a school board filed a lawsuit seeking monetary damages for the cost of removing hazardous asbestos material from school buildings. The company argued that the board had violated a court order by removing asbestos from one of the schools before the company could examine it.[564] The company moved for summary judgment based on violation

---

561. *Id.* (quoting *Kurczy*, 820 A.2d at 947).
562. *Id.*
563. 306 S.E.2d 390 (S.C. 1990).
564. *Id.*

of this court order. Although the trial court denied the motion, it did give a jury instruction that:

> permitted [the school board] to explain the circumstances surrounding its failure to notify [the company] and instructed the jury that when evidence is lost or destroyed by a party, an inference may be drawn by the jury that the evidence which was lost or destroyed by that party would have been adverse to that party.[565]

The court of appeals affirmed the trial court's decision as appropriate under the state discovery rules. The appellate court held, particularly given the absence of any showing that there was intentional misconduct or undue prejudice to the gypsum company, that dismissal of the board's claim, as sought by the company, was too severe a sanction.[566]

In cases of willful destruction, South Carolina courts may impose more severe sanctions. For example, a South Carolina trial court sanctioned a defendant by striking his pleadings in a non-compete case when the defendant altered a computer hard drive after the court had issued an order requiring him to surrender it.[567] The sanction resulted in a finding of liability against the defendant, which he challenged on appeal. Observing that a default judgment is "harsh medicine" that should not be administered lightly, the appellate court affirmed. It explained that a sanction that is tantamount to a default judgment requires the moving party to show bad faith, willful disobedience, or gross indifference to its rights.

Criminal Sanctions

South Carolina does not have a criminal statute governing destruction of evidence. However, under Appellate Court Rule 407, 3.4(a), a lawyer shall not "unlawfully obstruct another party's access to evidence or unlawfully alter, destroy or conceal a document or other material having potential evidentiary value," and "[a] lawyer shall not counsel

---

565. *Id.* at 372.

566. *Id. See also* Gathers v. S.C. Elec. & Gas, 427 S.E.2d 687, 689 (Ct. App. 1993) (allowing adverse inference in an electrocution case where the utility disconnected and discarded a power line).

567. QZO, Inc. v. Moyer, 594 S.E.2d 541 (Ct. App. 2004).

or assist another person to do any such act."[568] The comments to this provision indicate that its purpose includes "[f]air competition in the adversary system" and notes that "items of evidence are often essential to establish a claim or defense."[569] Accordingly, it appears that attorneys may be subject to sanctions under this rule in either civil or criminal cases for destroying or concealing evidence.

SOUTH DAKOTA

Independent Causes of Action for Destruction of Evidence

It does not appear that the Supreme Court of South Dakota or any state court in South Dakota has directly addressed whether an independent cause of action exists for spoliation of evidence.

Civil and Evidentiary Sanctions

South Dakota Codified Law section 15-6-37 permits a court, in the exercise of its discretion, to sanction noncompliance with a discovery order. This statute "is designed to compel production of evidence and to promote, rather than stifle, the truth finding process."[570] A court must temper the severity of the sanction it imposes with consideration of the equities.[571]

A South Dakota statute also permits a trial court to exercise discretion in determining what, if any, sanction to impose.[572] Of course, less drastic alternatives should be employed before sanctions are imposed that would hinder a party's day in court and defeat the underlying objective of litigation—to seek the truth from those who have knowledge of the facts.[573] Thus, Codified Law section 15-6-37 gives a trial court judge broad latitude to penalize a party who has failed to comply with a discovery order.[574]

---

568. S.C. App. Ct. R. 407, 3.4(a) (1998).

569. *Id.* at cmt.

570. Magbuhat v. Kovaric, 382 N.W.2d 43, 45 (S.D. 1986), *modified in part,* 445 N.W.2d 315 (S.D. 1989) (internal citations omitted).

571. *Id.*

572. S.D. Codified Laws § 15-6-37 (2004).

573. Wasserburger v. Consol. Mgt. Corp., 502 N.W.2d 256, 262 (S.D. 1993).

574. Haberer v. Radio Shack, 555 N.W.2d 606 (S.D. 1996).

South Dakota also recognizes the "adverse inference rule." This rule "provides that if a party has evidence under its control and does not present that evidence, an inference may be drawn that the evidence would not support that party's claim."[575] Therefore, when a relevant document is not offered in support of a claim, the court "will assume it will not provide such support."[576]

But to obtain an adverse inference instruction for spoliation, South Dakota courts require evidence of intentional conduct. For example, in *First Premier Bank v. Kolcraft Enterprises, Inc.*,[577] the South Dakota Supreme Court reviewed the trial court's issuance of an adverse inference instruction to a jury based on a plaintiff's loss of two pieces of evidence. The court concluded that the trial court should not have given the instruction because there had been no showing of bad faith or intentional conduct by the plaintiff.[578] The court observed that the defendants had an opportunity to examine the missing evidence before it disappeared, and their experts had photographs to use in place of the actual evidence.[579]

The *Kolcraft Enterprises* court referenced its earlier decision in *State v. Engesser*,[580] where it held that in both criminal and civil cases, a spoliation instruction is not appropriate absent intentional destruction of evidence.[581]

Criminal Statutes

South Dakota law prohibits the knowing destruction of any book, document, paper, record, or other matter or thing that might be evidence with the intent to prevent a party to an action from obtaining or producing such evidence.[582] There does not appear to be any South Dakota case where the state prosecuted a person for destruction of evidence in connection with a civil proceeding.

---

575. Estate of John Klauzer, 604 N.W.2d 474, 478 (S.D. 2000); *see also* Wuest v. McKennan Hosp., 619 N.W.2d 682 (S.D. 2000).

576. Klinker v. Beach, 547 N.W.2d 572, 576 n.2 (S.D. 1996).

577. 686 N.W.2d 430 (S.D. 2004).

578. *Id.* at 448.

579. *Id.*

580. 661 N.W.2d 739 (S.D. 2003).

581. *Id.*

582. S.D. CODIFIED LAWS § 19-7-14 (2003).

TENNESSEE

Independent Causes of Action for Destruction of Evidence

The Tennessee Supreme Court has not considered whether to recognize an independent cause of action for spoliation of evidence.

Civil and Evidentiary Sanctions for Destruction of Evidence

Tennessee courts have the discretion to sanction destruction of evidence and to impose sanctions appropriate under the circumstances of each case. The severity of the sanctions necessarily depends upon the circumstances of each case. Therefore, a Tennessee court must determine whether the evidence was lost negligently, inadvertently or intentionally.

Thurman-Bryant Electric Supply Company v. Unisys Corporation[583] involved a products liability action where a customer purchased a computer system that caught fire and ignited the customer's building and its contents. The customer's agent examined the fire artifacts, including the computer equipment, and then disposed of them. The trial court granted the manufacturer's motion for summary judgment, in which it had argued that since the agent destroyed the allegedly defective equipment, the customer forfeited the right to rely on the evidence and could not produce evidence that defective computer equipment caused its damage.

On appeal, the customer argued that the innocent spoliation of nonessential evidence did not justify dismissal of its claim or bar the testimony of its expert. The reviewing court found that the trial court has discretion to impose sanctions for the destruction or loss of evidence, but noted that the severity of the sanctions must depend upon the circumstances of each case. The court then reversed entry of judgment in favor of the manufacturer based upon the finding that the trial court appropriately excluded evidence resulting from examination of the remains of the computer, but that summary judgment was not an appropriate sanction.[584]

The Tennessee Court of Appeals has suggested that courts proceed cautiously before granting summary judgment based on spolia-

---

583. No. 03A01-CV-00152, 1991 Tenn. App. LEXIS 870 (Tenn. Ct. App. Nov. 4, 1991).
584. *Id.*

tion of evidence.[585] In *Foley v. St. Thomas Hospital*,[586] a medical malpractice case, a plaintiff authorized an autopsy to determine whether to bring a lawsuit. After the autopsy, the pathologist cremated the decedent's organs pursuant to his standard practice. Finding summary judgment too harsh a sanction because the plaintiff and the pathologist acted reasonably under the circumstances, the *Foley* court observed:

> [t]o impose a rule of law that requires the exclusion of all autopsy evidence upon the failure [to preserve] any organs when there is a possibility of litigation would "effectively require retaining organs in nearly all autopsies, since litigation following death is always a possibility."[587]

More recently, a Tennessee court refused to sanction a railroad's alleged alteration of some track wire in *Bronson v. Norfolk Southern Railway Company*.[588] There, the court observed that it had the authority to draw a negative inference against a party for intentional spoliation. But the court rejected the claimant's request for sanctions, finding that there was no evidence to support the claim that the railroad had altered the wire in a manner that prevented testing.[589]

Criminal Statutes

Tennessee criminalizes the alteration, destruction, or concealment of evidence with the intent to impair an official proceeding or investigation.[590] There are no reported cases applying this statute in a civil action.

TEXAS

Independent Causes of Action for Destruction of Evidence

The Texas Supreme Court has declined to recognize a tort action for spoliation of evidence. In *Trevino v. Ortega*,[591] a hospital destroyed medical records prior to litigation, supposedly making it impossible

---

585. Foley v. St. Thomas Hosp., 906 S.W.2d 448 (Tenn. Ct. App. 1995).
586. *Id.*
587. *Id.* at 453.
588. 138 S.W.3d 844 (2003).
589. *Id.*
590. TENN. CODE ANN. § 39-16-503 (2004).
591. Trevino v. Ortega, 969 S.W.2d 950, 952 (Tex. 1998).

for the plaintiff's expert to render an opinion in a malpractice claim. The trial court dismissed the spoliation of evidence claim because it found that Texas did not recognize an independent tort. However, an intermediate court of appeals reversed, becoming the first Texas court to recognize spoliation of evidence as an independent tort.[592]

The hospital challenged the appellate court's determination in the Supreme Court of Texas, which refused to recognize the tort. The Texas Supreme Court held that spoliation causes an injury only in relation to another cause of action; therefore, the appropriate place to deal with spoliation is within that case. The court reasoned that allowing a cause of action for spoliation would give a plaintiff a second opportunity to bring the same case but under a different theory. Since spoliation does not give rise to independent damages, the court held that damages caused by destruction of evidence are best remedied within the lawsuit affected.[593]

Texas Supreme Court Justice Baker concurred, but addressed in detail the plaintiff's claim that existing remedies for spoliation of evidence in Texas are inadequate. Justice Baker examined the duty to preserve evidence, breach of that duty, and prejudice to the spoliation victim's ability to put forth its case. Justice Baker then proceeded to examine a party's available remedies for destruction of evidence in pending litigation.[594]

Civil and Evidentiary Sanctions

Texas courts use a variety of methods to discourage and remedy spoliation of evidence including: (1) sanctions for discovery abuse under the Texas Civil Rules,[595] or (2) instructions that the jury must presume the destroyed evidence would not have been favorable to its destroyer.[596]

---

592. *Id.*

593. *Id.* The Texas Supreme Court has skirted the question of whether an independent tort action is available against a non-party spoliator. *See* Steven R. Selsberg & Melissa Rauer Lipman, *"My Dog Ate It": Spoliation of Evidence and the Texas Supreme Court's Ortega Decision,* 62 TEX. B.J. 1014 (Nov. 1999).

594. 969 S.W.2d 950.

595. TEX. R. CIV. P. 215 (as amended by new Rule 193.6, effective January 1, 1999).

596. Browning v. Minyard Food Stores, Inc., No. 05-97-00537-37, 1999 Tex. App. LEXIS 7723 (Tex. Ct. App. Oct. 18, 1999).

As Justice Baker noted in *Trevino v. Ortega,*[597] remedies for spoliation are designed to punish the spoliator, deter future spoliators, and serve an evidentiary purpose. Therefore, the legal inquiry involved is: "(1) whether there was legal duty to preserve evidence; (2) whether the alleged spoliator either negligently or intentionally spoliated evidence; and (3) whether the spoliation prejudiced the non-spoliator's ability to present its case or defense."[598] Since a party may have a statutory, regulatory or ethical duty to preserve evidence, once a duty is identified, a court should look to when that duty arose. Under Texas law, a duty to preserve evidence may arise prior to commencement of litigation, if a reasonable person would have anticipated litigation and would rely on such evidence.[599]

Once a court determines whether there has been a breach of duty, it must determine whether the destruction of evidence has injured the non-spoliating party. When a spoliator has negligently destroyed evidence, it may show no prejudice resulted to the non-spoliating party.[600] After these determinations, the court may consider an appropriate remedy.

In Texas, courts may impose sanctions to remedy discovery abuses, pursuant to their inherent authority.[601] Among other things, a court may dismiss an action when the spoliator's conduct was egregious, the prejudice to the non-spoliating party was great, and imposing a lesser sanction would be ineffective to cure the prejudice.[602] Texas courts also recognize exclusion of evidence or expert testimony regarding the destroyed evidence as appropriate sanctions.[603]

But Texas courts will not automatically impose sanctions for spoliation of evidence. For example, the Texas Supreme Court recently found that a trial court abused its discretion by giving a spoliation instruction in *Wal-Mart Stores, Inc. v. Johnson.*[604] The *Wal-Mart* court focused on the store's duty to retain the evidence and held that the creation of an "incident report" did not create a duty to preserve

---

597. 969 S.W.2d 950.
598. *Id.* at 954-55.
599. *Id.*
600. *Id.* (citing Brewer v. Dowling, 862 S.W.2d 156 (Tex. Ct. App. 1993)).
601. *Trevino,* 969 S.W.2d 950.
602. *Id.* at 954.
603. *Id.*
604. 106 S.W.3d 718 (Tex. 2003).

evidence. Specifically, the court found there was no showing that Wal-Mart disposed of the evidence after it knew, or should have known, that there was a substantial chance of litigation and that the "incident report" would be material to it.[605] The court also referenced prior appellate decisions, finding no notice of possible lawsuit where the destruction of evidence occurred in the course of regular business.[606]

A Texas court may also give a spoliation presumption instruction to the jury. Courts generally apply two rules to presumptions arising from the non-production of evidence. The first rule applies in cases of intentional spoliation and results in a presumption that the evidence would have been unfavorable to the spoliator, that is, a rebuttable presumption that the destroyed evidence was unfavorable to the spoliator.[607] The presumption may be rebutted with a showing that the evidence was not destroyed with a fraudulent intent or purpose.[608] Application of this presumption remains within the trial court's discretion.[609]

The second and less severe instruction is "an adverse presumption that the destroyed evidence would have been disfavorable to the spoliating party."[610] This presumption has probative value, but the non-spoliating party must still prove each element of its case.[611] That is, the jury need not heed the instruction.[612] But if the non-

---

605. *Id.*

606. *Id.; see, e.g.,* Doe v. Mobile Video Tapes, Inc., 43 S.W.3d 40, 55 (Tex. Ct. App. 2001) (refusing spoliation instruction where videotapes were recorded over prior to notice of claim in the normal course of business); Aguirre v. South Tex. Blood & Tissue Ctr., 2 S.W.3d 454, 457 (Tex. Ct. App. 1999) (finding destruction of records in the regular course of business and without notice of their relevance to future litigation did not raise spoliation presumption).

607. *Trevino,* 969 S.W.2d at 954; Wal-Mart Stores, Inc. v. Middleton, 982 S.W.2d 468, 470 (Tex. Ct. App. 1998) (reversing and remanding where no evidence of deliberate destruction of evidence and reasonable explanation for absence as well as what was depicted provided through testimony).

608. Hight v. Dublin Veterinary Clinic, 22 S.W.3d 614, 619 (Tex. Ct. App. 2000).

609. *Id.*

610. *Id.* at 960.

611. *Id.*

612. *Id. See* chapter 4 for a more detailed discussion of Texas's treatment of adverse inference instructions.

producing party testifies about the substance or content of the missing evidence, the presumption does not apply.[613]

Criminal Statutes

The Texas Penal Code does not provide relief to spoliation victims; however, it does provide that a person commits the offense of tampering with physical evidence if, knowing that an investigation or official proceeding is pending, that person alters, destroys or conceals any record, document or other thing with the intent to impair its use in that proceeding.[614] However, as one commentator noted, "Even if the victim of spoliation can convince a district attorney to prosecute a spoliation case, which is unlikely because section 37.09 has rarely, if ever, been applied in a civil case, a conviction only punishes the spoliator. It does not compensate the victim."[615]

UTAH

Independent Causes of Action for Destruction of Evidence

The Supreme Court of Utah has yet to address whether it will recognize an independent cause of action for the destruction of evidence. The one Utah appellate court that addressed this question declined to recognize the tort of spoliation of evidence.[616]

Civil and Evidentiary Sanctions for Destruction of Evidence

A Utah appellate court has discussed the spoliation inference in *Burns v. Cannondale Bicycle Company*.[617] In that product liability case, a

---

613. *See, e.g.,* Brumfield v. Exxon Corp., 63 S.W.3d 912 (Tex. Ct. App. 2002) (refusing spoliation instruction where videotape was destroyed in regular course of business and Exxon provided reasonable explanation for its absence and testimony that the missing video would have shown what occurred on the day of the incident).

614. TEX. PENAL CODE ANN. § 37.09 (1999).

615. Steven R. Selsberg & Melissa Rauer Lipman, *supra.*

616. Burns v. Cannondale Bicycle Co., 876 P.2d 415 (Utah Ct. App. 1994); *see also* Cook Associates, Inc. v. PCS Sales (USA), Inc., 271 F. Supp. 2d 1343 (D. Utah 2003) (holding that the claimant had no legal basis for asserting a claim for the tort of spoliation because the *Burns* court had considered and rejected such a claim).

617. 876 P.2d 415 (Utah Ct. App. 1994).

plaintiff had a bicycle repaired following an accident. Although he was not initially contemplating filing litigation, three years after the accident, he filed a suit against the manufacturer and distributor.

In the interim, the distributor had lost or disposed of the "defective" part. The defendants moved for summary judgment, claiming the plaintiff could not prevail on his claim as a matter of law because he lacked evidence of a defect that could have caused the accident. Although the plaintiff conceded that he lacked such evidence, he claimed that because the defendant had disposed of the defective part, the doctrine of spoliation should establish the defect. Rejecting this argument, the trial court awarded summary judgment to the defendants, concluding that the plaintiff's inability to furnish evidence of causation failed to establish a factual basis for his spoliation claim.[618]

The appellate court noted the absence of authority recognizing a spoliation inference by Utah courts. However, the court observed that the doctrine would not apply to the facts of this case in any event, because the plaintiff had not filed suit or even notified the defendants that he was considering filing a lawsuit when the part was destroyed. Therefore, the defendants were not parties to the lawsuit brought by the plaintiff or even on notice of impending litigation. Moreover, the *Burns* court reasoned that, in the absence of a general duty to retain the allegedly defective part, the defendants did not act inappropriately even if they did discard the part. Accordingly, the appellate court found that, even assuming the part was discarded, it could not be inferred that it was defective because the defendants lacked notice of the pendency of a legal claim and therefore a duty to retain the part on any other basis.[619]

Although no Utah court appears to have applied Utah Rule of Civil Procedure section 37(B) to sanction a party for destruction of evidence, this rule permits a court to exercise discretion to impose sanctions for noncompliance with discovery orders. This provision appears to have been modeled after its federal counterpart.

Criminal Statutes

Under Utah law, a person commits the crime of tampering with evidence if that person alters, destroys, conceals or removes anything

---

618. *Id.*
619. *Id.*

with a purpose to impair its veracity or availability in a proceeding or investigation.[620] Although there appear to be no civil cases imposing criminal liability for destruction of evidence, one Utah court recently affirmed a tampering with evidence conviction of a defendant who destroyed cocaine by swallowing it.[621] Interestingly, the Utah court permitted the conviction to stand despite the fact that the evidence itself would not have been admissible because it had been obtained with an invalid search warrant.[622]

VERMONT

Independent Causes of Action for Destruction of Evidence

No Vermont court appears to have considered whether an independent cause of action of any kind exists for destruction of evidence.

Civil and Evidentiary Sanctions for Destruction of Evidence

In Vermont, a superior court may, in the exercise of its discretion, impose sanctions for failure to comply with discovery orders.[623] In addition, the Vermont Supreme Court has recognized the inherent power of a court to sanction a party for abuse of the judicial process.[624]

Although there are no reported opinions where a Vermont court has imposed sanctions for destruction of evidence under Vermont Rule of Civil Procedure section 37, it appears that this rule provides a court with such authority. The severity of a sanction under this rule is a matter of judicial discretion.[625] The court must consider whether the party seeking the sanction has been prejudiced, and, at least where the ultimate sanction of dismissal is invoked, the trial court must indicate by findings of fact that there has been bad faith or willful disregard of the court's orders.[626]

The Vermont Supreme Court has long upheld the use of an adverse inference or presumption in the case of spoliation of evidence. As the court explained in *F.R. Patch Manufacturing Company v. Pro-*

620. UTAH CODE ANN. § 76-8-510.5 (2003).
621. State v. Wagstaff, 846 P.2d 1311 (Utah Ct. App. 1993).
622. Id.
623. VT. R. CIV. P. 37 (2005).
624. In re Sherman Hollow, Inc., 641 A.2d 753 (Vt. 1993).
625. In re R.M., 549 A.2d 1050 (Vt. 1988).
626. John v. Med. Ctr. Hosp. of Vt., Inc., 394 A.2d 1134 (Vt. 1978).

tection Lodge No. 215, International Association of Machinists,[627] "If the defendant had books which it suppressed, and which it failed to produce after having been notified to do so, the jury might 'find or presume that the claim of the plaintiff is true, and that the claim of the defendant is false.'"[628] However, the presumption does not relieve the other party of the duty to introduce evidence tending affirmatively to prove his case. The presumption approved by the *F.R. Patch* court is regarded merely as a matter of inference in weighing the evidence.[629]

Criminal Statutes

Vermont has no state statute that criminalizes the destruction or spoliation of evidence in a civil matter.

VIRGINIA

Independent Causes of Action for Spoliation of Evidence

In *Austin v. Consolidation Coal Company,*[630] the Supreme Court of Virginia answered the following certified question: "Whether Virginia law would recognize intentional or negligent interference with a prospective civil action by spoliation of evidence as an independent tort . . . [.]"[631] There, the plaintiff was injured while working in a coal mine. He was barred by the workers' compensation statute from filing suit against his employer. Instead, he pursued a product liability action against the manufacturer and distributor of the allegedly defective hose that caused his injuries.[632]

After the employee filed a lawsuit in state court, the court ordered his employer to preserve the hose as evidence until the employee's experts had examined it. Instead, the employer allegedly destroyed the hose before the experts could examine it. The employee claimed that he was prejudiced in proving his claim, including identifying the identities of the manufacturer and the distributor. Subsequently, the employee identified the manufacturer and distributor and filed suit

---

627. 60 A. 74 (Vt. 1905).
628. *Id.* at 83.
629. *Id.*
630. 501 S.E.2d 161 (Va. 1998).
631. *Id.*
632. *Id.*

against these two entities in federal court. The federal court certified the spoliation issue to the Supreme Court of Virginia.[633]

The Supreme Court identified the elements of spoliation as:

> (1) pending or probable litigation involving the plaintiff; (2) knowledge on the part of the defendant that litigation exists or is probable; (3) willful destruction of evidence by the defendant designed to disrupt plaintiff's case; (4) disruption of plaintiff's case; and (5) damages proximately caused by the defendant's acts.[634]

The court identified the key issue before it as "whether an employer has the duty to preserve evidence for the benefit of an employee's potential tort action against a third party," which "is a matter of first impression in this Commonwealth."[635]

The court held that the employee did not have a cause of action against the employer because it had no legal duty to preserve the hose. It further reasoned that the employee had not cited any statutes or authorities requiring an employer to preserve personal property for use in a third-party tort action. Moreover, the workers' compensation statute also did not impose any such duty. Accordingly, the court answered the certified question in the negative and declined to recognize a cause of action for spoliation.[636]

Civil and Evidentiary Sanctions for Spoliation of Evidence

Virginia courts also will impose civil and evidentiary sanctions for spoliation of evidence during pending litigation. In Virginia, spoliation "encompasses conduct that is either intentional or negligent."[637]

Where an expert witness has negligently or intentionally destroyed evidence, a court may prohibit the party retaining that expert from

---

633. *Id.*

634. *Id.* at 162.

635. *Id.* at 163.

636. *Id. See also* Bass v. E.I. duPont de Nemours & Co., No. 01-1073, 2002 U.S. App. LEXIS 474 (4th Cir. Jan. 10, 2002) (holding Virginia does not recognize a tort based on spoliation of evidence).

637. Ward v. Texas Steak, Ltd., No. 7:03cv00596, 2004 U.S. Dist. LEXIS 10575 (W.D. Va. May 27, 2004) (citations and internal quotation omitted).

introducing testimony regarding the missing evidence.[638] For example, in *Delaney v. Sabella*,[639] a woman filed a medical malpractice case based on the alleged failure of her doctor to diagnose an ectopic pregnancy. The doctor sent a Pap smear for analysis to a New York laboratory operated by his expert witness. The expert's laboratory lost the slide containing the specimen before the woman's experts had a chance to examine it.[640]

The injured woman argued that it would be unfair for her doctor to be able to introduce evidence relating to the Pap smear because it was lost while in the possession and control of the doctor's expert, and moved to exclude all evidence regarding the slide. The court agreed, citing cases from other jurisdictions in which evidence was barred under similar circumstances. Accordingly, the *Delaney* court concluded, "The preclusion of all testimony, expert or otherwise, about the misplaced Pap smear slide (including [the expert's] report about the Pap smear slide) is the appropriate remedy for the prejudice suffered by the plaintiff due to the inability of her experts to examine this crucial evidence that was lost while in the exclusive possession or control of defendant and/or her experts."[641]

When evaluating whether to impose a spoliation inference, Virginia courts apply a reasonably foreseeable test. In *Wolfe v. Virginia Birth-Related Neurological Injury Compensation Program*,[642] the court held, "[a] spoliation inference may be applied in an existing action if, at the time the evidence was lost or destroyed, 'a reasonable person in the defendant's position should have foreseen the evidence was material to a potential civil action.'"[643] Remanding the case, the Virginia Court of Appeals held that the commission should have considered the spoliation inference when determining whether an infant was entitled to benefits under the birth-related neurological injury compensation program where documents tracking blood gases and oxygen

---

638. Delaney v. Sabella, 1995 Va. Cir. LEXIS 1329 (Va. Cir. Ct. 1995).

639. *Id.*

640. *Id.*

641. *Id.* at *7-8.

642. 580 S.E.2d 467 (Va. App. 2003).

643. *Id.* at 475 (citing Boyd v. Travelers Ins. Co., 652 N.E.2d 267, 270-71 (Ill. 1995)).

levels measured during a child's delivery were missing from the hospital records.[644]

Although a court has broad discretion in imposing sanctions for spoliation of evidence, this discretion is not limitless. In *Gentry v. Toyota Motor Corporation*,[645] the plaintiffs sued several Toyota entities for injuries allegedly sustained in a Toyota truck. The plaintiffs' expert examined the truck and concluded that a temperature control cable had impinged on the accelerator pedal rod, thereby causing the accident. Thereafter, without any authorization or permission, the expert removed the cable and the accelerator pedal rod from the vehicle.[646]

After the plaintiffs filed the lawsuit, Toyota moved to dismiss the action for spoliation of evidence, claiming that the damage to the truck by the plaintiffs' expert had deprived it of its right to examine the truck and severely prejudiced its defense. Following a hearing, the plaintiffs moved to have the truck tested by another expert. That expert concluded that a defect in the carburetor had caused the accident. Thereafter, Toyota's expert examined the carburetor and determined that the carburetor had been functioning properly. He also concluded that his ability to examine the truck had not been affected by any spoliation by plaintiffs' initial expert. Toyota renewed its spoliation motion, which the trial court granted and dismissed the case with prejudice.[647]

The Supreme Court of Virginia reversed. Although it noted that a trial court has discretion to impose appropriate sanctions for spoliation of evidence, it found that the trial court had abused its discretion. In particular, the supreme court noted that neither the plaintiffs nor their attorney had acted in bad faith, and the expert had acted with neither consent nor knowledge of the plaintiffs or their attorney. Accordingly, dismissal would not serve to punish the wrongdoer, the plaintiffs' expert. Moreover, the court noted that Toyota was not prejudiced, since the theory on which the plaintiffs sought to recover (an

---

644. *Id.* at 477. The *Wolfe* court further explained the spoliation inference should be applied to the program even though it was actually the non-party physician who was responsible for the missing evidence.

645. 471 S.E.2d 485 (Va. 1996).

646. *Id.*

647. *Id.*

allegedly defective carburetor) was unrelated to the part of the vehicle that the plaintiffs' expert had destroyed. Accordingly, the court reversed and remanded the case.[648]

Criminal Sanctions

Virginia statute[649] prohibits any person from knowingly obstructing, or knowingly intimidating by threats or force, judicial officers, jurors, lawyers, witnesses, or law enforcement officers in the performance of their duties. Violation of this statute can be either a misdemeanor or a felony, depending on the surrounding circumstances. There are no reported Virginia decisions in which courts have imposed criminal sanctions for spoliation of evidence in civil proceedings.

WASHINGTON

Independent Causes of Action for Destruction of Evidence

Washington courts have not addressed whether to recognize an independent cause of action for intentional or negligent destruction of evidence.[650]

Civil and Evidentiary Sanctions for Destruction of Evidence

The traditional method for remedying spoliation of evidence in Washington is through an adverse inference instruction. For example, in *Walker v. Herke*,[651] the plaintiff alleged that the defendants had contracted to deliver steers to the plaintiff. After the lawsuit was filed, a receipt for the steers was destroyed allegedly at the request of the defendants. The plaintiff argued that a conclusive presumption should have been given that the receipt would have been prejudicial to the defendants. The trial court declined to apply the presumption.

On appeal, the Supreme Court noted that the true rule is not that missing evidence gives rise to a presumption, but merely permits the

---

648. *Id.*

649. Va. Code Ann. § 18.2-460 (2004).

650. In *Henderson v. Tyrrell*, 910 P.2d 522 (Wash. Ct. App. 1996), the court noted that courts from other jurisdictions have recognized a separate tort of intentional or negligent spoliation. The court did not cite to any Washington cases in which such a claim was recognized, nor was it called upon to decide that issue in the case before it.

651. 147 P.2d 255 (Wash. 1944).

jury to draw an inference that, if produced, the evidence would be unfavorable to the spoliator.[652] Moreover, this rebuttable presumption does not relieve a party from the obligation of putting on evidence to prove its case. Turning to the facts before it, the supreme court noted that even if the memorandum had been destroyed by the defendants, there was ample secondary evidence to prove the content of the memorandum.[653]

Washington courts have held that whether to apply a rebuttable presumption shifting the burden of proof depends upon two controlling facts: "(1) the potential importance or relevance of the missing evidence; and (2) the culpability or fault of the adverse party."[654] In *Marshall v. Bally's Pacwest, Inc.,*[655] the plaintiff claimed that, based on the defendants' failure to preserve a treadmill on which she allegedly was injured, a rebuttable presumption should have been given by the trial court. On appeal, the court of appeals rejected this argument and noted that the plaintiff did not request to inspect the treadmill until more than four years following her accident. Moreover, since she had never requested that defendants preserve this evidence, she could not establish that they acted in bad faith.[656]

Once a lawsuit has been dismissed, a party has no obligation to retain evidence from that lawsuit. In *Ellwein v. Hartford Accident & Indemnity Co.,*[657] the plaintiff filed a bad-faith lawsuit against the defendant insurance company. Following the dismissal of this lawsuit by the plaintiff, the insurer destroyed its home office file. Thereafter, the plaintiff refiled a lawsuit and claimed he was entitled to an adverse inference based on the destruction of this file. The trial court declined to give this instruction, and the court of appeals affirmed, holding that "destruction of notes in a file after a lawsuit has been dismissed does not establish a claim for spoliation."[658]

Recently, a Washington appellate court affirmed a trial court's decision to exclude all evidence relating to faulty windows destroyed by

---

652. *Id.* at 259.

653. *Id.* at 261.

654. Marshall v. Bally's Pacwest, Inc., 972 P.2d 475, 480 (Wash. Ct. App. 1999) (quoting *Henderson,* 910 P.2d at 532).

655. *Id.*

656. *Id.*

657. 976 P.2d 138 (Wash. Ct. App. 1999).

658. *Id.* at 145.

a builder.[659] There, the court determined that the builder failed to offer an innocent explanation for the destruction of the window evidence, and there was no doubt it was in control of this evidence. The appellate court affirmed, finding that the trial court reasonably concluded that the builder acted intentionally in destroying the evidence.[660]

Other sanctions also may be available in Washington, including civil discovery sanctions, like dismissal,[661] an award of attorneys' fees,[662] and punitive damages.[663] Before imposing the severe sanction of dismissal, Washington courts must consider on the record (1) whether the spoliation was willful and deliberate, (2) whether the opponent's case was prejudiced, and (3) whether a lesser sanction than dismissal would be sufficient to remedy the destruction of evidence.[664]

Criminal Statutes

Under Washington's tampering with evidence statute,[665] a person commits the crime of tampering with physical evidence if, "having reason to believe that an official proceeding is pending or about to be instituted," the person "destroys, mutilates, conceals, removes, or alters physical evidence with intent to impair its appearance, character, or availability in such pending or perspective official proceeding."[666] "Physical evidence" is defined as "any article, object, document, record, or other thing of physical substance."[667] It is unclear whether "official proceeding" can include civil proceedings.

---

659. Newhall Jones, Inc. v. Classic Cedar Constr., Inc., No. 43477-2-I, 2000 Wash. App. LEXIS 262 (Feb. 14, 2000).

660. *Id.*

661. Mieldon v. Univ. of Wash., No. 49763-4-I, 2002 Wash. App. LEXIS 2949 (2002) (citing Rivers v. Wash. State Conference of Mason Contractors, 41 P.3d 1175 (Wash. 2002) (remanding lawsuit dismissed as a sanction for employee's willful and repeated discovery violations and spoliation for explicit findings by the trial court regarding whether a lesser sanction than dismissal would have sufficed)).

662. A&W Farms v. Sunshine Lend and Lease, Inc., No. 20504-5-III, 2003 Wash. App. LEXIS 1363 (2003) (permitting an award of attorneys' fees where party altered evidence).

663. *Henderson*, 910 P.2d at 531 n.3.

664. *Mieldon*, No. 49763-4-I, 2002 Wash. App. LEXIS 2949 (2002) (citing Rivers v. Wash. State Conference of Mason Contractors, 41 P.3d 1175).

665. Wash. Rev. Code Ann. § 9A.72.150 (2004).

666. *Id.* at § 9A.72.150(1)(a).

667. *Id.* at § 9A.72.150(2).

The language of the statute suggests that criminal sanctions may potentially apply to destruction of evidence during a civil proceeding. Moreover, in *Henderson v. Tyrrell*,[668] the court specifically recognized that "criminal sanctions" may be available to remedy spoliation of evidence in civil litigation.[669] Despite that ruling, the authors found no reported authority imposing criminal sanctions for conduct in civil litigation based on Washington Revised Code Annotated section 9A.72.150.

WEST VIRGINIA

Independent Causes of Action for Destruction of Evidence

Answering questions certified to it by a West Virginia circuit court, the West Virginia Supreme Court of Appeals addressed the viability of independent torts for spoliation of evidence. In *Hannah v. Heeter*, the West Virginia Supreme Court held that West Virginia recognizes the torts of intentional spoliation for first and third parties and negligent spoliation, but only for third parties.[670] In that employment discrimination case, an applicant taped a conversation with the president of a company in which the president allegedly offered her a job in exchange for a sexual relationship. The applicant could not produce the original tape recording and the president's expert could not determine whether the copy produced in the litigation had been altered. The president brought a counterclaim for intentional and negligent spoliation and the circuit certified three questions to the Supreme Court.

First, the *Hannah* court concluded that West Virginia did not recognize first-party negligent spoliation as a stand-alone tort. The court reasoned the adverse inference instruction and sanctions available under West Virginia Rule of Civil Procedure 37 provided sufficient remedies for negligent failure to preserve evidence.[671]

Next, the court found that West Virginia did recognize third-party negligent spoliation as a stand-alone tort where the third party had a special duty to preserve evidence. Acknowledging there is no duty to preserve evidence as a general rule, the court noted that such a duty

---

668. 910 P.2d 522 (Wash. Ct. App. 1996).
669. *Id.* at 531 n.3.
670. 584 S.E.2d 560 (W.Va. 2003).
671. *Id.* at 568.

may arise through a contract, agreement, statute, administrative rule, voluntary assumption of the duty, or other special circumstance.[672] The *Hannah* court then outlined the elements of the tort [673] which, once established, create a rebuttable presumption "that but for the fact of the spoliation of evidence, the party injured by the spoliation would have prevailed in the pending litigation or potential litigation."[674] The court emphasized that the third party must have actual, rather than constructive, knowledge of the pending or potential litigation.[675]

The *Hannah* court then answered the third question, whether West Virginia recognizes a first- or third-party intentional tort for spoliation of evidence as a stand-alone tort, in the affirmative.[676] Critical to establishing this tort is the showing that "the evidence was destroyed with the specific intent to defeat the pending or potential lawsuit."[677]

Civil and Evidentiary Sanctions for Destruction of Evidence

The West Virginia Supreme Court of Appeals recently held that a circuit court's imposition of sanctions under West Virginia Rule of Civil Procedure 37(B) for a party's failure to obey a court's order to provide

---

672. *Id.*

673. The first five of these elements alone establish the rebuttable presumption: "1) the existence of a pending or potential civil action; 2) the alleged spoliatior had actual knowledge of the pending or potential civil action; 3) a duty to preserve evidence arising from through a contract, agreement, statute, administrative rule, voluntary assumption of the duty or other special circumstance; 4) spoliation of evidence; and 5) the spoliated evidence was vital to the party's ability to prevail in the pending or potential civil action; and 6) damages." 584 S.E.2d at 569. Damages are determined in the same manner as negligent spoliation claims. *Id.* at 573.

674. 584 S.E.2d at 570.

675. The *Hannah* court's remarks regarding causation and damages are discusses in chapter 4, *supra.*

676. 584 S.E.2d at 571. The elements of the tort are: "1) a pending or potential civil action; 2) knowledge of the spoliator of the pending or potential civil action; 3) willful destruction of the evidence; 4) the spoliated evidence was vital to the party's ability to prevail in the pending or potential civil action; 5) the intent of the spoliator to defeat a party's ability to prevail in the pending or potential civil action; 6) the party's inability to prevail in the civil action; and 7) damages. *Id.* at 569-70. The first six elements of a claim for intentional spoliation create a rebuttable presumption that but for the spoliator's actions, the injured party would have prevailed in the pending or potential lawsuit. *Id.*

677. 584 S.E.2d at 573.

or permit discovery is reviewable only for abuse of discretion.[678] Therefore, a circuit court's ruling on the admissibility of evidence and the
appropriateness of a particular sanction for discovery violations is
committed to the discretion of a trial court.[679] Although the *Adkins v.
KMart Corporation*[680] court did not address the question of destroyed
documents, it did reach a conclusion in a case where a party failed to
provide discovery concerning insurance coverage after the close of
discovery. Therefore, it appears that a trial court in West Virginia would
have similar discretion to impose sanctions for failure to comply with
a court order or with a party's discovery request.

The West Virginia Supreme Court of Appeals also has recently
addressed the question of whether a trial court may give an adverse
inference or impose other sanctions against a party for spoliation of
evidence.[681] In *Tracey v. Cottrell,*[682] the court held that a trial court
may not give an adverse inference jury instruction or impose other
sanctions against a party for spoliation of evidence unless and until it
considers the following factors:

1. The party's degree of control, ownership or authority over the
   destroyed evidence;
2. The amount of prejudice suffered by the opposing party as a
   result of the missing or destroyed evidence and whether such
   prejudice was substantial;
3. The reasonableness of anticipating that the evidence would be
   needed for litigation; and
4. If the party controlled, owned, possessed, or had authority over
   the evidence, the party's degree of fault in causing the destruction of evidence.[683]

The *Tracey* court further held that the party requesting an adverse
inference instruction on this basis bears the burden of proof on each
element of the four-factor spoliation test. The court also held that the

678. Arnold Agency v. W. Va. Lottery Comm., 526 S.E.2d 814 (W. Va. 1999).
679. *Id.* at 824.
680. 511 S.E.2d 840.
681. Tracey v. Cottrell, 524 S.E.2d 879 (W. Va. 1999).
682. *Id.*
683. *Id.* at 890.

analysis ends and no adverse inference instruction may be given or other sanction imposed if the trial court finds that the party charged with spoliation of evidence did not control, own, possess, or have authority over the destroyed evidence.[684]

The *Tracey* court also observed that a party who reasonably anticipates litigation has an affirmative duty to preserve relevant evidence.[685] Under appropriate circumstances, the court further observed that when evidence has been destroyed, it is within a trial court's discretion to sanction the offending party by dismissing its claims, excluding countervailing evidence, or giving a jury instruction on spoliation.[686] "This inference permits the jury to assume that "the destroyed evidence would have been unfavorable to the position of the offending party."[687]

The *Tracey* court considered two of the bright-line tests that trial courts have used when making a decision as to whether an adverse inference instruction or other sanction was appropriately imposed on a party as a result of spoliation of evidence. The first test, adopted by the Third Circuit Court of Appeals in *Schmid v. Milwaukee Electric Tools Corporation,*[688] requires a trial court to perform a three-step analysis examining the degree of fault of the party who altered or destroyed the evidence, the degree of prejudice suffered by the opposing party, and the availability of lesser sanctions that would protect the party's rights and further deter similar conduct.[689]

The *Tracey* court also analyzed a five-factor test used by some courts to determine whether a party should have an adverse inference instruction or other sanction imposed upon it because of spoliation of evidence. Under this test, observed the court, a trial court must consider (1) prejudice to the defendant, (2) whether prejudice can be cured, (3) the practical importance of the evidence, (4) whether plaintiff was acting in good or bad faith, and (5) the potential abuse in not sanction-

684. *Id.*
685. *Id.* at 887 (citing Baliotis v. McNeil, 870 F. Supp. 1285, 1290 (M.D. Pa. 1994)).
686. *Id.*
687. *Id.* (quoting Howell v. Maytag, 168 F.R.D. 502, 505 (M.D. Pa. 1996); (Schmidt v. Milwaukee Elec. Tools Corp., 13 F.3d 76, 78 (3d Cir. 1994)).
688. 13 F.3d 76 (3d Cir. 1994).
689. *Id.* at 79. Some courts refer to this test as the *Schmid* test.

ing a plaintiff.[690] Based on the West Virginia Supreme Court of Appeals' review of decisions from other jurisdictions and those by that court, it adopted the following factors that courts must consider before imposing sanctions for spoliation:

1. The party's degree of control, ownership possession or authority over the destroyed evidence;
2. The amount of prejudice suffered by the opposing party as a result of the missing or destroyed evidence and whether such prejudice was substantial;
3. The reasonableness of anticipating that the evidence would be needed for litigation; and
4. If the party controlled, owned, possessed or had authority over the evidence, the party's degree of fault in causing the *destruction of evidence.*[691]

Criminal Statutes

Under the West Virginia Code, a person commits a crime against public justice by causing or inducing a person to alter, destroy, mutilate, or conceal a record, document or other object impairing its integrity or availability for use at an official proceeding.[692] To be actionable, a person must use or threaten intimidation, physical harassment or fraudulent legal process.[693] In addition, West Virginia Code section 61-5-29 provides:

A person who violated this section is liable in a civil action to any person harmed by the violation for injury or loss to person or property incurred as a result of the commission of the offense and for reasonable attorney's fees, court costs and other expenses incurred as a result of prosecuting a civil action commenced under this subsection, which is not the exclusive remedy of a person who suffers injury or loss to person or property as a result of a violation of this section.[694]

---

690. 529 S.E.2d at 889.
691. *Id.* at 890. By degree of fault, the court stated that it meant "a determination of whether the destruction of evidence was negligent or intentional." *Tracey*, 524 S.E.2d at 890 n.7.
692. W. Va. Code § 61527(b)(4)(B) (2005).
693. *Id.*
694. W. Va. Code § 61-5-27(f) (2005).

The authors found no reported cases where this statute was the basis for awarding any person with attorneys' fees in connection with a civil proceeding.

WISCONSIN

Independent Causes of Action for Destruction of Evidence

Wisconsin has not decided whether to recognize a cause of action for independent or negligent spoliation of evidence.

Civil and Evidentiary Sanctions for Destruction of Evidence

In determining whether to impose sanctions for destruction of evidence, Wisconsin courts evaluate the five factors.[695] Courts consider:

> (i) identification, with as much specificity as possible, of the documents which were destroyed; (ii) the relationship of those documents to the issues in the present action; (iii) the extent to which such documents can now be obtained through other sources; (iv) whether [the party responsible for the document destruction] knew or should have known at the time it caused the destruction of the documents that litigation against [the opposing parties] . . . was a distinct possibility; and (v) whether, in light of the circumstances disclosed by the factual inquiry, sanctions should be imposed upon [the party responsible for the document destruction] and, if so, what the sanction should be.[696]

The Wisconsin Court of Appeals also has set forth a two-step framework for a trial court to use when considering sanctions based on spoliation of evidence:

---

695. Milwaukee Constructors II v. Milwaukee Metro. Sewerage Dist., 502 N.W.2d 881, 884 (Wis. Ct. App. 1993) (citing Struthers Patent Co. v. Nestle Corp., 558 F. Supp. 747, 756 (D.N.J. 1981)). *See also* Ins. Co. of N. America v. Cease Elec. Inc., 674 N.W.2d 886, 891 (Wis. Ct. App. 2004) (citing *Milwaukee Constructors II*), 502 N.W.2d 881 (observing that "common sense dictates that the purposes of the [spoliation] doctrine are served only if the offending party has notice that the evidence is or is likely to be relevant to pending or foreseeable litigation and proceeds to destroy it anyway").

696. 502 N.W.2d at 884.

[W]e conclude that when a trial court is faced with a motion for sanctions for the destruction of evidence, it must engage in a two-step process. It must first determine the nature of the conduct that gave rise to destruction of the evidence, and then decide whether the absence of this evidence so handicapped the moving party that an unfair advantage was gained by that party's inability to provide a basis for the claim or defense. Common sense dictates that both prongs of the exercise ought to be complete before a sanction is proper. Findings of fact will be reviewed pursuant to . . . [the] clearly erroneous standard.[697]

Some Wisconsin courts have suggested that "[w]hether the conduct was intentional or negligent may not be as crucial as whether, under the circumstances, it was prejudicial."[698] But for a trial court to consider dismissal as a sanction requires "a finding of egregious conduct, which means a conscious attempt to effect the outcome of litigation or flagrant knowing disregard of the judicial process."[699]

When there is a factual finding that evidence was not intentionally destroyed, and the non-spoliating party was not fairly prejudiced, a trial court acts within its discretion by declining to sanction spoliation.[700] In *Reed v. Andrew Automotive Group*,[701] the court of appeals considered whether the trial court properly granted summary judgment and dismissed the case based on spoliation of evidence. The plaintiffs had advised the defendant of their intention to have a mechanic inspect an allegedly defective car engine. The defendant also indicated that it wished to inspect the cylinder head, which was in the possession of the plaintiffs. Following a disagreement regarding timing of the inspection, and while the case was pending, the plaintiffs sold the car, including the cylinder head, for salvage.[702] The trial court

697. Foat v. The Torrington Co., 577 N.W.2d 386 (Wis. Ct. App. 1998) (internal citations omitted).

698. *Id.* at *10-11.

699. City of Stoughton v. Thomasson Lumber Co., 675 N.W.2d 487, 500 (Wis. Ct. App. 2003) (citing Garfoot v. Fireman's Fund Ins. Co., 599 N.W.2d 411 (Wis. Ct. App. 1999)).

700. *Id.*

701. 610 N.W.2d 511 (Wis. Ct. App. 2000).

702. *Id.*

granted summary judgment and dismissed the action, based on spoliation of evidence.

On appeal, the court of appeals noted that "'[t]here is a duty on a party to preserve evidence essential to the claim being litigated' and the 'failure to take adequate steps to preserve evidence that was totally within [a party's] control is sufficient to justify the imposition of sanctions' leading to dismissal."[703] The court of appeals concluded that the trial court had "properly exercised discretion in determining that, because the [plaintiffs'] disposal of essential evidence precluded Andrew from defending the case, dismissal of the [plaintiffs'] action was appropriate."[704]

The Supreme Court of Wisconsin also has held that in the appropriate circumstances, an adverse inference instruction may be given based on spoliation of evidence. In *Jagmin v. Simonds Abrasive Company*,[705] the trial court refused to give an adverse inference jury instruction. The court reasoned that such an instruction was proper only upon a showing that evidence had been intentionally destroyed, which was not supported by the facts. On appeal, the Supreme Court of Wisconsin agreed, holding that "the operation of the maxim *omnia praesumuntur contra spoliatorem* [all things are presumed against a destroyer of evidence] is reserved for deliberate, intentional actions and not mere negligence, even though the result may be the same as regards the person who desires the evidence."[706]

Criminal Statutes

In Wisconsin, a person commits the crime of destruction of documents subject to subpoena when the person "intentionally destroys, alters, mutilates, conceals, removes, withholds, or transfers possession of a document, knowing the document has been subpoenaed by a court," a district attorney or the attorney general,[707] or by use of "force, threat, intimidation or deception" causes another to do such an act.[708] There

---

703. *Id.* at *6 (quoting Sentry Ins. v. Royal Ins. Co. of Am., 539 N.W.2d 911 (Wis. Ct. App. 1995)).

704. *Id.* at *8.

705. 211 N.W.2d 810 (Wis. 1973).

706. *Id.* at 821.

707. WIS. STAT. § 946.60(1) (2004).

708. *Id.* at § 946.60(2).

is no case law to support whether this statute potentially reaches acts of spoliation committed during civil proceedings.

WYOMING

Independent Causes of Action for Spoliation of Evidence

Wyoming does not appear to recognize an independent cause of action for spoliation of evidence. In *Coletti v. Cudd Pressure Control,*[709] the plaintiff alleged that she was improperly terminated for filing a workers' compensation claim against her former employer. The plaintiff claimed that her employer fraudulently created evidence, a claim the district court dismissed. Considering whether a Wyoming court recognized such a claim, the Tenth Circuit observed that Wyoming courts have not recognized claims for fraudulent creation of evidence or analogous claims for spoliation of evidence. Instead, under Wyoming law, courts are "permitted to draw an adverse inference against a party responsible for losing or destroying evidence."[710]

Civil and Evidentiary Sanctions for Destruction of Evidence

As noted above, the sanction for spoliation of evidence in Wyoming is generally an adverse inference instruction. But Wyoming courts have other options, including granting summary judgment or dismissing a complaint because critical evidence has been destroyed to the prejudice of the non-destroying party.[711] Such sanctions, however, should be the least onerous appropriate under the circumstances.[712]

Criminal Statutes

Under Wyoming statute,[713] a person is an accessory after the fact if, "with intent to hinder, delay or prevent the discovery, detection, apprehension, prosecution, detention, conviction, or punishment of an-

709. 165 F.3d 767 (10th Cir. 1999).
710. *Id.* at 775; *see also* Aramburu v. Bowing Co., 112 F.3d 1398 (10th Cir. 1997) (bad-faith destruction of relevant document gives rise to adverse inference).
711. Abraham v. Great Western Energy, LLC, 101 P.3d 446 (Wyo. 2004).
712. *Id.*
713. Wyo. Stat. Ann. § 6-5-202 (2004).

other for the commission of a crime, he renders assistance to the person."[714]

The Wyoming legislature has defined "renders assistance" to mean "conceal, destroy, or alter any physical evidence that might aid in the discovery, detection, apprehension, prosecution, conviction, or punishment of the person."[715]

There is no case law suggesting that Wyoming courts would interpret this statute to apply criminal sanctions for spoliation of evidence in a civil proceeding.

---

714. WYO. STAT. ANN. § 6-5-202(a).
715. WYO. STAT. ANN. § 6-5-201(a)(iv)(E).

The Developing Law of Spoliation in Federal Courts

8

This chapter surveys the available remedies and sanctions for spoliation in pending civil litigation in federal courts throughout the United States. Most federal courts sanction deliberate spoliation, and many courts impose sanctions for negligent or reckless spoliation. No federal courts have yet recognized independent tort claims for spoliation under federal law, although some federal courts have held that the states in which they sit would recognize such a claim.

The following summary highlights the current law in all the federal circuits. It is not intended to be an exhaustive statement of the law and should not be relied upon as such.

FIRST CIRCUIT COURT OF APPEALS

The First Circuit Court of Appeals addressed spoliation on numerous occasions in a variety of contexts. Courts within this circuit sanction spoliation using the Federal Rules of Civil Procedure and the inherent authority of courts. Generally, bad faith or intentional conduct is not essential for the imposition of sanctions. Instead, courts may impose sanctions for reckless or negligent destruction of evidence that results in prejudice to the opposing party. Courts in this circuit consider fairness to the opposing party the primary consideration for determining the appropriate sanction.[1]

As in most jurisdictions, potential sanctions in the First Circuit include dismissal, exclusion of expert testimony, and an adverse inference jury instruction. In addition, before imposing an adverse inference, courts must find that the party who destroyed the evidence had prior notice of both the potential claim and of the evidence's potential relevance. Once this finding is made, the adverse inference is permissive, not mandatory.[2]

The First Circuit has routinely relied upon its inherent authority to exclude evidence that has been improperly altered or damaged when necessary to prevent prejudice to the non-offending party. For example, in *Sacaramona v. Bridgestone/Firestone, Inc.*,[3] the court upheld the entry of summary judgment in an action arising from a tire explosion. Three years after the accident, the wheel underwent a "somewhat destructive" examination, and the original tire and mounting machine disappeared. The testing precluded discovery of whether the tire was mismatched with its wheel. The district court excluded evidence of the wheel after finding that defendants' experts had no opportunity to inspect the evidence. The First Circuit affirmed, emphasizing that bad faith is not essential to sanction spoliation of evidence.[4]

---

1. McLaughlin v. Denharco, Inc., 129 F. Supp. 2d 32 (D. Me. 2001) (noting that conscious wrongdoing by plaintiff and sufficient *prejudice to support outright exclusion are the two most important factors with respect to spoliation issues). See also* TNT Road Co. v. Sterling Truck Corp., No. 03-37-B-K, 2004 U.S. Dist. LEXIS 13462 (D. Me. July 19, 2004) (denying spoliation sanction of expert exclusion against third-party supplier sought by third-party installer who was "less than vigilant" in notifying supplier of fire and where requested sanction/adverse inference would unduly punish plaintiff); Koken v. Auburn Mfg., Inc., No. 02-83-B-C, 2004 U.S. Dist. LEXIS 205 (D. Me. Jan. 8, 2004) (denying motion for summary judgment premised upon spoliation arising from welding blanket being discarded after fire where insurance company expressly waived subrogation between general contractor and subcontractors).

2. Blinzler v. Marriott Int'l, 81 F.3d 1148 (1st Cir. 1996) (affirming trial court's admission of evidence relating to the destruction of telephone logs). *See also* Pelletier v. Magnusson, 195 F. Supp. 2d 214 (D. Me. 2002) (ruling defendants were obliged to keep medical records and destruction was intentional).

3. 106 F.3d 444 (1st Cir. 1997).

4. *See also* Trull v. Volkswagen of America, Inc., 187 F.3d 88 (1st Cir. 1999) (upholding exclusion of post-accident condition of vehicle because it was discarded by the insurance company and unavailable for inspection).

Although generally in this circuit sanctions for spoliation of evidence are based upon the court's inherent power to impose sanctions for such conduct, in *Century ML-Cable Corporate v. Conjugal Partnership*,[5] the court relied upon Federal Rule of Civil Procedure 37(d). There, it entered a default judgment, awarding lawyers' fees and costs for pursuing the issue of destroyed evidence.[6] The plaintiffs established by clear and convincing evidence that the defendant discarded his laptop computer and business records in an intentional effort to destroy proof of his liability, which violated an existing restraining order. In addition to the default judgment, the court awarded costs, including lawyers' and investigative fees incurred in documenting the party's actions and preparing the motion for default.

Although courts within the First Circuit will dismiss actions for egregious and contemptuous behavior, this sanction runs contrary to the general policy favoring disposition of cases on the merits. For instance, in *Collazo-Santiago v. Toyota Motor Corporation*,[7] the court upheld the denial of a motion to dismiss after the plaintiff failed to preserve an automobile in a design defect action. The plaintiff allowed her insurance company to sell the vehicle at a public auction prior to allowing the manufacturer's experts to inspect the vehicle. The court emphasized that the allegation of design "as opposed to manufacturing" defect was relevant to the degree of prejudice suffered. Prejudice was minimal because the defect claim could be refuted by evidence other than the vehicle. Moreover, the *Collazo-Santiago* court acknowledged that the plaintiff never attempted to preclude the manufacturer from accessing the vehicle.[8]

Many district courts in this circuit employ a five-factor test in reviewing a request to exclude evidence. However, the First Circuit has not expressly adopted this test. These factors include:

---

5. 43 F. Supp. 2d 176 (D.P.R. 1998).

6. *Id.* at 186.

7. 149 F.3d 23 (1st Cir. 1998).

8. *Id.* at 20-21. *See also* Perez-Velasco v. Suzuki Motor Co., 266 F. Supp. 2d 266 (D.P.R. 2003) (granting motion for sanctions and excluding expert where plaintiffs failed to preserve vehicle for inspection action involving manufacturing defect claim); Chapman v. Bernard's Inc., 167 F. Supp. 2d 406 (D. Mass. 2001) (holding that a daybed in which an infant died was not crucial since the action was for design defect rather than manufacturing defect).

1. Prejudice to the defendant;
2. Whether the prejudice can be cured;
3. The practical importance of the evidence;
4. Whether the plaintiff was acting in good faith or bad faith; and
5. The potential for abuse.[9]

In *Northern Assurance Company v. Ware*,[10] a case involving a subrogation claim by an insurance company, the defendants moved to suppress the insurer's expert and applied this multi-factor test. There, a subrogated insurer allowed a burned house to be destroyed before the insurer initiated litigation. The destruction of the burned house and other relevant evidence prejudiced the defendants by precluding a proper investigation. In excluding the expert testimony of the insurer regarding the destroyed evidence, the court emphasized that because an insurance company should be familiar with this kind of litigation, it should have made reasonable arrangements to prevent the destruction of the house, and the wire installed in the house. The failure to preserve this evidence severely prejudiced defendants in developing and presenting a defense on causation.[11]

SECOND CIRCUIT COURT OF APPEALS

The Second Circuit has addressed the issue of spoliation of evidence in several contexts, sanctioning spoliation under both the Federal Rules of Civil Procedure and the inherent powers of federal courts. Courts in this circuit require that spoliation sanctions be tailored to accomplish the following remedial goals:

1. Deter parties from engaging in spoliation;
2. Place the risk of an erroneous judgment on the party who wrongfully created the risk; and

---

9. Driggin v. American Security Alarm Co., 141 F. Supp. 2d 113 (D. Me. 2000) (denying dismissal as a sanction in an action alleging improperly installed electrical equipment); Corales v. Sea-Land Service, Inc., 172 F.R.D. 10 (D.P.R. 1997) (concluding dismissal or exclusion of expert testimony (which would produce same result) is inappropriate sanction where bad faith but insufficient prejudice exists); Mayes v. Black & Decker (U.S.), Inc., 931 F. Supp. 80 (D.N.H. 1996) (denying dismissal as a sanction where no willfulness or bad faith exists in a product liability action against an electric coffeemaker manufacturer).

10. 145 F.R.D. 281 (D. Me. 1993).

11. *Id.* at 283-84.

3. Place the prejudiced party in the same position it would have been in, absent the wrongful destruction of evidence by the opposing party.[12]

Sanctions imposed for spoliation of evidence can range from an imposition of costs to an adverse inference instruction to a dispositive sanction.[13] The requirements for imposing sanctions become more demanding as the severity of the sanction increases. This framework and discretion affords courts leeway to tailor appropriate sanctions to ensure that wrongdoers do not benefit from their actions and upholds the remedial purpose of this sanction.

Dispositive sanctions may be given only if the spoliation was willful or in bad faith, and if no lesser sanction would effectively remedy the prejudice to the other party. In *West v. Goodyear Tire & Rubber Company*,[14] the court reversed a lower court decision dismissing the plaintiff's claims because of spoliation of physical evidence. The plaintiff had been injured when a tire he had overinflated exploded. The plaintiff and his expert witnesses deflated another tire on the affected vehicle, and then sold the tire-mounting machine and air compressor without notifying opposing counsel.[15]

The district court dismissed the complaint, finding that no lesser sanction would redress the prejudice against the defendants. On appeal, the court reversed the district court and remanded for consideration of a lesser sanction. The court held that outright dismissal of a lawsuit is appropriate only if there is a showing of willfulness, bad faith, or fault on the part of the party responsible for spoliating the evidence.[16] Moreover, because the sanction is so severe, it should be

---

12. Kronisch v. United States, 150 F.3d 112 (2d Cir. 1998).
13. *See, e.g.*, Reilly v. Natwest Mkts. Group, Inc., 181 F.3d 253 (2d Cir. 1999) (upholding adverse instruction after finding a party acted with gross negligence in searching for and preserving certain files in a breach of employment contract action); Shaffer v. RWP Group, Inc., 169 F.R.D. 19 (E.D.N.Y. 1996) (imposing adverse inference under inherent power to sanction destruction of relevant and discoverable evidence where the party breached its duty to preserve certain documents, and noting that conduct may not have risen to the level of bad faith, but demonstrated a conscious and reckless disregard for discovery obligation).
14. 167 F.3d 776 (2d Cir. 1999).
15. *Id.* at 778.
16. *Id.*

imposed "only in extreme circumstances, usually after consideration of alternative, less drastic sanctions."[17] The *West* court concluded that these lesser sanctions would be sufficient to meet the tripartite goals of spoliations sanctions as laid out in *Kronisch*:[18]

1. Instructing the jury to assume that the exemplar tire was over-inflated;
2. Instructing the jury to assume that the tire-mounting machine and air compressor malfunctioned; and
3. Precluding plaintiff from offering evidence on these issues.[19]

The court remanded to the district court to determine a more appropriate sanction.

Courts in the Second Circuit apply a fairly liberal standard to the imposition of adverse inference instructions as sanctions for spoliation. A party seeking an adverse inference instruction based on spoliation must establish:

1. that the party having control over the evidence had an obligation to preserve it at the time it was destroyed;
2. that the records were destroyed "with a culpable state of mind";
3. that the destroyed evidence was "relevant" to the party's claim or defense such that a reasonable trier of fact could find that it would support that claim or defense.[20]

With respect to the first requirement, recent case law in courts of the Second Circuit suggests a broad duty to preserve evidence. The Southern District of New York has held that an obligation to preserve evidence may exist prior to the filing of a lawsuit where a party knows that litigation is reasonably foreseeable.[21]

The "culpable state of mind" the Second Circuit requires to impose spoliation sanctions is not intentional conduct or gross negligence, even

---

17. *Id.* at 779-80 (citation omitted).
18. *See West*, 167 F.3d 776.
19. *Id.* at 778.
20. Byrnie v. Town of Cromwell, 243 F.3d 93, 107-12 (2d Cir. 2001).
21. *See* Fujitsu Ltd. v. Federal Express Corp., 247 F.3d 423, 436 (2d Cir. 2001); Zubulake v. UBS Warburg LLC, 220 F.R.D. 212, 216 (S.D.N.Y. 2003). For an extended discussion of the scope of the obligation to preserve evidence and its application in the electronic discovery context, see chs. 1 and 3.

though earlier case law suggested otherwise.[22] Currently, the Second Circuit permits the imposition of spoliation sanctions based solely on a finding of negligent conduct by the spoliating party—gross negligence or intentional conduct is not required.[23] Instead, all that is required is a "showing that the evidence was destroyed 'knowingly, even if without intent to [breach a duty to preserve it], or *negligently*.'"[24]

However, when it comes to meeting the third prong of the test—"relevance" of the spoliated evidence—the state of mind becomes relevant. As an initial matter, at least one court in this circuit has held that the term "relevant," for the purpose of the above test, is narrower than the traditional definition of "relevance" under Federal Rule of Evidence 401. For spoliation purposes, the party seeking the adverse inference instruction must show that "the destroyed . . . evidence would have been of the nature alleged by the party affected by its destruction."[25]

The party alleging spoliation ordinarily bears the burden of proof on the question of "relevance."[26] However, courts relieve a party of much of this obligation when "a party seeking an adverse inference adduces evidence that its opponent destroyed potential evidence . . . in bad faith or through gross negligence."[27] Specifically, it allows the court to accept the evidence of the bad faith or gross negligence as sufficient evidence that the destroyed evidence was favorable to the party.[28]

THIRD CIRCUIT COURT OF APPEALS

Courts within the Third Circuit find support for imposing spoliation sanctions in the Federal Rules of Civil Procedure, the Federal Rules of Evidence, and the inherent authority of federal courts. Sanctions im-

---

22. *See, e.g.*, *Kronisch*, 150 F.3d 112; Cine Forty-Second St. v. Allied Artists Picture Corp., 602 F.2d 1062 (2d Cir. 1979) (holding gross negligence is required to impose the sanction of evidence suppression).

23. Residential Funding Corp. v. DeGeorge Fin. Corp., 306 F.3d 99, 107-09 (2d Cir. 2002). While the *Residential Funding* decision did not specifically address spoliation, courts have applied this test to the spoliation context. *See, e.g.*, Pace v. Nat'l Ry. Passenger Corp., 291 F. Supp. 2d 93 (D. Conn. 2003).

24. *Residential Funding*, 306 F.3d at 108 (internal citation omitted; emphasis added).

25. *Id.* at 108-09 (quoting *Kronisch*, 150 F.3d at 127; *Byrnie*, 243 F.3d at 110).

26. *Id.*; *see also Zubulake*, 220 F.R.D. at 220.

27. *Residential Funding*, 306 F.3d at 108-09.

28. *Id.*

posed in this circuit include monetary fines, an adverse inference, and exclusion of evidence, as well as judgment against the offending party.[29] The Third Circuit uses distinct tests to determine whether to impose different types of spoliation sanctions. The Third Circuit does not appear to recognize a negligent spoliation claim.[30]

For the most serious sanctions, including exclusion of evidence, courts in this circuit employ the following three-factor balancing test:

1. The degree of fault of the party that altered or destroyed the evidence;
2. The degree of prejudice suffered by the opposing party; and
3. Whether there is a lesser sanction that will avoid substantial unfairness to the opposing party and, where the offending party is seriously at fault, will serve to deter such conduct by others.[31]

In *Schmid v. Milwaukee Electric Tool Corporation,*[32] the court created this balancing test when it reviewed a decision to exclude testimony by the plaintiff's expert after he altered the allegedly defective product during an examination. The *Schmid* court reversed and noted that because the underlying claim was for defective design, "the ability to determine whether the design of [the] saw permits sufficient infiltration to impair the guard's effectiveness and whether a safer design is feasible are matters that can be determined as well or better by inspecting or testing multiple saws of the same design than by inspecting the particular saw involved in the accident."[33] Therefore, the resulting prejudice from the spoliation did not warrant the exclusion of

29. *See* MOSAID Tech., Inc. v. Samsung Elec. Co., 348 F. Supp. 2d 332, 334 (D.N.J. 2004).

30. *See, e.g.,* Brewer v. Quaker State Oil Refining Corp., 72 F.3d 326, 334 (3d Cir. 1994) ("no unfavorable inference arises when the circumstances indicate the document or article in question has been lost or accidentally destroyed, or where the failure to produce it is otherwise properly accounted for"); Parkinson v. Guidant Corp., 315 F. Supp. 2d 760, 763 (W.D. Pa. 2004) (explaining "for the spoliation inference to arise, it is essential both that the evidence in question be within the party's control and that there has been an actual suppression or withholding of the evidence").

31. Schmid v. Milwaukee Elec. Tool Corp., 13 F.3d 76, 79 (3d Cir. 1994).

32. 13 F.3d 76 (3d Cir. 1994).

33. *Id.* at 79-80.

the expert's testimony. Moreover, because a lawsuit had not been filed prior to the expert's examination, the exclusion sanction was not commensurate with the limited fault and prejudice.[34]

In addition to resulting prejudice, Third Circuit courts also consider the degree of fault of the destroying party. In *Baliotis v. McNeil*,[35] the court considered a motion for summary judgment based upon the destruction of a fire scene or, in the alternative, to exclude expert testimony by the property owners' insurer. Applying the *Schmid* test, the *Baliotis* court found that although demolition of the fire scene resulted in the destruction of otherwise relevant evidence, no evidence supported a determination of bad faith. In considering prejudice, the court noted that it goes "too far" to assert that the demolition of the fire scene "rendered it impossible for the defendants to defend themselves," since there were scores of photographs and a lengthy videotape of the fire scene to mitigate the prejudice.[36]

In denying the requested relief, the court explained that where there is no bad faith on the part of the spoliating party and the prejudice is not severe, excluding the expert's testimony or entry of judgment is unwarranted.[37] The *Baliotis* court concluded that a spoliation inference instruction was the proper relief.[38]

More recently, in *Medina v. Rosa Art Industries*,[39] the court considered the appropriateness of a dispositive sanction where the parents of a child allegedly injured by a soap-making kit failed to produce the cup that allegedly caused the injury. While the plaintiffs had discarded the cup, they had saved the packaging and other kit compo-

---

34. *But see* Bowman v. American Med. Sys., Inc., No. 96-7871, 1998 U.S. Dist. LEXIS 16082 (E.D. Pa. Oct. 9, 1998) (upholding dismissal in manufacturing defect action where product at issue was unavailable); Williams v. American Surplus, Inc., No. 02-7655, 2003 U.S. Dist. LEXIS 15468 (E.D. Pa. Aug. 4, 2003) (holding that where plaintiff replaced a grate in a manufacturing defect claim before defendant could inspect it, defendant was severely prejudiced, and excluding plaintiff's expert testimony on the grate was an appropriate sanction).

35. 870 F. Supp. 1285 (M.D. Pa. 1994).

36. *Id.* at 1290.

37. *Id.*

38. *Id.* at 1293. *See also* Simons v. Mercedes-Benz of North Am., Inc., No. 95-2705, 1996 U.S. Dist. LEXIS 2695 (E.D. Pa. Mar. 7, 1996) (finding insufficient fault by plaintiff, who traded in her vehicle before defense experts could examine it, to support excluding the evidence).

39. No. 2:02-CV-1864, 2003 U.S. Dist. 3203 (E.D. Pa. Feb. 28, 2003).

nents. In arguing against the imposition of a spoliation sanction, the plaintiffs emphasized that this was a design defect claim as opposed to something unique to the individual cup.[40]

In determining the appropriate sanction, the *Medina* court noted that because product sampling would be sufficient to prove or disprove the plaintiffs' case, summary judgment would be appropriate only if the defendant could prove fraudulent behavior by the plaintiffs. Because the manufacturer failed to show fraudulent behavior, the court concluded that an adverse inference (spoliation) instruction was the appropriate sanction.[41]

Third Circuit courts have imposed dispositive sanctions where the circumstances warrant them. For example, in *In re Complaint of Wechsler*,[42] the court considered the appropriate sanction in a case arising out of the destruction of a fire-damaged ship. Following the fire, the ship was raised, but interested parties were unable to inspect the damage and determine the cause of the fire. During the raising, the parties videotaped and photographed the ship. The ship's owner ultimately destroyed the ship before conducting any further inspection or testing.[43] The court justified imposing a dispositive sanction on the ship owner for three reasons: (1) the ship was intentionally destroyed; (2) the destruction severely prejudiced the claimants; and (3) the sanction was necessary to deter such conduct in the future.[44]

More recently, certain courts in the Third Circuit have followed a separate four-part test to determine the appropriateness of a spoliation inference. In *Veloso v. Western Bedding Supply Company, Inc.*,[45] the court held that the following four factors must be shown before a spoliation inference may be given:

1. The evidence must be under the adverse party's control;
2. There must be actual (i.e., intentional) suppression or withholding of the evidence;
3. The evidence must be relevant; and

40. *Id.* at *7.
41. *Id* at *8.
42. 121 F. Supp. 2d 404 (D. Del. 2000).
43. *Id.*
44. *Id.* at 428-29.
45. 281 F. Supp. 2d 743 (D.N.J. 2003).

4. It must have been reasonably foreseeable at the time the document was created that it would later be discoverable.[46]

The *Veloso* court held that failure to produce certain "card files" did not warrant a spoliation inference because the plaintiffs failed to prove the loss was intentional.[47] This four-factor test has been used in other courts in the District of New Jersey and may eventually be adopted by the entire Third Circuit.[48]

FOURTH CIRCUIT COURT OF APPEALS

Courts in the Fourth Circuit impose sanctions for spoliation of evidence based upon their "inherent powers."[49] Sanctions employed in this circuit can include adverse inferences, the entry of summary judgment, and dismissal. In addition to the court's inherent power to impose sanctions, courts in the Fourth Circuit also look to Rule 37 of the Federal Rules of Civil Procedure.[50] However, a district court in this circuit recently held that when spoliation of evidence does not occur in the course of pending litigation and a federal court exercising diversity jurisdiction is required to apply those spoliation principles, the forum state would apply.[51]

---

46. *Id.* at 746 (internal citations omitted).

47. *Id.*

48. *See also MOSAID Tech.*, 348 F. Supp. 2d at 336; *Parkinson*, 315 F. Supp. 2d at 763; Crowley v. Chait, No. 85-2441, 2004 U.S. Dist. LEXIS 27235, at *28-29 (D.N.J. Dec. 27, 2004).

49. *But see* Ward v. Texas Steak, Ltd., 2004 U.S. Dist. LEXIS 10575 (W.D. Va. May 27, 2004) (applying Virginia law and allowing adverse inference to sanction spoliation).

50. *See* Bradley v. Sunbeam, 378 F.3d 373 (4th Cir. 2004) (reversing imposition of monetary sanctions premised upon spoliation because of criminal nature of award); Thompson v. United States Dep't of H.U.D., 219 F.R.D. 93 (D. Md. 2003) (imposing preclusion of evidence sanction where 80,000 e-mails that were said to be lost or destroyed were discovered shortly before trial).

51. *Ward,* 2004 U.S. Dist. LEXIS at *7 (citing State Farm & Cas. Co. v. Frigidaire, 146 F.R.D. 160, 162 (N.D. Ill. 1992) ("We can only conclude the issue of State Farm's pre-suit duty to preserve material evidence is substantive and, as such, Illinois law governs.")).

In the Fourth Circuit, the spoliation doctrine is a rule of evidence that gives broad discretion to sanction improper conduct.[52] *Vodusek v. Bayliner Marine Corporation*[53] is illustrative. This case involved negligence and product liability claims against a boat manufacturer and its retail dealer arising from a fatal explosion. The destructive examination of a boat by the boat owner's expert precluded the manufacturer's and dealer's experts from conducting a complete inspection. Therefore, the district court allowed the manufacturer and dealer to amend their answer to the complaint to include an affirmative defense based upon spoliation of evidence. The trial court also gave an adverse inference instruction to the jury, which found for the defendants.[54]

On appeal, the Fourth Circuit observed that bad faith is not essential to impose an adverse inference against a party that destroys evidence. Rather, to draw an adverse inference, the evidence must have appeared to be relevant to an issue at trial and, barring its loss or destruction, admissible at trial. The *Vodusek* court permitted an affirmative defense, even though application of the spoliation of evidence rule could prove critical to a party's recovery on a claim.[55]

Fourth Circuit courts have concluded that, absent bad-faith destruction of evidence, dismissal is too severe a remedy for spoliation. For example, *Cole v. Keller Industries, Inc.*[56] involved a product liability suit arising from an employee's fall from a ladder manufactured by the defendant. Experts for all parties examined the ladder and agreed

---

52. Hodge v. Wal-Mart Stores, Inc., 360 F.3d 446, 450 (4th Cir. 2004) (affirming summary judgment and refusing to provide sanction of adverse inference where store allowed witness to accident to leave accident scene); Hartford Ins. Co. v. American Automatic Sprinkler Sys., Inc., 23 F. Supp. 2d 623 (D. Md. 1998) (noting the spoliation doctrine is a rule of evidence that allows the court discretion to sanction improper conduct involving the loss or destruction of evidence by ordering a dismissal, granting a motion for summary judgment, or permitting an adverse inference to be drawn against the spoliation party); Moore v. General Motors Corp., No. 6:95CV00383, 1996 U.S. Dist. LEXIS 16089 (M.D.N.C. Sept. 12, 1996) (denying summary judgment in negligent design action where plaintiff's expert conducted destructive testing, and explaining the spoliation of evidence rule is a rule of evidence, to be administered at the discretion of the trial court).
53. 71 F.3d 148 (4th Cir. 1995).
54. *Id.* at 152.
55. *Id.*
56. 132 F.3d 1044 (4th Cir. 1998).

a rivet failed, but disagreed about the time, effect, or cause of the failure. During the inspection of the ladder, one of the plaintiff's experts lost two of the rivets. Thereafter, the district court dismissed the action after finding that the plaintiff's destructive testing substantially prejudiced the defendant.[57]

The court vacated the dismissal and remanded the case, holding that the unintentional destruction of the evidence and lack of bad faith made the exclusion of the evidence and the granting of summary judgment an abuse of discretion. In addition, because the defendant's experts had examined the evidence, no prejudice could be associated with the destruction.[58] The *Cole* court noted that although the plaintiff's innocent destruction of the evidence might have prompted a jury instruction allowing an adverse inference, that question was not before it.[59]

Likewise, in *Anderson v. National Railroad Passenger Corporation*,[60] the court examined a spoliator's intent. This case arose from a train derailment caused by vandals intentionally directing the high-speed train onto a side track. Federal investigators at the scene either tested or took possession of the switching equipment. Concurrently, all counsel agreed that plaintiffs would be given access to the accident scene within the week. But one of the defendants did not receive notice and began to move the damaged track. By the time the plaintiffs stopped this defendant, it had moved the switching equipment at issue from its original location. The plaintiffs opposed the defendants' motion for summary judgment because the defendants' intentional alteration of the evidence required an application of the evidentiary spoliation doctrine, which precludes summary judgment.

After acknowledging its power to permit a "spoliation inference," the *Anderson* court noted that the rule's application necessarily involves consideration of the blameworthiness of the offending party and the prejudice suffered by the opposing party. The court found that

---

57. *Id.* at 1046.

58. *See also* Ellicott Machine Corp. Int'l v. Jesco Const. Corp., 199 F. Supp. 2d 290, 294 (D. Md. 2002) (noting that in the Fourth Circuit, a showing of bad faith is necessary before summary judgment will be imposed for spoliation).

59. 132 F.3d at 1046; *see also* Jackson v. Fedders Corp., No. 94-0344, 1995 U.S. Dist. LEXIS 7306 (D.D.C. May 21, 1996) (denying motion for sanctions and dismissal where party discarded air conditioner unit after a fire, noting that actions were not in bad faith and caused little prejudice).

60. 866 F. Supp. 937 (E.D. Va. 1994).

the district court has discretion about how much weight should be given to the spoliation inference. Because the defendant's actions were not seriously blameworthy and any prejudice the plaintiffs suffered was speculative, the *Anderson* court found imposing a spoliation inference to be an issue of discretion. The court observed that, although the defendants were blameworthy to the extent they started moving the damaged track before the plaintiffs could investigate the scene, this resulted from miscommunication, not a desire to destroy evidence. In addition, the court found that the plaintiffs could have tested the switch at issue on several earlier occasions.[61]

More recently, in *Silvestri v. General Motors Corporation*,[62] a Fourth Circuit court upheld dismissal as a sanction in a case involving the failure to preserve a vehicle involved in an accident. Following the accident, the plaintiff hired two accident reconstructionists to inspect the vehicle and the accident scene and render opinions regarding the cause of the plaintiff's injuries. The vehicle owner transferred it to his insurance company. The insurer ultimately sold the vehicle to a repair firm that repaired and resold the damaged vehicle.[63]

Three years after the accident, the plaintiff filed suit against the manufacturer. Because the vehicle had been repaired and resold, the manufacturer was denied the opportunity to conduct any inspection. The plaintiff argued that he did not have a duty to preserve the vehicle, since he was not the owner. The court explained that even if he did not have a duty to preserve the evidence, he still had an "obligation to give the opposing party notice of access to the evidence or of the possible destruction of the evidence if the party anticipates litigation involving the evidence."[64] Although the destruction may have been inadvertent or simply negligent, the *Silvestri* court concluded that dismissal was an appropriate sanction given the "highly prejudicial" effect the destruction had on the manufacturer's ability to muster a defense.[65]

---

61. *Id.*
62. 271 F.3d 583 (4th Cir. 2001).
63. *Id.* at 587.
64. *Id.* at 591.
65. *Id.* at 594.

FIFTH CIRCUIT COURT OF APPEALS

The Fifth Circuit has addressed allegations of spoliation of evidence primarily in the context of tort actions.[66] To impose sanctions for spoliation of evidence, the Fifth Circuit requires a showing of bad faith or intentional conduct.[67] Negligent conduct will not support a sanction for spoliation. In addition, the destroying party must have been on notice of the evidence's relevance to potential litigation and thus subject to a duty to preserve such evidence.[68] Courts within this circuit recognize that trial courts may sanction spoliation under both the Federal Rules of Civil Procedure and a federal court's inherent authority.[69] Sanctions employed by courts in this circuit include presumptions, burden shifting, monetary awards, and dismissal entries.

In determining the appropriate sanctions for intentional destruction of evidence, courts focus on the actions of the spoliator as opposed to the prejudice of the injured party. *Caparotta v. Versus Entergy Corporation*[70] is illustrative. There, the Fifth Circuit reversed a decision allowing a party to present another party's inadvertent destruction of documents to the jury in an age discrimination suit. During discovery, the defendant's counsel possessed a box containing the plaintiff's employee and supervisor's records, which disappeared before being produced. After finding no bad faith, the district court refused to give an adverse inference instruction, but allowed the plaintiff to present evidence of the inadvertent destruction to the jury.[71]

---

66. *See, e.g.,* Stahl v. Wal-Mart, No. 4:98CV16LN, 1998 U.S. Dist. LEXIS 21926 (S.D. Miss. Dec. 7, 1998); Nowlin v. Miller Elec. Mfg. Co., No. 02-993, 2003 U.S. Dist. LEXIS 12407 (E.D. La. July 11, 2003).

67. Baker v. Randstad N.A., N0. 04-20924, 2005 U.S. App. LEXIS 22161 (5th Cir. Oct. 13, 2005); Caparotta v. Versus Entergy Corp., 168 F.3d 754 (5th Cir. 1999); Vick v. Tex. Employment Comm'n, 514 F.2d 734, 737 (5th Cir. 1975).

68. Catoire v. Caprock Telecomm. Corp., No. 01-3577, 2002 U.S. Dist. LEXIS 23389 (E.D. La. Dec. 2, 2002) (citing Anderson v. Prod. Mgmt. Corp., No. 98-2234, 2000 U.S. Dist. LEXIS 56968, *4 (E.D. La. 2000)).

69. *See, e.g.,* Bell v. CSX Transp., Inc., No. 97-2941, 1997 U.S. Dist. LEXIS 17843 (E.D. La. Nov. 7, 1997) (applying Louisiana law in tort action and acknowledging that Fed. R. Civ. P. 37 allows the court to sanction parties that spoliate evidence, and courts may make presumptions against the spoliating party or shift burdens to remedy spoliation).

70. 168 F.3d 754 (5th Cir. 1999).

71. *Id.*

On appeal, the Fifth Circuit found the district court had erred by submitting evidence to the jury and giving an instruction that the defendants had inadvertently destroyed employment documents. The appellate court determined that allowing the jury to hear that the defendants had inadvertently destroyed the evidence was unfairly prejudicial under Federal Rule of Evidence 403.

Likewise, *Stahl v. Wal-Mart*[72] involved a personal injury action arising from a fall in a store resulting from liquid that seeped out of a bottle. Although the store disposed of the leaky bottle before the defendant had an opportunity to examine it, there was no evidence of bad-faith destruction.[73]

The *Stahl* court examined both Fifth Circuit and Mississippi law and denied the plaintiff's request to exclude the store's use of the leaky bottle or to allow an adverse inference instruction. The court reasoned that although the proper sanction for spoliation of evidence is an adverse inference, it will not give such an instruction absent evidence of bad faith. Therefore, the court concluded that unless there is a showing of bad faith, there can be no sanction for the spoliation of evidence even if an innocent party is prejudiced by such spoliation.[74]

SIXTH CIRCUIT COURT OF APPEALS

In the Sixth Circuit, "[t]he rules that apply to the spoiling of evidence and the range of appropriate sanctions are defined by state law. . . ."[75] For example, in *Nationwide Mutual Fire Insurance Company v. Ford Motor Company*,[76] the plaintiffs, an insurer and its insureds, filed a lawsuit against an automobile manufacturer alleging that a defect in their automobile started a fire in the insureds' garage. The plaintiffs' expert examined the automobile and the garage. Several days later, without notifying the manufacturer, the insurer moved the automobile to another location. Thereafter, the manufacturer had an opportunity to photograph the automobile. Two months later, another expert of the insurer removed an electrical wire harness from the automobile that

---

72. No. 4:98CV16LN, 1998 U.S. Dist. LEXIS 21926.

73. *Id.* at *3.

74. *Id.*

75. Nationwide Mutual Fire Ins. Co. v. Ford Motor Co., 174 F.3d 801, 804 (6th Cir. 1999).

76. *Id.*

he believed caused the fire. Again, the insurer failed to notify the manufacturer before removing this evidence.[77]

The manufacturer moved to exclude the insurer's expert based on spoliation of evidence. While the district court found that the insurer's actions constituted spoliation, it ruled that the expert could testify if his opinions were based on evidence equally available to the manufacturer and the plaintiffs. The jury returned a verdict for the manufacturer.

On appeal, the plaintiffs claimed the expert testimony should not have been excluded and they had been denied a fair trial. The Sixth Circuit agreed, reversed as to both issues, and ordered a new trial.

With regard to the spoliation issue, the Sixth Circuit held that "the test, under Ohio law, is whether [the insurer] intentionally altered or destroyed its evidence, causing prejudice to the [automobile manufacturer]."[78] To qualify as "intentional" conduct, warranting exclusion of evidence, the harness had to be "removed for the purpose of rendering it inaccessible or useless to the defendant in preparing its case; that is, spoiling it."[79] The court held that there was no evidence the manufacturer had been prejudiced, since it had had two months to inspect the automobile, including the harness, before the harness was removed. Moreover, the manufacturer could still establish a defense, including one based on its theory that a faulty garage door opener had caused the fire. Accordingly, the Sixth Circuit held that the district court had abused its discretion in excluding expert testimony based upon spoliation.[80]

In addition to exclusion of evidence,[81] an adverse inference instruction may also be an appropriate sanction for spoliation under appro-

---

77. *Id.*

78. *Id.*

79. *Id.*

80. *Id.* at 804-05. The court of appeals also reversed and remanded for a new trial based on the district court's conduct during the trial, which the appellate court found was improper and prejudicial to plaintiffs. *Id. See also* Busch v. Dyno Nobel, Inc., 40 Fed. Appx. 947, 2002 U.S. App. LEXIS 14724 (6th Cir. July 18, 2002) (applying Michigan law and finding no abuse of discretion where magistrate judge denied plaintiff's motion for hearing on spoliation because it found plaintiff failed to create a genuine factual question as to whether evidence was deliberately destroyed).

81. In *Nationwide*, the court cited to Ohio decisions, including *Cincinnati Insurance, infra,* for the propriety of excluding expert testimony as a sanction for spoliation. *Nationwide,* 174 F.3d at 804.

priate circumstances.[82] In *Rogers v. T.J. Samson Community Hospital*,[83] the Sixth Circuit vacated and remanded a verdict in favor of the defendant hospital in a negligence action. The *Rogers* court considered the evidentiary value of certain missing tissue, that is, whether it was in a condition that would have permitted a worthwhile examination. Ultimately, the court found that the hospital breached a regulatory duty to preserve the tissue and therefore the plaintiff was entitled to an adverse inference instruction regarding the "missing" evidence.

The Sixth Circuit instructed that when considering whether to give an adverse inference instruction under Federal Rule of Civil Procedure 37, a court must look to state law regarding any presumptions that may arise from spoliation.[84] In Ohio, for example, an adverse inference instruction is proper only when the spoliating party has destroyed evidence in bad faith, or at least with a state of mind that rises to the level of "gross neglect."[85] However, one court in this circuit held that, under Michigan law, a "sanction may be appropriate 'regardless of whether the evidence is lost as the result of a deliberate act or simple negligence, [as] the other party is unfairly prejudiced because it is unable to challenge or respond to the evidence. . .[ ].'"[86]

---

82. *See* Lindsey v. M&M Restaurant Supply, 170 F. Supp. 2d 788 (N.D. Ohio 2001) (explaining the test for determining whether to impose sanctions is whether evidence has been intentionally altered or destroyed by a party or its expert before the defense has an opportunity to examine the evidence).

83. 276 F.3d 228 (6th Cir. 2002).

84. Austral-Pacific Fertilizers, Ltd. v. Cooper Indus., Inc., Nos. 94-4255/95-4287, 1997 U.S. App. LEXIS 5383 (6th Cir. Mar. 18, 1997) (dismissal held an abuse of discretion); Helmac Products Corp. v. Roth (Plastics) Corp., 814 F. Supp. 560, 571 (E.D. Mich. 1992) (noting default only imposed when less severe sanctions will not redress wrongdoing). *But see* Communities for Equity v. Michigan High School Athletic Ass'n, No. 1:98-CV-479, 2001 U.S. Dist. LEXIS 16019 (W.D. Mich. Sept. 21, 2001) (holding that because court had jurisdiction by federal question and not diversity, the "federal law on spoliation of evidence will be applied" and referencing decisions of other federal circuits, not state law, in reaching its decision the spoliation did not approach a level that warranted the sanction of exclusion of evidence).

85. Tucker v. General Motors Corp., No. 91-3019, 1991 U.S. App. LEXIS 23184, at *6 (6th Cir. Sept. 30, 1991) ("In general, a court may not allow an inference that a party destroyed evidence that is in its control, unless the party did so in bad faith."); Sullivan v. General Motors Corp., 772 F. Supp. 358 (N.D. Ohio 1991) (Ohio courts require bad faith or at least gross neglect before giving adverse inference instruction).

86. Roskam Baking Co. v. Lanham Mach. Co., 71 F. Supp. 2d 736 (W.D. Mich. 1999) (quoting Brenner v. Kolk, 573 N.W.2d 65, 70 (Mich. Ct. App. 1998)).

Generally, sanctions may be imposed only under Rule 37 during the pendency of a lawsuit.[87] According to the Sixth Circuit, for pre-litigation destruction a "remedy must be found in the substantive law of the case."[88] However, one district court has held, applying Michigan law, that it may sanction prelitigation destruction of evidence because Michigan courts would do so under their inherent power.[89]

In *Helmac Products Corporation v. Roth (Plastics) Corporation*,[90] the court reasoned that even when Rule 37 may be inapplicable because a court order has not been violated, a court can rely on its inherent power to sanction willful destruction of documents that are responsive to discovery requests.[91] It is, perhaps, questionable whether the Sixth Circuit, in holding that state law applies to spoliation, also intended for state law to apply to the initial issue of whether a federal court has the power to impose sanctions when the spoliation occurs before commencement of litigation.

Dismissal with prejudice and the entry of a default judgment also may be imposed as sanctions for spoliation. However, these are "the sanctions of last resort," to be imposed only in the most extreme of circumstances.[92] The failure of a district court to provide the alleged spoliator with an opportunity to rebut any presumption of spoliation, so that the court may have all relevant facts before concluding that dismissal is the appropriate remedy, is an abuse of discretion.[93]

However, in *Austin v. Mitsubishi Electric American, Inc.*,[94] a magistrate judge recommended that summary judgment be granted and the case dismissed. In that case, the plaintiffs destroyed all of the relevant evidence before the defendant could examine it, thereby rendering the plaintiffs' theory regarding the cause of fire "mere conjecture."[95] Accordingly, the dismissal was appropriate.[96]

---

87. Beil v. Lakewood Eng'g & Mfg. Co., 15 F.3d 546, 552 (6th Cir. 1994).
88. *Id.*
89. *Roskam Baking*, 71 F. Supp. 2d at 738.
90. 814 F. Supp. 560 (E.D. Mich. 1992).
91. *Id.* at 571.
92. *Austral-Pacific*, 1997 U.S. App. LEXIS 5383, at *8.
93. *Id.* at *12-13.
94. 966 F. Supp. 506 (E.D. Mich. 1996).
95. *Id.* at 517.
96. *See also* Citizens Ins. Co. of America v. Juno Lighting, Inc., 635 N.W.2d 379 (Mich. 2001) (finding dismissal sanction appropriate when spoliation prevented defendant from putting forth a defense).

Finally, the Sixth Circuit has not addressed whether an independent cause of action exists for spoliation of evidence under federal law. However, one district court within this circuit has specifically rejected an argument that an independent tort claim exists for spoliation of evidence under federal law. In *Lombardi v. MCI Telecommunications Corporation*,[97] the plaintiff claimed that the defendant employer's destruction of certain critical personnel records in violation of 29 C.F.R. § 1602.14 supported an independent claim for spoliation of evidence under federal law.

The *Lombardi* court disagreed and held that no such claim exists. It reasoned that, first, the language of the statute did not support the finding that an employer's failure to retain these records supported a damage claim. Second, the appropriate remedy when an employer has failed to preserve records under these circumstances is a [rebuttable] "presumption that the destroyed documents would have bolstered her case."[98] Finally, the court also noted that the plaintiff might be entitled to sanctions, including punitive damages for this conduct.[99]

SEVENTH CIRCUIT COURT OF APPEALS

Seventh Circuit decisions considering spoliation of evidence generally focus on the existence of independent causes of action, as well as the imposition of sanctions pursuant to the Federal Rules of Civil Procedure and courts' inherent authority. Imposition of a sanction, such as an adverse inference, requires a demonstration of "bad faith," which requires a showing of more than intentional conduct.[100]

Broadnax v. ABF Freight Systems, Inc.[101] involved a claim for negligent spoliation of evidence in a wrongful death action arising from a motor vehicle accident. The plaintiff filed a third amended complaint seeking punitive damages for the destruction of records. The court dismissed the claim as insufficiently pleaded and referenced *Boyd v.*

---

97. 13 F. Supp. 2d 621 (N.D. Ohio 1998).

98. *Id.* at 628 (quoting Hicks v. Gates Rubber Co., 833 F.2d 1406, 1419 (10th Cir. 1987)).

99. *Id.* and n.8.

100. *See, e.g.,* Mathis v. John Morden Buick, Inc., 136 F.3d 1153 (7th Cir. 1998).

101. No. 9601674, 1998 U.S. Dist. LEXIS 4662 (N.D. Ill. Mar. 30, 1998).

Travelers Insurance Company,[102] which required a plaintiff to plead the following elements in a negligent spoliation claim:

1. The existence of a duty owed by the defendant to the plaintiff;[103]
2. A breach of that duty;
3. An injury proximately caused by that breach (that is, the loss or destruction of evidence causing the plaintiff to be unable to establish his claim in the underlying suit);[104] and
4. Damages.[105]

In dismissing the claim, the court found no evidence that the plaintiff was unable to establish his claim in the underlying suit and related damages.[106]

The *Broadnax* court also reaffirmed the elements for an intentional spoliation claim:

1. Existence of a potential civil action;
2. The defendant's knowledge of the potential action;
3. Destruction of relevant evidence;
4. Intent;

---

102. 652 N.E.2d 267 (Ill. 1995).

103. *See, e.g.,* Welch v. Wal-Mart Stores, Inc., No. 04 C 50023, 2004 U.S. Dist. LEXIS 12165 (N.D. Ill. June 30, 2004) (granting motion to dismiss negligent spoliation claim because Wal-Mart had no duty to preserve videotapes from its in-store security cameras).

104. A recent decision in the Northern District of Illinois suggests when courts are strictly enforcing this requirement. In *Johnson v. Russell-Stanley Corp.,* No. 03 C 3400, 2004 U.S. Dist. LEXIS 11416 (N.D. Ill. June 22, 2004), the court held in a wrongful termination suit in which the plaintiff was terminated for allegedly falsely claiming to have tested drums, the destruction of the drums by the defendant was not deemed to be spoliation because the relevant question was not whether the drums were tested, but whether the employer believed they had not been.

105. *But see* Williams v. General Motors Corp., No. 93 C 6661, 1996 U.S. Dist. LEXIS 10555 (N.D. Ill. July 25, 1996) (denying motions to dismiss negligent spoliation claim filed by both defendants and following *Boyd* regarding the negligent spoliation claim, holding the plaintiff did not have to lose the underlying suit before bringing a spoliation claim).

106. *See also* Farrar v. Yamin, 261 F. Supp. 2d 987 (N.D. Ill. 2003) (dismissing negligent spoliation claim because plaintiff could not allege causation).

5. A causal connection between the destruction of evidence and the plaintiff's inability to prove the lawsuit; and

6. Damages.[107]

Ultimately, after defining the requisite elements for these two claims, the court struck the spoliation claim without prejudice.[108]

Mathis v. John Morden Buick, Inc.[109] discussed the intent requirement for spoliation claims. This case involved an employment discrimination action in which the plaintiff learned during discovery that the defendant had discarded certain documents that it was required to retain under federal regulations.[110] The plaintiff sought these documents under Federal Rule of Civil Procedure 34, but did not file a motion for sanctions under Rule 37.

In its decision, the Seventh Circuit noted, "Litigants who are not diligent in the defense of their own interests cannot expect rescue by appellate courts."[111] On the subject of sanctions, the court stated that in the absence of Rule 37 sanctions, the possibility exists of obtaining an adverse inference. To obtain an adverse inference, the party must demonstrate that the evidence was destroyed in "bad faith." The court observed that the documents clearly were destroyed *intentionally,* but, held by the court, "bad faith" means "destruction for the purpose of

---

107. 1998 U.S. Dist. LEXIS 4062, at *11. *See also* Mohawk Mfg. & Supply Co. v. Lakes Tool Die & Eng'g, Inc., No. 92C1315, 1994 U.S. Dist. LEXIS 2960 (N.D. Ill. Mar. 14, 1994) (interpreting Illinois law and defining the elements of the intentional spoliation of evidence claim as (1) existence of a potential civil action, (2) the defendant's knowledge of the potential action, (3) destruction of relevant evidence, (4) intent, (5) a causal connection between the destruction of evidence and the plaintiff's inability to prove the lawsuit, and (6) damages, the court dismissed plaintiff's intentional spoliation claim without prejudice in a copyright infringement action when party destroyed computer files, holding the claim was premature absent showing of any actual damages as a result of the loss of the evidence).

108. *Id.*

109. 136 F.3d 1153 (7th Cir. 1998).

110. "Federal regulations require employers to preserve documents relevant to claims of discrimination—in particular, records concerning persons hired (or not hired) for the position sought by the complainant." *Id.* at 1155 (citing 29 C.F.R. § 1602.14).

111. *Id.*

hiding adverse information."[112] Recent decisions suggest that more than mere speculation is necessary to find that spoliated documents contain adverse information, but courts may consider the circumstances surrounding the destruction to determine if the non-producing party acted in bad faith.[113] Moreover, "bad faith is a question of fact like any other, so the trier of fact is entitled to draw any reasonable inference."[114]

EIGHTH CIRCUIT COURT OF APPEALS

The Eighth Circuit has addressed spoliation of evidence in the context of commercial disputes, product liability actions, and employment discrimination actions.[115] When imposing sanctions for spoliation of evi-

---

112. *Id. See also* Kucala Enters., Ltd. v. Auto Wax Co., Inc., No. 02-C-1403, 2003 U.S. Dist. LEXIS 8833 (N.D. Ill. May 23, 2003) (dismissing action as sanction after finding plaintiff acted in bad faith by using computer program to delete documents from his computer and "clean" the hard drive); American Family Ins. v. Black & Decker (U.S.), Inc., No. 3:00cv50281, 2003 U.S. Dist. LEXIS 16245 (N.D. Ill. Sept. 16, 2003). *But see* Schaffner v. Rush Presbyterian St. Luke's Hosp., No. 9402471, 1996 U.S. Dist. LEXIS 12897 (N.D. Ill. Sept. 4, 1996) (upholding grant of summary judgment in an employment discrimination case on negligent destruction of evidence claim where party could not demonstrate the destruction caused her to be unable to prove underlying claim); Philips Med. Sys. Marrocco v. General Motors Corp., 966 F.2d 220 (7th Cir. 1992) (upholding dismissal where plaintiffs willfully disregarded specific discovery orders regarding vehicle inspectors and destructive testing and such testing made certain material determinations impossible).

113. Rummery v. Ill. Bell Telephone Co., 250 F.3d 553 (7th Cir. 2001); Wiginton v. C.B. Richard Ellis, No. 02-C-6832, 2003 U.S. Dist. LEXIS 19128 (N.D. Ill. Oct. 24, 2003) (despite defendant's bad-faith destruction of relevant electronic documents, court determined that sanctions would be premature, as the existence of backup tapes made it possible to determine the effect of defendant's actions on plaintiff's case). *But see* DirecTV, Inc. v. Borow, No. 03 C 2581, 2005 U.S. Dist. LEXIS 1328 (N.D. Ill. Jan. 6, 2005) (allowing adverse inference for defendant's bad-faith destruction of relevant electronic documents).

114. *Mathis*, 136 F.3d at 1155. *See also* Boneck v. City of New Berlin, 22 Fed. Appx. 629 (7th Cir. 2001) (upholding verdict for defendant employer and denying plaintiff's claim on appeal that he was entitled to default judgment in light of spoliation, finding "spoliation that sabotages a strong case supports default judgment, spoliation that destroys collateral evidence in a weak case does not require the same penalty").

115. *See, e.g.*, Sylla-Sawdon v. Uniroyal Goodrich Tire Co., 47 F.3d 277 (8th Cir. 1995) (imposing spoliation sanctions in a product liability action); SDI Operating P'ship, L.P. v. Neuwirth, 973 F.2d 652 (8th Cir. 1992) (affirming spoliation sanctions in commercial action arising from destruction of evidence at fire scene);

dence, Eighth Circuit courts rely upon both Federal Rule of Civil Procedure 37 and the court's inherent authority to regulate litigation.[116] Under either source of authority, courts may impose a wide array of sanctions, such as excluding expert testimony; imposing a default judgment; dismissing an action; awarding sanctions, costs, or attorneys' fees; and providing an adverse inference instruction to the jury.[117]

Courts in this circuit do not require a showing of bad faith for the imposition of spoliation sanctions.[118] Instead, sanctions are appropriate when the "party destroying the evidence knew or should have known the evidence was relevant to potential litigation."[119] This inquiry requires a determination of the relevance of the destroyed evidence and the resulting prejudice to the opposing party.[120] Significantly, given the severity of dismissal, courts in this circuit require a finding of bad faith for its imposition as a sanction.[121]

Recently, the Eighth Circuit held that "there must be a finding of prejudice to the opposing party before imposing a sanction for de-

---

Anderson v. Crossroads Capital Partners, LLC, No. 01-2000, 2004 U.S. Dist. LEXIS 1867 (D. Minn. Feb. 10, 2004) (refusing to dismiss sexual harassment action based upon spoliation of evidence but imposing adverse inference following discovery violations involving plaintiff's computer); Capellupo v. FMC Corp., 126 F.R.D. 545 (D. Minn. 1989) (imposing spoliation sanctions in an employment action). *But see* Blandin Paper Co. v. J&J Indus. Sales, Inc., No. 02-4858, 2004 U.S. Dist. LEXIS 17550 (D. Minn. Sept. 2, 2004) (declining to impose sanctions for destruction of evidence where no showing of prejudice or that the machine owner knew or should have known the destroyed items were relevant to the litigation).

116. *See, e.g.,* Stevenson v. Union Pac. R.R. Co., 354 F.3d 739, 745 (8th Cir. 2004) (noting court has discretion to impose spoliation sanctions under its inherent authority).

117. *See, e.g.,* Bass v. General Motors Corp., 150 F.3d 842, 851 (8th Cir. 1998) (refusing to dismiss action as spoliation but precluding testimony of experts who examined vehicle at issue prior to its destruction and issuing an adverse inference instruction to the jury).

118. Lord v. Nissan Motor Co., No. 03-3218, 2004 U.S. Dist. LEXIS 25409 (D. Minn. Dec. 13, 2004) (citing Dillon v. Nissan Motor Co., 986 F.2d 263, 267 (8th Cir. 1993).

119. *Id.*

120. *Id.* (citing *Stevenson,* 354 F.3d at 748).

121. *Lord,* 2004 U.S. Dist. LEXIS 25409, at *9 (citing *Capellupo,* 126 F.R.D. at 552 (finding dismissal as a spoliation sanction unwarranted because no content evidence destroyed intentionally).

struction of evidence."[122] In *Stevenson v. Union Pacific Railroad Company*, the defendant railroad company destroyed a voice tape of conversations between the train crew and dispatch at the time of the accident and track maintenance records predating the accident. The district court issued a permissive adverse inference instruction, awarded attorneys' fees as a sanction for the destruction, and precluded the railroad from presenting any evidence that the destruction occurred pursuant to a routine document retention policy. The jury awarded the plaintiffs more than $2 million and the district court awarded $164,410.25 in costs and fees as a sanction for the destruction.[123]

On appeal, the court found that the lower court properly issued an adverse inference jury instruction, but abused its discretion in not permitting a reasonable rebuttal to the inference.[124] In upholding the instruction, the *Stevenson* court emphasized that the tape was the only contemporaneous recording of the conversations and was "highly relevant."[125] In considering whether there was a showing of bad faith, the court noted that bad faith can be implied by a party's behavior. For example, a party's decision to selectively preserve some evidence while failing to retain other, or a party's use of the same type of evidence to their advantage in prior instances, may be used to demonstrate a party's bad faith.[126]

In reviewing the sanction, the court held that "a bad faith finding is specifically required in order to assess attorneys' fees."[127] Applying this standard, the appellate court vacated the sanction award because the district court based it upon prelitigation destruction of evidence that was not supported by a bad-faith finding.[128]

The decision in *Sylla-Sawdon v. Uniroyal Goodrich Tire Company*[129] outlines how courts in this circuit assess prejudice. This wrongful death and strict liability action arose after an automobile tire blowout caused the plaintiff to lose control of her vehicle. The manufacturer's inability

---

122. Stevenson v. Union Pac. R.R. Co., 354 F.3d 739 (8th Cir. 2004).

123. *Id.* at 743.

124. *Id.* at 746-48.

125. *Id.* at 748.

126. *Id.* at 747-48.

127. *Id.* at 751.

128. *Id.* The court remanded for recalculation and consideration under the bad-faith standard.

129. 47 F.3d 277 (8th Cir. 1995).

to examine the vehicle's tires became an issue during discovery when it learned the plaintiff had purchased two of the four tires one year earlier. At trial, the manufacturer sought to establish that the failed tire was older and had more mileage. The manufacturer also moved to exclude any evidence that the damaged tire was purchased in 1988. The district court granted this motion, finding that the plaintiff knew that the front tires existed in December 1989, but failed to preserve them. The court instructed the jury that the damaged tire was purchased on July 6, 1987. The plaintiff appealed a jury verdict for the manufacturer.

On appeal, the *Sylla-Sawdon* court considered the imposition of a sanction for the plaintiff's failure to preserve the three tires that had not exploded during the accident. In affirming, the Eighth Circuit explained:

> [T]he tires remaining on the vehicle were critical to this litiga-
> tion because only an examination of all four tires conclusively
> established the date of purchase of the failed tire and the mile-
> age that was on it at the time of the accident. During the De-
> cember 1989 inspection, plaintiff's former counsel was well
> aware that the cause of the fatal accident was tire failure and
> that the attorneys were contemplating a lawsuit claiming tire
> manufacturing defect. Therefore, they knew or should have
> known that all the tires would be relevant and should be pre-
> served as evidence.[130]

Finally, the decision in *SDI Operating Partnership, L.P. v. Neuwirth*[131] suggests how courts in the Eighth Circuit evaluate intent when imposing sanctions for spoliation. There, plaintiffs alleged that the negligent design and maintenance of the electrical system inside a building caused damage. The electrical contractor denied negligence and argued that an electrical service line located above the roof outside the building caused the fire. The plaintiffs challenged a district court's ruling that held certain expert testimony regarding the cause and origin of the fire admissible.

Following the fire, a fire marshal representative investigated the site and gathered certain evidence, including portions of internal elec-

---

130. *Id.; see also* Dillon v. Nissan Motor Co., 986 F.2d 263 (8th Cir. 1993) (relying on court's inherent power to sanction plaintiff's prelitigation destruction of evidence).

131. 973 F.2d 652 (8th Cir. 1992).

trical wiring. The building owner's insurance carrier retained an investigator, who conducted an on-site investigation. After the fire marshal had concluded his investigation, the electrical contractor's investigator obtained custody of the physical evidence from the fire marshal's investigation. Thereafter, the contractor's investigator told the insurer he intended to dispose of the evidence.

Neither the plaintiffs nor their expert ever examined either the internal wiring or the electrical service line. The magistrate judge determined that the destruction of evidence placed the plaintiffs at a severe disadvantage because it precluded them from examining the wires. Thus, the plaintiffs would likely be prejudiced. However, no evidence demonstrated that the defendants had destroyed the evidence willfully. Nevertheless, the magistrate judge granted the plaintiffs' motion for sanctions, including exclusion of testimony by two of the plaintiffs' experts and prohibiting the use at trial of evidence, opinion, or inference arising from the physical examination by the plaintiffs' experts of the destroyed evidence.[132]

The district court modified this order by allowing the use of certain evidence, opinions, or inferences arising from the physical examination, but not those arising from the microscopic examination of destroyed evidence. Following a bench trial, the court entered judgment in favor of the contractor.

On appeal, the plaintiffs argued that the district court erred in declining to enforce presumption that the lost evidence would be favorable to them. The Eighth Circuit upheld the sanction order, stating that a presumption "may arise where the destruction of evidence was intentional, fraudulent, or done with a desire to conceal and, thus, frustrate the search for truth."[133] Since the magistrate judge's decision explicitly indicated the lack of bad faith, the court found that the refusal to create a presumption in this instance was reasonable.[134]

In imposing sanctions, the court relied upon its inherent authority because the actions extended beyond the scope of Federal Rule of Civil Procedure 37. In addition to entering the sanction of dismissal, the court noted it must at least find that:

---

132. *Id.*
133. *Id.* at 655.
134. *Id.*

1. the employer acted willfully or in bad faith;
2. the plaintiffs were prejudiced by the employer's actions; and
3. alternative sanctions would fail to punish and deter future discovery violations adequately.[135]

After declining to enter a default judgment, the *Capellupo* court ordered the employer to pay the plaintiffs' attorneys' fees and costs incurred in investigating, researching, preparing, arguing, and presenting all motions touching upon the issue of document destruction. The court also found that it was appropriate to multiply the plaintiffs' fees and costs by a factor of two and require payment to the Clerk of Courts for the court's time.[136]

NINTH CIRCUIT COURT OF APPEALS

In the Ninth Circuit, a litigant has a duty to preserve evidence it knows, or reasonably should know, is relevant to a claim.[137] However, evidence may be permissibly destroyed in the ordinary course of business pursuant to a document retention policy, unless litigation is pending or the party is "on notice" of potential litigation for which that evidence may be relevant.[138] Courts in this circuit find authority for imposing spoliation sanctions both in Federal Rule of Civil Procedure 37(b)(2)[139] and from their inherent discretionary authority to make "appropriate evidentiary rulings in response to the destruction or spoliation of relevant evidence."[140]

Courts in the Ninth Circuit impose a variety of sanctions for spoliation of evidence, including excluding evidence (including expert

---

135. *Id.* at 552.

136. *Id.* at 553.

137. United States *ex rel.* Aflatooni v. Kitsap Physicians Service, 314 F.3d 995, 1001 (9th Cir. 2002) (holding that defendants only engage in spoliation of documents if they "had some notice that the documents were potentially relevant" to the litigation before being destroyed). *See also* Toste v. Lewis Controls, Inc., No. C9501366MHP, 1996 U.S. Dist. LEXIS 2359 (N.D. Cal. Feb. 28, 1996).

138. 314 F.3d at 1001.

139. *See* Unigard Security Ins. Co. v. Lakewood Eng'g & Mfg. Corp., 982 F.2d 363, 367-68 (9th Cir. 1992) (holding that Rule 37(b) sanctions may be imposed if a court order regarding discovery is violated).

140. Med. Lab. Mgmt. Consultants v. American Broadcasting Cos., Inc., 306 F.3d 806, 824 (9th Cir. 2002) (quoting Glover v. BIC Corp., 6 F.3d 1318, 1329 (9th Cir. 1993)).

testimony), giving an adverse inference instruction, and, where the spoliation is particularly egregious, dismissal or default.[141] However, to be sanctionable, the spoliation of evidence must damage the right of a party to bring an action.[142]

In determining whether to grant the extreme sanction of default judgment, a court will consider a number of factors, including:

1. Whether willfulness, bad faith, or fault can be attributed to the offending party;
2. Whether certain extraordinary circumstances exist;
3. Whether lesser sanctions would be efficacious; and
4. The relationship or nexus between the misconduct and the matters in controversy in the case.[143]

In *Unigard Security Insurance Company v. Lakewood Engineering & Manufacturing Company,*[144] the plaintiff insurance company brought subrogation claims against the manufacturer of an electric space heater. The heater allegedly caused a fire that destroyed a moored boat. Investigators for the insurance company concluded that the heater caused the fire. Unigard paid the claim brought by the insured. Believing that a subrogation claim was unavailable, the Unigard investigator in possession of the heater authorized its disposal.[145]

Two years later, a new lawyer for Unigard, who disagreed with the prior assessment regarding the propriety of a subrogation claim, filed a complaint based on the fire. The manufacturer counterclaimed for intentional spoliation of evidence, moved for summary judgment on

---

141. *See, e.g.,* Glover v. BIC Corp., 987 F.2d 1410, 1417 (9th Cir. 1993) (noting that "trier of fact may draw an adverse inference from the destruction of evidence relevant to a case") (internal citation omitted); *Unigard,* 982 F.2d at 369 (excluding evidence and granting summary judgment to defendant because plaintiff could not establish a prima facie case absent that evidence); Cabnetware, Inc. v. Sullivan, No. CIV S-90-313 LKK, 1991 U.S. Dist. LEXIS 20329, at *12-13 (E.D. Cal. July 16, 1991) (granting default judgment and holding that because "defendant's conduct strikes at the heart of the judicial process, . . . no sanction less than default judgment will be sufficient to serve both the necessary deterrent and punitive functions").

142. *Unigard,* 982 F.2d at 371.

143. *Cabnetware,* 1991 U.S. Dist. LEXIS 20329, at *7.

144. 982 F.2d 363 (9th Cir. 1992).

145. *Id.* at 365.

its spoliation claim, and sought sanctions for spoliation. The district court found that all evidence regarding the heater and vessel should be excluded and that, absent this evidence, Unigard could not prevail on its claims.[146] Accordingly, it granted summary judgment against Unigard on all claims.

On appeal, the Ninth Circuit affirmed the grant of summary judgment. The *Unigard* court held the district court was within its discretion in determining that a rebuttable presumption was insufficient to cure the prejudice to the defendant. Accordingly, the appellate court held that the district court correctly concluded that evidence should be excluded and, given that defendants could not establish a *prima facie* case without this evidence, summary judgment was proper.[147]

When a defendant willfully destroyed significant evidence after being served with a request for production, one district court has concluded that no lesser sanction than default judgment would serve to satisfy both the deterrent and punitive functions of spoliation sanctions. The *Cabnetware* court reasoned:

> Defendant's conduct in the instant action, cast in its most charitable light, is an affront to the integrity of the judicial system. Knowing full well the significance of the initial source codes to plaintiff's suit for copyright infringement, defendant willfully destroyed essential evidence after being served with a request for production. Although I have served many years on the federal bench, this court has never before been confronted with such a flagrant example of contempt for the judicial system . . . . I hold that nothing less than default judgment on the issue of liability will suffice to both punish this defendant and deter others similarly tempted.[148]

In contrast, the imposition of an adverse inference instruction based on spoliation of evidence does not require of bad faith. Rather, "simple notice of 'potential relevance to the litigation'" will support giving of the instruction.[149] That said, "[w]hen relevant evidence is lost acci-

---

146. *Id.* at 365-66.
147. *Id.* at 369.
148. *Cabnetware*, 2002 U.S. Dist. LEXIS 20329, at *11-12.
149. *Glover*, 6 F.3d at 1329 (quoting Akiona v. United States, 938 F.2d 158, 161 (9th Cir. 1991)).

dentally or for an innocent reason, an adverse evidentiary inference from the loss may be rejected."[150]

In *Medical Laboratory Management Consultants v. American Broadcasting Companies*,[151] the Ninth Circuit held that the trial court did not abuse its discretion in denying a request for an adverse inference instruction based on the defendant's loss of three medical slides. The case involved a television exposé regarding alleged errors in Pap smear testing by the plaintiff. The defendant's expert witness apparently lost three slides the plaintiff had intended to examine to determine whether they were, in fact, read incorrectly. The district court held that an adverse inference instruction was inappropriate because of the absence of bad faith or intentional conduct on the part of defendant and its expert.[152] The Ninth Circuit affirmed, holding that "under the totality of the circumstances, an unfavorable inference was not warranted because a rational jury would not infer that Defendants' loss of the slides indicated that the slides threatened Defendants' legal position and needed to be covered up."[153]

TENTH CIRCUIT COURT OF APPEALS

The Tenth Circuit addressed the issue of spoliation of evidence in the context of employment, commercial, and products liability actions. In sanctioning spoliation, courts in this circuit have relied on both the Federal Rules of Civil Procedure and the inherent authority of federal courts. Courts in this circuit generally require a showing of bad faith to impose sanctions.[154] Negligence, in losing or destroying records or other documents, generally will not warrant sanctions because neglect does not suggest consciousness of a weak case.[155]

---

150. *Med. Lab.*, 306 F.3d at 824.
151. 306 F.3d 806 (9th Cir. 2002).
152. *Id.* at 824.
153. *Id.*
154. Procter & Gamble Co. v. Haugen, No. 03-4234, 2005 U.S. App. LEXIS 22447 (10th Cir. Oct. 19, 2005) (reversing dismissal of claim as a discovery sanction based upon spoliation of evidence where court failed to address the requisite factors and no basis for concluding plaintiff acted willfully, in bad faith, or with culpability).
155. *See, e.g.*, Coletti v. Cudd Pressure Control, 165 F.3d 767 (10th Cir. 1999) (upholding judgment denying retaliatory discharge claim); Novell, Inc. v. Network Trade Ctr., Inc., 25 F. Supp. 2d 1233 (Utah 1998) (upholding special master's

In the Tenth Circuit, courts consider a variety of factors when determining the appropriate sanction, including prejudice imposed by the spoliation and intent. However, the primary focus is the spoliator's culpability and the degree of actual prejudice caused by the loss of evidence.[156] Applying these factors, Tenth Circuit courts follow the majority and impose the least onerous sanction that will effectively redress the prejudice, if the facts and circumstances warrant such action.

Only one court in this circuit has relied expressly upon the discovery rules to redress destruction of evidence. In *Barker v. Bledsoe*,[157] the court considered a motion to dismiss after discovery revealed that the plaintiff's expert had performed an autopsy that prevented further examination of relevant evidence by the opposing party. The court emphasized that all sanctions defined in Rule 37(b) are available for the total failure to comply with discovery requests. After acknowledging its discretionary authority to protect the pretrial discovery process, the court denied the motion but prohibited introduction of any evidence from the autopsy, including expert testimony.[158]

Considering a trial court's use of its inherent power, in *Jordan F. Miller Corp. v. Mid-Continent Aircraft Service, Inc.*,[159] the Tenth Circuit addressed dismissal of certain claims due to the spoliation of evidence. There, the claims arose out of the purchase of a twin-engine airplane from the defendants. During a landing, the landing gear collapsed, causing major damage to the airplane. Following this accident, the plaintiff notified its insurer and made a claim against its policy. The insurer in-

conclusion allowing adverse inference where party intentionally destroyed financial documentation in an effort to keep damaging information from the plaintiff); Hertz Corp. v. Gaddis-Walker Elec., Inc., Nos. 96-6022, 96-6136, 1997 U.S. App. LEXIS 27138 (10th Cir. Oct. 2, 1997) (upholding district court's finding that in the absence of bad faith, evidence was insufficient to warrant spoliation instruction where evidence at issue was controlled by third party at time of destruction).

156. *See, e.g., Hertz*, 1997 U.S. App. LEXIS 27138. *See also* Rowe v. Albertsons, Inc., 116 Fed. Appx. 171, 2004 U.S. App. LEXIS 20959 (10th Cir. Oct. 7, 2004) (applying Texas law and reversing grant of summary judgment and remanding for consideration of whether adverse presumption arose from spoliation of videotape by owner).

157. 85 F.R.D. 545 (W.D. Okla. 1979).

158. *Id.* at 549.

159. No. 97-5089, 1998 U.S. App. LEXIS 2739 (10th Cir. Feb. 20, 1998).

spected the plane and then made repair payments. While making post-accident repairs, repairmen found other defects in the plane.

Thereafter, the plaintiff filed suit alleging breach of contract, breach of warranty, negligence, and products liability claims based on the collapse of the landing gear and various other alleged defects in the plane.[160] During discovery, the defendants requested production of the "actual landing gear, component parts thereof or other apparatus which you claim as relevant to your claims."[161] Ultimately, all but one of the component parts of the landing gear had been lost or destroyed.

The defendants sought to dismiss the damage claims relating to the landing gear based on spoliation of evidence, arguing that the plaintiff had the duty to preserve evidence it knew would be relevant in the litigation. They also charged that failure of the plaintiff's agent to preserve the evidence irreparably prejudiced their ability to defend against the plaintiff's claims. The plaintiff responded that it had no involvement in the loss of the evidence and that it had suffered as much prejudice as the defendants because its own experts had not inspected the landing gear.[162]

Following a hearing and submission of affidavits from the parties' respective experts concerning actual physical examination and testing of the missing left landing gear, the court dismissed the plaintiff's claims arising from the collapse of the landing gear.[163] The court noted, "Hands-on inspection and testing is critical to a fair trial and due process for the defendants."[164]

The Tenth Circuit heard this question of first impression and noted that federal courts possess inherent powers necessary to "manage their own affairs so as to achieve the orderly and expeditious disposition of cases."[165] The *Jordan F. Miller* court noted that other courts have not generally imposed a requirement of bad faith when considering sanctions for the spoliation of evidence. Instead, when deciding whether to sanction a party for spoliation of evidence, courts focus on (1) the degree of culpability of the party who lost or destroyed the evidence, and (2) the degree of actual prejudice to the other party.[166]

---

160. *Id.* at *4.
161. *Id.* at *6-7.
162. *Id.* at *20.
163. *Id.*
164. *Id.*
165. *Id.*
166. *Id.* at *13.

In reaching its decision, the *Jordan F. Miller* court reasoned that the plaintiff knew that the damaged landing gear was relevant to its claims against the defendants, and therefore had a duty to preserve the evidence. The appellate court also emphasized the finding that destruction of the landing gear severely prejudiced the defendants, because visual inspection and testing of all components of the landing gear was critical to the defense. Noting that the district court had considered and rejected an adverse inference instruction because it would not restore the defendants' right to a fair trial, the appellate court found no abuse of discretion and upheld the dismissal.[167]

ELEVENTH CIRCUIT COURT OF APPEALS

The Eleventh Circuit has addressed spoliation in several contexts.[168] Although these courts will impose a variety of sanctions, dismissal will be entered only upon a showing that no lesser sanction will suffice. Courts in this circuit also focus on the intent of the spoliating party and the prejudice suffered by the nonspoliating party, and the existence of a duty to preserve the evidence at issue.[169]

Recently, in *Flury v. Daimler Chrysler Corporation*,[170] the Eleventh Circuit reversed the district court's decision regarding a spoliation issue and ordered that judgment be entered for the manufacturer. This case involved a claim for enhanced injuries arising from an allegedly defective airbag system in a vehicle. After the underlying acci-

---

167. *Id.* at *23.

168. *See generally* Greenleaf Nursery v. E.I. duPont de Nemours & Co., 341 F.3d 1292 (11th Cir. 2003) (concluding that "concealment does not form a basis for a claim for spoliation"); Bashir v. Nat'l R.R. Passenger Corp., 119 F.3d 929 (11th Cir. 1997) (concluding adverse inference not warranted in a wrongful death action where no evidence of bad faith regarding tampering with the train's speed tape); Stanton v. Nat'l R.R. Corp., 849 F. Supp. 1524 (M.D. Ala. 1994) (imposing adverse inference in ruling on summary judgment based on excessive speed where dispute regarding whether destruction of train's speed tape done in bad faith); Telectron, Inc. v. Overhead Door Corp., 116 F.R.D. 107 (S.D. Fla. 1987) (entering default judgment after evidence revealed intentional destruction of documents believed to contain damaging evidence).

169. *See, e.g.*, Silhan v. Allstate Ins. Co., 236 F. Supp. 2d 1303 (N.D. Fla. 2002) (granting motion to dismiss intentional spoliation claim where no finding of intentional conduct and negligent spoliation claim after finding no duty to preserve or notice of possible litigation).

170. No. 0415182 (11th Cir. Oct. 5, 2005).

dent, the plaintiff's counsel advised the manufacturer in writing about the accident and the airbag's failure to deploy.[171] This communication advised the manufacturer not to contact the plaintiff without counsel's consent and did not identify the location of the vehicle. The manufacturer then requested an inspection of the vehicle.[172] The plaintiff's counsel never responded to this request, and his insurance company ultimately sold the vehicle for salvage. The plaintiff filed suit against the manufacturer six years after the accident.

Before trial, the manufacturer moved for summary judgment based upon spoliation. The district court applied a balancing test that weighed the culpability of the spoliator against the prejudice to the opposing party.[173] The court denied the motion, concluding that the manufacturer shared some of the culpability for the spoliation because it had not followed up on the inspection request.[174] Accordingly, the district court found dismissal unwarranted and gave the jury an adverse inference instruction at trial. After the jury awarded the plaintiff $250,000, the court denied the manufacturer's renewed motion for judgment as a matter of law.[175]

The Eleventh Circuit reversed, explaining that the "extraordinary nature of plaintiff's actions coupled with the extreme prejudice to the defendant warrants dismissal."[176] As the appellate court noted, the plaintiff knew that the manufacturer requested an inspection of the vehicle, and even "without such a request should have known that the vehicle, which was the very subject of his lawsuit, needed to be preserved and examined as evidence central to his case."[177] The Eleventh Circuit also found the adverse inference instruction to be "weak" because it allowed the jury to balance the conduct of the parties.

Applying Georgia spoliation law, the Eleventh Circuit found that the district court improperly attributed fault to the manufacturer for not following up on the inspection request notwithstanding the plaintiff's failure to respond to this request.[178] Moreover, the resulting signifi-

---

171. *Id.* at *2.
172. *Id.* at *5.
173. *Id.* at *7 (citing Bridgestone/Firestone North American Tire, LLC v. Campbell, 574 S.E.2d 923, 927 (Ga. App. 2002)).
174. *Flury*, 0415182, at *7.
175. *Id.* at *8.
176. *Id.* at *9.
177. *Id.* at * 2.
178. *Id.* at *14.

cant prejudice could not be cured by a jury instruction. Finally, the appellate court considered the potential for abuse and the resulting "trial by ambush" caused by the delayed filing after the destruction of reliable evidence.[179] Overall, the Eleventh Circuit found that the plaintiff's spoliation of "critical evidence" prevented the manufacturer from putting on a complete defense."[180] In entering judgment for the manufacturer, the court noted the "resulting prejudice" is "incurable by any sanction other than dismissal.[181]

Likewise, in *Sedrati v. Allstate Life Insurance Company*,[182] the district court considered a motion for sanctions for destruction of evidence in a dispute involving a life insurance policy. Specifically, the parties contested whether the insured was dead after discovering fingerprints on documents generated after the insured's alleged death. This discovery resulted from the defendants' expert's examination, which rendered the original documents unacceptable for further analysis.

The district court considered the five-factor test applied in *Northern Assurance Company v. Ware*[183] and especially emphasized the potential prejudice to the adverse party. Applying this principle, the court found that the destructive testing resulted in considerable prejudice because the plaintiff's expert could not duplicate the conditions of the original documents and account for the existence or absence of fingerprints. Moreover, the court found that the prejudice could not be cured. Although the court found no bad faith, it emphasized the need to preserve fairness to all parties during discovery. Therefore, the court precluded any introduction of evidence relating to the fingerprint evidence.[184]

In contrast, *Goulah v. Ford Motor Company*[185] involved a negligent design claim arising from a motor vehicle rollover accident. During trial, the plaintiffs introduced evidence of the destruction and/or absence of certain documents by the vehicle's manufacturer relating to the vehicle's stability. The district court refused to enter a default judgment or provide a jury instruction regarding bad-faith destruction of evidence and entered judgment for the car maker defendant. On

179. *Id.* at *16.
180. *Id.* at *17.
181. *Id.*
182. 185 F.R.D. 388 (M.D. Ga. 1998).
183. 145 F.R.D. 281 (D. Me. 1993).
184. *Id.* at 394.
185. 118 F.3d 1478 (11th Cir. 1997).

appeal, the court affirmed, finding no evidence that the documents had been destroyed in bad faith.[186]

By way of further example, *Hessen v. Jaguar Cars, Inc.*[187] involved a subrogation action alleging defective design claims arising from a car fire. Following the fire, the insurance company's inspectors investigated the cause of the fire and determined that a "bad fuel hose" was the probable cause. The manufacturer then sent an inspector who conducted a brief inspection. Thereafter, the owner discarded the vehicle.[188]

At trial, the jury returned a verdict in favor of the insurance company. On appeal, among other things, the manufacturer contested the district court's refusal to exclude the plaintiff's expert testimony due to destruction of evidence. In affirming, the Eleventh Circuit noted that, after receiving notice of the fire, the manufacturer had sent a representative to inspect the vehicle and, shortly thereafter, disclaimed any liability for the fire. The court held that the failure to conduct a more in-depth examination could not be attributed to the insurance company.[189]

DISTRICT OF COLUMBIA CIRCUIT COURT OF APPEALS

Courts in the D.C. Circuit Court of Appeals have the discretion to impose a full range of sanctions for the spoliation of evidence, including fines, exclusion of evidence, spoliation inference instructions, and dispositive sanctions. In addition, the District of Columbia recognizes an independent cause of action for negligent and reckless spoliation.

In *Shephard v. American Broadcasting Co., Inc.*,[190] the court reviewed an entry of default judgment pursuant to the district court's inherent authority as a sanction for litigation misconduct. At issue was the alteration of documents in an employment discrimination action, including a confidential memorandum describing a meeting of minority employees that allegedly was altered to conceal attendance at that meeting by the plaintiffs.

After finding Federal Rule of Civil Procedure 37(b) inapplicable, the *Shephard* court focused on the district court's inherent authority.

---

186. *Id.* at 1487.
187. 915 F.2d 641 (11th Cir. 1990).
188. *Id.* at 651.
189. *Id.*
190. 62 F.3d 1469 (D.C. Cir. 1995).

Initially, the court considered the appropriate burden of proof for awarding sanctions under this power. The court found the preponderance of the evidence standard improper and analyzed the purposes and requirements for a heightened "clear and convincing" standard of proof. Acknowledging this heightened standard, the court noted that since an adverse inference is an "issue-related" sanction with a remedial as opposed to punitive purpose, it does not require such an exacting standard.[191]

However, the *Shephard* court also held that the heightened standard of proof is appropriate where a district court imposes the sanction of dismissal or default judgment. Applying the heightened standard, the court found dismissal unwarranted because the document at issue, if unaltered, would not have provided direct evidence of any discrimination. Moreover, absent an explanation from the district court regarding why a lesser sanction was insufficient, granting default judgment was improper.[192]

A similar situation arose in *United States v. Philip Morris U.S.A., Inc.*[193] There, various high-level Philip Morris officials lost e-mail messages following the imposition of a preservation order entered by the court at the outset of the litigation. The United States asked for four sanctions: an adverse inference instruction, the exclusion of the testimony of a Philip Morris official who was among those who failed to comply with the preservation order, a monetary sanction and attorneys' fees, and a sanction that would estop Philip Morris from asserting a defense.[194]

The court held that although it had the authority to impose an adverse inference instruction, it would not do so, because, "with knowledge of the breadth of issues involved in this lawsuit, . . . such a far-reaching sanction is simply inappropriate."[195] Instead, the "choice of sanctions should be guided by the 'concept of proportionality' between offense and sanction"; the adverse inference instruction failed

191. *Id.* at 1478.
192. *Id.* at 1478-79; *see also* William v. Bensten, No. 93-5192, 1993 U.S. App. LEXIS 33839 (D.C. Cir. Nov. 5, 1993) (explaining destruction of files does not warrant sanction when files not of primary importance to claims and no evidence of willful or bad-faith destruction).
193. 327 F. Supp. 2d 21 (D.D.C. 2004).
194. *Id.* at 25.
195. *Id.*

this test and the court accordingly refused to impose it.[196] That said, the court did exclude the testimony of "any . . . individual who has failed to comply with Philip Morris' own internal document retention program. . .[ ]."[197] The court also imposed a monetary sanction of $2.75 million and required Philip Morris to reimburse the government for the cost of conducting a Rule 30(b)(6) deposition on e-mail destruction issues.[198]

In addition to imposing sanctions for spoliation, this circuit allows independent spoliation claims. In *Holmes v. Amerex Rent-A-Car*,[199] the D.C. Circuit responded to a certified question regarding whether negligent or reckless spoliation of evidence is an independent tort actionable in the District of Columbia. The court held that the District of Columbia recognizes a cause of action for negligent or reckless spoliation. To start, a plaintiff must establish that (1) a potential civil action existed and (2) a legal or contractual duty on the part of the entity to preserve evidence relevant to said action.[200] Moreover, the court held that a plaintiff, to prove such a claim, must establish a "reasonable inference" that, due to the spoliation, (1) the plaintiff's ability to prevail in the underlying lawsuit was significantly impaired because of the absence of the spoliated evidence, and (2) there had been a "significant possibility" of success in the underlying claim.[201] Applying this standard, the court found that the district court erred in granting summary judgment in the negligent spoliation claim and rendered the case for further proceedings.[202]

FEDERAL CIRCUIT COURT OF APPEALS

The Federal Circuit has addressed spoliation of evidence in relatively few cases. The cases addressing this issue focus on the effect

---

196. *Id. But see* Arista Records, Inc. v. Sakfield Holding Co. S.L., 314 F. Supp. 2d 27 (D.D.C. 2004) (imposing adverse inference regarding personal jurisdiction where defendant destroyed electronic records that would have shown whether the defendant had sufficient contacts to grant the court personal jurisdiction).

197. *Id.*

198. *Id.* at 26.

199. 180 F.3d 294 (D.C. Cir. 1999).

200. *Id.* at 297.

201. Holmes v. Amerex Rent-A-Car, 710 A.2d 846, 947 (D.C. 1998).

202. *See also* Fletcher v. District of Columbia, No. 01-0297 (RMU), 2005 U.S. Dist. LEXIS 5013 (D.D.C. Mar. 22, 2005).

of the destruction. Given the distinct nature of the claims addressed by this circuit, it tends to review cases involving imposition of severe sanctions.[203] When reviewing sanction orders, the Federal Circuit applies the law of the circuit from which the case arose.[204]

Acknowledging the jurisdictional split on the requisite intent in *Slattery, Jr. v. United States*,[205] the court observed that in the Federal Circuit, "bad faith is an indispensable element of the spoliation doctrine."[206]

---

203. *See generally* Seal-Flex, Inc. v. Athletic Track and Court Constr., 172 F.3d 886 (Fed. Cir. 1999) (upholding dismissal of counterclaims and award of lawyers' fees relating to the withholding and destruction of documents in patent infringement case in appeal from District Court for the Eastern District of Michigan and applying Sixth Circuit law); Litton Sys., Inc. v. Ssangyong Cement Indus. Co. Ltd., Nos. 96-1034, 96-1047, 1997 U.S. App. LEXIS 2386 (Fed. Cir. Feb. 13, 1997) (reversing entry of default judgment in Lanham Act action when district court failed to conduct adequate hearing regarding document destruction by multiple parties); Eaton Corp. v. Appliance Valves Corp., 790 F.2d 874 (Fed. Cir. 1986) (upholding judgment in patent infringement action when document destruction not dispositive of issue of liability when original documents were produced during discovery before being destroyed).

204. Monsanto Co. v. Ralph, 382 F.3d 1374, 1380 (Fed. Cir. 2004).

205. 46 Fed. Cl. 402 (2000).

206. *Id.*

Bibliography

DOCUMENT RETENTION

Armen Artinyan, *Legal Impediments to Discouraged Destruction of E-Mail*, 2 LEGAL ADVOC. & PRAC. 95 (2000).

Ian C. Ballon, *Spoliation of E-Mail Evidence: Proposed Intranet Policies and a Framework for Analysis*, 4 CYBERSPACE LAW 2 (Mar. 1999).

Steven C. Bennett and Thomas M. Niccum, *Two Views from the Data Mountain*, 36 CREIGHTON L. REV. 607 (June 2003).

Matthew J. Bester, Comment: *A Wreck on the Info-Bahn: Electronic Mail and the Destruction of Evidence*, 6 COMM. LAW CONSPECTUS 75 (1998).

Rolin P. Bissel and James M. Holston, *Document Spoliation Claims Require Timely Investigation*, NAT'L L.J., Feb. 5, 1996.

Mary Kay Brown and Paul D. Weiner, *Digital Dangers: A Primer on Electronic Evidence in the Wake of Enron*, 74 PA. BAR ASSN. QUARTERLY 1 (Jan. 2003).

Christopher R. Chase, *To Shred or Not to Shred: Document Retention Policies and Federal Obstruction of Justice Statutes*, 8 FORDHAM J. CORP. & FIN. L. 721 (2003).

Richard L. Claypoole and Gladys Queen Ramey, *Guide to Records Retention in the Code of Federal Regulations* (Diane Pub. Co. 2004).

Christopher V. Cotton, *Document Retention Programs for Electronic Records: Applying a Reasonableness Standard to the Electronic Era*, 24 IOWA J. CORP. L. 417 (1999).

Christopher S. D'Angelo, *Creating and Managing Documents*, 65 DEF. COUNS. J. 494 (1998).

Denlinger, Rosenthal & Greenberg, LPA, *Electronic Mail: No Year Risks*, Vol. 9, Issue 11 OHIO EMPLOYMENT LAW LETTER (Nov. 1999).

Kevin Eng, *Spoliation of Electronic Evidence*, 5 B.U. J. SCI. & TECH. L. 13 (1999).

Patrick R. Grady, *Discovery of Computer Stored Documents and Computer Based Litigation Support Systems: Why Give Up More Than Necessary?*, 14 J. MARSHALL J. COMPUTER & INFO. L. 523 (1996).

Maurice B. Graham and Michael D. Murphy, *Spoliation of Medical Records*, 52 J. OF MO. BAR 87 (1996).

Gary G. Grindler and Jason A. Jones, *Please Step Away From the Shredder and the "Delete" Key: §§ 802 and 1102 of the Sarbanes-Oxley Act*, 41 AM. CRIM. L. REV. 67 (Winter 2004).

Daniel S. Hapke, Jr., *Developing and Implementing Record Retention Programs in Business Organizations*, American Corporate Counsel Assn., RECORDS RETENTION MANUAL (1st ed. Supp. 1995).

Michael P. Harvey, *Essential E-Law*, 13 OHIO LAWYER 10 (Nov./Dec. 1999).

Gregory Joseph, *Expert Spoliation*, 15 THE PRACTICAL LITIGATOR 7 (Nov. 2004).

Jeffrey S. Kinsler and Anne R. Keyes MacIver, *Demystifying Spoliation of Evidence*, 34 TORT & INS. L.J. 761 (1999).

Virginia Llewellyn, *Planning with Clients for Effective Electronic Discovery*, THE PRACTICAL LITIGATOR 7 (July 2003).

Charles A. Lovell and Roger W. Holmes, *The Dangers of E-Mail: The Need for Electronic Data Retention Policies*, 44 R.I. B.J. 7 (Dec. 1995)

Joseph P. Messina and Daniel B. Trinkle, *Document Retention Policies After Andersen*, 46 BOSTON BAR J. 18 (Sept./Oct. 2002).

Martin C. Redish, *Electronic Discovery and the Litigation Matrix*, 51 DUKE L.J. 561 (2001).

Gordon M. Shapiro and Brian A. Kilpatrick, *E-Mail Discovery and Privilege*, 23 CORP. COUNS. REV. 201 (2004).

Brenda Paik Sunoo, *What If Your E-Mail Ends Up in Court?*, 77 WORKFORCE 36 (July 1998).

Ken Withers, *Digital Discovery Starts at Work*, NAT'L L. J., Nov. 4, 2002.

Stephen Zovickian and Geoffrey Howard, *Electronic Discovery and Construction Litigation*, 18 J. CONSTR. L. 8 (July 1998).

REMEDIES AND SANCTIONS IN PENDING LITIGATION

Jerrold Abeles and Robert J. Tyson, *Spoil Sport*, 22 L.A. LAW. 41 (May 1999).

David A. Bell, et al., *An Update on Spoliation of Evidence in Illinois*, 85 ILL. B.J. 530 (1997).

David A. Bell, et al., *Let's Level The Playing Field: A New Proposal for Analysis of Spoliation of Evidence Claims in Pending Litigation*, 29 ARIZ. ST. L.J. 769 (1997).

Wayne D. Brazil, *Civil Discovery. Lawyers' Views of Its Effectiveness, Its Principal Problems and Abuses*, 1980 AM. B. FOUND. RES. J. 787 (1992).

Charles C. Cohn, *Tort and Other Remedies for Spoliation of Evidence*, 81 ILL. B.J. 128 (1993).

Steve E. Couch, *Spoliation of Evidence: Is One Man's Trashing Another Man's Treasure?*, 62 TEX. B.J. 242 (1999).

Donald H. Flanary, Jr. and Bruce M. Flowers, *Spoliation of Evidence. Let's Have a Rule in Response*, 60 DEF. COUNS. J. 553 (Oct. 1993).

Thomas G. Fischer, Annotation, *Intentional Spoilation of Evidence, Interfering with Prospective Civil Action, as Actionable*, 70 A.L.R. 4th 984 (1999).

Richard J. Heafey and Don M. Kennedy, PRODUCT LIABILITY: WINNING STRATEGIES AND TECHNIQUES, §11.02 (1996).

Brian E. Howard, *Spoliation of Evidence*, 49 J. OF MO. BAR 121 (1993).

Edward J. Imwinkelried, *A New Antidote for an Opponent's Pretrial Discovery Misconduct. Treating the Misconduct at Trial as an Admission by Conduct of the Weakness of the Opponent's Case*, 1993 B.Y.U. L. REV. 793 (1993).

Iain D. Johnston, *Federal Courts' Authority to Impose Sanctions for Prelitigation or Pre-Order Spoliation of Evidence*, 156 F.R.D. 313 (1994).

S. Katz, *Spoilage of Evidence—Crimes, Sanctions, Inferences, and Tort*, 29 TORTS & INS. L.J. 51 (1993).

John F. Kuppens, *There Is No Substitute: Spoliation of Evidence in Product Liability Suits*, S.C. LAW (Mar./Apr. 1994).

Kenneth R. Lang, et al., *Spoliation of Evidence: The Continuing Search for a Remedy and Implications for Aviation Accident Investigations*, 60 J. AIR L. & COM. 997 (1995).

Sean R. Levine, Note, *Spoliation of Evidence in West Virginia: Do Too Many Cooks Spoil the Broth?*, 104 W. VA. L. REV. 419 (Winter 2002).

Maria A. Losavio, *Synthesis of Louisiana Law on Spoliation of Evidence—Compared to the Rest of Country, Did We Handle It Correctly?*, 58 LA. L. REV. 837 (1998).

Christopher B. Majors, *Where's the Evidence? Dealing with Spoliation by Plaintiffs in Product Liability Cases*, 53 S.C. L. REV. 415 (Winter 2002).

Robert R. Merhige, Jr., CIVIL PRACTICE AND LITIGATION TECHNIQUES IN FEDERAL AND STATE COURTS OUTLINE OF SPOLIATION OF EVIDENCE ISSUES, 28 ALI-ABA 533 (Aug. 1999).

Charles R. Nesson, *Incentives to Spoliate Evidence in Civil Litigation. The Need for Vigorous Judicial Action,* 13 CARDOZO L. REV. 793 (1991).

Margaret O'Mara Frossard and Neal S. Gainsberg, *Spoliation of Evidence in Illinois, The Law After Boyd v. Traveler's Insurance Company,* 28 LOY. U. CHI. L.J. 685 (1997).

Chris William Sanchirico, *Evidence Tampering,* 53 DUKE L.J. 1215 (2004).

Angelo G. Savino, *Sanctions for Negligent Spoliation of Evidence,* 70 N.Y. ST. B.J. 28 (1998).

Brian Slaughter, *Spoliation of Evidence: A New Rule of Evidence Is the Better Solution,* 18 AM. J. TRIAL ADVOC. 449 (1994).

Robert L. Tucker, *The Flexible Doctrine of Spoliation of Evidence: Cause of Action, Defense, Evidentiary Presumption, and Discover Sanction,* 27 U. TOL. L. REV. 67 (1995).

Monte E. Weiss, *Spoliation of Evidence: A New Defense in Products Liability Cases,* 70 WIS. LAW. 18 (May 1997).

Spoliation Rule Does Not Require Bad Faith, 11 FED. LITIG. 93 (May 1996).

Pillage and Plunder in Aircraft Accidents: Potential for Spoliation Penalties for Spoliation of Evidence Can Be Serious, Including Exclusion of Evidence, Adverse Inferences and Liability for an Independent Tort, 60 DEF. COUNS. J. 280 (1993).

INDEPENDENT TORTS

Jerrold Abeles and Robert J. Tyson, *Spoil Sport,* 22 L.A. LAW. 41 (May 1999).

Linda L. Addison, *Civil Evidence: The Tort of Spoliation,* 60 TEX. B.J. 656 (1997).

David A. Bell, et al., *An Update on Spoliation of Evidence in Illinois,* 85 ILL. B.J. 530 (1997).

David A. Bell, et al., *Let's Level the Playing Field: A New Proposal for Analysis of Spoliation of Evidence Claims in Pending Litigation,* 29 ARIZ. ST. L.J. 769 (1997).

Ruth Cornell, *Negligent and Reckless Spoliation of Evidence,* 1 LEGAL AD. VOC. & PRAC. 212 (1999).

Thomas G. Fischer, Annotation, *Intentional Spoliation of Evidence, Interfering With Prospective Civil Action as Actionable*, 70 A.L.R. 4th 984 (1999).

Maurice B. Graham and Michael D. Murphy, *Spoliation of Medical Records*, 52 J. OF Mo. Bar 87 (1996).

Brian E. Howard, 1993 *Spoliation of Evidence*, 49 J. OF Mo. Bar 121 (Mar./Apr. 1993).

S. Katz, *Spoilage of Evidence—Crimes, Sanctions, Inferences, and Torts*, 29 TORTS & INS. L.J. 51 (1993).

Maurice L. Kervin, *Spoliation of Evidence: Why Mississippi Should Adopt the Tort*, 63 MISS. L.J. 227 (1993).

Monica L. Klug, *Should Arizona Adopt the Tort of Intentional Spoliation of Evidence—LaRaia v. Supreme Court?, 150 Ariz. 118, 722 P.2d 286 (1986)*, 19 ARIZ. ST. L.J. 371 (1987).

Rebecca Levy-Sachs, et al., *Spoliation of Evidence: The Trend to a New Tort*, 49 FED. OF INS. & CORP. COUNSEL Q. 225 (1999).

Maria A. Losavio, *Synthesis of Louisiana Law on Spoliation of Evidence—Compared to the Rest of Country, Did We Handle It Correctly?*, 58 LA. L. REV. 837 (1998).

Nancy Melgaard, *Spoliation of Evidence—An Independent Tort?* 67 N.D. L. REV. 501 (1991).

Steffen Nolte, *The Spoliation Tort: An Approach to Underlying Principles*, 26 ST. MARY'S L.J. 351, 353 (1995).

Margaret O'Mara Frossard and Neil S. Gainsberg, *Spoliation of Evidence in Illinois, The Law After* Boyd v. Traveler's Insurance Company, 28 LOY. U. CHI. L.J. 685 (1997).

Theresa M. Owens, *Should Iowa Adopt the Tort of Intentional Spoliation of Evidence in Civil Litigation?*, 41 DRAKE L. REV. 179 (1992).

Jay. E. Rivlin, *Recognizing an Independent Tort Action While a Spoliator*, 26 HOFSTRA L. REV. 1003 (1998).

Stefan Rubin, *Tort Reform: A Call for Florida to Scale Back Its Independent Tort for Spoliation of Evidence*, 51 FLA. L. REV. 345 (1999).

Steven R. Selsberg and Melissa Rauer Lipman, *"My Dog Ate It:" Spoliation of Evidence in the Texas Supreme Court's Ortega Decision*, 62 TEX. B.J. 1014 (1999).

J. Brian Slaughter, *Spoliation of Evidence: A New Rule of Evidence Is the Better Solution*, 18 AM. J. TRIAL ADVOC. 449 (1994).

Terry R. Spencer, Ph.D., *Do Not Fold, Spindle or Mutilate: The Trend Towards Recognition of Spoliation as a Separate Tort*, 30 IDAHO L. REV. 37, 40 (1993).

John K. Stipancic, *The Negligent Spoliation of Evidence: An Independent Tort Action May Be the Only Acceptable Alternative*, 53 Ohio St. L.J. 1135 (1992).

James F. Thompson, *Spoliation of Evidence: A Troubling New Tort*, 37 Kan. L. Rev. 563, 564 (1989).

Robert L. Tucker, *The Flexible Doctrine of Spoliation of Evidence: Cause of Action, Defense, Evidentiary Presumption, and Discover Sanction*, 27 U. Tol. L. Rev. 67, 67 (1995).

Monte Weiss, *Spoliation of Evidence: A New Defense in Products Liability Cases*, 70 Wis. Law. 18 (May 1997).

Bart S. Wilhoit, Comment, *Spoliation of Evidence: The Viability of Four Emerging Torts*, 46 U.C.L.A. L. Rev. 631 (1998).

Eric M. Wilson, *The Alabama Supreme Court Sidesteps a Definitive Ruling in Christian v. Kenneth Chandler Construction Co.: Should Alabama Adopt the Independent Tort of Spoliation?*, 47 Ala. L. Rev. 971 (1996).

CRIMINAL SANCTIONS

Joseph V. DeMarco, *A Funny Thing Happened on the Way to the Courthouse: Mens Rea, Document Destruction, and the Federal Obstruction of Justice Statute*, 67 N.Y.U. L. Rev. 570 (1992).

S. Katz, *Spoilage of Evidence—Crimes, Sanctions, Inferences, and Torts*, 29 Torts & Ins. L.J. 51 (1993).

STATUTORY RECORD KEEPING

Steven W. Huang and Robert H. Muriel, *Spoliation of Evidence: Defining the Ethical Boundaries of Destroying Evidence*, 22 Am. J. Trial Advoc. 1991 (Summer 1998).

TREATISES/BOOKS

Couch on Insurance §§ 84, 99 (1999).

Paul C. Giannelli and Barbara Rook Snyder, Baldwin's Ohio Practice Evidence § 401.8, *Adverse Inferences: Spoliation* (West 1999).

J. Gorelick, et al., Destruction of Evidence (1994 and Supp. 2005).

Richard J. Heafey and Don M. Kennedy, Product Liability: Winning Strategies and Techniques (2000).

William L. Prosser, Handbook of the Law of Torts (4th ed. 1971).

John William Strong, McCormick on Evidence 265 (4th ed. 1992).

Charles A. Wright & Arthur R. Miller, FEDERAL PRACTICE AND PROCEDURE: CRIMINAL, CIVIL, JURISDICTION AND RELATED MATTERS (1999).
CALIFORNIA JURY INSTRUCTIONS—CIVIL (8th ed. 2000).
2 WIGMORE ON EVIDENCE (1999).
29 AM. JUR. EVID. §§ 202-300 (1999).

MISCELLANEOUS

Kristin Adamski, Comment, *A Funny Thing Happened on the Way to the Courtroom: Spoliation of Evidence in Illinois*, 32 J. MARSHALL L. REV. 325 (1999).
Anthony C. Casamassima, Comment, *Spoliation of Evidence and Medical Malpractice*, 14 PACE L. REV. 235 (1994).
Charles C. Cohn, *Tort and Other Remedies for Spoliation of Evidence*, 81 ILL. B.J. 128 (1993).
J. Donovan and J. Hamill, *Sabers Continue to Rattle in the Evidence Spoliation Battle*, 3 PRODUCT LIA. L. & STRATEGY 5 (Sept. 1996).
William S. Duffey, Jr., *Corporate Fraud and Accountability: A Primer on Sarbanes-Oxley Act of 2002*, 54 S.C. L. REV. 405 (2002).
Margaret A. Egan, *Spoliators Beware, but Fear Not an Independent Civil Suit*, 24 U. ARK. LITTLE ROCK L. REV. 233 (Fall 2001).
Hank Grzlak, *Federal, State Courts at Odds on Spoliation*, PA. L. WKLY., July 22, 1996.
William A. Hancock, E.D., GUIDE TO RECORDS RETENTION (Business Laws, Inc. 1993).
Dana E. Hill, *Anticipatory Obstruction of Justice: Pre-Emptive Document Destruction Under the Sarbanes-Oxley Anti-Shredding Statute, 18 U.S.C. § 1519*, 89 CORNELL L. REV. 1519 (Sept. 2004).
R. Kahn and K. Vaiden, *If the Slate Is Wiped Clean (Spoliation: What It Can Mean for Your Case)*, BUSINESS LAW TODAY (May/June 1999).
Kathleen Kedigh, *Spoliation: To the Careless Go the Spoils*, 67 UMKC L. REV. 597 (1999).
S. Lamanna, *Courts Take a Harder Line on Spoliation*, NAT'L L.J., July 26, 1993.
Joseph J. Ortego, et al., *Spoliation Concerns for the 21st Century Toxic Tort Litigator*, 10 MEALEY'S LITIG. REP. 14 (Feb. 2000).
Robert Gray Palmer, *Altered and "Lost" Medical Records*, TRIAL (May 1999).
Sarah Roadcup, *Obstruction of Justice*, 41 AM. CRIM. L. REV. 911 (2004).
L. Solum and S. Marzen, *Truth and Uncertainty: Legal Control of the Destruction of Evidence*, 36 EMORY L.J. 1085 (1987).

W. Russell Welsh and Andrew C. Marquardt, *Spoliation of Evidence*, 23 WTR BRIEF 9 (1994).

P. Wilson, *Doctrinal Malfunction—Spoliation and Product Liability Law in Pennsylvania*, 69 TEMPLE L. REV. 899 (1996).

The Sedona Conference, *The Sedona Guidelines: Best Practice Guidelines—Commentary for Managing Information—Records in the Electronic Age* 18 (Sept. 2004).

Recent Legislation: Corporate Law—Congress Passes Corporate and Accounting Fraud Legislation, 116 HARV. L. REV. 728 (Dec. 2002).

Table of Cases

305

Foster v. Lawrence Mem'l Hosp., 809 F. Supp. 831, 837 (D. Kan. 1992)
88 n.45; 170 n.254; 171 nn.255-257

Fox v. Cohen, 406 N.E.2d 178 (Ill. Ct. App. 1980)   102 n.117

Fox v. Country Mut. Ins. Co., 7 P.3d 677 (Or. Ct. App. 2000)   222
n.532

Fujitsu Ltd. v. Federal Express Corp., 247 F.3d 423, 436 (2d Cir. 2001)
5 n.19; 10 n.37; 262 n.21

Galanek v. Wismar, 69 Cal. App. 4th   1417 (1999)   140 nn.87, 88

Gamerdinger v. Schaefer, 603 N.W.2d 590 (Iowa 1999)   168 n.240;
169 241-245

Gardner v. Blackston, 365 S.E.2d 545, 546 (Ga. Ct. App. 1988)   154
n.158

Garfoot v. Fireman's Fund Ins. Co., 599 N.W.2d 411 (Wis. Ct. App.
1999)   252 nn.699, 700

Gargan v. State, 805 P.2d 998 (Alaska Ct. App. 1991)   131 n.37

Gates Rubber Co. v. Bando Chem. Indus., 167 F.R.D. 90 (D. Colo.
1996)   41 n.76; 53 n.1; 54 n.4; 59 nn.25,.28; 61 n.36-41; 62 nn.42,
43, 45; 77 n.114

Gathers v. S.C. Elec. & Gas, 427 S.E.2d 687, 689 (Ct. App. 1993)   228
n.566

Gentry v. Toyota Motor Corp, 471 S.E.2d 485 (Va. 1996)   66 n.66; 67
n.67; 242 n. 645-647; 243 n.648

Gilleski v. Cmty. Med. Ctr., 765 A.2d 1103 (N.J. Super. Ct. App. Div.
2001)   5 n.17; 207 n.453

Glotzbach v. Froman, No. 45A03-0307-CV-264, 2005 Ind. App. LEXIS
797 (Ind. Ct. App. May 11, 2005)   82 n.9

Glover v. BIC Corp., 6 F.3d 1318, 1329 (9th Cir. 1993)   56 n.11; 65
n.57; 284 n.140; 285 n.141; 286 n.149

GNLV Corp. v. Service Control Corp., 900 P.2d 323, 325 (Nev. 1995)
202 nn.427-429

Goff v. Harold Ives Trucking   Co., 27 S.W.3d 387 (Ark. 2000)   104
n.127; 134 nn.48, 49; 135 n.50

Goldman v. Goldman, 883 P.2d 181 (Okla. Ct. App. 1992)   221 n. 530

Goulah v. Ford Motor Co., 118 F.3d 1478 (11th Cir. 1997)   292 n. 185;
293 n.186

Linnen v. A.H. Robins Co., Inc., No. 97-2307, 1999 Mass. Super. LEXIS 240 (Mass. Dist. Ct. June 16, 1999) 39 n.63; 183 n.318

Linscott v. Foy, 716 A.2d 1017 (Me. 1998) 179 nn.297-299

Litton Sys., Inc. v. Ssangyong Cement Indus. Co. Ltd., Nos. 96-1034, 96-1047, 1997 U.S. App. LEXIS 2386 (Fed. Cir. Feb. 13, 1997) 296 n.203

Lombard v. MCI Telecomm. Corp., 13 F. Supp. 2d 621, 627 (N.D. Ohio 1998) 3 n.7; 5 n.11; 121 n.19; 276 nn.97-99

Lombardo v. Broadway Stores, Inc., 2002 Cal. App. LEXIS 262, at *22-23 (Cal. Ct. App. Jan. 22, 2002) 50 n.109

Loomis v. Ameritech Corp., 764 N.E.2d 658 (Ind. Ct. App. 2002) 167 n.231

Lord v. Nissan Motor Co., No. 03-3218, 2004 U.S. Dist. LEXIS 25409 (D. Minn. Dec. 13, 2004) 280 nn.118, 120

Lucas v. Christiana Skating Ctr., Ltd., 722 A.2d 1247, 1248 (Del. Super. 1998) 85 n.33; 145 nn.108, 110; 146 n.118

Lueter v. State of California, 115 Cal. Rptr. 2d 68, 79 (Ct. App. 2002) 139 n.75

Lynch v. Saddler, 656 N.W.2d 104, 111 (Iowa 2003) 168 n.239

Madden v. Wyeth, No. 3-03-CV-0167-R, 2003 U.S. Dist. LEXIS 6427 (N.D. Tex. Apr. 16, 2003) 45 n.85

Magbuhat v. Kovaric, 382 N.W.2d 43, 45 (S.D. 1986) 229 nn.570, 571

Manorcare Health Servs., Inc. v. Osmose Wood Preserving, Inc., 764 A.2d 475, 482 (N.J. Super. Ct. App. Div. 2001) 2 n.3; 208 n.460

Manpower Inc. v. Brawdy, 62 P.3d 391 (Okla. Ct. App. 2002) 220 nn.523- 525

Marinelli v. Mitts & Merrill, 696 A.2d 55 (N.J. Super. Ct. App. Div. 1997) 208 n.457

Marrocco v. General Motors Corp., 966 F.2d 220, 223 (7th Cir. 1992) 55 n.8; 190 n.352, 353

Marshall v. Bally's Pacwest, Inc., 972 P.2d 475 (Wash. 1999) 79 n.126; 244 nn.654-656

Martin v. Intex Recreation Corp., 858 F. Supp. 161, 163 (D. Kan. 1994) 60 n.34

Philips Med. Sys. Marrocco v. General Motors Corp., 966 F.2d 220 (7th Cir. 1992)   279 n.112

Phillips v. Covenant Clinic, 625 N.W.2d 714, 721 (Iowa 2001)   168 n.239

Pia v. Perrotti, 718 A.2d 321 (Pa. Super. Ct. 1998)   225 n.549

Pirocchi v. Liberty Mut. Ins. Co., 365 F. Supp. 277, 281 (E.D. Pa. 1973)   89 n.49

Pittsfield v. Barnstead, 40 N.H. 477, 496 (1860)   205 n.442

Playboy Enters., Inc. v. Welles, 60 F. Supp. 2d 1050 (S.D. Cal. 1999)   49 n.104

Pomeroy v. Benton, 77 Mo. 64 (Mo. 1882)   64 n.54; 194 n.385; 195 n.386

Powers v. Eichen, 961 F. Supp. 233, 236 (S.D. Cal. 1997)   120 n.14

Pratt v. Payne, 794 N.E.2d 723 (Ohio Ct. App. 2003)   217 n.508

Procter & Gamble Co. v. Haugen, 179 F.R.D. 622 (D. Utah 1998)   41 n.76; 78 nn.122, 123; 79 124, 125

Procter & Gamble Co. v. Haugen, No. 03-4234, 2005 U.S. App. LEXIS 22447 (10th Cir. Oct. 19, 2005)   287 n.154

Proske v. St. Barnabas Med. Ctr., 712 A.2d 1207 (N.J. Super. Ct. App. Div. 1998)   208 n.457

Public Health Trust of Dade Cty. v. Valcin, 507 So. 2d 596 (Fla. 1987)   151 n.142, 153 nn. 153-155

Quinn v. Riso Investments, Inc., 869 So. 2d 922 (La. Ct. App. 2004)   175 n.281; 176 nn.282-284

Quint-Cities Petroleum Co. v. Maas, 143 N.W.2d 345, 348 (Iowa 1966)   169 n.242

QZO, Inc. v. Moyer, 594 S.E.2d 541 (Ct. App. 2004)   228 n.567

R.A. Siegel Co. v. Bowen, 539 S.E.2d 873 (Ga. Ct. App. 2000)   156 n.168

R.S. Creative, Inc. v. Creative Cotton, Ltd., 89 Cal. Rptr. 2d 353, 360 (Ct. App. 1999)   140 n.84

Rafferty v. Halprin, No. 90 CIV 2751(CSH), 1991 U.S. Dist. LEXIS 10344 (S.D.N.Y. 1991)   114 n.28

Rambus, Inc. v. Infineon Tech. AG, 222 F.R.D. 280 (E.D. Va. 2004)   26 n.6; 27 n.12; 28 n.13; 30 n.28; 31 n.29

Index